MASSIMO D'AZEGLIO

Massimo d'Azeglio
Oil painting by Francesco Hayez

MASSIMO D'AZEGLIO

AN ARTIST IN POLITICS

1798–1866

RONALD MARSHALL

LONDON
OXFORD UNIVERSITY PRESS
NEW YORK   TORONTO
1966

Oxford University Press, Ely House, London W. 1

GLASGOW NEW YORK TORONTO MELBOURNE WELLINGTON
CAPE TOWN SALISBURY IBADAN NAIROBI LUSAKA ADDIS ABABA
BOMBAY CALCUTTA MADRAS KARACHI LAHORE DACCA
KUALA LUMPUR HONG KONG

Printed in Great Britain by
The Camelot Press Ltd., London and Southampton

76040

IN
MEMORIAM
GEORGE ARTHUR WAREHAM
4 April 1907–9 December 1963

ACKNOWLEDGEMENTS

THOUGH Azeglio's political writings and speeches were edited by Marcus de Rubris, there is unfortunately no collected edition of his letters: the various volumes of them that have been published are not always complete or reliable. The equally interesting letters of his sister-in-law Costanza to her son Emanuele have not been published *in extenso*, though there are excellent collections of extracts from them, the most recent, by Mario Schettini, having come out as lately as 1960. His brother Prospero has been luckier in this respect, Father Pietro Pirri having edited his letters for the 'Biblioteca di Storia Italiana Recente'. Thanks to Professor Alberto M. Ghisalberti of the University of Rome there is at last a definitive edition of Azeglio's Memoirs, but no satisfactory collected edition of his novels and essays seems to exist.

Besides editing the political works and some of Azeglio's letters, Marcus de Rubris wrote essays on various aspects of his life, but these tend to be too uniformly flattering to Azeglio's statesmanship and too discreet in their treatment of some of his opinions and lapses from virtue. The biographies by Vaccaluzzo and Santangelo (this latter primarily a study of Azeglio's writings and influence) are not only more recent but better balanced. More recent, still better balanced, and also more entertaining, containing much material not previously published, is the volume of essays by Professor Ghisalberti, *Massimo d'Azeglio, un moderato realizzatore*. The publication of Professor Vincent's translation of Azeglio's Memoirs (*Things I Remember*, Oxford University Press, 1966) is a most welcome event, and the author of this biography is keenly aware of the advantage it would have been to it had he been able to draw upon this new version for his quotations from the Memoirs; unfortunately the timing of its preparation for the press did not allow this.

In the course of his work the writer has been greatly helped by the staffs of the British Museum Reading Room, of the Public Record Office, and of the Linenhall Library in Belfast, and very particularly by its librarian, Mr. James Vitty. Much as he values their kindness and the wealth of material that their institutions possess, he would also like to record his especial indebtedness to the London Library, since without its help the writing of this book would have been immeasurably more difficult.

In Italy he owes debts of gratitude to the staffs of the Biblioteca Reale and of the Archivio di Stato in Turin. To Doctor Rodolfo Pellion di Persano, who granted him the unusual privilege of access to the papers of Admiral Count Persano, he is especially grateful. The pleasantest of all experiences was that of working in the Archive of the Opera Pia Taparelli in Saluzzo, where the papers of the main line of the Azeglio family are preserved. The Reverend Mother Superior and the sisters of the Cottolengo Order were unfailing in their countless little daily acts of kindness to the stranger in their midst, as was the Institute's secretary, Dr. Riccardo Ambrogio.

Finally the writer's thanks are due to all who have given encouragement to the actual writing of this biography: to his colleagues in the Social Studies Department of Stranmillis College, Belfast: to Mrs. Kathleen McCloy, who read the typescript and commented most helpfully: and to Dr. Nesca Robb, who from time to time interrupted her own more substantial work on William III to read and comment on the manuscript: and to the late Elena de Bosis Vivante for the hospitality of the Villa Solaia, Siena, where some of the following chapters were written.

R. M.

Belfast
August 1965

CONTENTS

LIST OF ILLUSTRATIONS

(*All reproduced by permission of The Mansell Collection*)

I

PRELUDE TO A FIRST CAREER

When Massimo d'Azeglio was appointed Prime Minister of Piedmont-Sardinia in May 1849, *Fischietto*, the Torinese satirical paper, published a caricature of his arrival on the threshold of his office carrying an unfinished canvas, a box of paints, an easel and palette, with a violoncello slung over his shoulder and sheets of music fluttering in his wake; he had a pile of substantial books under his arm and a quill pen stuck behind his ear. Beneath the drawing was the caption, 'With knowledge of so many trades, though he will not be greatest [*massimo*] in all, he will achieve something'. The 'cello was a flight of fancy, for the new Prime Minister played the piano and guitar, and these as a general rule only to accompany his own singing; but the other emblems of his versatility were justifiable. And yet the caricature was seriously incomplete, for the artist, musician, novelist, and publicist had had experience as a soldier, not merely as a scapegrace young officer in 'Piemonte Reale' but as second-in-command to Durando when he was in charge of the Papal Army during the War of Liberation in 1848: at Monte Berico Azeglio had commanded his men in a desperate stand against a much larger army and received a wound from which he was to suffer for many years still to come.

His secondary interests were as varied as his major ones. He was passionately fond of riding, and to be unable to keep a horse of his own was one of the greatest deprivations of his days of poverty as a student in Rome. He swam, and in old age sailed a boat on Lake Maggiore. He was virtually trilingual, using Piedmontese in familiar speech and, like most of his social class, French on formal social occasions and in much of his correspondence: he wrote and spoke better Italian than most Piedmontese, including Cavour, even though he used Roman and Milanese locutions regarded as provincial in Tuscany.

It was perhaps his knowledge of his country rather than the variety of his talents that led him to be described as 'the most complete man of the Risorgimento'. Whilst he was a child the family lived in Florence: during the twenties he was for seven years in Rome, and then after a period in Turin he settled for some fourteen years in Milan. He had even visited Sicily on three occasions, making one long tour of the island despite the incredibly primitive conditions that made travel there not just difficult but positively dangerous. After his withdrawal from an active political life he spent most of his time outside Piedmont, in Tuscany, or in Lombardy after its liberation from the Austrians. In all this he contrasts very strongly with Cavour, who knew much more about Europe but very much less about Italy than Azeglio.

Moreover he knew his Italy at many different levels. In Turin he had moved only amongst his own social class, whose limitations irked him unendurably. In Rome he was with artists and students because of his vocation: but his family background gave him access to the palaces of the lay aristocracy, whilst through his uncle, Cardinal Morozzo, he knew something of the backstage events in the world of ecclesiastical politics. During the summer he would leave Rome for one of the villages in the Alban Hills— Rocca di Papa, Genzano, Albano, or Castel Gandolfo. There he would spend his time painting out of doors and lodging when he could afford it in the village inn with waggoners and peasants as his table companions, or in less affluent seasons camping in an abandoned cottage or in some part of a crumbling and deserted mansion. In Milan he lived in a background of intellectual activity. The Brera with its annual exhibitions made the city the artistic capital of Italy and Azeglio was surrounded by fellow-painters: but Milan was also the scene of intense literary activity, with Manzoni at its centre; and as Manzoni's son-in-law, and later as a novelist in his own right, Azeglio was living in a world of literature. There too was the Scala, and the theatre and its personnel were always a source of fascination to him. In effect, until he was forty-six years of age, the only type of activity with which Azeglio, on the whole deliberately, had made no contact was that of politics.

A 'complete man' cannot fail to be a complex one: the Azeglio of reality is far more paradoxical than the self-portrait of the *Ricordi*: in private life he was fanatically scrupulous in money matters, but an incorrigible amorist. As a politician he cannot be pigeon-holed once and for all: not only did his opinions change radically with time, but at any given moment they were a mixture of conflicting views and prejudices. He saw no virtue in any political system other than a parliamentary one: but it did not follow that Parliament must be democratic. Ministers must be in harmony with the majority in Parliament or government becomes impossible: but whether ministers are created by the majority or create it is the significant question. Royal powers must be limited: yet when occasion demands they must be stretched to the very limit—and a good way beyond. Azeglio created the legend, and invented the term 'Re Galantuomo' for Victor Emmanuel: but after 1855 he became in private the King's most embittered critic. As novelist, publicist, painter, soldier, and politician he did all he could to stimulate Italians to the great mission of expelling the foreigner: yet he not only had no zeal for the ideal of a united Italy, but on the contrary dreaded and opposed it. He had lived in and had loved Rome, but he hated the thought that it might one day become the capital of a unified country. He was bitterly critical of Cavour's policy in private, disliking the ends he had in view and shocked by the means by which he pursued them: but in each great crisis from 1855 onwards he rallied to him and offered and gave him his loyal service. He had, as he thought, revolted against the limitations of his own social class, and had been happy to lead a bohemian life, at home with men of all ranks of society: but as he saw the emergence of a class of professional politicians drawn from the middle class, usually from the practice of law, and often from central and southern Italy, his prejudices hardened, and much of his opposition to the policies of Cavour's successors seems to have been based on social snobbery. He was philanthropic but a programme of social reform such as that adumbrated by Garibaldi and Mazzini in Rome, or by Garibaldi in Sicily, revolted him. And at the heart of it all, Azeglio the Italianate became less and less able to see any virtue in any part of Italy outside Piedmont: only very reluctantly did he eventually vote for the transfer of the capital to Florence from Turin, though he could hardly bear to live in his native city.

His nephew Emanuele, for many years Sardinian and later Italian Minister in London, was remarkably like him in character and tastes and there was extremely close sympathy between them: but Massimo and his two brothers were an unusually dissimilar trio. Roberto, the eldest, had been a Carbonaro, involved in the 1821 Revolution in Piedmont; but after that he virtually withdrew from politics. He was active as an educationist and social reformer, and Director of the Royal Picture Gallery. He was austere and somewhat humourless, religious with an inclination towards Jansenism, and instrumental in gaining religious and civic rights for Jews and Waldensians in Piedmont. Prospero, the other brother to survive into mature years, became a Jesuit, better known as Father Luigi Taparelli. He was a Thomist in philosophy, a voluminous writer on political philosophy, and, somewhat unjustly, was regarded as the most eminent theoretical defender of the absolutist and Papalist cause in politics. He was a man of engaging simplicity of life and character, and though in his way of life and in his views the very opposite of Massimo, he was loved by him as Roberto never was.

Their family, destined to die out in the male line with the Marchese Emanuele, was by tradition of French origin. According to one account they came into Italy in the wake of Charles of Anjou in or around 1264, but in fact they were established in Piedmont earlier than that date, for their name has been traced as far back as 1180 in Savigliano. They gradually accumulated estates, none of them very large, and titles, becoming in sequence Consignori di Savigliano, Signori del Maresco, Conti di Cortandone, Marchesi di Montanera, Conti di Genola, di Lagnasco, and finally Marchesi d'Azeglio. It was by this latter title that they became known, though the Azeglio estate and castle were of little value, and Genola was their main home. The archives of their estates, preserved at Saluzzo, fill 342 cases, and what would appear to be the oldest deed dates from 1028, before the Taparellis had entered into possession of Savigliano. The roll-call of their estates and titles may be misleading: the family was never wealthy or important and in the traceable course of some six centuries before the birth of the Marchese Cesare they only produced one person of any note at all, the Blessed Aimone Taparelli (?1400–95), of the Dominican Order of Preachers. Famous in his day as theologian, preacher, and ascetic, he became Professor in the University of Turin, Confessor to the Duke of Savoy, Amedeo IX, who was likewise beatified, and Inquisitor-General for Piedmont, Liguria, and Lombardy. Not untypically of the Taparellis he fell just short of real eminence—in his case by having failed to earn canonization.

Cesare Taparelli d'Azeglio, father of Massimo, was the only surviving son of the Marchese Carlo Roberto, who by a second marriage had a daughter: she married Count Prospero Balbo and their son, Cesare, author of *Le speranze d'Italia*, was thus not only the dear friend but also cousin of Massimo d'Azeglio. Of

Carlo Roberto we know little except that he had an enthusiasm for the English language that, however it had been gained, and however shallow it may have been, earned him a reputation for eccentricity in Turin, according to his grandson. But one suspects that even a minimal interest in any literature might have gained one such a reputation in that city if one were of noble birth—at least that was Massimo's opinion two generations later.

Cesare his son had a conventional enough upbringing. At the age of eleven he was enrolled as a cadet in the Piedmontese army, in the Reggimento della Regina: at seventeen he returned from Sardinia, where his regiment had been posted, to take up appointment as Equerry to the Duke of Aosta. In 1784, having apparently done nothing previously in the least degree unconventional, he in his turn surprised Torinese society by a sudden religious conversion as a result of hearing a Lenten sermon by a Dominican. His illumination was as sudden, and, it must be added, as permanent, as that which his later acquaintance Alessandro Manzoni was to experience in the Church of St. Roch in Paris on 2 April 1810. In 1788 Cesare married Cristina Morozzo di Bianzè, who proved to be fully his equal in firmness of religious conviction and strength of character, though delicate in physique. Their first son died in infancy, but the second, Roberto, born in 1789, lived until 1862: Prospero, the next, lived from 1793 until 1862: Enrico, the fourth, who died in 1824, was born in tragic circumstances in 1795.

In 1794 the French revolutionary armies began to move towards Italy, occupying the Alpine passes. Cesare, as Lieutenant-Colonel of the Vercelli Regiment, was in action in the Val d'Aosta, and after a defeat on the Little St. Bernard Pass he and his manservant were taken prisoner. In Turin it was reported that he had been killed—an eye-witness having given a graphic account of his death.

Weeks went by before news reached Cristina that he was still alive. She had been prostrated by grief, and it was in a state of intense nervous depression that she had given birth to Enrico. Cesare had in fact been doubly lucky to survive. His regiment had suffered very heavy casualties during the battle, and he might well have been amongst them: but he had been in even greater danger after falling into the hands of the revolutionary soldiers. It was obvious to them that he was a fluent French-speaker; from this it was an equally obvious deduction that he must be a

B

Frenchman: and a Frenchman fighting in the enemy army must be an émigré—and therefore fit to be shot out of hand.

Having escaped this fate he came near to dying of starvation: for prisoners of war had to fend for themselves. It is true that they were given an allowance, but this was in assignats whose value had depreciated to such an extent that they were almost worthless. Cesare and his servant were reduced to begging for their food. Such as they got they shared equally. But his most intolerable deprivation was not this material one: it was the difficulty of hearing Mass. This was still proscribed in France, though from time to time he was able to attend secret celebrations at night in the homes of recusants: had he been discovered it would have gone hard with him.

After a couple of months news reached Turin that he was alive. The Sardinian Government negotiated for his release, and this was offered to him on condition that he would not take up arms against the French Republic until a reciprocal exchange of prisoners had been made. Such a condition was usually regarded as perfectly honourable, but to him it was totally inacceptable as a limitation of his oath of loyalty to his King. He consequently remained a prisoner of war until the Cherasco Armistice of 1796, when he was released unconditionally.

For Piedmont-Sardinia the peace was of short duration. In 1798 the French occupied Turin: King Charles Emmanuel abdicated the throne of Piedmont and withdrew to Sardinia, and the newly-established Republican Government began to extend to Piedmont the social reforms already promulgated in France. There is a trivial record of this in the Azeglio Archives in Saluzzo. There Citizen Giuseppe Blengino (who was once Cavaliere Blengino) gave a receipt to Citizen Cesare Taparelli for 'fifteen writings on sheets of parchment and other writings to the number of twenty-six on paper, which are investitures, diplomas, patents, and concessions concerning Lagnasco'. 'Given in Turin, 2 February 1799: 14 Pluvioso anno 7.' On the cover is the note 'That they may be burnt'. It was essential to the destruction of feudalism that the documentation on which that social system was based should be destroyed in liberated countries as it had so largely been in France in the château-burning period of the Revolution. Luckily the bulk of the family archives remained unscathed.

In this same year the Allied forces drove the French out of

Piedmont: but Napoleon's victory at Marengo the following year made it clear that French domination of north Italy was likely to be of long duration. Cesare therefore decided to leave his country, and he took with him into exile his family, which now included a daughter, Melania, and a fourth son—Giuseppe Maria Crisostomo Rafaelle Massimo, known to us simply as Massimo—born in 1798. The family settled in Florence, where a considerable number of Piedmontese, including the Balbos, had preceded them. Over his desk Cesare hung a view of Turin, with the word *Fuit* carved on the frame.

Massimo's earliest recollections were therefore of Florence. In his *Ricordi* he concentrates especially on his memories of the household of the Countess of Albany, widow of the Young Pretender, who used to give a children's party each week. She was now ageing and stout, dressed always in the style affected much earlier by Marie Antoinette. She was still living with Alfieri, but they had ceased to matter to each other. 'Count Alfieri at nine o'clock each evening went out to join a lady with a French name that I now forget. . . . But when he returned to the house, woe to the footmen if they closed the door and shot the bolt in his hearing. . . . "I am slave enough without having to hear myself locked in!" '[1] The Countess in turn was being wooed by the painter Fabre, and Massimo's first vivid memory was of himself as a naked child of four being told to keep still by a tall thin man in black: this was Alfieri, and Massimo was being used as a model of the infant Christ by Fabre for a picture that, he believed, finally went to a church in Montpellier.

Azeglio in due course went through a period of enthusiasm for the tragedies of Alfieri, and though he came to find Alfieri's style less to his taste than Metastasio's, he continued to regard him as having 'discovered Italy, as Columbus discovered America, and initiated the idea of Italy as a nation'. His mother and his father admired Alfieri as dramatist, but deplored his lack of religion and were gratified that on his death-bed he sent for a priest, and saddened that the priest, hesitating to commit himself, went first to consult his bishop, and arrived at the poet's bedside to find his penitent already dead.

With no public activity to distract him Marchese Cesare concentrated on his own studies and on the education of his

[1] *I miei ricordi*, ed. A. M. Ghisalberti (Einaudi, Turin, 1949), p. 85. All references in this book to the *Ricordi* are to this edition.

family. Immediately after his marriage he had taken his wife's education in hand and had guided her in an intensive course of reading: now it was the children's turn. But his concern was genuinely for their education and not solely for their instruction, and training of character was his chief preoccupation.

As it is described in the *Ricordi* this process seems in some aspects appallingly severe. But Massimo makes it clear that even the sternest discipline was accepted by him as being a normal thing: and the children could not fail to see that under the Spartan severity was a deep love. As Massimo approached his majority he revolted bitterly against his father's control—an incident not at all clearly revealed in the *Ricordi*: but when he came to write his memoirs he had swung round again: in his own words he 'discovered his father after his death', and as an old man he was grateful for the strictness with which his early years had been controlled.

The children were never dressed in such a way as to make them conspicuous amongst other children: they were given few playthings: public demonstrations of affection or admiration for them were avoided by their parents and discouraged in visitors. It was only after their return to Turin that Massimo first heard himself addressed as 'Cavaliere', an honour to which he had not known himself entitled. Minor virtues such as punctuality were insisted on. Arriving one day late for lunch, his second sister Metilde and her governess were made to take their soup out on the balcony of the dining-room, in six inches of snow. Immediate and unquestioning acceptance of parental authority seemed to Massimo in later life, as it had done to his parents, to be essential. 'Children by a law of nature should be moulded by authority and not by their own judgements. I distrust a father, and more especially a mother, who can reply to all a child's "Why's" otherwise than with a "Because I say so".'

Uncomplaining endurance of physical pain was regarded as a notable virtue. 'When a Piedmontese has had his arms and legs broken, and two sword-thrusts through his body, then, and not till then, he may say "Really, I don't feel well",' his father would say. That this Spartan endurance of pain was not a Piedmontese monopoly Massimo was to learn later in the Roman Castelli: but he tells one incident to illustrate it that seems more than a little shocking to us, even though his father's intention was well-meant. Walking one day in the hills with his father he chanced to fall heavily: his father rushed to him, and saw that his arm was broken. 'Listen, Mammolino, your mother is ill: if she sees that you have hurt yourself she will be upset. You must be brave. Tomorrow we will go to Florence and have it attended to, but for tonight you must not let anything be noticed.' And Massimo nursed his broken arm cleverly enough for his mother to be hoodwinked: but it gave him trouble for years afterwards. At the time, however, 'I did not seem to have done anything very important or difficult'.[1]

Cesare was more concerned for the physical development of his children than was usual at that time. They were taken for long walks: Massimo remembered one that began in the late evening, continued through the night, and only ended in the late forenoon of the next day. They were taught to ride and to swim, and all the boys were made to practise some acrobatics, using the trampoline and spring-board. Massimo recalls the sight of his brother Prospero, destined for the priesthood and already wearing the cassock, whirling in an aerial somersault after a take-off from the spring-board, his flowing robe flying around him in his trajectory.

By contrast Cesare had some quite exceptionally solicitous customs. He did not approve, for instance, of children being wakened too suddenly. So he would arouse them by singing to them, at first softly and then gradually more loudly. Their religious education was entrusted to the family chaplains, of whom they had a succession during Massimo's childhood. They over-reached themselves, for Massimo always ascribed his later scepticism to an overdose of religion in early life. The second of this series (for the first was sent packing the moment Massimo innocently told his father something of his extra-curricular practices) had to be endured for five years. For him an ideal day started with a Mass, served by Massimo, who in mid-morning had a 'spiritual reading', with an 'examination of conscience' before lunch. This meal was followed by Benediction or a visit to a church: and the evening was not too short to preclude a triduum or novena. The worst experience for Massimo was a series of special devotions for children in one of the city churches; the happiest, but, like all such idylls, too short-lived, was a period of excommunication imposed on him for having struck his chaplain. This joyous holiday was ended by a formal pardon from

[1] *Ricordi*, p. 98.

no less a person than the Archbishop of Turin. Then and afterwards he believed that the whole business of excommunication and pardon was 'a pure comedy intended to make a deep impression on my soul . . . it was in short a pious fraud, but a fraud is like brandy, at the moment it seems to give one strength, only to leave one weaker than before'.[1]

Massimo's theory that this excess of religion gave him a lifelong distaste for its outward practice seems convincing enough but he does not point out that Roberto and Prospero underwent the same discipline, without experiencing the same reaction. Massimo explains it away too easily: for one could not imagine him ever being as pious or as conventional as his brothers, no matter how differently he had been brought up.

His schooling began in Florence: his elder brothers had been sent as boarders to the Collegio Tolomei in Siena, but Massimo went as a day-boy to be taught in Florence by the Scolopi (Friars of the Scuole Pie). He was one of a class of three, placed in charge of the doorkeeper ('my first professor, of most humble academic status and perfectly matched by his pupil'). He was extremely happy there—as he was almost all the time in Florence, which as a result always seemed to him to be his native city, rather than Turin. The period, however, was that of Napoleon's apogee, and the fortunes of the great Emperor could affect even the small boys sitting at the feet of the Florentine school-doorkeeper. In 1805 Piedmont, as part of the Kingdom of Italy, was brought under the Emperor's direct rule and a decree was soon issued forbidding his Italian subjects to send their children to be educated abroad, 'and Siena was abroad'. A second one summoned the nobility back to their native provinces and a third demanded of them that they take an oath of allegiance to Napoleon. Roberto and Prospero were brought back to Florence and their father began to arrange for the family's return to Turin. He himself was loath to go. The oath of allegiance was something that he could not conscientiously subscribe to, and he wrote to his exiled King, offering to join him in Sardinia. Victor Emmanuel had the good sense to advise his devoted subject not to leave his family but to go with them to Turin and take the oath as required. So, from Pisa, where they had awaited the King's reply, they travelled back to Florence and thence by way of Bologna, Piacenza, and Milan to their home in Turin in Via d'Angennes, after a fortnight

[1] *Ricordi*, pp. 142–4.

on the way. Here Massimo was thrilled to be addressed as 'Signor Cavaliere' and to discover what seemed to him the glorious splendour of their unremembered home.

A school was found for him in Turin, where once again he was one of a class of three: and of the three, by his own confession, by far the least apt scholar. True he won a prize for Greek composition, but this was due to a stratagem that made him despise the prize, his masters, and himself. For whilst the examination was in progress the master of studies looked over his shoulder and was horrified at 'the schismatic Greek I was bringing to birth'. Acutely aware that this illiterate barbarian was nephew of Prospero Balbo, Rector of the University, the master, without the other candidates noticing, dextrously dropped on to Massimo's desk a fair copy of the Greek version. Massimo copied this and handed it in as his own, gained a complete edition of Homer as a reward, and felt the whole affair to have been the greatest humiliation that he could ever receive. Looking back on his formal education he found little that was good in it, for apart from the failure of his teachers to stimulate him to any interest, he found it hard to defend a curriculum that concentrated on Latin and Greek but taught no English or German, and whose course in History was restricted to pre-classical and classical times, and made no reference to Italy in Medieval or later times. But at least he was not physically ill-used as was his friend Grossi at a school of the Oblates near Lecco: he was so often and so severely beaten that 'his skull was something incredible: scars and dents alternated all over it', and when Suvorov's Cossacks rode into the town and stabled their horses in the College, Grossi by sign language besought one of them to take a swipe with his sabre at an especially obnoxious brother.[1]

In 1811, at the age of thirteen, Massimo was enrolled as a student at the University of Turin. At home the family chaplain continued to coach him in Latin, and his father guided him in a wide reading of the Italian classics, but of his studies, such as they were, at the University he has left no record. The best legacy it gave him was the friendship of a lecturer in physics, Giorgio Bidone, who won Massimo's confidence and became a great influence for good at a time when he was in danger of ruining his life by his follies.

For the Azeglio family these years between their return to

[1] *Ricordi*, pp. 489–91.

Turin and the Restoration were gloomy for a variety of reasons. The political situation was heart-breaking to a patriot of Cesare's stamp: his legitimate King was in exile and the Pope was a prisoner of the Emperor. Cesare, it is true, had been able to succour some prelates in their captivity: but to him Napoleon must have seemed like anti-Christ enthroned. To add to this, in 1809 both Roberto and Prospero were called to enter the service of the Emperor. Roberto was not compelled to join the army, but he was employed as a civil servant in France, Rome, and Germany successively. After the Battle of Leipzig he left his unwanted employment and made his way back to Turin. Prospero, the intended priest, by the inscrutable working of the imperial machine, was drafted into the army and was ordered to present himself at St. Cyr. As an act of grace and favour he was permitted to defer his entry for a year, but then he set out for Paris, accompanied by his father. His declared intention of taking orders had interested the Church in his fate, and the intervention of friends, almost certainly including the Archbishop of Turin, secured his release and father and son returned home. There seems no doubt that intercession by Church dignitaries had been backed by bribery, but who paid, how much, and to whom is not known.[1] Greater griefs came from the deaths of their daughters. Melania had always been known to be delicate, and she had been left in Turin with her grandmother when the family went to Florence. She died there at the age of twelve. Metilde, born in 1791, lived long enough to marry, becoming Countess Pallio di Rinco: but she in turn died of phthisis at their castle near Asti in August 1813 at the age of twenty-two.

The following year, 1814, saw the collapse of Napoleon's power in Italy: the wild rejoicing in Turin was tempered somewhat by the presence of Allied forces, who seemed to presage that Piedmont might have changed one master for another: and there was also the fear that the people might get out of hand. To preserve law and order a Civil Guard was enrolled, and Massimo, aged sixteen, now entered it. His university career, such as it had been, was ended, and it seemed that the army would become his profession: after all for a younger son of a family such as the Taparellis the Church and the army were the only decorous alternatives: and one son already had been destined for religion. As a member of the Civil Guard on duty in Piazza Castello

[1] Article by A. G. Tononi in *Rassegna Nazionale*, June 1884.

Massimo had a splendid view of the entry into Turin of his legiti-mate sovereign. The King and his staff received a tumultuous welcome. For so long now Piedmont had been a channel for the torrential activities of Napoleon: that it should become once again a tranquil backwater, ruled over by King Log, must have seemed a desirable event. But Massimo, like others in Turin that day, could not fail to see how antediluvian the King and his companions seemed. 'With powder and pigtails, and hats in the style of Frederick the Great, they were figures of fun.' The term 'codino' (pigtail) became the regular nickname for political reactionaries from this moment. That same evening the King toured the city enjoying the popular excitement, and having neither coach nor horses of his own he accepted the loan of Marchese Cesare's state-coach, 'all gilding and crystal with dropsical cupids above the windows'.

The full meaning of the term 'Restoration' became clear the following day in a Royal Edict: 'Setting aside all other laws, henceforward our subjects shall obey the Royal Constitutions of 1770 together with the Statutes made by Our Royal Predecessors before 30 January 1800.' And the King took the Court Almanac of the year of Charles Emmanuel's departure from Piedmont: he reinstalled all officials in the ranks they had then occupied, replaced the dead as best he could, and in the army, whilst keep-ing in the force those who had served in it under Napoleon, degraded them all by one rank, so that a newly-commissioned officer—like Massimo himself shortly—might be higher in rank than a veteran who had seen Moscow in flames and been at the crossing of the Beresina.

The political oppression that was the policy of the restored governments in Italy earned, and has continued to receive, general disapproval. Little if anything could possibly be said in defence of the administrations of Lucca, Modena, the Papal States, and the Kingdom of the Two Sicilies, though, bad as government was in Rome, a man who was unaware of politics—'un homme moyen sensuel' like Massimo d'Azeglio before 1845—could live quite happily there. The Government of Tuscany was notoriously easy-going, and this duchy became an asylum for malcontents. The Imperial Government of Lombardy-Venetia was, in normal times, the most tolerant of all: such, at least, was Azeglio's impression, and his experience seemed to confirm it. 'If I wished to breathe freely I had to return from Turin to Milan. Why?

Because of the subtle skill with which the Austrian authorities knew how to allay and soften commands from Vienna and allow the widest freedom to the Milanese to grumble, to fool the "pollini" [literally 'lice'—i.e. police], make definite pronouncements not only on the spectacles at the Scala but even on politics: only—it was essential not to shout too loud; with prudence one could say anything. . . .'[1] Azeglio's dealings with the censorship seemed to justify this opinion. But in times of stress the Austrian Government, liable on both sides of the Alps to take panic, acted with severity and even brutality. Rightly enough it is the sporadic fierceness it showed on such occasions against men like Pellico that is remembered and condemned: the long years of slipshod, somewhat contemptuous tolerance are forgotten.

The Government of Piedmont-Sardinia was more consistent than the Austrian. It was uniformly leaden: agitators were imprisoned or driven into exile: the lives of men like Mazzini bore witness to this: but there were not the waves of harshness alternating with slackness that characterized Austrian behaviour. Even after the 1821 revolutionary movement only one death sentence was carried out: and to nickname Carlo Felice 'Carlo Feroce' was an exaggeration.

The restored rulers had now to resume normal diplomatic relations with each other: and the Marchese Cesare was chosen to convey the King's congratulations to the Pope on his restoration. No one more appropriate for this mission could have been selected, for during the Napoleonic persecution of the clergy Cesare had been unremitting in his aid to prelates passing through Piedmont on their way to prison or to exile, even at risk to his own liberty. Among them had been Cardinal de Gregorio, whom he had visited in his confinement in the grim fortress of Fenestrelle, a kindness that the Cardinal was to repay on later occasions by assistance to Massimo in Rome. Cesare took with him Massimo and Prospero, who was now firmly decided to seek entry into the Society of Jesus.

Their father was instructed to stay in Rome until the Marchese di San Saturnino should arrive to take up his post as permanent Sardinian Minister to the Papal Court. Until then the Taparellis, father and sons, paid a round of visits. Massimo was introduced to many of the hierarchy—to the Pope, with whom on one occasion he played a game of billiards, to Cardinals Pacca,

1 *Ricordi*, p. 509.

Somaglia, and de Gregorio: and they renewed acquaintance with his uncle Monsignor, later Cardinal, Morozzo. After the persecutions that these clergy, from the Pope downwards, had endured from Napoleon rather than make concessions against their conscience, they were at this moment more respected than perhaps at any other time since the Renaissance, though this sympathy was to be dissipated by Papal political repression. The palaces of the great lay aristocrats were also open to Cesare—the Torlonia, Piccolomini, Patrizi, and Massimi: whilst he was equally at home with artists like Canova and Thorwaldsen and such poets and dramatists as Rome then possessed. Massimo was not allowed to waste his time in Rome, and he was sent out to visit the antiquities of ancient, and the monuments of Christian Rome. The first guide chosen for him was an antiquary and Massimo was made to absorb culture unremittingly. But the second one, a Signor Malvotti, was quickly summed up by Massimo as a man after his own heart. 'With the lively Malvotti, having seen statues and paintings, I began the study of the originals.' So Massimo entered on a new phase of life, one of riotous indiscipline that was to last for five years. If this reaction against parental and priestly control had not happened in Rome under Malvotti's guidance it would have come a few months later when Massimo was a young officer in Piemonte Reale amongst similar young hotheads. He was never to outgrow his love of womanizing, though he learnt to conduct himself with a decent measure of discretion: but the more reputable interest acquired in Rome, a taste for painting and for music, also stayed with him all his life. This at least fitted in with the background of his family, for his father was interested in the fine arts and in music, being a competent pianist able to play the piano from an orchestral score. Massimo was not alone in developing executive ability: Prospero also was a pianist and became a composer, while Roberto, who seems to have had no interest in music, was an amateur painter and became a historian of art. So, however unusual these interests might be amongst the Piedmontese aristocrats of their day, they were widely shared by the Taparellis.

With the arrival in Rome of San Saturnino and the end of his mission, Cesare set off back to Turin with Massimo but not with Prospero, who had been admitted to the novitiate of the Society of Jesus. Massimo was not to see him again for twenty-seven years. The journey home seemed endlessly long to Massimo, for he had learned of his award of a commission in Piemonte Reale, and his anxiety to join his regiment was only surpassed by his craving to know whether this regiment wore helmets. Back in Via d'Angennes he awoke Enrico at two o'clock in the morning to have this question answered, and slept triumphantly when he learnt that they did.

The Royal Piedmont Regiment was a new formation and presented the odd spectacle of non-commissioned officers and other ranks that included seasoned veterans under officers many of whom were treading a barrack-square for the first time in their lives. Massimo saw enough examples of young officers making fools of themselves by their public display of ignorance of the most elementary techniques of military drill to determine to learn, and as quickly as possible, enough of its procedure to avoid such ludicrous humiliation. He worked hard—and he played hard too: for one thing he felt the exhilaration of having a good horse to ride: and off duty there was the company of officers as young and gay as himself. Writing his Memoirs over forty years later he neither conceals nor palliates his follies of this epoch: reading his account of them one feels that they were acts of defiance rather than outbursts of frivolity, as when he drove into Turin in an open carriage with one of the most notorious women of the town on each side of him at the time when all polite society was taking its Sunday afternoon walk, or when, in order to finance a trip to Milan with some of his companions, he took with him two portraits by Rigault of an ancestor and his wife of the period of Louis XIV, stolen by him from his home and sold in Milan. His parents were able to buy them back a dozen years later, and were forgiving enough to refer to this as his 'outing with his ancestors'. But forgiveness could not have come easily. The only person who, on his own showing, exercised any moderating influence over him at this time was his former university teacher, Giorgio Bidone. There were times in plenty when, without any promptings, Massimo felt disgust with himself as he thought of his stupid exploits. And there was a growing, more continuous self-questioning about the career he had chosen. His outbreaks were due in part to a wish to behave even more conspicuously than his fellow-officers, but also in part they were perhaps a reaction to a way of life whose dull routine gave him no satisfaction. For one of his class it was natural to be an army officer and to have no further ambition for a whole lifetime; but was he, he wondered, going to be content to go on for thirty years supervising the currying of horses and the measuring out of fodder to the amount prescribed by the Ministry of War? Even with the helmet of Piemonte Reale it hardly seemed worth while. And as his dissatisfaction with this life grew, so also did the longing to become an artist— and to become one not in Turin but in Rome. To the family, art as an interest was natural and admirable: but even to them, enlightened as they were compared to most of their class, art as a career was unheard of. As Massimo grew more and more determined the tug-of-war inside the family became more obstinately contested. The *Ricordi* do not clearly indicate how long and how bitter this contest was, lasting from 1817 to 1820. During this time it was Costanza, Roberto's wife, who was peacemaker in the family: and on 27 April 1819 Massimo's mother wrote to her: 'You may imagine how often I have tried to change Massimo's ideas: do you know what he answers? "I *do* love my father and the fact that I have been willing to give up my plans in order to obey him proves it: I have promised and I will not go back on it. But confidence and affection cannot be commanded and the past has made an impression on me that cannot be wiped out." '[1]

Cesare's reluctance to yield to his son's importunity was not based solely on a class-conscious feeling that for a nobleman to make a living (if he managed even to do that) by painting was demeaning. To Cesare the first duty of a Taparelli d'Azeglio, as of every aristocrat, was to serve the State or the Church as he, Roberto, and Prospero had done or were doing; and as their ancestors had done, and had felt it their duty to do as part of the social contract implicit in their occupation of a privileged position in society. Massimo himself could not deny this and even when he came to write his Memoirs, as a fairly successful painter, he still felt that 'in so far as the interests of his country are the main concern of a citizen . . . for society's sake a general, an economist, an administrator, even though mediocre in ability, are more useful than a painter, musician, or poet even of the first rank'.[2] As against this, however, in the Sardinia of his day he saw no certainty that he could serve even himself by taking up an artistic career. Added to the doubt about the fitness of such a career for him was the equally serious doubt about his fitness for

[1] Letter of 27 April 1819 in Archives of the Opera Pia Taparelli, Saluzzo (hereafter referred to as O.P.T.).
[2] *Ricordi*, p. 219.

the career. An interest in art such as he had did not guarantee ability to practise it. And, were he competent, would he be willing to live by selling paintings? Would he find this dependence on pleasing patrons, and having, it might be, to haggle with them, more dignified than supervising the care of cavalry-horses? And in addition, for Cesare, there was the lack of confidence in his son's moral stability. If he was capable of such monstrous follies in Turin how wildly might he behave in Rome freed from all tutelage? It is no wonder that a father hesitated long before giving consent to such a fantastically risky proposal. The marvel is that he gave it in the end—and with a good grace into the bargain.

Massimo gained his objective stage by stage. The first step was to gain his father's consent to his transferring from Piemonte Reale to the Brigata Guardie. This was an infantry regiment. From this he was able to pass into the Reserve. The next step was to convince his parents that he was capable of working steadily and living soberly. He broke completely and permanently with his former army friends, spent his time indoors reading seriously, or in the houses of his father's friends copying paintings in their collections. For some months he worked so hard as to bring on a break-down in health: and this demonstration of self-control and industry did more than all his arguments had done to convince his parents that his determination to become a painter was genuine. They decided to make the experiment of taking him to Rome for a trial period. In 1818, despite her ill-health, his mother set out heroically on the tedious journey to Rome with Massimo and Enrico. Her brother, Monsignor Morozzo, had found accommodation for them in Piazza Colonna, with an aged priest in the Papal civil service as their landlord, until one night they heard unwonted movement in the house, and learnt the next morning that he had been taken off to prison for falsifying his accounts. For Massimo a studio had been found and he set to work with zeal but, as he came to see before long, with no sense of direction. During this winter in Rome he rarely frequented society and, unlike the Romans, rose and went to bed early. Not content with trying to master the art of painting, he tried his hand at writing. He confected an epic fragment, half a comedy, a handful of odes and sonnets, and launched himself into a tragedy on the story of Dido. This was to be in the regulation five acts. In the first of them Aeneas summoned his companions and told them that the gods had commanded him to abandon Dido and to continue his journey. But having written so much Massimo realized that it was going to be difficult to interest even himself, let alone an audience, in four more acts whose action had already been announced. 'And so I sent Aeneas, Dido, Anna, and the whole lot to the devil.' He then tried a one-act comedy and went 'in Arcadian simplicity' to the theatre to show it to the actor Vestri, whom he found rehearsing his company. He introduced himself as best he could and handed the actor his neatly-copied manuscript: but Vestri looked at him pityingly, made some excuse, and turned back to his rehearsal: and that was final, for Massimo there and then abandoned all ambition to write comedies.

From Rome he made an excursion to Naples to join Enrico. They visited all the customary places of interest: but more importantly he came to know a small group of men who were to be associated with him all his life. One was Clemente Solaro della Margarita,[1] who, though politically opposed to Azeglio later, was to keep his admiration and affection for ever. Another was Marchese Domenico Ricci, who was also studying art and music: they lost sight of each other until 1852, when Ricci's son sought the hand of Azeglio's daughter. He spoke more kindly of him in his Memoirs than he was to do in his letters.

In spring Massimo and his mother moved to Castel Gandolfo, where they were joined by his father. There also they found interesting company; there were diplomats from Rome, the Torlonia at their villa, and amongst others was Miss Cornelia Knight.[2] She had been lady-companion to the Prince-Regent's daughter Princess Charlotte (Azeglio mistakenly calls her Caroline) and had lived for many years in Italy, for much of that time in Naples, where she had known Nelson, for whom her hero-worship was unbounded, Collingwood, Acton, and Troubridge, whom, according to Azeglio, she would have married had he not been lost at sea. She was known to all the Azeglio family, though it is not possible to discover how often or when they met. In 1862, when he had received a copy of her posthumous memoirs, Roberto wrote: 'J'ai beaucoup connu Miss Knight dont je goûtais beaucoup la conversation et le good-natured [sic] du caractère.'[3] Massimo seems to have had some tuition from her in English: and he records his envy of her pride in being English:

---

[1] Or della Margherita.   [2] 1757–1837. Her Memoirs were published in 1861.
[3] Letter of Roberto to Emanuele, in O.P.T.

for already he observed that no Italian could find similar pride in his nationality, Italy being just the name of the country in which he had been born.

Massimo's artistic studies were now becoming better organized: instead of working on his own he had now become a pupil of Martin Verstappen, a Flemish painter of high repute in Rome at that time, and he was to return to work under his somewhat spasmodic tuition again after his short return to Turin. Massimo and his fellow-pupil (Verstappen never had more than two, and seemed to regret having any at all) worked in the outermost of the master's rooms, in which he kept his finished canvases whilst they were awaiting dispatch: their sole occupation was to copy these. Verstappen himself worked in an inner room into which no one but himself ever penetrated. He would emerge at night only, to make long perambulations through the city simply for the sake of exercise, and for days the pupils might not see him. Then he might come out to them, look over their shoulders, and make the briefest of comments in his guttural Italian. But sometimes he would be shut in for days on end, emerging hollow-eyed. In the summer he would migrate to some village outside Rome and make sketches galore, from which he would work up finished pictures during the rest of the year, a method that Azeglio also was to follow. Whatever Cesare might think of painting as a career, he now would discuss Massimo's efforts dispassionately and helpfully, avoiding discouraging him, but equally seeking not to give too much stimulus to him to think of art as a possible lifetime's occupation.

In the spring of 1820 the entire family returned to Turin. It was made into a leisurely journey, for they went by way of Modena and Mantua to Venice before turning westwards to their home. But Massimo's one great aim was to return to Rome: it was not to be expected that either of his parents would go back with him —if he did go back—and it was therefore essential that he should convince them that he had a real vocation, that he had promise of success, and that he had enough moral stability to be allowed to live alone. So he spent the summer in Turin working hard, as he had done before, copying paintings in private possession. He did not notice that there was a mounting interest in politics: organizations like the Carbonari and the Adelfi were gaining adherents, especially amongst the administrative and learned professions, and amongst army officers. His own brother Roberto was certainly involved in the Carbonari movement: but Massimo knew and cared nothing about all this: his sole concern was to go on painting in Turin in order to gain permission to paint in Rome. His industry and his progress finally convinced his father: before the end of the year he was allowed to resign his commission and go to Rome; but it was on terms that would mean absolute poverty: he was given an allowance, but it was exactly what he had had whilst living at home, enough, but only enough, to buy his clothes. This minimum, with liberty, was a wonderful concession, and Massimo set off southwards again, alone.

II

ROME, 1820-1826

As a result of his return to Rome, Massimo avoided any implication in the 1821 Carbonari movement, though even had he been in Turin he might not have been involved. His friend Bidone wrote urging him to come back to take part in the attempt to wrest a constitution for Sardinia: but his father also wrote forbidding him to leave Rome; and in case he should be already on his way other letters were sent to await him in Florence and Genoa to order him back. As he admitted, he had not a particle of interest in constitutions for Sardinia or for anywhere else and it had never entered his mind to go back to Turin, which bored him, to urge the granting of something that meant nothing to him. But when Austrian troops were being sent to suppress the risings in the Kingdom of the Two Sicilies he went to the Neapolitan Minister in Rome to offer his services in the Neapolitan army should there be any resistance to the Austrians.[1] The offer was sincere but unsophisticated since the Neapolitan Government was inviting the Austrians in, not planning resistance to them: his services as a result were not called for. Yet his action, however impractical, was typical of his general outlook: he might have no interest in constitutional experiments such as those planned for his own state: but he already felt deeply enough about foreign intervention in Italian affairs to be willing to fight against it. As long as he lived the liberation of Italy was to be more important to him than liberalism or unification.

Enrico, who had a commission in the artillery, took no part in the rising, his regiment remaining loyal to the Crown, to the satisfaction of his father; and Massimo also approved, for he thought that the intervention of the army in politics was a greater evil than popular insurrection. Roberto, however, was deeply involved. He was already a member of the Carbonari: we have his own word for that. In a letter of 12 February 1849 to his son he refers to himself as an 'ex-Carbonaro'.[2] It is also known that it was he who introduced Asinari, Santarosa, Lisio, and

---

[1] *Ricordi*, p. 282.
[2] Letter of that date in O.P.T.

Collegno to Charles Albert at the interview of 6 March when they urged him to use his influence with King Victor Emmanuel to persuade him to grant a constitution to Piedmont.[1] This was the first of a series of interviews in which the demands of the Carbonarists increased, and Charles Albert hesitated, advanced, and then retreated. Roberto seems to have played no further part in the process of bringing pressure to bear on the Prince, and he later took no part in the popular uprising. After the failure of the constitutionalist movement, when Charles Albert's succession was left in doubt, and when he turned bitterly against the liberals, who, he believed, had misrepresented him, used him as a tool, and deceived him, he made an exception for Roberto, with whom he remained on friendly terms. But Cesare found it harder to forgive his son and it was a long time before they were fully reconciled. When the movement ended with the abdication of Victor Emmanuel I and the arrival in Turin of Charles Felix, Roberto was advised to leave the country for a time. From then until 1826 he lived abroad, in Geneva and later in Paris. But from 1821 he took little active part in politics and never aspired to any position of influence in national affairs, though he was active in municipal and philanthropic matters.

For Cesare himself only one course of action was conceivable at a time when the throne seemed to be in danger: his loyalty to the House of Savoy must be demonstrated all the more openly after the equivocal part played by his eldest son. When it became known on 11 March that the garrison in the citadel of Turin was in revolt and demanding a constitution the Marchese put on his uniform, buckled on his sword, and rode to the palace, where others of his age, class, and opinions were gathered to defend their sovereign. But Victor Emmanuel was unwilling either to grant the constitution or to cause bloodshed, and during the night signed a deed of abdication. On the morning of the 13th he drove out of Turin, unmolested, unworried, and without rancour. Cesare, learning of the abdication, had returned home, depressed and apprehensive. Most of those who had rallied in vain around their King were conservatives of the deepest eighteenth-century dye— 'codini' to a man—and to the ordinary people, as well as to his son, Cesare seemed no different from the rest of them. But Victor Emmanuel and Charles Felix were by no means so sure of him; and their doubts were justified: he was not the reactionary that

[1] Piero Pieri, *Le società segrete ed i moti del 1820–1821 e 1831* (1948), p. 168.

the less perceptive thought him. In a letter to Roberto he stated his beliefs.

Certainly I would oppose revolutionaries with whatever I might have of wisdom, skill, strength, and reputation . . . but if revolution should succeed by royal assent, whether this were the result of persuasion or through fear of some greater evil, I would adapt myself to the royal ordinance, and, the new system once established, I would be its tenacious supporter. To obey whoever rules is one's duty, saving certain limitations: and it would be almost without limitations if the king should have conceded another form of monarchy, mixed or constitutional.[1]

Although Massimo knew many in Rome who were interested in politics and who belonged to political societies he never joined any such organization, nor, according to his Memoirs, was he ever invited to do so. His account of these years is the most entertaining and the most detailed part of his autobiography, though one is inclined to doubt whether he worked quite as unremittingly as he alleges: when he was writing his novels he suggests that he worked like a galley slave: yet he spent so long on their composition that one wonders if he did not exaggerate his industry.

For a time in the winter of 1820–1 he was taking lessons in the early morning in English and history from a Genoese named Garello, who, he says 'had found new and useful applications of mnemonics to these studies'. Apart from his lessons from Miss Knight, and later conversation with Countess Fanny Persano (née Bacon), there is no record of his study of English before he began to write his novella[2] in that language, so it is possible that he really worked quite hard with Garello. After these lessons he took exercise by riding. It was quite impossible for him to have a horse of his own, but by tipping a groom he could sometimes get a mount on one of the horses of the Rospigliosi family, which had in any case to be exercised every day.

He would then go to a studio to practise drawing from life: one studio that he frequented was run by a certain Antonio, a model of magnificent physique and kindly disposition, though it was true that 'in a moment of vivacity he had killed his brother; but no one can be perfect'. After such a day, weary and with little

---

[1] *Ricordi*, p. 430.
[2] This story, published in *Italian Studies*, Vol. XII, 1957, is first mentioned in a letter of 18 January 1847 to Persano (C. Persano (ed.), *Lettere di M. d'A. a Carlo di Persano*, Turin, 1878).

to spend even if he had been in the mood for amusement, he would go to bed at a time when Roman society was beginning to bestir itself. All the same it was not to be imagined that a man of twenty-two could be capable of being the industrious apprentice all day and every day—especially in Rome, and Massimo had a wide circle of friends, laymen and ecclesiastics, some of them aristocrats with whom his acquaintance dated back to the time of his father's mission to Rome, or to the family visit of 1818–20. He had a succession of love affairs, mostly transitory and unidentifiable: but one was to last for some years and to have permanent importance in his life. He refers to it, and to its abrupt termination, when his mistress jilted him for a wealthier and still more nobly-born lover, in his Memoirs, but he naturally concealed the lady's name: nor was this his only concealment.[1] She was a member of the Roman aristocracy, Carolina Morici. She bore him a daughter, Bice, whom he acknowledged, and who was much with him in the later years of his life. The many references to her in his letters are naturally either excised or concealed under initials in the published versions. Duchessa Margherita Lante was also for a time his mistress: but most of his affairs were with women of less exalted rank.

Such liaisons as these with the Morici and the Lante were not likely to arouse much unfavourable comment in the Rome of that age, if Azeglio's accounts are at all reliable; and they are borne out by the comments of many other observers. Though the government of Rome was through priests and for priests, the ethical standards of society were lax. The administration was rotten with corruption, and asceticism was far from the rule amongst the clergy: Antonelli, Cardinal Secretary of State during the Pontificate of Pius IX, was to surpass all others in the size of the fortune and of the family he left behind him, both acquired irregularly. The lay aristocracy were easy-going: marriages were arranged and in consequence marital fidelity was not to be expected; it was not even held to be a social virtue and when it was conspicuous it aroused no admiration. 'What a Cossack!' exclaimed a Roman mother when she learnt that a young husband had resented her son's paying court to his wife. During the Carnival period that preceded Lent standards of behaviour became even more elastic as opportunities for intrigues became easier during those parts of the day when masks and cloaks were

1 See A. M. Ghisalberti, *M. d'A., un moderato realizzatore* (1930), p. 170.

worn. But at least by this time one of the most objectionable features of the Roman Carnival had been discontinued—the public humiliation of the Jews of Rome, who had once been rolled in barrels down Monte Testaccio—the fantastic heap of ancient potsherds outside the city walls—then, later, made to run foot-races along the Corso: and finally, as an act of charity, simply required to send their Rabbi to the City Council to present a declaration of submission and be ceremonially kicked by the Mayor, who in the end made a gesture of kicking the Rabbi without actually connecting with his person: this Christian custom lasted until 1830. Much of the merrymaking of the Carnival was harmless—even ingenious. On one occasion Azeglio, Rossini, and Paganini made up a trio. They composed a burlesque begging-poem that Rossini set to music. Then, dressed as women, Rossini already stout, Paganini skeletally emaciated, they went from house to house along the Corso singing and playing guitars: but Azeglio says he soon became bored and went home to bed!

As the Papal Government was a total despotism its subjects had to content themselves with gossip. Countless stories were in circulation about the irregular lives of the nominally celibate clergy: corruption among the clergy in high and low places was notorious: the police were inefficient and brutal, the judges, as the saying is, the best that money could buy. Azeglio tells how a sculptor was cheated out of an antique statue that he had bought quite honestly; he had restored it, as the custom then was—sometimes by destroying another antique to provide materials for the restoration. But after the expenditure of money, time, and skill it was then sequestrated from him by its first owner, an aristocrat, who, having influence with the Government, was able to compel the artist to return the remodelled statue to him for its original purchase price and an arbitrarily-fixed recompense for his work. At the other end of the scale of injustices were the imprisonments, the tortures, and the executions for political and criminal offences, some of them of a most venal nature.

For what that mattered, the Church did, however, provide a magnificent and permanent pageant and on important occasions its ceremonial could be absorbingly interesting. It was like this on the death of a Pope. There was the verification of his death, the tapping on his forehead with a silver hammer, the calling of him by name, and his subsequent lying in state, with the fascination of a conclave to follow. About all this Massimo is interesting, though he has few revelations to make, writing as an outsider: but he does tell us of the confusion that could arise when a Pope was known to be moribund.

When the Pope is nearing his end, and the chance of a recovery is impossible all the ties that bound his household are broken . . . no time is to be lost. It is a question of hours at most, and they must be used to the full. So each and all set about taking and stowing away all that is their own and much that is not, private papers, jewels, money, robes: it is a general sauve-qui-peut and many a time the unhappy old man dies alone. . . . So it happened to Gregory XVI. . . . I quote the words of a friend whom I know to be reliable. 'A poor gardener who loved the Pope knew that he was on the point of death. The man took it into his mind to see him once again: he finds the private staircase open, goes up and arrives at an ante-room; knocks; no one; he goes through and finds himself in the Pope's bedroom: but he is lying as though he had been trying to raise himself in a fit of choking, lying curled up on his side, with his head dangling over the side of the bed. The poor gardener rushes to help him and lifts him back on to the bed as best he can: he calls to him, feels his pulse, and finds him cold: he goes down on his knees weeping and recites a *de profundis* for the dead Pope. Just then one of the household enters, perhaps just back from hiding things away: he is taken by surprise, shouts and threatens the man lest he should tell tales, and chases him out. But the gardener talked. . . .'[1]

The death of a Pope gave rise to exciting speculation as to his possible successor: but it also involved a period of public mourning, the closing of theatres, and the cancellation of public and private festivities. When a Pope died during Carnival his lack of tact was bitterly resented. Leo XII did this and his death was celebrated in a doggerel that might be translated:

> Holy Father, you've thrice done us wrong
> By accepting the Throne, and by living too long
> Until so unreasonably dying unseasonably.

Leo's least forgivable action on his election in 1823 had been to proclaim 1825 a Jubilee Year, 'which meant Rome transformed for twelve months into a great factory of spiritual exercises; no theatres, no festivals, no dances, no receptions: not even puppet-shows in the streets: instead, sermons, missions, processions, functions'.[2] Even Turin was preferable to Rome in such a year, and Azeglio went home.

It was his custom in any case to leave the city each spring.

---

[1] *Ricordi*, p. 410.   [2] Ibid., p. 413.

Vincent p.265

This was not a fashionable custom, for the aristocracy stayed in the city during the summer. The high ceilings, marble floors, and closed shutters of their houses gave respite from the heat of the day and their active social life began in the cool of the late evening. Only in the autumn would they go to some resort in the hills or on the coast. Azeglio's reasons for not following their practice were partly to avoid the enervating heat of Rome, but more particularly to go where he could spend the daylight hours out of doors painting or sketching from nature. His preference was for the Castelli Romani, the villages in the hills that ring Rome to the east and south-east. Between them and the city lay a flat plain made picturesque by the broken aqueducts striding across it and by the Appian Way with its roadside monuments and scattered massive ruins. But this flat ground was marshy and malarial. Travellers crossed it only by day when the mosquitoes were inactive—or as they explained it, when the earth was not exhaling its evil air, its *mal'aria*. The carters who brought the wines of the hills into Rome travelled by night, and must have been immune to the infection: but it was dangerous for the unaccustomed to take this risk. Azeglio often did, travelling at a gallop. But to move slowly or to stay at one of the wayside inns was madness. Azeglio did so on one occasion and found the mosquitoes to be of phenomenal size and voracity: he had one bout of malaria, but it did not last long nor, luckily for him, did it recur.

The hill-slopes were, and still are, covered with deciduous trees as well as pines, so there was abundant shade. At Tivoli the air was cooled in the Villa d'Este by the sophisticated fountains installed for that purpose, but the natural cascades also sounded cool even if they did not actually lower the temperature. Castel Gandolfo looked down on the circular mirror of Lake Albano, and from Genzano one saw the more mysterious water of the Lake of Nemi, each lake in its crater of an extinct volcano. Grottaferrata had its abbey of Basilian monks observing the Greek rite: Rocca di Papa, a castle, once the stronghold of the Borgia Pope Alexander VI. Marino had a palace of the Colonna family, Castel Gandolfo villas of the Pope and of the Barberini, Ariccia a palace of the Chigi, and Genzano one of the Cesarini. The villages were pleasant and unassuming. But what made, and makes, them so attractive was their situation. Well above sea-level, they enjoy fresh air when Rome is sweltering, and from them one looks sideways along the range of wooded hills, or at

Albano as from a veranda over a vertical drop across the Latian plain. The view is loveliest in the evening as one looks into the setting sun. Then one can see the cupola of St. Peter's and, beyond, a grey shimmer that might be haze, or might be the Tyrrhenian Sea: and all bathed in that amber light that harmonizes so well with the red-sandstone, ochre stucco, or honey-coloured travertine of Roman buildings.

Azeglio lived in each of these villages in the summers from 1821 to 1826. The first in which he stayed was Castel Sant'Elia, chosen because he knew that Martin Verstappen was there and on this occasion he was accompanied by a fellow art-student, Michele Pacetti, a nephew by marriage of Verstappen. He and Michele were to be friends for many years, and he became god-father to Pacetti's son Stefano: although he and Michele ceased to be friends, he looked upon Stefano almost as a son.[1] Verstappen had not expected them, in fact had tried to keep his retreat a secret, and he made no attempt to hide his lack of enthusiasm for their company: they saw little of him, and never succeeded in seeing him at work. The two youths had to find shelter of some kind: neither could pay for lodging at even the meanest inn, and they installed themselves in a ruined cottage that had been deserted for a generation. Michele, luckier than Azeglio, had a donkey and this also had to be lodged indoors for safety. Sacks filled with straw served as mattresses, sheets they already had, a table was borrowed, and a few pots and pans bought. Every other day one would go to Nepi, the nearest market town, to buy bread and stuff to make a soup, though it is hard to say what, since he says they managed without vegetables, fruit, milk, and butter. They were gradually accepted by the villagers, and houses were opened to them in the evenings: they would entertain their hosts by singing and playing the guitar: and on Sundays Massimo played the organ for the village priest.

Azeglio describes his method of working during this and other periods in the Castelli.

I used to paint from nature in canvases of fair size, trying to finish the study as a painting on the spot without adding a brush-stroke indoors. I did smaller studies of details, trying always to make them as finished as possible. That was the morning's work. After lunch I did drawings, also from nature, finishing them with great care and studying every

<hr />

[1] Ghisalberti, op. cit., p. 72.

detail of relief. By this means my two months' stay at Castel Sant'Elia led me to make my first real progress and got me out of the technical difficulties of a beginner. Finishing from nature on the scene, as one would finish a painting in a studio, makes one achieve a background with the simple aid of nature and not with the forced contrasts of mannered art. Remembering always, however, that our means are limited whilst those of nature are infinite. For she has light on her palette, whereas we have pigment. So we are forced to use artifice, and thus to create 'art'. It is easy to make up a background of a misty and sky-coloured distance, with a huge dark tree thrusting forwards, in the style of the mannerists: but it is not easy to create such a background with the infinite gradations found in nature, which so often is bright in the foreground and darker in the distance. It is not just less easy, but in fact impossible to draw them together unless one modifies the sky-scene to a certain extent, setting the distance back and bringing forward the foreground a little more than in actuality. Even this artifice must be kept within certain limits. How are these fixed? By talent and taste. These are the mainsprings of art. Inspiration is the ray of light that makes the seed germinate. For landscape painting precepts and advice can be given, but if it is not the creation of imagination all will be useless. For this reason great landscape painters have been fewer than great masters of other branches of art.[1]

In July, annoyed because his rank had become known owing to the arrival of a packet addressed to the Marchese Massimo d'Azeglio, he left Castel Sant'Elia for Rocca di Papa, where he was unknown. The summer was passing, the exodus from Rome beginning, and a party of his friends, led by a Princess whose name he conceals—Princesse Trois Étoiles—found him there as they passed through on their way to her villa. The 'Princess' may have been the Countess Morici, or, perhaps, the Duchess Lante. But though both have been suggested as possible originals neither carries full conviction: the Princess is described as in her forties, heavily in debt as a result of her extravagances, and mistress of a series of plebeian lovers: this certainly does not indicate the Morici, who can only have been in her mid-twenties at this time, and who in any case was his mistress, according to him, for seven years. For a time he interrupted his work to camp out with this party in their villa on the hill above Rocca di Papa. His stay here was tinged with tragedy; he encountered a group of men who were passing themselves off as brigands, falling in with them as they were practising their marksmanship in a wood near where he

[1] *Ricordi*, p. 270.

Vincent, p. 161

was painting: he found their leader a sympathetic person, of unusual background: his story might have been interesting, but Azeglio never heard it, for a few days later he was treacherously killed in an inn. More disturbing was the fate of the married pair with whom he lodged: the husband, Carluccio Castri, kept a café, and village gossip began to link the names of Carluccio's wife with Azeglio. Azeglio insists on his innocence in this matter, and Carluccio certainly seems to have believed him, for when Azeglio left Rocca di Papa, Carluccio accompanied him down the hill for some way across the plain: they parted with complete trust in each other: but when Carluccio returned to the village it was to meet a wave of mockery as a complacent husband: and that night he killed himself. Azeglio does not draw a direct contrast between this village code of honour and the way of life of the Princesse Trois Étoiles—and of her daughters, one of whom he says he saw years afterwards as a camp-follower of the Papal army after a life as dissipated as her mother's.

As a result of the summer's activity Azeglio had three or four large canvases, a score or so of smaller ones, and many drawings; so after taking these to Rome he felt he deserved a holiday, and in October he went to Albano to rest. As Albano was more easily accessible though no nearer Rome than Rocca di Papa and had already become a sizeable small town, it had a more respectable as well as a larger population of holiday-makers from Rome, civil servants and members of the professions, whose country holiday was devoted to an evening stroll and gambling till dawn.

The following year he went to stay in Genzano, a little beyond Albano, a smaller and simpler town. He arrived in time to see the 'Infiorata', when the whole length of the main street leading up to the church is carpeted with flowers arranged in a succession of rich and fragile patterns: this is done for the Feast of the Assumption, in preparation for the procession that goes to the church by way of this street. Naturally at such a time the few inns were packed and Azeglio was given hospitality for a night by a villager. The next day he took up his residence in what were to be his quarters for the summer—in the palace of Duke Salvatore Sforza. This sounds imposing: but the palace, though vast, was dilapidated and unfurnished. Azeglio established himself in a small room reached by way of the grand staircase and a suite of state apartments where family portraits still hung on the walls. In the village the palace had the reputation of being haunted, but Azeglio's nerves were strong and he was troubled by nothing more insubstantial than bats and rats. This summer he was not so poor as to have to make his own meals, and he ate at the local inn. As in the previous year, 1821, he moved to Albano in October before going back to Rome for the winter. Succeeding summers were spent in Marino (1823 and 1824), Tivoli (1825), and Ariccia (1826); but in all these years he was able to stay either at an inn or with a better-off peasant family.

These periods of residence in the Castelli were the most idyllic and picturesque episodes of his whole life: they gave him the material for his vivid 'Sketches of Italian Life', published by his friend Torelli in his paper *Cronista* in 1856 and 1857, rewritten as Chapters 17 (Part 1) and 1 to 10 (Part 2) of his *Ricordi*. Of the characters portrayed in them the most memorable is Sor Checco Tozzi, with whom he lodged in Marino. As a boy Checco had left home in the wake of the French armies heading south to Naples. He returned as a man possessed of capital, though how acquired no one was ever to learn. He went back to work in the stone quarries but within three years had become owner of vineyards, wine-cellars, and cottages. He married a widow, also not without means, and being by then Marino's most substantial citizen was accorded the honorific title of 'Sor'. He had one child, a daughter—'a snail in human form', Azeglio called her—on whom he doted and for whom he managed to find a husband of much higher social class, totally harmless if equally totally useless for any purpose except to walk once a day through Marino in his blue coat with brass buttons. To all except his daughter and son-in-law Checco was an unqualified tyrant, none the less ruthless for his superficial joviality. Sor Fumasoni, the local advocate, business adviser, and letter-writer, was on the other hand a really attractive personality. No wedding was complete without him for his special gift was for the improvisation of verses in honour, or more often in mockery, of the guests at the banquet. The real measure of the man was shown one night when he was ambushed by enemies and shot. There was nothing remarkable in this: it would have been more singular not to have enemies, and one had to expect them to shoot: but though a charge of shot had entered his back near the kidneys and gone right through him he managed to walk home and without telling his wife in what way or how badly he was hurt sent her for the doctor, saying he would get himself to bed whilst she was gone.

Violence was never very far away and knife-play might flare
up for any reason or for no reason at all. A lad might impetuously
draw his knife, scrape a line in the dust of the street, and challenge
anyone to cross it. Motivated quarrels over points of honour were
settled more formally. For these it was the custom in Marino for
the disputants to go down to the river-bed where dense masses of
reeds grew higher than a man. The duellists, each with his knife
in his right hand and his jacket rolled round his left forearm as a
sort of shield, would enter the reeds at opposite points and stalk
each other through the dense growth: it was rare for both to
emerge alive from this type of encounter.

For him who had killed his man there was only one course of
action—to take to the hills as a bandit. Azeglio considered himself
lucky, for as he escaped malaria in his night crossings of the plain
so he went unmolested by brigands during his solitary excursions
by day into the hills. Such meetings as he had with them were
amicable, and on one occasion he found them co-operative: for
Azeglio and two friends had promised to decorate the apse of a
church with mural paintings in return for a picnic lunch to be
given them by the parish priest. They arrived early at the church
and found it already occupied by three brigands who had sought
asylum there. It was not unknown for such refugees to spend
months in sanctuary, passing their time loafing, gambling, and
quarrelling and for these three the arrival of the painters was a
most welcome diversion. They made themselves useful grinding
colours and doing odd jobs, so that the painting was finished
by lunch-time.

Banditry was not disapproved of by the majority of the
peasantry who knew that a man took to it as a result of some
unfortunate circumstance—a murder committed in a 'moment of
vivacity' or in pursuit of a legitimate vendetta. To Azeglio it
seemed to be the result of an indefensible social structure and an
oppressive, corrupt, and inefficient political and judicial system.
The response of the middle and upper classes to these grievances
was the development of secret societies. Azeglio, like everyone else,
knew of their existence and could usually guess which of his
acquaintances were likely to belong to one. He was not interested
in their aims and implacably hostile to their procedures. Fearful
as such societies must always be of traitors amongst their numbers,
they were for ever purging themselves of men suspected or guilty
of informing. At Marino in 1824 there was Prince Luigi Spada,

hiding from a society to which he had belonged, though in Azeglio's view he was half mad. Far different was Doctor Leonida Montanari, the medical doctor of Rocca di Papa, an altruist and political idealist at whose execution in Piazza del Popolo Azeglio was present. He had been chosen by lot to kill an informer, had run him through with a dagger, but had failed to kill him: his victim had accused him, and Montanari with an accomplice was sentenced to death. The real sensation however did not lie in the execution but in the refusal of the condemned men to accept the last rites of the church, though their beheadings were postponed for hours whilst priests pleaded with them. To Azeglio it was a tragedy that men of Montanari's stamp should inflict and suffer death to preserve the secrecy of any organization, however admirable its ultimate end might be or however necessary its secrecy.[1]

These summers in the Castelli Romani were of decisive importance to Azeglio's professional career, since it was this serious practice of painting from nature that made him into a competent and, in due course, successful artist. But they did more than that. His life amongst the peasants and small-town middle-class people, complementing his familiarity with his own aristocratic milieu, gave him an understanding of his fellow-Italians that was unusual in anyone of his period, especially so in a Piedmontese, and extraordinary in a member of the Piedmontese nobility.

[1] For Azeglio's life in the Castelli see *Ricordi*, pp. 367–406; for Checco Tozzi, pp. 371ff; for Fumasoni, pp. 383–4; for Montanari, pp. 399–400.

III

TURIN AND MILAN, 1826-1845

THE Roman period of Azeglio's life ended with an unforeseeable abruptness in 1826. During the later part of it he had been becoming more and more deeply involved in his love of the Morici. To be absent from Rome all the summer months when she was still there became a purgatory, and he began to compromise by working all week in his village retreat and then riding down to Rome on Saturday evening, going into society from his arrival until Sunday night, then returning to his country home at the gallop across the dreaded plain. His passion for her had become an obsession. It must have been purely physical, for he realized that she had had no education and had little intelligence and, as it proved, little constancy: but she was beautiful, and when he met her in 1842 after a break of sixteen years she was still so lovely that he was amazed that he did not fall in love with her all over again. He who found it hard to be faithful to any one woman declared that this was one of the few periods of his life when he found constancy possible.

At the end of 1826 he had just come back from a long holiday in Naples and Sorrento, where he had been sent for the sake of his health. The change had done him little good, and indeed in Naples he had become so ill as to be almost panic-stricken: at Sorrento he had improved just sufficiently to be able to return to Rome, no sicker, but no better than when he had left. The Morici received him with storms of rage, accusing him of unheard-of infidelities: her confidante advised him to stay away from her until she should have cooled down. This he did. But in Rome no secrets were inviolable, and he soon learnt that in his absence she had in fact taken a new lover—a Duke, no less—and the tantrums had been a pre-arranged comedy, the confidante's advice a stratagem, to be off with the old love in order to be unrestrainedly on with the new. His whole Roman life had collapsed and the only course of action open to him was to go right away and to stay away until he might feel able to move again in Roman society, certain that when he met her again, as meet her he must in so restricted a society, he would be able to do so without being tormented either by desire or by resentment.

Unutterably depressed, physically debilitated, with a bad cough, he set out in the depth of winter on the long coach journey to Turin. He arrived there, in a coach stuffed with straw to give some insulation against the cold, with his cough completely cured. Until after his father's death in 1830 he made Turin his home once more. The city interested him no more than it had done before his seven years of almost unbroken absence. After Rome it must have seemed dull enough to justify his often-repeated grumbles. But to look at, it must have been, as it still is, a pleasant if not an excitingly beautiful town. It had an attractive natural setting: in the distance were the Alps, and skirting the city was the Po, with open space between the built-up area and the river. Across it were low hills, densely wooded, and on one of them a couple of miles or so downstream rose the votive church of Superga, Juvara's masterpiece, the most notable Torinese architect of the baroque period having matched a magnificent site with a most beautiful domed church whose imposing splendour is due to a perfection of proportions that makes one forget that it is really quite modest in size. In its crypts are the tombs of the House of Savoy. The church of the Gran Madre di Dio is also on the far side of the Po, but looking across towards the centre of the city, a church in a pure classical style, but colder in its purity. And on the hills a little upstream from the Gran Madre were villas of the Torinese aristocracy, including the Rubatto, home of the Balbo family, to which Azeglio was a frequent visitor.

The city itself was small. What is now its main axis, the Via Roma, had already been laid out, roughly parallel to the river, and running from the Royal Palace through the harmonious and to this day still unspoilt Piazza San Carlo to the Piazza del Re (now Piazza di Carlo Felice, with the Porta Nuova Railway Station looking across it and down the Via Roma). The Via Po, now less important and much less smart than then, ran at an angle from the Royal Palace down to the river, debouching opposite the Gran Madre. But on the side of the Via Roma opposite to the river the expansion of modern Turin had barely begun, and most of this area was occupied by a parade ground and by the Citadel of Turin. This, with its multi-angular defence works, has gone, but its former existence is recalled by such names as the Via dell'Arsenale, the Giardino della Cittadella, and the Maschio della Cittadella.

Turin had no great buildings, ecclesiastical or lay, to rival those of Florence, Venice, or Milan. The Royal Palace, though pleasant enough, was unpretentious, low, and somewhat rambling. The Palazzo Madama, formerly used as a Dower House, in the square in front of the Royal Palace, was architecturally much more interesting: it had an imposing grey façade in Juvara's best baroque style, but behind this the building was higgledy-piggledy: the main part dated from the early thirteenth century, but incorporated the towers of the Roman Porta Decumana, and seen from behind the palace looked like a fortified manor-house. The Palazzo Carignano, home of the cadet branch of the House of Savoy, and occupied at this time by Charles Albert, Prince of Carignano, was a gloomy palace, its baroque façade of patterned brick-work made darker by the use of black mortar. The court-yard and the interior of the palace surpassed even the exterior in depressing darkness.

The streets and squares of the city are unspectacular but attractive in their planned harmony, and the use of colonnades is eminently practical, so that in the rains of the autumn and winter or in the brilliance of the summer sun one can walk the city in shelter or in shade. The enormous bulk of the towering Mole Antonelliana, begun as a synagogue and completed as a monu-ment to Victor Emmanuel II, of whose size and height modern Turin is inordinately proud, had not then arisen to dominate the skyline as it now so unhappily does. A pleasant town, but to Azeglio a dull one to look at.

And to him a dull one to live in. There was so much that Italian towns have that Turin had not. There was nothing to correspond to the great art galleries of Florence or Milan. It was only in 1832 that the newly-acceded King, Charles Albert, under the promptings and guidance of Roberto d'Azeglio, cleared the Office of the Public Debt out of the Palazzo Madama and placed the royal collection of paintings there on view to the public, with Roberto as Director of the Gallery. As a collection, though it had good Piedmontese primitives, it was very limited, and the organ-ization of the Gallery had not the funds to allow for many new acquisitions. There was no theatre to rival the Scala of Milan or the San Carlo of Naples. It is true there was the Teatro d'Angennes, and the Teatro Carignano, facing the Palace, but they had no

D

great traditions or reputation. For at least part of the season French companies gave performances of plays in the French language. Charles Felix, it is true, was a devotee of the theatre: and it was one of the accepted sights of Turin to see him eating his frugal supper in the royal box during the intervals, especially as he had a singular knack in eating grissini, the characteristic Piedmontese bread-sticks, by a process of continuous ingurgitation.

In matters of learning Turin's prestige fell as far below that of cities like Bologna as it was inferior to others in painting, architecture, and music. It had a university, but it had not the traditions and could not boast a roll of illustrious names to rival those of other great Italian centres of learning from Padua to Naples.

To Azeglio the religious atmosphere was the main cause of his feeling of 'moral suffocation' in Turin. Laymen and priests took religion seriously, and, as he had experienced as a child, it could develop into a fervour unknown to the easy-going, more cynical Romans. Within the Roman Catholic community in Piedmont Jansenism was not extinct. His sister-in-law spoke of herself, not altogether in jest, as a Jansenist: Mazzini's mother, as is known, had similar tendencies: they were not peculiar to Piedmont: Manzoni himself has been charged with Jansenism and the church in Paris in which he had his experience of illumination was notoriously Jansenist. Marchese Cesare on the other hand was rigidly orthodox and in 1826 was one of the founders of a journal, *Gli Amici d'Italia*, and from 1821 to 1829 secretary of 'Amicizia Cattolica', both avowedly opposed to Jansenism: he had in fact been described as one of the 'most active scourges of Jansenism in Piedmont'. Outside the fold of the Church, Waldensianism still survived, not only in Alpine valleys but in Turin, where they had a Temple with a growing congregation. One could not trace any influence of Jansenism or Waldensianism on Piedmontese policy: but their continued existence indicates a particular idiosyncrasy of the Piedmontese character.

What further added to Azeglio's depression was the philistine conservatism of the Piedmontese aristocracy. In a most amusing chapter of his Memoirs he illustrates this by inventing an imaginary evening's conversation, in the broadest Piedmontese (of which he supplies a very necessary translation for his Italian readers) at a reception in the drawing-room of the Marchesa Irene d'Crsentin (i.e. di Crescentino).[1] News has reached them

[1] *Ricordi*, pp. 236–47.

of Massimo's determination to leave the army and take up painting as a career and all are as scandalized as if he had decided to become a house-painter. It is true that Count Alfieri had written tragedies, but since he had made no money by them, even having to print them at his own expense, that was excusable, though odd. In England, it is said, gentlemen and even noblemen write for the press and publish books—all for money: but what is there in England that is not for money? As for the Azeglios, the father ought to instil some sense into his son, keep him in the army, and, if he must paint, let him paint as a gentleman, not as a tradesman.

Though intensely class-conscious the Piedmontese aristocracy were not in general very wealthy: there were exceptions such as the Cavours, but their money had been made in speculation. That many of them were, as landlords, fairly enlightened is suggested by the general prosperity that Piedmontese agriculture shared with that of most of northern Italy, as well as by the numerous societies for promoting new ideas in agriculture, though many of these had unavowed political undertones: even a philharmonic society might be suspected of political motives, and to interest one's self in any form of novelty might lay one open to gossip. All the same this period of stagnation in Piedmont was to lead into one of intense economic activity, as in the building of railways, and of interest in the free trade theories of Cobden.

The rigidity of class distinction is amusingly illustrated by one of Azeglio's anecdotes. During the cholera epidemic of 1835 the story went around that the nobility were giving the doctors twenty francs for each person who died. The Marchesa Villanova, hearing this from her washerwoman, assured her of the absurdity of such a story. . . . 'Mais je vous assure que vous ne valez pas autant.'[1] For the noble caste, then, only two professions were conceivable—the Church and the army: but both were taken seriously and there was a tradition of loyal service to the King and to the state that made the Piedmontese aristocracy admirable despite all their faults. 'If it [the nobility] had its defects, it had also its good qualities, and kept itself hard-working and energetic . . . for it was continually engaged in war (in the last century Piedmont took part in three) and war is morally more stimulating to people than long periods of peace. Dedication to a difficult and

[1] Roberto d'Azeglio (ed.), *Souvenirs historiques de la Marquise Constance d'Azeglio* (1884) (hereafter referred to as *Souv. hist.*), p. 18.

dangerous duty tempers the character and renders it competent to act with noble intentions and courage in matters other than military ones.'[1] So wrote Azeglio in 1863, and the reiteration of such views in his Memoirs reveals how peculiarly Piedmontese, and un-Italian, he really was: for these are essentially the opinions, not just of one member of a noble caste, but of a nobility of a border-state dependent on its military resolution, not on its strength of numbers, for the maintenance of its independence.

Renewal of contact with his family might bring Massimo some sense of security but could not add to his gaiety. Prospero was, of course, in Rome and later in Sicily. Enrico, nearest to him in age, had died of consumption in 1824, at the age of twenty-nine. He is a shadowy figure in the background of the family history. Massimo wrote of him as though he had been a 'late developer', of tardy and somewhat limited intelligence. He describes him as having been aware of this and depressed and melancholy as a result. But in the *Ricordi* he quotes from a memoir of self-analysis written by Enrico, and though this certainly reveals him as unhappy and self-critical it is not the work of a dim-witted person. He seems to have had no interests outside his army career.[2]

Their mother the Marchesa Cristina was now ill for long periods, and was apt to lose her memory and her powers of speech: yet she outlived her husband by eight years, dying in 1838. Cesare had little to cheer him in these years. Roberto had returned from his exile in 1826 but full intimacy and understanding between him and his father were never restored after his deviation in 1821. In a document preserved in the archives at Saluzzo, and printed by Colombo, Cesare on 5 April 1830 signed, in the presence of a judge and of two lawyers as witnesses, a deed formally granting to his sons Roberto and Massimo emancipation from 'patria sua podestà'.[3] He appreciated Massimo's growing success as an artist and presented one of his paintings to King Charles Felix. Whilst still in Rome Massimo had set to work on what he intended to be his masterpiece, to be sent to Turin for this presentation. He had chosen as its theme the battle of Thermopylae and the last stand of Leonidas. He completed the picture to his own great satis-faction: but his father pointed out that this subject might seem

---

[1] *Ricordi*, p. 53.   [2] Ibid., pp. 389–94.
[3] A. Colombo, *Carteggi e documenti diplomatici inediti di Emanuele d'Azeglio* (1920), Vol. I, p. xxx.

dangerously liberal to Charles Felix; so Massimo set to work on an alternative picture, 'The Death of Montmorency: an incident of the Crusades'. We know of this from a letter of that time to his brother Roberto: but when he came to write his Memoirs he confused the story and suggested that both pictures were given to the King, first the 'Leonidas'[1] and, later, the 'Montmorency'.[2] It is a pity he forgot the true story, for he could have written a sparkling page in his Memoirs about the dangerous liberalism of the heroes of Thermopylae. However, the 'Montmorency' gave great pleasure to the critics in Rome, and 'in Turin it seemed a marvel. My dear father was convinced that all the diamonds of Golconda were not worth as much as my picture.' Despite this success, his father was still not fully convinced that Massimo should be a painter and nothing else and as late as 1825 he was still attempting to persuade him to accept a court appointment: but the prospect of becoming a 'gentiluomo di bocca' to Charles Felix—or to any other king if it came to that—had no attraction for Massimo, especially now that artistic success seemed to be coming his way.

His conquest of the Torinese lovers of art was completed by the publication of his 'La sacra di San Michele'. On a visit to the Val di Susa he had been impressed by the sight of the monastery: travellers entering Italy by the Mont Cenis will be familiar with it, perched spectacularly on an immense pinnacle overlooking the valley along which the railway winds to Turin. He decided to compose a book, with an essay on the history of the monastery and a series of lithographs. As a piece of book-production it appeared most imposingly, with pages of generous size, handsome if rather heavy typography, and superb paper. In later life he judged his lithographs unfavourably; 'they achieved a certain amount of effect as a result of effort, but of artistic imprint they had little'. His verdict is fair enough: they are in fact laboured, showing technical competence, but in a hard and overwrought style. This is especially noticeable in the drawings of architectural details of the monastery to which several pages are devoted. The tracery of windows and the decorative details of door-frames are rendered with a geometrical perfection, as though with ruler and set-square. In drawings of the abbey itself he tends to over-dramatize: the buildings are made to stand out against lurid skies: verticals are over-emphasized to stress the Gothic effect

[1] *Ricordi*, p. 395.   [2] Ibid., p. 413.

of soaring height, and trees, always his favourite subjects, are too often romanticized by heavy gnarling and contortion. Into several pictures groups of figures are introduced with distracting effect: in one it is a party out hawking in medieval costume, in others figures in nineteenth-century dress, peasants in one case, or cavalcades of travellers of the upper class. Monks naturally appear in some drawings, or a hermit-like figure crouches gloomily in a recess of the rocks: and elsewhere the artist himself is to be seen, with his easel under a parasol, and his servant and mule waiting patiently at a respectful distance. A half-page drawing is of the legendary La Bell' Alda, who leapt from a castle window over a precipice to avoid violation by a soldier at the seizure of the castle: one sees him battering down the door, whilst she, with an expression of smugness meant for rapture, is launched into the middle atmosphere. The text tells of her miraculous preservation, for the Blessed Virgin herself, in admiration of such devotion to chastity, buoyed her up and set her gently down on the earth. But in his Memoirs Azeglio tells us that in the sequel, to prove the truth of the story of her supernatural salvation, La Bell' Alda undertook the leap again before an audience: and no miracle was vouchsafed this time: 'and to this day they will tell you in the neighbourhood that "the largest piece of her they ever found was an ear" '.

The text accompanying the illustrations recounted the history of the monastery, and supplemented it with accounts of the battles and sieges fought in the district, and of local legends. The prose style is quite frankly terrible, as Azeglio noted with amusement in later life, in its laboured and pretentious rhetoric. 'Just imagine,' he says, 'my text begins "Through the long cycle of the centuries Italy wielded the sceptre of the universe"—*Per lungo volger di secoli resse Italia lo scettro dell'universo.*' Sentences abound such as 'Like all fertile ground which, overturned by the plough, yields the lovelier fruits, so arose all the greater our glory after the dark and bloody chaos of the barbarian invasions.' The book as a whole is the work of the industrious apprentice. The text is a succession of purple passages, with epithet piled on epithet and metaphor upon metaphor, inflated and billowing: the pictures, by contrast, painstaking, striving as hard as the text for effect, yet unlike it seeming hard or even scratchy. Still, it was a large book, expensive-looking, and doubtless imposing in its pompousness of text and mixture of mechanical verisimilitude and romanticism of drawings to impress the unsophisticated book-buyers of Turin, and to look well casually laid on the table of the salon. Azeglio's pride in it at the time and his mockery of it afterwards are both exaggerated: it was a stage that he had to go through as writer and as artist.

Already he had on the stocks what was to be a far more important literary work. He had done a large painting of an episode in the French invasion of Italy at the end of the fifteenth century —'La disfida di Barletta'—in which Italian knights had fought a tournament against a party of French. As he worked on the painting the idea entered his mind that this was a story to be told as well as painted. At first he thought of it as a subject for a poem: but then on reflection he decided that as it would be a tale to stimulate Italian patriotism it should be aimed at a wide circle of readers and for this prose would be more effective. 'Prose, prose—talk so as to be understood in the streets and market squares, not on Mount Helicon.'[1] By 1830 the opening chapters of his novel *Ettore Fieramosca* had been written, and he had read them to his cousin Cesare Balbo: Balbo had exclaimed: 'But this is really well-written!', and emboldened by this encouragement Massimo had told his father of his work in progress. Cesare asked to have the story read to him, but his health was failing and he heard little of his son's work.

Cesare had had other causes of grief besides the death of Enrico and the eccentric behaviour of Roberto and of Massimo. He had been active in 'L'Amicizia Cattolica', as has been mentioned; besides publishing a review, this society distributed religious books gratis—some 18,000 in the space of three years by one account, based on information supplied by his widow: she also said that King Victor Emmanuel I and Charles Felix in turn had subscribed to the Society.[2] But in 1828–9 it dissolved at the expressed wish of Charles Felix. In his *Ricordi* Azeglio depicts his father as having been used by others who had joined the Society to further ends of their own, and whose private machinations had led to the dissolution of the organization: this may well have been so, but though he had the feeling of having been hardly used he was unswerving in his loyalty to his King, and was still to the very end the same subject who had refused parole, who had lent his King his horses and coach, and in the hour of revolution had ridden to the Palace to offer his service.

[1] *Ricordi*, p. 462.   [2] Tononi, in *Rassegna Nazionale*, June 1884.

He complained, says his son, 'neither against the sentence nor its form. But not feeling himself blameworthy he sought neither to seek pardon nor to return to favour. He obeyed and kept silent. What he felt towards his miserable companions no one could learn.'[1]

He had continued to read deeply and widely and had corresponded with Manzoni, whose *Morale Cattolica* had so impressed him that he had invited him to collaborate in writing for *Gli Amici d'Italia*. Manzoni's important letter 'On Romanticism' was addressed to the Marchese Cesare, and after Cesare's death his widow paid at least one visit to Manzoni's home at Brusuglio in 1832, and she described life in the household there.[2] Now, however, Cesare was ill and was confined to his bed for some time in the autumn of 1830: he seemed to recover, and went with Cristina to Genoa to spend the winter, which in Turin was too severe for her. There he fell ill again and it was clear that his recovery was unlikely: Roberto and Massimo were sent for and arrived in time to see him before he died.[3]

In the spring of 1831 Massimo went to stay at the castle of Azeglio, some thirty miles north-west of Turin, which had been left him by his father: this is the one occasion when he is known to have been there and one wonders what state the castle was in. In autumn he returned to Turin, where he and Roberto signed a deed of division of their inheritance: from this Prospero was excluded. They might and did send him gifts of money, but by the rules of his Society he might not have a personal income. This had been ratified by a deed drawn up in August 1821, when he had decided to enter the Society. 'I, the undersigned, fully, absolutely, and permanently renounce every kind of lordship I may have or might come to have over anyone whatsoever, and all right to have or own anything in the future: all this according to the rule of the Institution of the Society of Jesus and to the decree of the most recent General Congregation.'[4]

Besides the castle of Azeglio Massimo received a share in Genola, a property some six miles south-east of Saluzzo: Roberto made his country home at the villa 'Il Roccolo' or 'Le Roc' not far from it. He developed this house into a charming, rather

Vincent p. 271

[1] *Ricordi*, p. 418.   [2] Colombo, op. cit., Vol. I, p. xlvi.
[3] He died on 26 November 1830 as stated on p. 58 of the *Ricordi*, not on 29 November 1831 as stated on p. 469. *but cent p. 313*
[4] Document in O.P.T.

'Strawberry Hill' Gothic, small-scale castle, and kept the Via d'Angennes house as his Turin residence. In 1835 Costanza told Emanuele that his father had money available to buy Massimo out of Genola,[1] but the deal must have fallen through, for in 1839 in a letter of 9 September Roberto wrote to Emanuele to say 'Maxime a vendu Azeglio 150,000 francs. Il espère maintenant en faire autant de Genolle avec le Novère qui a 350,000 francs à placer.'[2] Massimo did in fact sell his share in Genola but, like the castle of Azeglio, it was eventually bought in again so that all the family estates were reunited in the possession of Emanuele.

In the *Ricordi* Massimo explains that it is prudent for brothers to live apart. 'As long as the father is living, the household is united and one house can accommodate all brothers. But with the father dead the household is no longer one: there are in fact as many households as there are brothers. . . . I had to realize that it was opportune that I should set up on my very own.' As a further reason for this separation, 'to be in Turin was like dying of consumption: the arts were tolerated there as Jews in a ghetto: hence I transported my household gods to Milan'.[3] As usual in the *Ricordi* Massimo was concealing as much as he was revealing. In fact a distinct coolness developed between the brothers apparently over this division of property. It was recorded by Cantù: 'He [Massimo] had some disputes with his brother, not ended very quickly, but it gave him great consolation to be able to end them.' The reconciliation took place during a cholera epidemic (almost certainly that of 1835): their uncle Cardinal Morozzo acted as peacemaker: Roberto wrote to Massimo, who replied, and Roberto wrote again in affectionate strain, and so 'now we are great friends and a separation, or I should say, a war of four years' duration is over. When our mother knows of this reconciliation, who can guess what she will think?' The misunderstandings were sadly renewed: in 1851 Massimo was convinced that Roberto owed him 5,000 francs, and he unburdened himself on this topic to his nephew, though 'To you I let my pen run on without weighing my phrases: but you would give me great displeasure if directly or indirectly you took one step to bring that sum into my purse. I see it one way, Roberto differently. . . .'[4] He goes on to insist that he is not going to let a mere matter of money cause a breach with his brother, yet he was obviously nettled, and six months later he sang a paean of joy at the news that Roberto

[1] *Souv. hist.*, p. 3.   [2] O.P.T.   [3] *Ricordi*, p. 474.   [4] Letter in O.P.T.

was sending him the disputed sum. After Roberto's death Massimo was still regretful that relations between them had never been ideal. 'As you know,' he wrote to Emanuele, 'I am of an affectionate character and I was hurt because I could never find friendship with the elder branch . . . it will be through no ill-will on my part if we do not become greater friends than I ever managed to be with your father.'[1] It is sad that two brothers, neither of them at all mercenary, should have been divided by money questions: and it is even sadder perhaps that these questions would not have mattered if the two had not been so different in temperament: it is this rather than details about 5,000 francs that really prevented full sympathy. But there was never any quarrel, and almost every year during the 1830s Massimo spent some time with Roberto either in Turin or at Le Roc (Il Roccolo). And even if these coolnesses had not existed, Massimo would have left Turin for Milan for the sake of his career. Whether he realized it or not, his life was moving into a new direction: it was not just a change of cities that awaited him. In Rome he had gained sufficient respect from other painters to convince him that he might arrive at success: in Turin he had achieved what seemed spectacular success: but standards there were low and his triumph had, as he knew, been too easily won. The great centre of Italian art was Milan: it was there that reputations were to be made at the annual exhibitions at the Brera: after success there one might try Paris if one desired European fame: but this was vaulting ambition.

When Azeglio went to Milan it was not as a painter alone: he had a novel that was slowly getting itself written: and Milan was not only the capital of the visual arts and of music: it was also Italy's greatest literary centre, dominated by Manzoni, but also the home, or adopted home, of Grossi, Cantù, and other lesser lights. His years in Milan were to lay the foundations of an edifice whose structure he could not have foreseen. For they were to see his success as the author of patriotic novels, a success that carried his name much farther afield than his reputation as a painter: because of this he would be invited to undertake a mission in the Papal States in 1844, from which would stem his first political writings, and these in turn would lead him into an active part in the early events of the Risorgimento. Twelve years in Milan, after

[1] Letter in O.P.T., printed in part in N. Bianchi, *Lettere inedite di M. d'A. al Marchese Emanuele d'Azeglio* (1883) (hereafter referred to as *Lettere*), pp. 313–14.

his experience of Florence, Turin, and Rome, would continue his education in Italianism. And Milan would see him transformed from a carefree bachelor into a married man: in the end a very far from carefree married man. Some part of this he had in mind when he went to Milan. He knew that he was setting out to fight a hard battle to win recognition as a painter, and a new battle as a novelist. Even marriage was in his mind, though not conceived in the same austere terms. So he carried with him not only the beginnings of his *Ettore Fieramosca* but also a letter of introduction to Manzoni from his brother Roberto; and Roberto had suggested to him that amongst the daughters of Manzoni he might perhaps find a wife.

He presented himself at Brusuglio, Manzoni's home just outside Milan, on Thursday 6 April 1831. His hopes for a speedy and favourable verdict on his novel were damped almost at once, for when he disingenuously turned the conversation to historical novels he was surprised to hear Manzoni condemn them as a branch of literary art. This was not a *jeu d'esprit*: nor was it meant unkindly, since Manzoni had no cause to suspect that his visitor was working round to producing a manuscript. It was a considered verdict that the author of one of the greatest of such novels had formulated and by which he abode for the rest of his life. Azeglio said nothing about his own attempt and it was several months before Manzoni learnt of its existence. But Azeglio's matrimonial ambitions suffered no such delay, for having arrived on a Thursday he submitted to Manzoni on the Saturday a written request for the hand in marriage of his eldest daughter Giulietta. Her father asked for a week's grace to allow her to make up her mind, and Azeglio, taking a leaf out of his father's book, drew up, as Cesare had done, a short written statement analysing his character in generalized terms, and at the same time making clear that he was not, and was not likely to be, wealthy. Within the week Giulietta gave her answer—a definite refusal. Her suitor prepared to leave—with his novel unread and his hand refused. But then by a sudden change of mind she accepted him. They were married very soon afterwards and set up in Milan in a house bought by Azeglio from his father-in-law. In 1832 their only child Alessandrina (always known as 'Rina') was born: and on 20 September 1834 Giulietta died. A tragic fate seemed to overhang the girls of Manzoni's family. Three, Giulietta, Cristina, and Sofia, died young: only Vittoria and Metilde lived into the prime of life, and Azeglio was always afraid that Rina might have inherited some constitutional weakness.

Gossip had it that this marriage was not ideally happy. It was alleged that Giulietta was dull and Massimo inconstant. Both charges may have been true. But the second of them, though not inconsistent with Azeglio's character, is not necessarily well-founded. All suggestions to this effect seem to be traceable to Tommaseo, who condemned Azeglio's laxity in later life, and to Cesare Cantù's *Reminiscences of Alessandro Manzoni*, published in 1882. According to him Giulietta 'became a mother, and without having known complete happiness died at Brusuglio on 20 September 1834': Azeglio, he says, 'lived rather amidst outward triumphs than in domestic happiness'. Cantù may have been right: but from 1848 he was politically opposed to Azeglio and this may have coloured his views. He does describe Azeglio as having been affected by Giulietta's death: as they were out riding together on the Beccaria estates 'I shall never forget how, shivering in the winds of early winter, he exclaimed: "I cannot feel them without thinking how cold my Giulia must be there in the open".' Her mother was well pleased with their son-in-law. 'Nothing could equal the happiness that God has granted to our dear daughter, and to us as a result; we have found in her worthy husband the most considerate and affectionate son-in-law,' she wrote, a year after the wedding. After Giulietta's death Manzoni begged Cantù to 'try to cheer poor Massimo', and the confidence between Manzoni and Azeglio survived Azeglio's second marriage and was only broken in the 1860s when Azeglio was cool towards the older man because of his greater enthusiasm for the unification of Italy. Manzoni had been fascinated by Azeglio's versatility—music-making, singing, dancing, riding, fencing, and playing billiards and cards. Together they had ridden from Florence in the hills of Pistoia 'collecting words and sayings of the living language'.[1]

In September 1835, a bare year after Giulietta's death, Azeglio remarried. This was definitely a love-match: unlike his first marriage it was a passionate affair; and of this one we can have no doubts: it was to prove a total failure. His bride was a widow, Luisa Blondel, *née* Maumary, Swiss by birth and a Protestant all her life. Her husband's sister Enrichetta was Manzoni's first wife

---

[1] See C. Cantù, 'M. d'Azeglio', in *Collana di storie e memorie contemporanee* (Milan, 1868).

and mother of Giulietta. She too had been Protestant at the time of her marriage to Manzoni and a Dispensation had been necessary. It was this kinship by marriage that had brought Luisa into the Manzoni family circle. Vittoria Manzoni described her as elegant, beautiful, generous, and witty, 'most delightful company when she wished, but not always to be found in good humour. She could be restless, dispirited, and jealous, and on her bad days could show herself very disagreeable.' The estimate was just enough, as Azeglio was to find. It was rumoured that on the death of her husband she had tried to poison herself: it may not have been true, but she was passionate, impulsive, and sufficiently given to self-dramatization to make the story credible. Her religion made a slight complication, but Gaisruck, Archbishop of Milan, later Cardinal, was helpful and arranged that they should be married by the Bishop of Klagenfurt in his private chapel. Everything would be easy: the bishop spoke Italian, and as he had 17,000 Protestants in his diocese he was accustomed to mixed marriages.[1] So to Klagenfurt they went, and returned to settle down, dividing their time between the house in Milan and one Azeglio had bought at Loveno near Menaggio on Lake Como.

Azeglio was painting industriously and in most of the ten years from 1833 to 1843 he showed something in the annual exhibitions at the Brera: only in 1836 and 1842 did he refrain from showing; in other years he might have as many as ten or more pictures hung. Many were straightforward landscapes, but his more ambitious ones illustrated themes from history or from literature. Ariosto was his favourite source for the latter type of subject, and whether from fiction or from history a patriotic note was often dominant in his themes or in his treatment of them. In composing a picture of the Battle of Legnano (A.D. 1176) in which the Emperor Frederick Barbarossa was routed by the armies of the Lombard League, losing his shield and his standard, he 'did not hesitate to depict the Emperor on his inevitably white horse in such imminent danger that his survival could not have seemed imaginable'. His paintings were bringing him a useful income as well as reputation during this period and some were disputed amongst two or three would-be purchasers, whilst others were acquired for public galleries. Only towards the mid-forties did his success begin to diminish, but by that time he was ready for a change of activity.

[1] Letter of 20 July 1835 from Gaisruck to Azeglio, in Archivio di Stato, Turin.

A visit to Paris with Luisa in 1836 was a disappointment. He had taken pictures with him to show at the Salon, and for that reason had not exhibited at the Brera. But his works attracted no attention. He found there a style of painting quite strange to him —as later he was to be mystified in London by the prices Turner could command for utterly incomprehensible pictures. He himself attracted no more notice than his exhibits. It was to be far otherwise on later visits, but he was more than a little chagrined this time.

By 1840 irreconcilability of temperament was making it almost impossible for Luisa and him to continue to live together. He was going more often to Turin and staying there longer, with Roberto and Costanza, who in December 1840 summed up the conflict of their temperaments in a letter to Emanuele: 'Massimo is a bon-vivant, but he has little depth: his principles, feelings, opinions are all light and without roots, so that I sympathize with his wife whilst realizing that she behaves in a way that annoys him. She is too imperious in character and behaviour: she wants to control in all things, even in feelings, and that is the surest way to put an end to everything.' The next year they parted: to their friends and relations it seemed that the separation must be final, but Grossi, Azeglio's oldest friend and still influential with him, intervened as peacemaker. He wrote to tell Azeglio that Luisa had shown him two letters he had sent her and he thought they had been too severe, but he had advised her to answer cautiously, 'lest with her impulsiveness she create resentment in you . . . and so, I beg you, show yourself to her once more the good, dear, gracious, and affectionate Massimo that you used to be and at heart still are even though outwardly you seem changed a little. . . . Dear Massimo, write her a nice letter that may lead to a full reconciliation. . . .'[1]

In the hope of achieving such a reconciliation they planned a journey together to Sicily in 1842. Such a trip would be interesting, for to them as to any Italians of the mainland Sicily was *terra incognita*, strange in language, customs, and landscape. It would also be arduous and most uncomfortable, for roads in the island were appalling and the inns even worse. Brigandage was a reality and the innkeepers might not be the only ones to hold travellers up to ransom. It would almost seem that Massimo had decided on community in hardship as an experience to draw the

[1] Colombo, op. cit., Vol. I, p. xc, letter of Grossi to M. d'A., 13 December 1841.

two of them together. But he had an additional motive: he would be able to see Prospero again—for the first time since 1821. Their correspondence had been very intermittent but there was a deep sense of affinity between them. Prospero had been urging Massimo to come, for though he was only forty-eight he feared he was ageing rapidly and might not have many more years to live. So Massimo and Luisa left Milan on 25 January, embarked at Leghorn on the 28th, and encountered so fierce a storm that their ship had to put in at Civita Vecchia. Massimo, who was never a good sailor, and seems to have had the bad sailor's ill-luck of having more than his fair share of rough weather at sea, went ashore and vowed never to set foot in a boat again. But the next day they re-embarked and after a call at Naples landed at Palermo on 4 February—having taken a week on the voyage. Massimo went at once to see Prospero, and then, after some days of sight-seeing in the city, husband and wife set out to tour the island, going by boat to Messina and then to Catania and to Syracuse. Azeglio rode a mule and Luisa was carried in a litter: 'I could not have believed it possible to carry a litter—or even a rider—over breakneck places that our goats would not risk: but those mules never miss a footing!' '. . . those precipices that in Sicily pass for roads. . . .' 'To think that they have paid for roads four or five times over, and yet in 1842 in a country like Sicily in the centre of Europe one cannot travel even with a cart!' 'Syracuse that in the time of the Tyrant Dionysus had a million inhabitants has now fifteen thousand and a harbour that could hold all the world's shipping has four boats in it.'[1] Whilst Azeglio was sketching the cave of the fountain Arethusa local lads threw stones at his white parasol, but otherwise they received touching hospitality. As soon as they arrived in a town and word had gone round that strangers were there, all the local notables called upon them with presents and offers of hospitality. Azeglio's fame as a novelist had preceded him and his reception was so flattering that 'to make new friends in that country is to have the roses without the thorns—something unknown in the rest of the world'. From Syracuse they took ship for Naples, landing there on 26 March.

It had been wonderful to see Prospero, and interesting to visit scenes of antiquity and to come to know something of the least-known part of Italy. He had a bundle of sketches to show,

[1] From letters of Azeglio quoted by M. de Rubris, *Il cavaliere della prima passione nazionale* (1930), p. 72.

but the main objective of the journey, the effecting of a reconciliation with Luisa, had not been achieved, as he was soon to see.
For on their way home they went to Rome, although they had
originally intended to go on from Civita Vecchia to Florence.
Azeglio was anxious to revisit Rome, which he had not seen since
1827, and to renew some—but not all—old acquaintanceships.
Michelangelo Pacetti, his old friend of Verstappen's studio and of
the Castelli, arranged for their lodging. One person whom he saw
was his old flame Carolina Morici whom he had loved so
desperately: apparently he did not see their daughter on this
occasion, but he was comforted to discover on meeting the
Morici again that he was no longer in the least in love with her.
Whether all his old attachments had subsided into cold ashes we
cannot tell: certainly he assured Grossi that his behaviour in
Rome on this visit was irreproachable: 'I am positive that I
behaved like a good husband—and this is not a case of "or so it
seems to me"—for even in Rome I had no cause to reproach
myself.'[1] But poor Luisa was reading a chapter of Azeglio's past,
if not of his present, and the text did not please or reassure her.
Her jealousy was smouldering and burst into flame over a trivial
incident in which her husband was certainly guiltless. One afternoon in the Corso, at the time when all Rome was taking the air,
a flower-girl came alongside their carriage and, smiling at
Massimo, threw a flower to them. Luisa slapped his face in public:
he rose, stepped down out of the carriage, bowed to her, and walked
back to their lodging. He began to pack, and only with difficulty
was dissuaded from leaving Rome and Luisa at once. Instead of
making a final breach there and then he went away for a week,
to stay in the guest-house of the Benedictine monastery of Subiaco.
He passed the time reading history to help him with the background of the novel he was beginning, his unfinished third one,
and trying meanwhile to reorientate his mind about his marriage.
He returned to Rome and joined Luisa, and both of them, with
a party of friends, travelled south once more to Sorrento for a
seaside holiday. From there he crossed once more to Sicily,
alone this time, to visit Prospero again. Then he and Luisa
travelled back together to Milan. But Azeglio was now certain
that they could not continue to live together, and a year later
they separated finally. Their life from then onwards was described
by an acquaintance as a model of harmonious conjugal separa-

[1] From a letter of 23 May 1842 to Grossi, in Ghisalberti, op. cit., pp. 227–8.

tion. If this suggests that their separation was easy it is misleading. It is true that each found consolation elsewhere. Massimo had his transient affairs with ballet dancers and less estimable young women, besides a long and deep devotion in his closing years. He also gave increasing attention to his daughters, first of all to Rina and afterwards to Bice. Luisa also found distraction, especially in an open liaison with Giuseppe Giusti, who took up her cause with such fervour that he could assure her in 1844: 'Your [Luisa's] agitation has inspired me with such pity and fear, and my disdain for that man would have reached its culmination had I not held him more pitiable than you. On your side are reason, feeling, and zeal for your honour and that of your family: on his, I grieve to say, I see only errors, shame, and afterthoughts.' He even went so far as to advise her to think of Massimo as 'no longer master of himself', to be pitied as 'one deranged in mind'.[1] Years afterwards we shall see Azeglio's resentment of Giusti's betrayal flaring up again in savage letters to his nephew. But despite their separation powerful bonds between husband and wife subsisted. For some years she had charge of Rina, and as long as Azeglio lived he and she exchanged letters. His to her were affectionate and voluminous, and he kept her most completely informed of his opinions and of his political activities, writing to her in the utmost confidence, so that the published extracts from these letters are amongst the most valuable sources of information about his innermost thoughts. Yet he took good care to avoid meetings with her—ensuring, for instance, that she would not be in Milan when he went there as Governor. The indecent ferocity of his letter[2] to Emanuele on the subject of Giusti's intimacy with her reveals more than just wounded egoism—a depth of love turned into resentment by her infidelity.

Both his marriages had had Milan as their background and the unhappy end of each helped to draw him away from there and back to Turin and his own family. Massimo felt also 'the need of some big task to occupy mind and heart',[3] especially as his success as a painter seemed to have passed its zenith, and his third novel was dragging to a standstill. Renewal of contact with Roberto and Prospero showed him how different were their

---

[1] Ghisalberti, op. cit., pp. 78–88.
[2] Published only in part, for example by Ghisalberti, op. cit., p. 85. Original in O.P.T.
[3] *Ricordi*, p. 529.

E

cases, since each had found his life's work and was fully dedicated to it.

Prospero, Padre Luigi Taparelli, was at this date in Palermo teaching in a Jesuit school for boys. His career had suffered a setback that would have distressed a worldly man but he had fully accepted his Society's rule of obedience. Until 1829 he had been in Rome, becoming Rector of the Jesuit college there until he had been promoted Preposito of the Order for the Province of Naples. But from this position he was transferred to Palermo to teach in the school. The only apparent cause of this demotion was the opposition of his superiors to his zeal in furthering the study of Aquinas. He gained the devotion of the Palermitans during the cholera epidemic of 1835 by his attendance on the sick and dying, and when revolution came in 1848 he was specifically exempted by the new régime from the general banishment of Jesuits from the island, though he characteristically threw away this favour by defying the revolutionary government and visiting and ministering to the Bishop of Girgenti, who was under arrest. After his expulsion he made his way to Turin, where he arrived on Roberto's doorstep in civil dress, gaunt and at first unrecognized.

As an educationist he had ideas far ahead of his time: he limited the time given to the Classics and extended that assigned to modern languages. He introduced geography, modern history, and natural history into the curriculum, employing specialist teachers. But when in 1853 he was called back to Rome all his innovations in Palermo were abandoned. He was an ingenious craftsman and a cultivated musician as executant and composer: all these gifts he used in his endeavour to create a new musical instrument with a keyboard like that of a pianoforte but in which the strings were to be bowed as with a violin, not plucked or struck. His 'violicembalo' or 'symphoneum' was tested by Liszt, who praised it but never played it in public, and it never achieved any artistic or commercial success. Despite the calls on his time as a member of a religious order and as a schoolmaster he completed his substantial works on political philosophy and because of them he has been considered one of the ablest, if not the ablest, of Catholic political theorists of the nineteenth century.[1] But the studied moderation of his views was misunderstood. His brother Massimo, Gioberti, and Cesare Balbo, all on the liberal side,

[1] For example by B. Brunello in *Il pensiero politico italiano dal Romagnosi al Croce* (1949), p. 138.

regarded him as the supreme exponent of clerical reaction: whilst at the same time Solaro della Margarita, most reactionary of Piedmontese politicians, wrote to Roothaan, General of the Society, protesting at Father Luigi's inflammatory encouragement of liberalism and virtually asking that he be allowed to publish no more.[1]

These apparent setbacks were mere worldly matters and Prospero was unshakably serene and unmurmuring. Massimo, who was with him in July and August 1842 and again in November 1844, felt for him a warmth of affection that he confessed to Emanuele he had never been able to feel for Roberto: he described the joys of their companionship in some of the most moving passages of his *Ricordi* and more revealingly still in letters to Luisa.[2]

Roberto had strength of convictions, integrity of character, and social conscience in the same measure as Prospero. But one understands why Massimo's heart could not warm to him in the same degree as to Prospero. There is a close parallelism in the activities of the two brothers. In 1835 Roberto was working in Turin in the cholera epidemic as unsparingly as Prospero in Palermo—organizing hospitals, collecting funds for them, supervising their management, and arranging for patients to be brought in. It is true that the poorer classes were distrustful, for they regarded admission to a hospital as a death sentence (not without some justification) and believed that if a man must die the natural and preordained place for him to do so is in his own bed surrounded by his family. The governing class, more concerned to prevent contagion, were more appreciative and the city struck a special gold medal for Roberto to commemorate his services.

Besides having charge of the royal picture gallery Roberto was active in elementary education, which he wished to see made available to the less privileged classes of society: to achieve this he and others in Turin studied and adopted the monitorial method developed in England by Bell and Lancaster. Roberto first of all founded—largely at his own expense—a school for adolescent girls where they might learn enough to be able to

---

[1] Letter of 1 March 1847. In Padre P. Pirri, *Carteggi del R. P. Luigi Taparelli d'Azeglio* (1932).

[2] *Ricordi*, pp. 125–7, and G. Carcano (ed.), *Lettere di M. d'A. a sua moglie Luisa Blondel* (1870), pp. 81–90, 146–8.

teach younger children. When this had been safely established he began a similar school for boys: and these 'Schools of Mutual Instruction', or 'Lancasterian Schools', as Massimo called them, were then completed by the setting up of an infants' school.

These projects were very dear to him. To them he devoted not only his money but his time, spending hours and days in the schools supervising and teaching. This was admired by Massimo, who was equally convinced of the need for extending and improving Italian education, and who also from means more slender than Roberto's gave money to elementary schools. But in the *Ricordi* we can sense that, genuinely as Massimo admired Roberto's self-sacrifice, he felt that his brother demanded too much of Costanza. 'The time for school would come: Roberto would say to his wife "It is time to go". One could read from her expression the effort it cost her: but she would rise with a little sigh and go forth, be it in fog, snow, or rain, to shut herself away for the evening in the infragrant and stuffy atmosphere of the school.'[1]

[1] *Ricordi*, pp. 474, 475. There is in the Risorgimento Museum in Turin an engraving showing Pellico and others visiting one of these 'Lancasterian Schools', whose general organization is such that it might well have been a school of the National Society of the Church of England or of the British and Foreign Society of the nonconformists.

IV

AZEGLIO AS PAINTER AND NOVELIST

THE year 1844 was one of decision for Azeglio, with the failure of his second marriage, his reputation as a painter past its zenith in Milan, and his third novel hanging fire. Soon he was to be away on a completely new tack; but before charting its course one might pause to see just how far he had come as painter and novelist.

The simplest, shortest, and perhaps most honest if not the most flattering way to account for the success his pictures had had in Milan, and would later have in Turin, might be to say that he was a good if not great painter in a dull period. Of his contemporaries, Hayez is the one whose work, especially as a portraitist, is still admired: but when one stops in front of his best-known portraits in the Brera it is perhaps rather because these are portraits of Rosmini, Rossini, Manzoni, or Azeglio than because of the attraction of the style of portraiture, the photographic likeness, the warmth of flesh tones against the conventional bituminous black backgrounds. Many competent painters of that time were content to turn out picture after picture of *contadini* and *contadine* in romantic costume or to paint and repaint scenes of obvious beauty, the cascades of Tivoli, the relics of ancient or the glories of Renaissance Rome. Compared with them one understands why Azeglio, sugary as some of his works may seem now, was considered a 'realistic' painter. A fine example of his work is 'La vendetta', in the Galleria d'Arte Moderna in Milan, quite a small canvas. A yellow sandy track runs across a gloomy upland moor. The sky is dark and louring: a really impressive atmosphere has been captured: but the landscape has been visualized in this way as part of the 'pathetic fallacy', for this is a story picture, as the title indicates, and nature has to suit the gloom of the anecdote: for in the middle of the track a man lies spread-eagled: his dog crouches near his body and his horse wanders off on to the moor, whilst over the crest of the hill a horseman vanishes into the distance. If not a great painting it is undoubtedly a good one.

In his still-life paintings by contrast Azeglio evidently aimed at photographic exactness. There are examples of them in the

Museo d'Arte Moderna in Turin. But the search for accuracy has ended in harshness, even clumsiness, and the results are unattractive. A window in a background will be drawn as if in an architect's elevation and one scents the ruler and set-square. The painting is an exercise, lacking spontaneity, lacking also self-confidence.

In his day it was with his big literary compositions that he was most successful with public and patrons. His 'Ulysses meeting Nausicaa', in Turin, is a typical example. The titling of these paintings exaggerates the importance of the anecdote, for in this picture, as in others like 'The Challenge at Barletta', the figure composition is far less important than the landscape setting. Though highlighted, the human action is confined to a very tiny proportion of the whole scene. In the 'Ulysses' a vast expanse of sea-shore landscape is shown, with cliffs and sea fading away into the misty light of the far distance. Soft, clear, rather too pretty blues are used for sky and for sea, that merge into one another gently. The trees are in gradations of equally soft greens. The bright colours of the costumes and the flesh-tints of the human figures prevent them from being lost in the large composition despite their very small size. The effects of lighting with pools of sunshine on grass and shallow water in the foreground and the misty haze of the background are quite charming: but one is aware of the artifice of the scene. The lighting, for which he was highly praised in his day, is contrived: the trees are too determinedly picturesque: he was proud of his skill in painting them, and had made innumerable studies of them, but he seems never to have painted a tree as it was: each one is a synthesis of singular features, and many are miracles of gnarling. The most excessively determined picturesqueness of this scene is in the natural rock-arches. Such geological features are not unknown: but to have two, one striding out to sea, and one on land, in the same scene is certainly one rock-arch too many.

One comes to the conclusion that his paintings have considerable charm, using that word with its usual rather faded connotations, as period pieces. And they are not the work of a dabbler—or of a 'Sunday-painter'. In many of his varied activities he was an improviser: but as a painter he had, if not genius, abundant talent, with evident signs of training and of care. There is a great gap between the hard meticulous drawing of his early works and the much more fluent technique of his later paintings.

What he lacked was the genius that allows a painter to create a picture that looks at one and the same time spontaneous and vital and yet as firmly constructed as a piece of architecture.

Azeglio suggests the same tendency to improvisation as a novelist. He has told of his sudden decision to write the story of *Ettore Fieramosca* and in his references to that novel he gives the impression that it was written at white heat. Certainly he began it with the minimum of preparation. He did only the most superficial reading of the history of the period, and he created his Barletta from a hasty look at a map.

I invented my Barletta, Castle, and Island of St. Ursula for my own use, and from there, on and on, straight as an arrow, bringing into the world one day this, and the next day the other of my characters, fathering, as I saw later, a far bigger family than was necessary. For what the devil was the necessity, I ask, for that personage Zoraide? All the same, the proverb 'Once on the road and the pack-saddle will settle down' never had fuller application than in the fabrication of that novel of mine, whatever may be its literary worth. . . . I can never describe the intimate pleasures, the inward joy I then felt in depicting these scenes and personalities, in entirely reliving that life of chivalry, totally forgetful of the present: that was assuredly one of the most wonderful periods of my life.[1]

This suggestion that *Ettore Fieramosca* was the result of rapid, continuous improvisation is partially misleading. Cesare Balbo had heard the opening chapters read in 1830: after his marriage to Giulietta Azeglio took courage to submit as much as he had then written to Manzoni for his opinion. His comment was dry but not discouraging. 'What a strange business this literary occupation of ours is: whoever wishes can take it up between one day and the next. Here is Massimo—the whim of writing a novel seizes on him, and behold him getting on with it, not so badly either.'[2] It was not until 1833, nearly three years after its beginning, that the novel was completed, yet it was not a long one, even by modern standards, and distinctly short by those of Azeglio's time. Work on it may have been, and probably was, as intensive as he declares, but for long periods it must have lain untouched. That would not be surprising, as he was in general averse from long continuous effort.

With its completion arose the question of publication. The

---

[1] *Ricordi*, p. 463. [2] Ibid., p. 483.

patriotic tone of the book would make it offensive to most of the governments of Italy: the role played in it by Pope Alexander VI and his son Cesare Borgia would hardly be pleasing to ecclesiastical authorities, and the main theme, the burning resentment of foreign intervention in Italy, would seem to suggest that the least likely place in which to have it published would be the Austrian-ruled provinces of Lombardy-Venetia. But knowing Austrian rule, as Azeglio did, in all its unforeseeability, he decided that there he had the best chance of getting his novel past a censor, though he expected that he might have to make modifications in it.

The censor, however, was an easy-going Abbé, one Bellisomi, and by choosing his moment carefully and using all the tact of which he was capable Azeglio succeeded in getting an Imprimatur for the novel with no changes. The Government realized what a blunder had been made and Bellisomi lost his job: but the novel was in circulation by then.[1] There could be no doubt of its success: it circulated widely, since no Italian government could very well forbid the distribution of a novel that had passed the Austrian censorship. It brought Azeglio more money than ever he dreamt of or hoped for—some 5,000 francs. But more importantly and more excitingly than this it created for him a more spectacular fame than ever he could have earned by the comparatively esoteric art of painting. It is true that this reputation was attained on political rather than on purely aesthetic grounds. As de Sanctis has said, 'To those who read it when it came out *Ettore Fieramosca* was important as a political tract on the theme "Viva l'Italia!"' For this reason this novel, and to a less extent its successor, by giving Azeglio this particular kind of fame, provided the key with which he was to open the door to a new career as a practising politician.

The historical novel at this time was as important a branch of literature in Italy as it had become in England with the Romantic Revival. The outstanding example, the only one to attain international significance, was, of course, Manzoni's *I promessi sposi*, first published in 1827: lesser practitioners included Grossi and Guerrazzi, with *Marco Visconti* and *L'assedio di Firenze* respectively as their main works. Grossi's novel of the fourteenth century was written with a purely artistic motive—to tell a tale that would arouse the reader's pity for its characters, and for its heroine

[1] *Ricordi*, pp. 487–8.

especially. A setting in the past was chosen to give credibility to events on a heroic scale. Manzoni's aim was to serve a religious purpose, to show the workings of divine providence, protecting the pure in heart and transforming and redeeming the wicked. Some of his characters are drawn from history, as are some of the incidents: but the persons on whom his attention is centred, Renzo, Lucia, or less prominent figures like Don Abbondio, are fictitious. Guerrazzi's *Assedio di Firenze* has the same historical background as Azeglio's second novel *Niccolò de' Lapi*, but with Guerrazzi history predominates, and his main characters are historical personages. His novels tend to be even more melodramatic than Azeglio's, their incidents more sensational and their rhetoric more clamant. It is odd that he and Azeglio should have been rivals in treatment of the same historical setting, for they were to be even more antagonistic to each other as politicians, Guerrazzi's radicalism being quite revolting to Azeglio.

In *Ettore Fieramosca* the authentic historical characters are in the background. Cesare Borgia is the chief of them, and his ravishing of the tragic heroine, Ginevra, the climax of the fictional part of the story. But he is not allowed to overshadow the action. To have brought into his tale a character who in so many romances has loomed up in vastly inflated wickedness and yet to prevent his playing all the other characters off the stage of the melodrama would seem to be quite an achievement on Azeglio's part.

The plot of the novel is a dual one—of Ettore's devotion to Ginevra, and of his championship of Italian renown in arms. Each moves to its climax—the dishonouring and death of Ginevra, and the challenge and tournament between the Italian knights and the French ones, with whom is the renegade, Ginevra's husband. The two climaxes are made to coincide exactly in time— Ettore's personal tragedy with his public triumph. The neatness of pattern that makes the two actions converge in this way is a sign of conventionality: such contrivance of structure was expected in the novel at that time, though it has ceased to be regarded as an artistic advantage. A major defect, of which Azeglio was aware as quotation from his Memoirs has shown, was the proliferation of unnecessary characters. His example, Zoraide, does not completely justify this criticism. It is true that she is necessary for one incident only, and that not an essential one. The more valid criticism would be of the wild improbability of her

presence in Italy: she is a Saracen girl, and a most fantastic
fabrication of incidents and coincidences is necessary to account
for her presence and her relations with the other characters. It is
her exoticism, rather than her superfluity, that is open to criticism.
Her presence is not, however, as unnecessary as might appear if
considered solely from her contribution to the action of the story.
Azeglio uses her somewhat as a Greek chorus. As she is a Moslem
she may be allowed to make observations that Azeglio himself
might wish to make but could not introduce through an Italian,
Christian persona. So, for example, when Ettore tries to explain
to her that the sovereignty of the French in Naples was justifiable
on historical grounds since they inherited it from Charles of
Anjou, who had it as a fief of the Church: 'Oh, splendid . . . and
who donated it to the Church?'—a question not of historical fact
alone but of legitimacy and one to which Ettore had no answer;
but the nineteenth-century reader might, and in Italy almost
certainly would, ask the same question as he read this passage,
about the Papal States. Again, it was easy enough to point to the
presence of the foreigner in Italy as the impediment to Italian
unity, as Ettore did: but it was into Zoraide's mouth that Azeglio
put the comment that it was divisions amongst the Italian themselves that brought the foreigner into the country and made his
continued presence there possible.

Azeglio's manipulation of the plot makes her observation
pertinent. He is not so naïf as to range wicked foreigners on one
side and pure-minded Italian patriots on the other; there were
men of honour on both sides, and on the French side the only one
to be actively hated was not La Motte, whose sneers provoked
the challenge, but Graiano d'Asti, the only Italian amongst them,
and he was the only one to be killed when the tournament took
place. Ettore, in excess of delicacy, would not range himself as
Graiano's opponent, since Ginevra, whom he loved, was Graiano's
wife, and to Ettore it would be dishonourable to fight and perhaps
to kill a man against whom he had a personal grudge and by
whose death he might gain personally. So Graiano was challenged
by Brancaleone, who was by no means overburdened with
scruples, for he alone knew that because of an earlier wound
Graiano had a vulnerable skull, and Brancaleone was willing to
make use of this private information. This he did and Graiano
was not only killed, but was further dishonoured by a casual
burial, unlamented even by those who had fought on the same

side in the tournament. Contrary to Azeglio's intentions one's sympathies are to some extent with him: not because of his hazardously thin skull, though a man with such a vulnerable headpiece should not undertake the occupational risks of fighting in tournaments. But Graiano was, according to his own lights and those of his day, an honest man. He was a professional soldier, serving the highest bidder, it might be, but serving him honestly and courageously: a mercenary, but a reliable one in an age of mercenaries not all as dependable as he. In short he was a figure of his times, not an anachronism as were those who were depicted as thinking of 'Italy' as more than a mere geographical expression. And it is hard that a man, regardless of the thinness of his skull, should get himself killed because he is not an anachronism.

Weaknesses in characterization are as evident as the flaws in the construction. Ettore and Ginevra fail to come to life, for Azeglio had not the genius of Manzoni to create characters of perfect moral goodness and make them convincing by having them fall short of perfection in other ways—by showing them acting rashly or foolishly in practical everyday matters, for instance. The most successful of his characters is Fanfulla, who enters the novel rather late but obviously captivated his creator, who introduced him again into his next novel. Fanfulla, a soldier of fortune, has loyalty, courage, simplicity, and, above all, a dry commonsense wit. Like Zoraide he is there to make the kind of practical, irreverent, sceptical comment that came naturally to Azeglio himself. If Ettore is an unamusing, seriously-meant Quixote, Fanfulla is a heroic Sancho Panza. *Ettore Fieramosca* is admittedly a second-rank novel: by comparison with English historical novels one might count it as well below the Scott level, but a very long way above Harrison Ainsworth: by Italian standards, though it falls short of *I promessi sposi*, as would seem inevitable, it is still much more readable than the works of Guerrazzi. Its immediate success was natural enough. The action has speed. The opening chapter is admirably contrived to capture interest, and the closing ones move with an exciting rapidity. One is convinced that they were written, as Azeglio says, with verve. Apart, however, from its purely literary merits, the ardent patriotism of the novel must have made it electrifying in 1833. Its essential point was that man for man the Italians were as heroic as the soldiers of other nations. When Don Prospero Colonna addressed the Italian champions before the tournament his words were addressed as much to the nineteenth-century reader as to his imagined knights, and would remind them of their country's present unhappy divided state and stimulate future hopes.

Gentlemen, do not imagine that I intend to urge you to fight like the men I know you to be. I see among you Lombards, Neapolitans, Romans, Sicilians. Yet are you not all equally sons of Italy? Will not the honour of victory be equally divided among you? There before you are the foreigners who called us Italians cowards! One thing I would say: behold there the infamous traitor Graiano d'Asti. He is fighting to keep his countrymen in infamy! Understand me well— let him not leave this field alive!

The action of the novel ends in personal tragedy for Ettore and Ginevra, yet its general tone is optimistic and inspiriting. *Niccolò de' Lapi* by contrast is darker in mood throughout: it is typical that in this novel, as in *Macbeth*, all the most impressive scenes take place by night. Its theme is heroic endurance, the unremitting fight for a cause doomed in advance, the acceptance of death or exile in preference to dishonour: yet, still in contrast with *Ettore Fieramosca*, its hero and heroine survive to live serenely when the storm and tumult are over. Unlike its predecessor as it is in mood, in morals it is as salutary and its patriotism even more dedicated. As a work of art it is far superior, but it never had the same popular success at a time when Italians wanted to be assured that their cause must triumph, rather than to be steeled to endure misfortune stoically.

It is not clear just how early Azeglio began to write this second novel. In his Preface he says it was begun in 1833 and 'laid aside a hundred times before its completion in 1841'. In the *Ricordi*[1] he suggests that it was started after he had gained permission to publish *Ettore*: but he also says a little later: 'When I could not but be convinced that not only was it [*Ettore*] accepted by the Italian public, but definitely making a furore . . ., I thought the time had come to set my hand to *Niccolò de' Lapi*, of which I had already written some chapters as early as 1831 or 1832.'[2] Even if one accepts the later date for the commencement, this novel was some eight years on the stocks. His slowness in completing it was not due to lack of application so much as to fear that it should prove inferior to *Ettore*: a too successful first novel is as likely to be intimidating as encouraging to the writing of a second. For

[1] *Ricordi*, p. 489.   [2] Ibid., p. 493.

this reason Azeglio worked much more seriously in studying the history of the period. This time he did not invent the natural settings: as these were in Tuscany it would not do to treat them as cavalierly as those in far-off Barletta. So he travelled to see for himself those which lay outside Florence. But this survey of the scenes of his novel was not made until 1838—some five years after he began to write. Then he left Milan with Luisa on 28 August, and went by way of Parma, Reggio, and Modena to Gavinana, scene of the battle that he would have to describe, and thence to Florence, arriving a fortnight after leaving Milan. After his return he resumed writing: but painting occupied most of his time and only after a period of intense application did he finish it in 1841. He had become embarrassed by the number of inquiries he was receiving about its progress, and finally to give himself an incentive he decided to complete it by March: this he achieved, not knowing, he says, whether he had written a creditable piece of work or miserable fustian, and lacking the confidence to re-read it appraisingly. The next hurdle was the censorship. This would not be leapt over as easily as before, for whoever was in poor Father Bellisomi's place would be aware of his downfall and would go through Azeglio's new work with a fine-tooth comb. Luckily for Azeglio, between 1840 and 1845 Austria was riding Lombardy-Venetia on a slack rein, and the censor, Father Mauro Colonnetti, was a scholar and a man of integrity. Summoned to his office to hear his verdict Azeglio was astonished to hear him say: 'Signor Cavaliere, your manuscript is too splendid for me to dare to touch it.' To safeguard himself the censor asked Azeglio to explain certain passages, and accepted the author's explanations. Positions were reversed, for then the censor justified himself to Azeglio. 'I believe that one can do one's duty without showing so much zeal as to injure others. I am an Italian and if it were proved to me that Lombardy would be better off without the Austrians I know what I would consider to be my duty. But that is not yet proved. I can even see that this is the best government that there is in Italy. Try to have this manuscript of yours published anywhere but here, and let me know how you succeed.'[1]

Colonnetti may have been justified in defending the mildness and commonsense of the Austrian Government at that particular moment of time. But both he and Azeglio overlooked one important point: even supposing that the existence of a censorship were

[1] *Ricordi*, pp. 511–13.

defensible in any general terms, in practice, like all Austrian administration in Italy, it was utterly unpredictable in its capriciousness. Azeglio judged it tolerantly since his two novels had both been sanctioned, but in the interval between their publication many other books had been forbidden—including such a harmless-sounding work as Tommaseo's *Dictionary of Synonyms*. One may learn, painfully, to come to terms with a government that behaves consistently in such matters; but the vagaries of the Austrians were baffling, and their furies in times of crisis were unforgivable. Azeglio assumed that, as Colonnetti suggested, no other government would permit the publication of *Niccolò*—not even the Tuscan one: yet his *Degli ultimi casi di Romagna*, a much more dangerous book directly indicting the Papal Government of its day, came out in Florence five years later. The fate of a book here and there might not be a major issue, but the oddities of censorship suggest that what was wrong with governments in Italy at this time was not their rigidity but their unpredictability: Charles Albert of Savoy, the 'walking hieroglyphic' as Azeglio called him, was the supreme example of this.

Niccolò de' Lapi is a story of the siege of Florence in 1529 and 1530, that ended in the overthrow of the Florentine Republic and the re-establishment of the rule of the Medici. Niccolò is the inspirer of the resistance, as leader of the 'Piagnoni' (the 'weepers' as they were mockingly termed), men of the artisan or shop-keeper class socially, devoted to the republican cause and to the memory of Savonarola, who had been sent to the stake in 1498. Savonarola's uncompromising asceticism, contrasting so strongly with the general worldliness of the Renaissance, and in particular with the degradation of the Church under the Papacy of Alexander VI Borgia, his contemporary and victor, was not burnt out in the flames that consumed his mortal body, but was imagined by Azeglio reincarnated in Niccolò, who in the cause that he believed right—a cause that was religious as well as constitutional —was willing to sacrifice his prosperity, that of the city, then the lives of his children, and of his partisans—and incidentally of Florentines involved in the siege without willing it—and in the end to go to his own death on the scaffold heroically and calmly. He is conceived by Azeglio on the grandest scale, single-minded, inflexible, inspired and inspiring, one to whom this world and all in it are as dust and ashes.

In dramatic contrast to him we have not just the out-and-out villains of the story—Troilo, or Baccio Valori, treacherous, petty-minded self-seekers, and Malatesta, the ruin of what might have been a great man, but, more subtly, Fanfulla, back once more from an unsuccessful attempt to live the religious life of a lay-brother after the events of the Barletta period. Fanfulla is still, as he was in *Ettore Fieramosca*, of the earth, earthy. He is in his way as good a man as Niccolò, loyal and honest, but his is the honesty that comes from fundamental decency: there is still not a particle of spirituality in his make-up: with his innate respect for decent people, and, it may be added, no more respect for property than may be expected of a mercenary soldier, he has an immense gusto. So he contrasts not just as another type of human goodness, but as a figure of comedy in a sombre background. Early in the novel, whilst he is still in the cloister, there is a conversation between him and his Prior that is a most entertaining and sustained piece of talk at cross-purposes, an excellent example of Azeglio's skill in the writing of comedy. Azeglio's wit sometimes got the better of him and led to misplaced sallies, as when describing the darkness of the Florentine streets at night he could not resist a parenthesis: 'At that time there were no street-lamps in Florence: today they go out at night but at least they are there, and that is progress.' Or, 'To control an army in that century the noose had to be used frequently; nor had military etiquette as yet laid it down that to die by hanging wounds one's honour, but by shooting leaves it unharmed. One must condole with the unfortunates of the sixteenth century who had perchance the idea that the shame lies in the crime, not in the form of punishment.'

If, as has been suggested already, Azeglio's natural bent may have been towards comedy, rather than the high romanticism of the historical novel, he is at his best in depicting scenes of swift action. His description of the tournament is much the most impressive part of *Ettore Fieramosca* and in *Niccolò* he deals most vividly with the naval battle (Chapter XIV) and the Battle of Gavinana (Chapter XXVII). For the former he has clearly read very carefully in order to be correct in his description of the manœuvring of a galley in a naval encounter and he is able to keep his reader conscious of the simultaneous actions of galley slaves, steersmen, fighting-men, chaplain, and captain at each stage of the battle. He does not attempt to give an over-all view of the battle of Gavinana: instead he lets Lamberto and Fanfulla each recount what he saw during the general confusion. Their stories are told conversationally, fragmentarily, with guesses, ejaculations, and speculations: we are aware that no one sees a battle as a whole, least of all those fighting in it: as it is a confusion, especially when it takes place in the narrow confines of tortuous medieval streets, it can only be described convincingly in a confused series of short impressions.

The atmosphere in Florence after the news of this defeat is described equally vividly.

The night following that gloomy day was full of anxiety, suspicions, and preparations for the Florentines awaiting the tragic events that they foresaw for the coming day. During those hours when, especially in the summer heats, sleep usually overcomes all worries and the memory of all toil, Florence stayed awake. No one was to be seen wandering the streets, but the gleam that issued from windows here and there, the noises and sounds of voices heard from inside the houses showed plainly that the doomed populace knew that the last act of a long and bloody tragedy was about to be played: and in men's hearts party-passions, hopes, and desires soon to be forever satisfied or betrayed boiled up more violently.

The Piagnoni, already aware of the internal divisions amongst the citizens of Florence, some of whom were honest partisans of the Medici whilst others were simply anxious for peace at any price, have now learnt of the extent of treachery in their own midst, for their appointed military leader, Malatesta, has gone over to the enemy. Niccolò keeps vigil in the chapel of the monastery of St. Mark, Savonarola's old convent, and here the more determined of the republicans rally round him to vow resistance to the end. This dark scene, interposed as the novel moves towards its climax, makes a deliberate re-evocation of the opening scene of the novel, when in this same chapel Niccolò and his family and friends prayed by night over the body of the second of his sons to have been killed in the fighting, as the siege artillery continued its methodical bombardment of the city.

Despite so many excellences of characterization, narrative, and description *Niccolò de' Lapi*, though less faulty than *Ettore Fiera-mosca*, is not an unflawed masterpiece. The lovers, Laodamia and Lamberto, are dull: he in particular, meant to be virtuous, ends up priggish and insensitive, capable of behaving like a prudish boor in his anxiety to keep his virtue. The story of Lisa, Niccolò's other daughter, seduced by Troilo by means of a faked

The Vendetta

Oil painting by Massimo d'Azeglio

Ulysses meeting Nausicaa
Oil painting by Massimo d'Azeglio

marriage, lapses from drama into melodrama. It is true that when she is driven forth into the street by her unrelenting father it is not into a blinding snowstorm as in classic melodrama: but it is into an icy rainstorm, through which she wanders in vain search of shelter, concerned only for her baby and not for herself.

And seemingly unable to profit by his own admitted mistakes, Azeglio introduced into *Niccolò* a strange character even more exotic than his Zoraide—La Selvaggia—an amazon fighting with the Medici party on sea and on land, a fierce daughter of nature, warrior and camp-follower, sworn to avenge herself on the father (a Hungarian Jew) who had sold her into debauchery. She fell in love, by the attraction of opposites presumably, with Lamberto, was treated like Potiphar's wife and became his enemy, not surprisingly in view of his horrified repulsion, and ended virtuously after an expiatory pilgrimage to the Holy Land. Azeglio was aware that his uncontrollable impulse to introduce these outlandish personalities into his stories was due to the influence of Victor Hugo, whose wilder romanticisms he was copying. Manzoni could bring so violent a character as the Nun of Monza into his novel and, though she might somewhat upset its proportions, she would not seem a creature as it were from outer space like the hard-riding, hard-fighting daughter of the Hungarian Jew.

On its publication *Niccolò* earned respect rather than enthusiasm; what would have been the reception of his third novel, had it been completed, is hardly worth conjecturing. What he did write of it is heavy going. In his *Ricordi* he made no mention of this new novel and one can only trace its progress through his letters. In September 1843 he wrote telling Luisa that he had finished the first, and started the second chapter, that is two years after completing *Niccolò*. In May 1844 he read the opening part to Balbo, who approved it, especially praising the breadth of its canvas. This must have pleased Azeglio, for he meant this novel to break new ground—to show the impact of historic events on men of all classes. It was also deliberately planned to portray the Church in a more favourable light than in his previous novels. And he had prepared himself even more carefully than for *Niccolò* in his study of the historical background. He read and transcribed from the great histories of the Italian Renaissance period, endangering this novel by an overburdening pedantry. His progress was slow. He reached the seventh chapter in 1845 and there it was abandoned, to be published only posthumously.

F

It has been believed that he was directed from it by his growing interest in politics, in which he was now becoming an actor and not just a spectator. But the novel had been moving very slowly even before he went into politics: and when he had left political life he did not take it up again. The simple explanation may be that he was bored by it, bored by the reading he had done—and maybe not encouraged overmuch by the reception given to *Niccolò*. We know that he had worked on the plot and that he was worried by the size to which his story threatened to grow if he was to cover all the incidents he intended: he was in difficulties about the method of weaving some of the historical incidents into the story —and not happy about his grasp of the historical background: and in addition he could not decide whether to write as he would wish and perhaps have such trouble with the censor as to have to publish in France, if at all, or to compromise so as to be more likely to pass the Italian censor: for he felt that the luck he had had with Bellisomi and with Colonnetti was not to be expected to be his for a third time. His seventh and longest chapter is a survey of Lombard history, and a very tedious one too for the reader: if it was as tedious for the author it is little wonder that he went no further. The fictional part is no more satisfying: in the space of seven chapters he has introduced more coincidence than one would hope for in a complete novel, and some of his characters resemble pasteboard.

His only other work of fiction, the beginning of a story in English, dates from the end of 1846 and early 1847. It was written for Countess Fanny Persano (*née* Bacon), the English wife of his friend Carlo (later Admiral) Persano, and as much of it as he had written was sent to her for correction. She worked over it most carefully, suggesting emendations, but apparently never returned the manuscript to him. Both he and she would seem to have forgotten about it, and it lay amongst the Admiral's papers until brought to light in 1955.[1] The story was to have been of brigandage in the Castelli Romani, for which Azeglio was able to draw upon recollections such as he used later in his *Ricordi*. In what he wrote of the story, the hero, Venanzio, has committed the crime that would compel him to take to the mountains: he has shot the son of a rich peasant, the oppressor of Venanzio's parents in the past. The son Natale is the favoured wooer of a lovely but ambitious village girl, Lalla, with whom Venanzio

[1] It was published in *Italian Studies*, Vol. XII, 1957.

is hopelessly in love. Natale has been challenged to a duel but refuses to fight an opponent for whom he professes contempt, and he drives Venanzio to desperation by distraining on him for his parents' debts, small enough in total, but far beyond the means of Venanzio and his widowed mother to pay after years of interest have mounted up. So Venanzio takes the law into his own hands, ambushes his rival, and shoots him. He returns to his home just long enough to kiss its portal and takes to the hills. Azeglio's English is remarkably correct grammatically, especially considering that a quarter of a century had elapsed since he was having some lessons from Miss Cornelia Knight and, later, from Garello in Rome. Professor Ghisalberti has found evidence of his taking further lessons in English from Charles Isidore Hemans, son of Charles Hemans and Felicia the poet, who lived in Rome. But Azeglio did not take these lessons until early in 1848, after having left off this English story. These two circumstances of writing and learning English are interesting because at this date he was becoming almost totally occupied by politics, and presumably suspected that it might be useful in his new career to have a knowledge of English.

Although correct enough, his English is, not surprisingly, stiff and characterless. One sentence is amusing and would seem typically Azeglian: 'It is said that Alexander the Great slept perfectly well the night before the battle of Arbella, which proved in the first place that he was sleepy, and then perhaps that he was quite decided upon what he was to do the next day. The same causes produced the same results with Venanzio, who also was more sure of himself than the conqueror of Darius was of his army.'

But Manzoni, alas, had anticipated him. 'It is said that the Prince de Condè slept profoundly the night before the battle of Rocroi: but in the first place he was very tired; secondly he had already made all the necessary arrangements and decided what was to be done the next morning.' So opens the second chapter of *I promessi sposi*.

V

ENTRY INTO POLITICS

His Italian biographers have considered the Milanese period to be the most obscure part of Azeglio's life. It is true that his *Ricordi* says little about it apart from listing paintings exhibited and describing the writing and publishing of his two novels. The *Ricordi* continues his life story to the interview with King Charles Albert at the end of his political fact-finding journey through the Papal States: and it appears to be as full as one could need, and, as one expects from its author, to be candid. But these final thirty pages omit information of considerable importance, and on some points they are misleading. This may be due in part to this section of the *Ricordi* having been pieced together for publication by his friend Torelli, after Azeglio's death, from fragments written at various times. Yet this is not a fully satisfactory explanation, for some of the disputable passages were straightforward transcriptions from Azeglio's own accounts, and one must conclude that even after a lapse of twenty years he did not wish to reveal some circumstances.

We begin with his return to Rome, recounted with apparent lucidity in Torelli's recension. Azeglio, we read, had been tempted to leave Milan for Rome, but for various reasons—the more influential ones being his family ties—he had decided to stay in Milan.

Whilst these thoughts were solidifying in my mind there arrived a letter from an old friend in Rome, begging and urging me to come at once to help him out of an awkward situation. The balance swayed in favour of setting out. Do not believe, however, that my departure was a little misdeed of which I had to repent later. I have already, I think, convinced a reader that in questions of faults or of temper I am no different from any other, yet from the moment I have had duties to perform I have never held back. That I repeat even here lest I seem to pass for a luckier sinner than in truth I was. I arrived in Rome. Reputation had arrived ahead of me and I was given my fill of compliments from men in black and men in purple. I ran at once to my friend and in a few days managed to extricate him from his quandary, thanks largely to the kindly help of Cardinal De Gregorio.[1]

[1] *Ricordi*, p. 522.

This passage is strangely verbose and strangely incomplete. Azeglio had in fact left Milan in 1843 and from then on was living in Piedmont, either at Envie or in Turin, his separation from Luisa having now become permanent. He was busily painting, intermittently writing *La lega lombarda*, and spending much of his time with his cousin Cesare Balbo. It was under Balbo's influence that Azeglio now began for the first time in his life to pay any attention to political matters. Much had been happening and much had been written since the abortive movements in the Two Sicilies in 1820 and in Piedmont in 1821. Confalonieri had been sentenced to death in 1821 after a mockery of a trial, reprieved as a result of his wife's petition, but sent to the Spielberg fortress in Moravia, the most dreaded of all prisons, his wife following him to live, and soon to die, in sight of his gaol. Silvio Pellico, a native of Saluzzo, a town with which the Taparellis were closely associated, came out of the Spielberg after ten years' imprisonment to write *Le mie prigioni*, which by its gentleness and avoidance of rancour in telling of the grim conditions did more perhaps than any other book to discredit Austrian rule. A rising in Salerno province in 1828 had been repressed with savagery by the Neapolitan soldiery, who had paraded the heads of their victims from village to village. In 1830 Menotti had led a rising in Modena that for a time threatened to drive Duke Francis IV from his throne: the French Revolution of that same year was the signal for revolt in Parma, Romagna, Emilia, and the Marches: in 1834 Ramorino led a desperate attempt to enter Piedmont from Switzerland to start a revolution against Charles Albert, the failure of which was paralleled by that of Garibaldi to raise a mutiny in the Sardinian fleet. Attempt after attempt in one region after another failed: Austria's military control was unchallengeable, her determination to suppress risings outside as well as inside her own provinces unswerving. The young Italy movement of Mazzini had been gaining adherents, but all it had seemed able to achieve was to keep idealism alive by the sacrifice of idealists, the last and most tragic of this series being the Bandiera brothers and their seven friends, shot in 1844 after a descent on the Calabrian coast, dying with the cry 'Viva l'Italia'.

For all his lack of interest in politics Azeglio could not be unaware of or unmoved by these events. But to him they seemed futile, however well-intentioned, and he refused to allow even good intentions to Mazzini. It seemed to him that from his own place of security in Paris or London Mazzini was remorselessly sending a succession of brave men to the scaffold. He expressed his disapproval of Mazzini in letters, but as an Italian he could not voice any public criticism of patriots who had shown such fanatical, if in his view ill-directed, heroism. What aroused him to a more active interest in politics was a theory, put forward by Gioberti in his *Del primato morale e civile degli Italiani*, published in 1843. The bulk of this vast politico-historical pamphlet is devoted to analysis of Italian achievements in the past, but Gioberti outlined his hopes for Italy's future, trying to avoid 'utopias which in any case I dislike; and to make one state out of Italy, though a most beautiful idea, is in our days a solemn utopia, whereas to link them in four sister monarchies, Piedmont, Tuscany, Rome, and Naples, and to drive out the abhorred Austrian is perhaps a utopia but less so than the other'.[1] Of the four monarchs the Pope, by virtue of his spiritual and universal office, would have to be president.[2] Events were quickly to show how utopian Gioberti's scheme was: but even as pure theory it was shaky. It assumed the dispossession of the smaller Italian rulers and the willingness of the greater ones to accept Papal overlordship: more challengeably it assumed the willingness of the Italian people to accept this half-way house as a permanent settlement. It also assumed that the Pope would be able to associate himself still more closely with Italy as a lay sovereign without detriment to his spiritual ecumenical authority, which could only be based on political non-alignment. But above all it failed by its silence about the way the problem of the abhorred Austrian might be solved: how and by whom Lombardy-Venetia might be liberated, and how these provinces might then be integrated into his federal Italy. The fine dedication to Silvio Pellico made clear his own anti-Austrian sentiment, but the omission of forthright discussion was intentional. In the *Gesuita Moderno* he wrote later: 'When I read the *Speranze* of Cesare Balbo I was glad that I had not forestalled him in a subject that gave my illustrious friend the occasion to publish a book that all Italy now considers a classic.'[3]

[1] From a letter of Gioberti to Mamiani, 18 December 1840, in V. Gioberti, *Del primato morale e civile degli Italiani*, Utet edition, Vol. I, p. xxiii.

[2] Gioberti, op. cit., Vol. I, pp. 107–11.

[3] Quoted in Introduction to Gioberti, op. cit., Vol. I, p. lxix.

The *Primato* had been eagerly read and discussed by Balbo and Azeglio at the Villa Rubatto and it was Azeglio who prompted the writing of the *Speranze d'Italia*. In a way Balbo redressed the balance. He offered no solution to the Roman question but concentrated on the hopes of liberation. These were four— voluntary action by the Italian princes, an uprising of the people, foreign intervention, or the evolution of favourable circumstances, whatever these might be. The first he believed unlikely, the second foredoomed to failure for purely military reasons, the third undesirable: so there remained only the vague fourth. This he thought might come with the continued disintegration of the Ottoman Empire, creating a vacuum in the Balkans into which Austria would be drawn if only to keep Russia out. This would create a new European situation in which Austria might consent or be prevailed upon to vacate Lombardy-Venetia. As it proved, the Ottoman Empire did continue to break up and Austria did find herself more and more deeply involved in Balkan affairs. But this involvement followed upon, and was partly a compensation for, the loss of her Italian provinces. Stimulating as Balbo's book was, it was therefore quite as much an exercise of the imagination as Gioberti's. One thing it had done: by switching off the spotlight that Gioberti had focused on the Pope it left the stage prepared for the entry on to it of the only other ruler worthy of such a highlight—the King of Sardinia.

The hitherto apolitical Azeglio had been mulling over such ideas for some months before he left Turin on the errand so dramatically described in the *Ricordi*. But there is still some mystification, for he did not go immediately to Rome, as stated there, but to Sicily.[1] A wish to see Prospero again may have been the only motive for this journey, as he said in a letter to Luisa;[2] though Azeglio always denied it, it was alleged even during his lifetime that he had had contacts with the secret societies some-where.[3] Whatever the reason he had had for going to Sicily, and whatever he was doing there, it was from Palermo that he went in mid-November by way of Naples to Rome.

After his arrival two mysterious attempts were made, according to his *Ricordi*, to lure him to assignations. Were these advances

[1] N. Vaccaluzzo (*Massimo d'Azeglio* (1930), p. 83) has him go to Rome and has antedated the Sicilian visit to 1843.
[2] Carcano, op. cit., p. 147.
[3] For discussion of this see Vaccaluzzo, op. cit., pp. 330 and 342.

being made by secret societies, or were they traps laid by the police? Or were they simple invitations to an amorous intrigue? Whatever they were, and one does not doubt that they were made, Azeglio was too canny to let himself be enmeshed. It was something of an anticlimax that after such 'cloak and dagger' assignations he should receive the overtures of the liberals in a Roman drawing-room. This was in the house of Clelia Piermarini, a former Lady of the Bedchamber to Queen Cristina of Spain, but now back in Rome, where she was fairly well-known as a political *intrigante* though considered by Pantaleoni to be a lightweight. Under her auspices Azeglio was introduced to two men whom in the *Ricordi* he refers to as Adolfo S. of Pesaro and Filippo A. of Cesena. The one was Count Adolfo Spada and the other Filippo Amadori, a doctor, who according to Minghetti had been 'so much inside the secret life of the Romagna that he could have written a book on the secret societies from 1796 to our days'. In 1848 he was to be a member of the Roman Constituent Assembly: exiled after the restoration of Pius IX he settled down to work devotedly in Liguria in the state medical service, pioneering vaccination there: after 1860 he returned to politics as a deputy in the Moderate party in the Italian Parliament. On this evening in 1845 he and Spada took Azeglio into an anteroom off Clelia's drawing-room under pretext of a medical consultation, to propound their scheme to him. Even now, however, the straightforward account given in the *Ricordi* and hitherto unquestioningly accepted is confused by a claim, generally overlooked, that it was not they but Pantaleoni who made the actual proposition. Like Amadori, Pantaleoni was a medical doctor in Rome, but unlike him a notably successful one. He had moderately liberal views on constitutional matters: but in national affairs he was one of the leaders of the Roman group who looked to Piedmont as the only hope for Italian liberation. A note in Pantaleoni's *Carteggio*, prepared for publication by himself and an unnamed editor, reads (ambiguously enough): 'He [Azeglio] was ripe for a political mandate and this he received from the mysterious Doctor Filippo A. of Cesena, who for the framework of a historical romance might be converted into Doctor Diomede Pantaleoni.'[1] Although he is not mentioned by Azeglio Pantaleoni might well have been

[1] '. . . che per la quadratura di un romanzo storico si potrebbe convertire nel dott. Diomede Pantaleoni.' D. Pantaleoni, *Diomede Pantaleoni e M. d'A., Carteggio inedito* (1888).

present at the interview: but, as the account just given might indicate, there is nothing unduly mysterious about Filippo Amadori, a real enough person and more likely than Pantaleoni to be able to introduce Azeglio into the network of the secret societies: Azeglio's story is probably substantially correct.

After a show of checking Azeglio's pulse Amadori explained the political situation as he saw it. The Pope, the detested Gregory XVI, was not likely to live much longer: his dominions, and the Romagna in particular, were liable to break out into insurrection on the news of his death. But a growing number of politically acute men were convinced that such risings could only provoke Austrian intervention and heavy reprisals. These people were looking for a new man, one who was not involved in the past history of Carbonarism and Young Italy, one who inspired confidence, to go round, to meet the more responsible leaders in the provinces, and to counsel caution. And it had been decided that 'this man, it seemed to them, dear Signor Azeglio, must be yourself'.[1]

Amazed, he tells us, at being offered the task of deciding the strategy of the societies, Azeglio pointed out that he had never had any part in them: but this, it was argued, was his supreme qualification. He took a few days to think over the invitation and then accepted it. What he actually did, though, was something different from what Amadori had proposed. Instead of arguing against action by the societies, a purely negative counsel hardly likely to arouse any enthusiasm, he went round the Romagna with a positive proposition, that the liberals should look to Piedmont for a lead. Amadori had not suggested that he should do this in such of their conversations as Azeglio recalled: but it was something that Pantaleoni might well have proposed.

On the first or second of September, in a hired carriage driven by one Antonio, Azeglio left Rome. For the first part of the journey he was accompanied by a man named Pompilii, one of Clelia Piermarini's circle and like her considered to be of little solid discretion, who was to go as far as Spoleto, his native town, in Azeglio's company, and whose function was to introduce Azeglio into the network of the societies. This was known as the Trafila, from the pierced steel plate through whose holes thin strips of metal were drawn in the process of making wire. It was a matter of great and justifiable pride that the members of the

[1] *Ricordi*, pp. 529–32.

societies had maintained this Trafila successfully and prevented secret agents of the Papal Government from insinuating themselves into it in order to be able to seize its members. The fact that Azeglio was passed along it is a sign of the confidence they had in him, whether or not he had had any previous connexions with any underground organization.

Azeglio tried out his argument on Pompilii as they were driving together to see how he would react to the proposal to align the societies behind Piedmont. The aim of all patriots was the expulsion of the Austrians and the overthrow of the 'government by priests'. This could not be achieved without the use of force. So far, so good.

'Have you the force? If you have not, you must find someone who has. And who in Italy has it—or, to speak more exactly, has some? Piedmont, for she at least has an independent existence, money in reserve, an army, and a navy.' At the word 'Piedmont' my fellow-debater grimaced (as everyone did, right to the very last, during my journey) and replied ironically 'Charles Albert! You want us to put some hope in him?' 'If you can't trust him, don't: but in that case you have no one to look to.' 'But what about 1821—and 1832?'[1]

That was the question Azeglio knew he had to expect, and to which it was hard to find any answer—even an unconvincing one. He was not at all convinced himself. The events of 1821 had been bad enough. They had given Charles Albert the reputation for irresoluteness that was to stick to him all his life and for ever after —'the Hamlet of Savoy', 'King Wobble' (Re Tentenna). And from that event men had drawn the still more damaging conclusion that he was treacherous. Worse still by far was the effect of the events of 1832 and 1833. On his accession in 1831 he had promulgated a number of reforms, in themselves of very minor importance, but interpreted by his subjects as auguries of things to come, and, they hoped, to come quickly and unswervingly. An atmosphere of optimism and goodwill pervaded Sardinia: and it was dissipated almost at once. The discovery of members of Young Italy amongst the officers of the army led to a series of investigations in which torture was used, to courts martial, and to the execution of nine of the accused. From that date 'King Wobble' was also 'King Executioner'—'Re Fucilatore'. Not only Piedmontese and Italian but also foreign opinion was shocked by the

---

[1] *Ricordi*, p. 537.

trials and executions. How could Azeglio ten years later hope to inspire liberals or anyone at all with any confidence in a King with such a record, especially as he had no such confidence himself either then or later? His task of converting the Pope's subjects to put their trust in Charles Albert was difficult enough and would become more so a year later when the Papal tiara had been assumed by Pius IX, in whom everyone, even his own subjects, had boundless confidence. Only the negative part of Azeglio's mission, the counselling of prudence and of abstention from action, had any chance of success. As for Charles Albert, the only argument that Azeglio could think of was that he might be relied upon to act, as any man would, in his own selfish interests, and that these must lead him to attempt, should the chance arise, to seek the aggrandizement of his territories at the expense of Austria. Yet could even this unflattering reasoning carry any conviction when the man's whole record was apparently one of subservience to Austria, or even, as in 1833, one of trying to surpass Austria in harshness? To sum up, it seems certain that Azeglio could not sincerely believe in his King nor persuade others to believe in him. He could believe in Piedmont because of people like his own father, his brother Roberto, Cesare Balbo, and others of that stamp of integrity, selflessness, and patriotism: but he could not transmit this faith to those to whom Piedmont meant Charles Albert.

The liberty that Azeglio allowed himself in promising Charles Albert's intervention against Austria when a possible occasion should arise leads naturally to the question whether the King had been consulted before Azeglio set out. In the *Ricordi* (p. 550) Azeglio specifically denied that he had been: but this may have been a half-truth. During 1843–5 he had been with Cesare Balbo: Balbo was intimate with the King: he may have acted as an intermediary and the King may have been told that liberals outside Piedmont were looking to him, and hoping for encouragement from him: all this is hypothetical and it is not in the least degree likely that the King had shown any initiative in this matter, for in the account that Azeglio wrote of his interview with Charles Albert informing him of his journey, an account that was written immediately afterwards, he records his own surprise at the King's unqualified approval of what he had done. One is so apt to see Piedmontese intrigue everywhere in Italy at this period that one is liable to suspect it where it was not merely unprovable but even unlikely.

Azeglio's route took him due north from Rome by Civita Castellana, Terni, Spoleto, and Foligno: then he turned to go by Camerino and Macerata to Ancona, and thence along the coast of the Marches into the Romagna via Rimini and from there inland to Forlì. This was his farthest north, for he then went southwest over the Apennines to Florence. After Pompilii had once introduced him into the Trafila the procedure was simple enough. In each town the key-man would give him the name of his corresponding number in the next town, whom Azeglio would seek out as unobtrusively as possible. Having met him Azeglio would expound his views as convincingly as he might. His propaganda for Charles Albert seemed to him to be carrying a certain amount of conviction.

I found everyone convinced that 'Young Italy' was folly, and folly all the conspiracies, petty revolutions with neither heads nor tails, that had been attempted previously, and convinced also that it was time to think of other means. Hearing of such means as I suggested all of them screwed up their faces: but being soon persuaded that without force nothing could be accomplished, and that as they had no such force it was necessary to find someone who had, they ended, after much grimacing, by putting up with the idea of Charles Albert.[1]

One may wonder how deep or sincere may have been even such grudging acceptance of Charles Albert as his listeners conceded him: in Rimini the other part of his mission was a total failure. Just such a 'petty revolution' as he had set out to discountenance broke out very soon after his visit. This rising had its aims expressed in the 'Rimini Programme' and its suppression called forth Azeglio's pamphlet *Degli ultimi casi di Romagna*. But though the Rimini rising may have been a sign of Azeglio's failure it may equally indicate that he had been almost too successful in one half of his mission, for his promise of intervention by Piedmont on some hypothetical future occasion may have had a stimulating influence outweighing his counsel of caution and submission. Aurelio Saffi, who took part in this very rising, certainly held Azeglio responsible, writing in 1860:

He [Azeglio] was not speaking at random; he could guarantee that Charles Albert was not unaware of the undertaking: Lombardy was prepared for great events: the Savoyard King was to supply arms and treasure in abundance. If he wavered, if he did not make up his mind

[1] *Ricordi*, p. 542.

to this magnanimous war the force of opinion would compel him: if he opposed this he would fall from his throne. The words of Cavaliere d'Azeglio seemed to them to be worthy of some attention as showing an important nationalist movement in the Sardinian states, and they thought it would be of great value to the common cause to establish correspondence and ties of solidarity between the strong sub-Alpine people and the enthusiastic people of Central Italy.[1]

In 1860, when he wrote this, Aurelio Saffi was a political opponent of Azeglio and he may have exaggerated the definiteness of Azeglio's advice: but it seems beyond doubt that Azeglio's promise that Piedmont would intervene when the chance should come carried far more weight with some auditors than his counsels of prudence and abstention from action. If Azeglio had had no encouragement, direct or indirect, from Charles Albert his suggestion of the certainty of such intervention is inexcusable. If he did argue, as Saffi alleged, that Charles Albert would be deposed should he fail to take action, he was not merely talking near-treason but was floating away towards realms of fantasy. He had always had the reputation of being a politican of singular candour, but on this occasion he may have spoken beyond his brief (if he had any brief). It is not improbable, for in 1848 he was to do just the same in publicly pledging Pius IX to a course of action that the Pope not merely had not approved, but never could approve. And this too was done in the interests of Piedmont. To Azeglio, as early as 1845, as to Cavour later, the establishment of Piedmontese hegemony in Italian affairs was the main aim; amongst the subjects of the Pope it might not be impossibly difficult to preach the Piedmontese cause convincingly, but in Tuscany, as Azeglio admitted in the *Ricordi*,[2] he had no success whatever. Apart from a natural unwillingness to subject, even in appearance only, a city as sophisticated as Florence to the simple provincialism of philistine Turin, no one who had lived under the rule of the Tuscan Grand Dukes and had read about the way power was exercised by the Kings of Sardinia would be in any hurry to submit to Piedmontese government. Azeglio broached his idea to two men in Florence, both unnamed in the *Ricordi* but one of whom was certainly Gino Capponi, a man of immense prestige: both cut him off at once, one saying 'What— Charles Albert as head of Italian liberals? Away with you!', and the other, more simply still—'That traitor!' It was to take a very

[1] Quoted by Vaccaluzzo, op. cit., p. 92 and note to p. 343.　　[2] *Ricordi*, p. 542.

determined Tuscan, Bettino Ricasoli, the 'Iron Baron', to swing Tuscany round to union with Piedmont, and by that time it was a Piedmont ruled by Victor Emmanuel, not by Charles Albert.

On his return to Turin Azeglio sought an audience of the King, who received him, as was his custom, at six o'clock in the morning, when his palace was the only building in the city with a window showing lights. He was ushered at once into the royal presence and he and the King sat in the embrasure of a window overlooking the still-sleeping city. Charles Albert's first question, 'And where have you been?', gave Azeglio his cue. He told of his tour of the Papal States and of the disillusionment with the secret societies that he had found there. He reported his attempts to counsel patience, though admitting that the rising that had taken place in Rimini had shown how incomplete his success there had been. In conclusion he asked the King whether he approved of what he had done and said. The King's reply was unhesitating and given with a warmth of feeling that seemed utterly alien to his character. 'Let those gentlemen know that they should wait quietly and take no action, since as yet nothing can be achieved: but let them also know that when occasion offers, my life, the lives of my sons, my arms, my treasure, my armies—all will be spent in the Italian cause.' Azeglio was taken by surprise at the directness of the answer, and repeated the King's opening words, 'I am to let them know . . .', and as he did so the King nodded his assent. The interview ended with that: both rose and in closing the audience the King placed both his hands on Azeglio's shoulders and kissed him on each cheek. But, says Azeglio, there was something so studied in this gesture that all his doubts returned, and his inner voice said 'Do not trust him!'[1]

His surprise at hearing Charles Albert's uncompromising declaration would not have been so great had he been more aware of the King's private opinions, for though outwardly a client of Austria he repeatedly expressed violently anti-Austrian views to his intimates. Vienna had every right to expect his loyalty, for when Charles Felix had been determined to exclude Charles Albert from the succession, or even to pass over the whole Carignano line in favour of Francis of Modena, only Austrian devotion to the principle of legitimacy, overcoming the Emperor's distrust of Charles Albert and preference for Francis, had saved the throne for him. By marriage alliances with the Habsburgs,

[1] *Ricordi*, pp. 550–5.

active participation in the Holy Alliance's intervention in Spain in 1823, and ruthless punishment of Piedmontese revolutionaries in 1833 he had done all he could to ingratiate himself with Austria in the sight of all Europe. Yet he was pro-Austrian only in so far as Austria was the champion of legitimacy and of royal autocracy. So long as Austria ruled over any Italian territory he bore her a deep resentment. In his diaries and in reported conversations with friends he might speak of 'taking his musket on his shoulder in another war with Austria' (1838) or of 'ringing every bell from the Ticino to Savoy to raise the cry of Lombard independence' (1843), and around 1843 he was giving to his friends a medallion on which the lion of Savoy trampled down the eagle of Austria, with the motto 'J'atens mon astre'. This dichotomy seems strange to us if we assume that in the Risorgimento period the ideals of national independence, unification, and representative government were inseparable. But this was not the case: patriots could be enthusiastic about one or two of these causes and apathetic about, or even hostile to, the rest. So Charles Albert wished to liberate Lombardy-Venetia, and probably annex them to Piedmont, but gave little apparent thought to the rest of the peninsula. As for liberalism, that was anathema to him since 1821. Knowing only the King's public image Azeglio naturally was surprised by his fervour. Even had he known him better he might still have doubted: for how could a man so morbidly distrustful of all save a very few gain general trust? It was not until after the tragic events of 1848–9 that Azeglio became ashamed of his reservations.

As soon as he had left the palace and returned to the hotel where he was staying Azeglio wrote in veiled terms an account of his interview. This, dated 12 October 1845, he sent to a Roman friend, Farini, who transmitted it to others, notably to Marco Minghetti. It was published in 1911 in the *Epistolario Farini* but de Rubris seems to have been the first to have seen its significance.[1] It began:

I have talked as you wished me to do, with the royal director of charitable institutions, hospitals, and nursing homes. He says he will gather together all the information you ask for, and that much of it is ready on demand, of which he will give delivery. . . . All his life he has concerned himself with nothing else and his one study is to free his administration from all abuses and I think there is no one else in

[1] Letter quoted by de Rubris in *Il cavaliere della prima passione nazionale*, pp. 90ff.

Italy his equal in such work. . . . He promises to assist and will certainly do so, with great seriousness, and when occasion arises he expects from you an exchange of information about different administrations. He says he wishes to know the regulations of the hospitals where you are and that you should be ready to give him a fairly minute account since it is only right that you should in your turn do something for him: and in this surely he is justified. . . . Returning to our director of hospitals, and not wishing to take too much responsibility on to myself, I should add that he spoke with warmth, showed great anxiety to help you, and, I believe, will do so, his interest lying in what he hopes from you: but, after all, God alone sees into his inner heart.

The final phrase remained in Azeglio's mind, for in the *Ricordi* he recalls it as having concluded his letter. This letter to Farini, with its date, seems decisively to dispose of a theory that has been put forward that Azeglio in fact had had his interview with the King before he went on his tour of the Papal States: it would not have been to his discredit if he had had the King's approval in advance for his promises of Charles Albert's aid: but one must accept the *Ricordi* as reliable in placing the interview after the journey.

Azeglio had now set his hand to the plough. The furrow he drove was a fairly straight one but it did not stop at the confines of the Piedmontese field, going on into fertile soil in Tuscany and the Papal States. Whether it was honest seed or dragon's teeth that he then sowed might have been a matter of debate.

His private activities are not easy to unravel. But he was staying in Turin: he was in frequent contact with the King and was writing to the liberals in Rome, Farini, Pantaleoni, and Minghetti, of whom at least Pantaleoni was already pro-Piedmontese and Minghetti was to be so if not already converted. He was also keeping in touch with them through intermediaries of whom one, a lawyer, Cornero, is known by name. Owing to the possibility of interception and censorship his letters are not revealing: what messages Cornero carried can only be guessed: but one's guess would be that they continued the argument that all depended on Piedmont and on Charles Albert, and that the King was virtually committed now: and that as a result all other action, such as local risings, must be prevented.

His open contribution to the development of the cause was the publication of his pamphlet *Degli ultimi casi di Romagna*. Gioberti's and Balbo's books had been important but this shorter work (though it was not difficult to write more shortly than Gioberti, whose prolixity was fantastic) had a far greater immediate effect. It was perhaps the first book to make any contribution to the Risorgimento as it really happened, instead of to some ardently longed-for but vaguely outlined future happy state.

As Balbo was writing his own book Azeglio was living with him and as Balbo had read his *Speranze* to him, so he now read *Degli ultimi casi* to Balbo, to hear his comments. Nor was Balbo the only one to be so favoured.

Balbo is pleased with it and so is *another person*, which is more important, and it seems it may be allowed to circulate here. . . .[1]

I am in a fury to finish my work. Yesterday evening I read from it to Balbo, Lisio, Villamarina, Sauli, and Provana. They had some comments to make but on the whole thought it should go ahead. I was trying to print it here, relying on a remark made in this sense by *our friend*, but when it came to tying things up I was left empty-handed. If I were to have printed it here I would have had to delay: so as soon as it is finished I am leaving and hope to be in Pisa or Florence by the 10th [of January 1846]. I hope that if at all possible I shall have everything settled by February.[2]

The King, for 'our friend' could be no one else, might well have approved the sentiments of *Gli ultimi casi*, but with his usual knack of blowing both lukewarm and icy cold he did not wish to seem at all responsible for its publication. So Azeglio took the manuscript to Florence. He had twice been lucky in his dealing with the Austrian censorship, but this third manuscript would have been totally unacceptable in Lombardy. The only hope lay in the most easy-going of all governments, in Tuscany.

Before its publication he read parts of it to the blind Gino Capponi, whose approval was immediate. 'That is the road to follow, the right tone: these are things that need to be said. God bless you!'[3] One modification Capponi asked for: Azeglio had described the behaviour of the Societies as culpable: Capponi thought this was offensive to men whose motives were patriotic if misguided: but Azeglio would go no further than to replace 'culpable' with 'blameworthy'. The *Ultimi casi* was published by Le Monnier in Florence on 11 March 1846. A second, corrected and enlarged, edition was printed a little later, nominally at least in Bastia, Corsica: but the Government of Tuscany, acting with belated efficiency, seized all copies of it: even Azeglio himself

---

[1] Carcano, op. cit., p. 195, 16 December 1845.
[2] Ibid., p. 196, from Turin, 26 December 1845.   [3] Ibid., op. cit., p. 199.

G

was unable to find one when in 1850 he was having his political writings reprinted in Turin, so that the Le Monnier edition is the one accepted as definitive. It circulated widely, and in Piedmont its sale was permitted 'with caution', which meant that booksellers might stock and sell, but not display it. Azeglio always believed that it was one of the books that the Cardinal-Bishop of Imola, Mastai Ferretti, took with him to the Conclave that was to elect him Pope as Pius IX: but in this, alas, he was wrong. Whilst still Bishop of Imola he said that Azeglio's book contained 'many abominable lies and defamations. [The author] is just worked up by the Italian delirium; . . . if others think like him there will be a good and a bad end. . . . The good will be that there will be no revolutions or seditions, which he condemns . . . the bad will be that we shall have a flood of writings attacking the administration.'[1] The books taken to Rome by Mastai were Balbo's and Gioberti's, both given to him by the Pasolinis in whose house he stayed on his journey.[2] It was read by Mazzini, however, in his London exile, and he, to whom Azeglio was so hostile, gave it its due. 'I do not agree with some of its views, but I respect its convictions for what they are. The great national idea is expressed in it with decisiveness, without reservations, and with a courage worthy of admiration.'

Unlike the *Primato*, the *Ultimi casi* started not from a theory but from a fact—the attempted uprising in Rimini, and the greater part of it was concerned with the actual state of Italy in 1845: Azeglio's recommendations for the future grew out of the situation as he exposed it. His concern was not with ends but with means. And precisely in this lay the force of his book.

He opened it with an uncompromising statement of his disapproval of the rising. In the first place, like all risings since 1820, it was purely local, not merely in its occasion and incidents but in its aims, and in that lay the causes of its failure. It was ill-timed, for the great European powers were all anxious to maintain European peace: thus France, Britain, Russia, and Prussia were not in the least likely to exert any pressure on Austria to restrain her from intervention in Italy. And whilst no support could be expected from outside, there was no effective strength in the opposition to Austria amongst the Italians themselves. 'The

---

[1] Quoted by J. Parris in *The Lion of Caprera* (1962), p. 67, from Serafini's *Pio Nono* (The Vatican, 1958).
[2] E. E. Y. Hales, *Pio Nono* (1954).

Italian people knows that to plan revolt in small numbers is useless: to rise in masses is impossible.' He admitted that the guerrilla warfare of the Spanish people against Napoleon seemed to support the possibility of a national uprising succeeding, but, as he pointed out, behind the Spaniards were the resources of Britain, and British armies led by the Duke of Wellington. What had Italy to set against the 200,000 men and 200 pieces of artillery that Austria could muster in Italy?

So far Azeglio had not gone beyond the bounds of cool common sense, but it was a novelty to have the situation analysed with such realism. It was also courageous on his part, for pity for the defeated after these risings had blinded the sentimental to their futility. However misguided they may have been, these movements were a reaction against a misgovernment so serious as to be felt intolerable, and Azeglio therefore launched into a scarifying indictment of the Papal administration. To begin with, he denied that arguments based on *raison d'état* had any validity. A government could only justify its actions by reference to its own established code of law, 'since right is indivisible, constrains all men equally to its laws, and admits no possible occasion for its transgression'.[1] One of his first accusations against the Papal system of rule was that it was chaotic. Powers were delegated to the Governors of the various Provinces without any co-ordination, and each was allowed so much latitude that the result was utter confusion. The Pope himself was almost unapproachable: absolute sovereigns usually had days of audience when complaints might be heard, but his subjects might only address the Pope on condition that they did not discuss state affairs. Next there was no equality before the law. Even in the Austrian provinces, apart from *raison d'état*, the rights of the humblest were safeguarded by a code of law applicable to all. But in the States of the Church there was one law for the clergy, who were the civil service, and another for the laity. In economic and commercial affairs the same inept and oppressive chaos prevailed. Indirect taxes were exorbitant and were farmed out, so that their incidence on the actual payer was made still heavier. Monopolies were an essential part of the fiscal system: prices were inflated as a result and the ónly industry to flourish was that of smuggling. Rome had refused to sanction the building of railways. Agriculture and trade were

---

[1] M. de Rubris (ed.), *Scritti e discorsi politici di M. d'A.* (1931), 3 vols. (hereafter referred to as *S.D.P.*), Vol. I, p. 30.

languishing as a result of these follies, wages were derisorily low, smallholders were all in debt, and misery was rampant. The Government maintained its control only by the employment of mercenary soldiers, and these would have been swept aside by the populace had it not known that if they went the Austrian armies would enter in their stead. Besides the visible forces of army and police the Government relied on its special secret police—the Sanfedisti—who were no more than organized and licensed rapacious bullies. Terrorism was a deliberate part of government policy and savage sentences were imposed in law courts where the same officials were accusers and judges. Azeglio cited lists of punishments after uprisings and contrasted them with the leniency shown in France towards Louis Napoleon after his attempt to seize power.

From this exposure of the state of affairs as it was Azeglio went on to formulate a policy, not to paint an idealized picture of some happy future prospect but to recommend something that could be initiated forthwith. This part of the book is especially significant not only for its effect but because it stated views from which Azeglio never afterwards departed. All his future political writings were a development of themes foreshadowed in this short book of 1846. It was his belief that public opinion was an irresistible force. Not as a result of pressure from minority groups of rebels, sectaries, or philosophers, but because of the upsurging of popular feeling, Louis XVI and Charles X were dethroned and Charles V forced to abdicate: in England it was this that led to Catholic emancipation and to parliamentary reform. The essential task in Italy was to create public opinion and to make it heard.

To protest against injustice, against all injustices, openly, publicly, in every way, on every possible occasion, is, in my opinion, the formula that best expresses the greatest necessity of our times, the most useful and the most potent action now. The first, the greatest protest, which we should never tire of making, which should sound on every tongue, flow from every pen, must be against foreign occupation, and in support of our right to full control over our own soil, of our nationality, and of our independence. Let protests follow against the injustices, the abuses and evil orders of our own governments.[1]

His aim was that of 'plotting in full daylight'—the 'open conspiracy'. The crystallization of public opinion, and, to make this

---

[1] *S.D.P.*, I, p. 90.

possible, the education of the Italian people, not by exhortation but by the example of honest responsible political leaders, willing to apply to their public acts the same standards of morality as should rule their private affairs, was to be the leading motive of all Azeglio's political teaching.

His book dealt with the situation as it actually was, dealt with it honestly and courageously, and set forth a scheme of immediate action based on a cool appraisal of what was possible. In that lay its importance at the time: but in that lay also the reason for Azeglio's ultimate decline into political ineffectiveness. His arguments appeal to historical precedents: and these do not bear him out. It would be difficult to prove that public opinion throughout France decided the execution of Louis XVI or the overthrow of Charles X: still more difficult to show how public opinion in his far-scattered realms of the Empire, Spain and the Americas, the Netherlands and North Italy forced abdication on to Charles V. The success of radical or revolutionary movements such as those for Catholic emancipation or parliamentary reform in England to which he referred, like the success of twentieth-century communist or fascist movements, was due to the action of well-organized pressure groups, who, if they had any approval from public opinion, had dragged it along in the wake of their apparent success. The whole of Azeglio's political programme was based on his cult of the possible: but the great national upsurges have been stimulated not by a call for 'le possible, encore du possible, toujours du possible', but for 'de l'audace, encore de l'audace, toujours de l'audace': the Dantons, the Garibaldis sweep events along. The possibilists, the Siéyès, the Balbos, the Azeglios, the Kerenskys, if not actually trodden down, are left behind when the march of events becomes a gallop.

The interest aroused by Azeglio's book alarmed the Tuscan government, and he was politely but firmly requested to leave Florence. Important members of Florentine society, and representatives of some foreign governments, including Lord Holland, who greatly admired *Gli ultimi casi*, interceded on his behalf: so, though in a very lukewarm way, did the Piedmontese Minister, but the Grand Duke had decided and in the end Azeglio had to go, though a banquet of farewell was given in his honour at which most of the diplomats were present, though not, needless to say, the Austrians. Back he went to Piedmont, and there he was when the world learnt with some surprise of the election to the Papal throne of Pius IX in June 1846. Because of the new Pope's well-known humanity all Italy was in a state of expectation. Rome itself was perhaps the least excited city of all until the proclamation of an amnesty by the new Pope. From that moment even his sceptical capital began to be worked into a ferment of emotional sympathy for the new Pontiff. With a man of supposedly liberal views, one believed to be a convert to the Giobertian neo-Guelf concept of an Italian Confederation under Papal presidency, sitting in the seat of St. Peter, Rome had become the great centre of interest. Turin was forgotten. Charles Albert was sinking back once more into the limbo of shadowy and inchoate figures. Azeglio himself came to the conclusion that if he wished to be in the centre of things he must go to Rome.

Before he was able to arrange this he published a second pamphlet, *A Letter to N.N.*[1] (N.N. being in this case Marco Minghetti). This was his contribution to the universal Italian hymn of praise in honour of Pius IX. But 'It is not the only purpose of this letter to join you in blessing and thanking God for the gracious gift of such a Pope': his real purpose was once more to counsel caution. There were, he thought, two immediate dangers confronting the Pope and his subjects. The first of them was that far too much might be asked of the Pope. He had initiated reforms, and appetite was growing with what it fed on: his subjects might ask for too much, too quickly. It was impossible to supersede an evil and corrupt system overnight: men as well as measures had to be found. Further, the reform of government was not the Pope's only care, for on his shoulders lay responsibility for current affairs of Church and State, and for relations with other powers. If the enthusiasts tried to push the Pope too far and too quickly the result might imperil their own hopes.

This was admirable advice. Had it been followed, by its author as well as by his readers, the disillusionment with Pius IX, the complaints that Pius IX the First was followed by Pius IX the Second might not have ensued. A sense of proportion was lost in this first wave of enthusiasm for him: but it was lost still more in the reaction against him when it was found that he would not follow a policy that was quite impracticable for any Pope, would not do what in fact he had from the very outset made it clear that he could not do. One respects Azeglio's commonsense in offering this wise counsel of moderation in 1846: one would respect him

[1] *S.D.P.*, I, pp. 97–122.

still more had he not two years later become one of those who were most blatantly trying to manœuvre Pius into a false position.

The second danger was that the Pope might not be able to control the machine in his charge. As Azeglio reminded people, the ruler acts through subordinates and these in this case were men of the old régime. He compiled a catalogue of misdeeds committed by them in the first months of Pius's reign in continuation of the old policy they had maintained under Gregory XVI.[1] Minghetti and others saw that however well-intentioned Pius might be it would take some time to steer the cumbrous vehicle of Papal government into new directions, and they feared that this delay, and the continuance of Gregorian policies and of Gregorian officials in office, might provoke resistance. It was this fear that led Minghetti to ask Azeglio to make his appeal for moderation.

The *Letter to N.N.* ('Massimo's Second Epistle to the Romans' his sister-in-law called it) was published clandestinely in Bologna in October 1846, and copies were given away. Whatever might have been its other successes it did not gain for its author an immediate grant of a visa to enter the Papal States. In that same month Azeglio told Minghetti that Charles Albert himself had twice interceded on his behalf with no result. However much he might preach moderation Azeglio was still thought to be a firebrand. His attacks on Papal administration in the past rankled in the minds of the new Pope and of the old guard of the Government. Charles Albert too was aware of the possible ultimate effects of this apparently moderate revaluation of the situation. After the publication of the *Ultimi casi* he noted in his private diary: 'The King saw Massimo d'Azeglio. He has spread revolutionary activity into Tuscany. The King is content. Alfieri and Revel are scared of him.'[2] To the King Azeglio was the apostle of revolution rather than of moderation: nor could he seem otherwise to the Pope.

At last, on 30 December, permission to enter the Papal States was given, as a result, Azeglio believed, of the Pope's satisfaction with the *Letter to N.N.* But Azeglio delayed his departure, staying in Genoa until the beginning of February, and arriving in Rome eventually on the 8th of that month. He had had quite a variety of things to do in the period of his delay. He had begun, and laid aside, his English 'novella', and he had presided at a banquet in honour of Cobden, making a speech and proposing the toast

[1] *S.D.P.*, I, pp. 116–18.   [2] Quoted by Vaccaluzzo, op. cit., p. 96.

in English. Azeglio was never an economist, and as Prime Minister showed little interest in economic and commercial questions. But he had heard of 'free trade' and always reverenced what little he understood of it and of Cobden its apostle.

For him these weeks were blighted by the publication of a pamphlet by his brother Prospero, *On Nationality*. Apart from its content there was the added annoyance that it came out over the name of Father Luigi Taparelli d'Azeglio, whereas in the past Prospero had always published as Padre Luigi Taparelli, and so might not have been recognized as one of Massimo's family. The essay had been planned as a chapter of a larger work, though Prospero had hoped to see it published separately in advance. His superiors prevented this and later disclaimed any responsibility for its appearance in print now. It would seem that someone in Rome had sent a copy of the manuscript to someone else —probably a fellow-Jesuit—in Turin, who arranged for its printing by Ponthenier in Genoa. The Jesuits in Rome had found it too liberal: Solaro della Margarita has been quoted in protest against it. Gioberti, shocked by its illiberalism, attacked it in one of the interminable footnotes in his *Gesuita Moderno*, and Massimo wrote 'Father Taparelli has played a dirty trick on me: he has written a little work on "Nationality" printed and published a few days ago in Genoa . . . it is something incredible, even the Ultras are making the sign of the cross because of it.'[1] It is hard to believe that they had all actually been reading the same book. But Massimo held the Society chiefly to blame for the publication: whilst Prospero denied their responsibility, admitted to having been taken by surprise by its appearance, and wondered why so many, for such different reasons, were attacking a theory that he believed was a reconciliation of the ideas of Gioberti with those of the moderate secular liberals.[2]

Massimo was determined not to start a public disputation with his brother and to let the essay sink into oblivion. His annoyance passed quickly and relations between the three brothers remained unaffected.

[1] Carcano, op. cit., pp. 273–4, letter of 3 February 1847.
[2] Pirri, *Carteggi del R. P. Luigi Taparelli*, pp. 237–9, letter of April 1847 to Roberto.

VI

AZEGLIO AND THE DEVELOPMENT OF ITALIAN NATIONAL OPINION, 1847-1848

HAVING arrived in Rome on 8 February 1847 Azeglio stayed there, apart from a visit to Turin in September and October of that year, until he left to join the Papal army on 24 March 1848. He had played his part as underground propagandist and as pamphleteer: now he was to be active in politics at the centre where history was apparently being made. If it is difficult to systematize his aims and activities during this period the reason lies in his own confusion. All this time he was striving to become an 'éminence grise' of Pius IX, ready with an abundance of advice, recommendations, and if necessary admonitions. There was nothing inconsistent in his trying simultaneously to put a brake on the more extreme liberal politicians, to prevent them, if he could, from asking for too much to be done too quickly. So far, so good. But one still doubts whether he really had any deep faith in the Giobertian scheme of a Pope as a champion either of liberalism or of nationality: one has cause to suspect—and later it became a certainty—that he was using the Pope as a lever to move the ever-hesitant Charles Albert. He was in continuous association with those in Rome, whether Roman or Piedmontese, who were determined to establish the leadership of Charles Albert in the national cause; but his behaviour showed one aspect that harmonized with neither a Giobertian nor a Piedmontese-centred policy: that was his association with some of the wildest demagogues in Rome, making a public display of friendly co-operation with them. This was so completely out of character as to be puzzling: he was to make amends later by his irreconcilable hostility to them. But for a while he and they were appearing at banquets together. It is hard to avoid the conclusion that celebrity and popularity had gone to his head, that he was enjoying activity for the sake of activity, and that like another horseman he had mounted his steed and was riding wildly off in all directions.

The very day after his arrival in Rome he made a speech at a banquet given in the Circolo dei Nobili, proposing the health of the Pope. In it he reiterated his plea for moderation in making demands of His Holiness, and ended on a note that was to be struck by him over and over again for years to come. 'The completeness of our regeneration can only be achieved by the co-operation of all as individuals. A nation cannot be strong if it is composed of weak individuals. The only way of reforming the nation is through our reforming ourselves personally. . . .'[1]

Four days later he was received in audience by the Pope. The interview was friendly but inconclusive, each being content to form an opinion of the other. Azeglio's enthusiasm for Pius was expressed in a letter to Balbo that was widely circulated in Piedmont in manuscript copies and was brought to the notice of the King, who wrote to Villamarina: 'The Pope has decided to advance along the road of progress and reforms. God bless him! His campaign is against Austria! Long may he live!' By sending forth such reports, by his public speeches, and by his occasional writings at this time, Azeglio was creating the legend of a liberal, national-minded Pope—a Pope in the Azeglian image. That the myth might not correspond to the truth was a possibility that either was simply not noticed or was set aside. Though Pius was already trying to show that he could not be a monarch with limited powers, and could on no account challenge the established order in other Italian states, his reservations were explained away as due to the influence of the old gang still strong in the Curia. But for the time being Azeglio's preoccupation was to gain and keep the Pope's confidence: to do this he wished to restrain the extremists, to prevent their excesses playing into the hands of the reactionaries. In his second audience on 10 March he was able to tell the Pope that he had been successful in discouraging a group associated with Sterbini from publishing a clandestine journal critical of Papal policy. And when the Government issued an Edict on 15 March organizing the control of the Press, Azeglio defended it in his *Letter to Professor Francesco Orioli*.[2] He argued that a responsible Press was the ideal to be sought after, control being necessary until self-control had developed: the control as now established had at least the new virtues of being open and public, entrusted to a Council of Censorship composed of only one ecclesiastic with four laymen. It was a practicable measure and 'I believe it can be affirmed that what harms a state is not so much

---

[1] *S.D.P.*, I, pp. 129–30.   [2] Ibid., I, pp. 133–59.

evil laws as the non-observance of existing ones whether good or evil'. All in all, the new Edict, cancelling all earlier ones on the Press, had set up 'such an ordinance as exists under no other Italian Prince'.

The other important matter in which his influence was for moderation was that of a Civic Guard. He was in favour of its establishment by the Pope and in early July drew up a petition that received many signatures asking for it, and also for some system of representation in the Papal States. But the Guard as he envisaged it was to be a defender of the existing social order, drawn as far as possible from, and to be officered only by, members of the property-owning middle class. In this there is nothing that conflicted with his earlier opposition to the presentation to the Pope of a petition for a Civic Guard that had been drawn up and signed by a number of men who had only recently emerged from confinement as political suspects. A bourgeois Civic Guard as imagined by Azeglio might exercise pressure on the Pope and Curia: but it would also serve as a check to the *sans-culottes* and their inspirers. Yet he was consorting with this very type; on more than one occasion he made public appearances with the two most notorious—Sterbini and Ciceruacchio, of whom the former, as the more intelligent, was the more dangerous. Both had been Carbonari and were now members of Young Italy, and their goal was a republic, to be established by revolution, and ultimately a social revolution to set up a classless society of some sort. The greatest threat to the success of the first stage of their journey to utopia lay, not in the clerical reactionaries, but in the moderates who might lead the Pope by steady but non-violent pressure to set up a transformed but bourgeois system of constitutional government. Pellegrino Rossi, the ablest and most statesmanlike minister that Pius found, was therefore a predestined victim, and Ciceruacchio's son was one of his murderers. Both were to be leaders in the short-lived Roman Republic: on its overthrow Sterbini escaped, but Ciceruacchio was caught and shot. For Sterbini no one seemed able to say a good word. 'I have known few men more evil in mind and soul and more horrid in appearance. There was no infamy of which he was not accused . . . he was neither esteemed nor loved but feared . . . an example of what might be called a political *maffioso*.'[1] The verdict is that of Minghetti, a political opponent, but it was not one that would

[1] Marco Minghetti, *I miei ricordi* (1888), Vol. I, p. 351.

have been seriously challenged. Angelo Brunetti, nicknamed 'Ciceruacchio' from his oratorical enthusiasm, was, by contrast, a good man gone wrong. He was a son of Trastevere—the working-class district on the 'wrong' side of the Tiber, a wine and hay carter who developed a livery-stable business. When Lord Minto was in Rome he, Azeglio, and Minghetti would ride in the Campagna on horses hired from Ciceruacchio, a jovial figure who had proved himself heroic during the cholera epidemic of 1837, and whose popularity with the poor and with the working class of Rome dated from that event.

On 23 February Ciceruacchio gave a banquet in honour of Azeglio, who was his guest at another at 'Tasso's Oak' on the Janiculum on 20 April, and on 16 May at still another at Zagarolo, north of Rome, organized by Ciceruacchio, with Azeglio presiding. There were toasts to Gioberti (*in absentia*, of course), Azeglio, and Ciceruacchio. Not all Azeglio's public appearances were in this questionable company. On 7 April he made a speech,[1] at the dinner in the Palazzo Galitzin to mark the opening of the 'Società Artistica Italiana'. This was a rapid and it must be said a very superficial discussion of the arts as reflection of the social and political systems of their day, and it ended with the customary hymn of praise to Pius IX. His most gratifying performance was at the dinner to celebrate the anniversary of the foundation of the city of Rome, with seven tables to represent the seven hills.

The previous evening I was told to make the opening speech, and I started work on it at seven in the morning, finishing at half-past ten. The celebration was most elegant and orderly. There were many speeches, mine through a change in the order being one of the last. When I went up to the platform I was afraid of a cool reception because of the Edict on the Press, but instead had a very warm one. At the passage in which I referred to the Emperor and Gregory I had many calls of 'Bis!', and at the end a curtain-call, just like Cerrita [a ballet-dancer].

His reference to the Emperor Henry IV and Gregory VII must have struck the audience by its appositeness.

The Emperor Henry was a tyrant who wearied God, till He said to Rome 'I yield thee Henry the Emperor', and from the hills that surround us here, Hildebrand, Pope Gregory VII, raised his austere and potent voice, saying 'God did not give thee Italy that thou mightest

[1] *S.D.P.*, I, pp. 163–70.

tear it in pieces', and Italy, Germany, and Europe saw its butcher prostrate at the feet of Gregory, begging his pardon. The first spark of liberty had been lit in the hearts of Italy, Germany, and Europe. (Naturally, Azeglio did not continue his reference further and describe the lonely death in exile of the disillusioned Pope.) For Pius IX he foretold glory to come.

Not my weak hand but the strong right hand of Pius IX rends the veil that hides the future: he has made himself the prophet not of his subjects alone but of all Christian civilization: it is he who announces our fates in store: I am unworthy to add my voice to the mighty word of the great Pontiff that resounds in the heart of each, and spreads the message of justice, peace, concord, and pardon throughout the whole world.[1]

No matter how anti-aristocratic Azeglio might have been in his bohemian days, the company of Sterbini and Ciceruacchio could not have been congenial to him in private: and he was spending time with men of his own social background and especially with those in Rome of Piedmontese origin. The Sardinian Minister in Rome at this time was the Marchese Pareto, who not only acted as official envoy of the government but was also in secret correspondence with the King and with those of his ministers who were in his confidence. Another Piedmontese was Giovanni Durando, who had been joined in Rome by his lawyer brother Giacomo. Giovanni had served in the Sardinian army until 1831: after the events of that year he had gone into exile and had stayed away from Piedmont until 1843: In August 1847, after the Ferrara incident, he was entrusted by Pius IX with the command of the Papal army and with its immediate reorganization. His acceptance of these duties had been specifically approved by Charles Albert. Pantaleoni, an eminent doctor, Roman by birth but wholly Piedmontese in his sympathies, was another of the group, as was Minghetti, a native of Bologna, a cultured and widely-travelled man, who had not only been to Ireland but had written perceptively about it. After the Papal Allocution had disillusioned so many who had placed such self-deluded hopes in Pius IX, Minghetti went right over to Charles Albert and joined his army with the rank of Captain.

See above p. 76-7

This Piedmontese clique was suspected then, and has been accused since, of underground activity on behalf of Charles

---

[1] *S.D.P.*, I, pp. 173–7.

Albert, and even the murder of Pellegrino Rossi was ascribed by
some to the manœuvres of the Albertists.[1] How busily they were
intriguing at this time, and with what success, it is impossible to say.
But did they in fact need to do anything? Piedmont had already
the most considerable army of the Italian states: she was more
prosperous than the others, with the possible exception of Tuscany:
all she needed to seize the moral leadership of Italy was the influence she would gain by her example in evolving towards a
representative system of government. If she could become a
liberal as well as a prosperous and well-armed state, under a
dynasty more Italian in the sense of being less Austrian than most
other ruling families in the peninsula at that time, her place as
leader in the movement for the liberation of Italy would be
assured. So far Charles Albert was hesitating. But if the Pope
could be manœuvred into making in Rome the kind of reforms
desired in Piedmont, Charles Albert would have to follow suit.
It did not need Piedmontese agents in Rome to urge the Pope
along: his own subjects would do that unprompted. Azeglio and
his friends might even have to use the bridle rather than the spur.
When the point was reached at which the Pope would say 'Thus
far and no farther', and such a point was bound to exist though
how far ahead it might be no one could tell, his reputation as a
liberal would decline and his popularity might vanish overnight.
For the time being all that the Sardinian clique in Rome needed
to do, assuming that their motives were purely selfish and concerned only with repercussions on Piedmont, was to keep the
cauldron gently simmering. Important as events in Rome seemed
to be to Azeglio, and flattering to him as his popularity was, he
could not afford to lose touch with what was happening at home,
and so he returned to Turin in September.

Before making this journey he had published two more political
essays. The first and shorter one was on *The Nobility of Italy and
Italian Opinion*,[2] and had come out in Turin in the *Antologia
Italiana* in May 1847, having been written as a prearranged
pendant to an earlier article by Farini. Azeglio's contribution was
at first rejected by the Piedmontese censorship, but a direct
appeal to Charles Albert had led to the ban being withdrawn, a
measure that was hailed as though it was a considerable victory
for the liberal cause. In itself the article is of no great interest.

[1] Bolton King, *A History of Italian Unity* (1934), 2 vols., Vol. II, Appendix D, p. 389.
[2] *S.D.P.*, I, pp. 193–212.

It is not likely that within a score of pages much light could be thrown on the relationships between the nobility, middle classes, and peasantry of all the different Italian states. In any case the purpose of the essay was not scientific sociological analysis but political propaganda. Convinced that co-operation between men of all classes throughout Italy was essential for national regeneration, he wished to prove that there was no gulf between the nobility and the other classes: but he could only assert, not prove, a common political interest and he ignored the possibility of social and economic tensions. He surveyed the states one by one and judged that in most of them relations between nobles and others were harmonious, especially in Florence, where the aristocracy engaged in commerce. Only in Piedmont was there a problem created by the rigidity of outlook of the nobility, due, he believed, to the historic fact that as a border state her very existence had depended on her military strength. In consequence the feudal system had been more deeply rooted and longer-lived there than elsewhere. Despite this, Piedmont had had a more peaceful internal history than any other Italian state. Azeglio was not preaching egalitarianism: a class system was not merely an historic inheritance but an inescapable condition of society. But 'inequality of classes will more easily be borne when those differences come to be controlled by known and equitable statutes, when it will be less possible for one class to usurp the rights of another, and when there will be the minimum of casual and arbitrary favours and distinctions'.[1]

Azeglio had barely finished the essay before he was busy on a much more important one provisionally entitled *Proposal of a Programme for Italian Moderate Progressive Opinion*, later more briefly but less revealingly replacing 'Moderate Progressive' by 'National'. This was intended not merely to formulate a policy for internal application but, equally important to its author, to be capable of influencing opinion abroad in favour of Italian liberalism. 'It will serve to consolidate ideas in Italy and outside, to show that we are not always in the realms of abstractions and poetry or of the secret societies.' Its publication in Florence on 19 August 1847 over Le Monnier's imprint was followed by the appearance of English[2] and German[3] translations. To achieve the maximum effect in Italy Azeglio had for a time hoped that

[1] *S.D.P.*, I, pp. 199ff.   [2] *The Present Movement in Italy* (London, Newby, 1847).
[3] *Vorschlag zu e. Programm der National Partei in Italien* (Leipzig, Spamer, 1848).

Minghetti, Balbo, and others would add their names to his on the title-page and manuscript copies were sent to them and to others in Pisa and Florence for comment. But in the end the pamphlet came out over Azeglio's name only, though it incorporated suggestions from the others.

The most important person to have seen the draft was Pius IX. Azeglio was determined to publish it outside the Papal States so as not to embarrass the Pope by laying him open to criticism either for permitting or for preventing its appearance. Even if it were to be published outside the Pope's jurisdiction, the continued presence of its author in Rome might seem to commit the Pope to tacit approval: hence Azeglio's submission of the manuscript to him, with an offer to leave Rome if the Pope should judge it expedient for his own sake. The Pope read and approved the essay, and told Azeglio that he saw no reason why he should not remain in Rome after its publication, a decision that Azeglio joyfully announced not only to his Italian friends but also to his new French correspondent, Doubet, who, with his nephew Rendu, was to be the recipient of many of Azeglio's confidences and also of some calculated indiscretions.[1]

To a large extent the 'Proposal' repeated opinions that Azeglio had already expressed, but there was a change in tone in his attitude to the secret societies. He still thought that their intentions were misguided and their use of force not only wrong but futile, but he wished to create harmony inside Italy and to avoid giving foreigners the spectacle of one Italian patriot condemning others who, by their heroic and self-sacrificing actions, had gained admiration even amongst many who were not especially sympathetic to their cause. So Azeglio now went so far in their defence as to argue that the violence of the sectaries was a natural, even an inevitable, human reaction to the oppressiveness of governments.

As the basis of his political creed Azeglio postulated that 'in politics the only real and pursuable objective is the possible and the practicable'. As has been argued, this was at best a doubtful proposition and one that could and, with Azeglio, did later tend to become an argument for doing nothing at all in circumstances involving even a minimal risk.

The first practicable goal was the establishment of confidence between rulers and their subjects, by the granting of reforms and

---

[1] E. Rendu (ed.), *L'Italie de 1847 à 1865: Correspondance politique de M. d'A.* (1867), letter of 6 July 1847, p. 7.

the overhauling of existing statutes and systems of justice. Taxes were too often arbitrary, excessive, and injurious to trade; insistence on outward conformity in religion as a proof of political reliability had led to hypocrisy; education had been neglected and the poor drained of initiative and industriousness by the pernicious state lotteries. Reform of these abuses would lead not only to the amelioration of social conditions but also to the development of national cohesion. Army reforms in the different states could create uniformity and make possible joint military action should need arise: educational reforms could be similarly co-ordinated so that a student might, for example, move easily from one university to another: the fiscal system could be so revised as to tend towards internal free trade in the peninsula: roads might be improved and a railway network planned for Italy as a whole as a further stimulus to prosperity and unity.

Nothing could be more reasonable or seem more practicable than these proposals. But that was because Azeglio stopped there. He did not consider ways and means to achieve any measure of political unification. Only once did he discuss the chance of one Italian state achieving hegemony, and that was in a reference to an opportunity missed in the past, with the failure of the other north Italian states to come to Piedmont's assistance when she was fighting for three years against the Revolutionary armies of France. Had they supported her then a measure of unification *de facto* might have been gained, sufficient to prevent the great powers planning such a settlement as was reached at Vienna. The liberation of Italy from the Austrians was similarly passed over, presumably as being one of those ideals only to be attained in circumstances utterly unforeseeable.

Having expatiated on the attitudes of Italian rulers towards each other and towards their subjects, Azeglio discussed the attitude of subjects to rulers. And here he had singularly little to offer beyond the hope that subjects might come to have trust in their princes. Such confidence might not only follow princely reforms but might stimulate further ones. 'We believe that to hasten this process the peoples must be attracted and loyally bound of their own free will to the princes, must be averse from any act that might have the appearance of trying to limit them in their powers, and must seek to lead them by moderate and open ways to such ameliorations as the needs of the age demand.'[1]

[1] *S.D.P.*, I, pp. 229–30.

H

In the very month of July 1847, whilst the 'Proposal' referring to the hope of 'our complete and absolute independence in an undetermined future' was still in manuscript, events happened that made it for a while seem possible that the crisis was actually imminent: Austria took action of such a nature that had it not been for Pius's statesmanship and Charles Albert's afterthoughts war in Italy might easily have broken out.

On 5 July Pius granted a Civic Guard, one of the three requests made in the petition organized by Azeglio and others at the Circolo Romano: their other pleas were for a new Press Law and for a system of representation. As a protest against the Pope's concession and as a warning to him against his continuing in this dangerous course, Austrian troops at Radetzky's orders moved into the fortress of Ferrara in the extreme north of the Papal States. This they had a right to do by treaty: but they also began to patrol the town of Ferrara as well, and this was not sanctioned by any treaty. The Cardinal Legate Ciacchi at once entered a formal protest against this unwarrantable extension of Austria's rights, and the Cardinal Secretary of State followed this with a note of protest to all the powers signatory to the Treaty of Vienna. Azeglio made his protest also in yet another pamphlet, *A Protest on the Events in Ferrara*. Austrian action, he argued, was a menace to every ruler in Italy: in the past she had extended her power by usurpation and invasion; now 'the shows of force, the operations of Austrian troops and diplomacy in Italy, seen and understood fully by all, are directed not at occupying a stretch of territory but at usurping the rights of sovereignty in all the independent states. . . . Let us express this in clear and precise terms: no Italian state will ever be able to try to improve its conditions for fear of disturbing the slumber of the Viennese ruling class and its police.' The Italians had shown dignity and restraint in the crisis, people and rulers alike, but the only answer to such action must be the drawing together of the princes in defence of their independence.[1]

Like the 'Proposal' this pamphlet had been shown to the Pope and had had his approval: according to the title-page it was published in Bastia—a sheer fiction: Azeglio later referred to it as having been published in Rome. Its importance was not considerable and it had interest only as showing Azeglio's views, and possibly as reflecting those of the Pope: Italian opinion about the

[1] *S.D.P.*, I, pp. 273–88.

crisis had crystallized and it did not need pamphlets to achieve this effect. Azeglio in fact was moving away from literature to action now.

The Papal Government had decided to concentrate its forces near Ferrara and some 100,000 men were gathering into an encampment at Forlì. On 20 August Azeglio wrote to his wife:

The Government has decided to mass its troops around Ferrara and prepare for defence. Not to do so would be shameful. The Pope is resolved to resist with all his means. You will realize that if a single battalion were to be enrolled and I not in it I should be dishonoured. In consequence I have volunteered and have been accepted: I leave tomorrow for Headquarters at Forlì . . . . I am convinced that we shall gain glory at bargain prices, for the Germans will sit watching us from Ferrara, and we shall stay at Forlì, watching them.[1]

What Azeglio saw of the army did not inspire him with much confidence in the military arrangements. To Pantaleoni he reported on 18 September that the Papal army was so widely scattered as to be ineffective in case of an Austrian attack. No reserves of supplies were being built up and volunteers from other Italian states were dispiritedly drifting home again. Azeglio himself was at Pesaro for the month of September. Originally he had planned to make a tour of the towns in the northern parts of the Papal States to urge, and advise on, the formation of Civic Guards, but the Pope had asked him not to do so lest the appearance of Azeglio, author of such provocative pamphlets, should lead to demonstrations that might give the Austrians the pretext for further extensions of their occupation. So instead Azeglio sent Tommasoni round them with a circular letter urging active preparations for self-defence.

Papal army, volunteers, Civic Guards all told did not add up to a total likely to cause serious alarm to Radetzky and his whitecoats. To create an effective force the co-operation of the princes to whom Azeglio had addressed his 'Proposal' was essential, and, as he admitted privately, when he spoke of 'princes' he really meant the King of Sardinia. This was not just the natural partisanship of a Piedmontese but cool commonsense, since only in Piedmont was there any army worthy of serious consideration. He decided therefore to go again to Turin to see what the situation was, to find whether Charles Albert was totally motionless or drifting with some current, and in this case in what direction.

[1] Carcano, op. cit., p. 287.

He paused on the way in Florence and then in Lucca, hoping to exert some influence there. In Florence he saw some leading citizens, whom he urged to demand a civic guard by petitions to the Grand Duke, and to demand also that it be effectively armed. At the same time he counselled against any actions or speeches that might alienate the ruler or provoke Austrian interference. Despite this moderation his meddling in Tuscan affairs was presumptuous; a less tolerant government might well have ordered him out merely because of his association with demagogues in Rome. What the important Grand Duke of Tuscany did not do, the relatively insignificant Duke of Lucca attempted.

Though Azeglio assured Minghetti that his purpose in going to Lucca had been solely to advise restraint, since the Duke's reactionary policy had so angered many of his subjects that a rising against him was possible, the Duke suspected him of being anything but a peacemaker and asked him to leave. Azeglio reported this in a typical letter to Persano.

After three days the Duke sent me word that I must go. I coolly asked why and was told 'Because the Lucchese government is on friendly terms with Tuscany, point number one, and because my political opinions are not the Duke's, point number two.' As you see, there was no answer to this, so instead of replying I have written to Carrega [Piedmontese Minister] in Florence. Now we shall see whether a subject of a friendly prince, with his passport in order, doing no harm to anyone, should be chased out as though he had been caught burgling, on the grounds that his views are not those of the Duke and because the Duke is in harmony with the Grand Duke. I shall defend myself and give my reasons, as I do not like to be bullied without showing some signs of life: but it matters very little having to leave this or that state —I am destined to be a gipsy.[1]

The letter's postscript was a slight anti-climax: the Duke had allowed him ten more days.

From Lucca he went to Turin and found he liked it no better than formerly. 'Imagine—after having seen Rome and Tuscany, finding myself in this cemetery!' The atmosphere seemed funereal because of the contrast between Rome in its ferment of political excitement and Turin bewildered by the unpredictability of Charles Albert, who had been giving demonstrations of his

---

[1] As printed by Persano, op. cit., p. 13, this letter is dated February 1847. On the original Persano had pencilled the date 15 August: but it must have been written on or very near to 15 October.

special paradoxical habit of 'sauter pour mieux reculer'. On 2 September he had made a declaration to a conference in Casale of his willingness to undertake the lead in a war of liberation. 'What a magnificent day it will be when we can raise the cry of national independence!' A week later he had had a tumultuous welcome in Genoa but, alarmed by this demonstration and afraid of being swept along by the enthusiasm of others, he had drawn back, even to the extent of explaining that by 'national' he had meant 'Piedmontese' independence.

Azeglio found himself in Turin to be merely an observer whom the King avoided receiving. He besought his friends in Piedmont, Rome, and France to petition the King for action, and made similar use of Lord Minto, who was on a roving commission on behalf of Palmerston as an observer but, not content to observe, was playing busy-body all over Italy encouraging liberals, who were apt to take his mission as more official than it was ever meant to be. It seemed that nothing was likely to happen in Turin so Azeglio set off back to Rome, 'the workshop and origin of whatever is being done in Italy'.

He had perhaps left too soon. In Florence he heard that Charles Albert had taken another leap forward. On 30 October he had announced a series of administrative reforms; control of the press, legal system, police, local government were all to be overhauled: civil rights were to be given to Waldensians and a Department of Education to be set up—two changes especially welcome to Roberto d'Azeglio. The announcements of these measures in the Official Gazette led to such intense excitement in the capital that the middle class, fearing lest the situation should get out of hand, had improvised a company of volunteers with Roberto as president and was protecting the places most likely to be menaced, the Jesuit headquarters, the Austrian embassy, and the home of the governor of the city. Through a scene of delirium the royal family left for a visit to Genoa: but when similar demonstrations welcomed the King back he made his carriage drive quickly through the streets, paid little heed to the cheering, and made only a perfunctory appearance on the palace balcony. His most positive reaction to his realization of the sentiments of his people was to dismiss the most conservative of his ministers—Solaro della Margarita: but to counterbalance so decisive an action he simultaneously dismissed his most liberal one, Villamarina.

The popularity of the Azeglio family had been very clearly shown during this time. Not only was Roberto the unofficial leader of the middle-class citizens, but the demonstrators drawn from the working classes had saluted him, when, after having gathered to cheer under the windows of the palace, 'they lit candle-ends on the ends of their walking-sticks and the enormous crowd of demonstrators went off behind a torchlight procession of apprentice printers down Via Po. . . . After a turn round Piazza Vittorio they came up Via d'Angennes and stopped in front of our house. . . . "Long live the house of Zei" [Azeglio], they shouted, waving their hats. . . .'[1] According to another account they called 'Viva Casa Zei, Viva Azeglio, Viva Massimo, Viva Roberto', and 'Long live the friend of the poor!'

News of these events, catching up with Azeglio in Florence and creating excitement there and arousing the hopes of the partisans of Piedmont, did not dissuade him from his intention of returning to Rome, though he stayed long enough to make contact with the Piedmontese clique and to speak at a banquet or two. Rome was still in his view the focus of attention and by mid-November he was there and had an audience with the Pope soon after his arrival. On 1 December he was one of the guests at a banquet given by Minto. Amongst the company were his friends Minghetti and Pasolini: a more surprising member of the party was Cardinal Antonelli, who was to become Pius's Cardinal Secretary of State, the wily and unscrupulous opponent of all liberalism in theology or politics. One hopes that Minto's spoons had long handles.

A dinner with Antonelli was not the strangest of Azeglio's activities in this November and December. He who had so often and so forthrightly condemned the machinations of secret societies and had preached the doctrine of the open conspiracy was now enmeshed in a scheme to arrange a popular revolt in Sicily: the very date had been fixed—it was to occur on the twelfth of January 'with the punctuality of a bill of exchange', as in the event it did.[2] Amongst the planners were Crispi, who hoped to see a simultaneous rising in Naples, La Masa, who had been in Florence in the hope of concerting action between Sicily and Tuscany, Pantaleoni and Minghetti, both subjects of the Pope,

---

[1] Letter of Costanza to Emanuele d'Azeglio, M. Schettini (ed.), *Giornale degli anni memorabili di Costanza d'Azeglio* (1960), pp. 172ff.

[2] For the unravelling of the preparation for this rising, and Azeglio's part in it, see G. F.-H. and J. Berkeley, *Italy in the Making, June 1846–1 January 1848* (1936).

and Giovanni Durando, who had come from Piedmont to Rome in September to take command of the Papal army, with Charles Albert's approval, and whose self-appointed mission it was to use that army, if occasion should arise, on behalf of his King: and, finally, Azeglio. One can say 'finally', for he was drawn into the plot rather late and apparently rather reluctantly. To assist, even to countenance, such a conspiracy was contrary to his avowed principles; and it was also a gamble. No one could foresee whether it could succeed, or what direction it would take. Any rising in Sicily was almost certain to be separatist in its tendency—at least at the start when it was seeking popular support: all the risings in the island's past had been essentially revolts against the mainland: and in 1848 as on earlier occasions this was the case. On 12 January, as arranged, the rising began, though in the end the exactness of the timing was accidental, and the rebels demanded the traditional Spanish constitution of 1812 and home rule for the island. After their initial success in liberating all the island except Messina, but after failing to gain any satisfactory concessions from Naples, on 13 April the Sicilian Parliament declared the Bourbons deposed from sovereignty over the island. They had good reason to suppose that their independence would be recognized by England and France: but a condition of this recognition was the establishment of an effective government under a king of their own choice. The only two ruling families whose scions could be acceptable to the Sicilians were those of Sardinia and of Tuscany. The role that the house of Savoy was playing in north Italy, and the high reputation as a soldier of Charles Albert's second son, the Duke of Genoa, were decisive and on 10 July the two houses of the Sicilian Parliament unanimously offered him the throne. The Albertist clique in Rome, Azeglio, Durando, Pantaleoni, and Minghetti, could not have foreseen how neatly their patronage of the planned rising in Sicily was to create the opportunity for the advancement of the house of Savoy. Sicily had been one of their appanages once before, from 1713 until 1720, when they had exchanged it for Sardinia: now in 1848 it seemed that they might enter into possession again in response to a Sicilian invitation and under the patronage of France and Britain. But the chance slipped by.

Charles Albert had declared war on Austria on 22 March, and from that moment events in Lombardy had monopolized the attention of all Piedmontese, of Azeglio and Durando as well as of the royal family. Milan and Venice were in a state of insurrection, Radetzky and his army on the defensive. If Lombards and Venetians could come to terms with Sardinian monarchism, and if Charles Albert could achieve swift victory in the field, the house of Savoy might extend its dominions to the Adriatic, but failure would endanger the very existence of the dynasty. At such a crisis Sicily was an irrelevance: and the defeat of Charles Albert at Custozza on 25 July ended any likelihood of his family establishing itself in Sicily. The Neapolitans began the reconquest of the island and their victory had become assured before the Duke of Genoa sent a message formally declining the offered throne.

The campaign in Lombardy had overshadowed and Custozza put an end to another project that had at one time seemed capable of leading Italy nearer to a close federation of her rulers. In moving cautiously towards an increased co-operation between Italian princes, Pius had been influenced by altruistic patriotism, but he could not have been unaware that such a scheme would redound to the increase of the political influence of the Papacy. He was too cautious to propose the establishment of a confederation as his immediate goal, and he planned to move by limited stages, each step being a positive gain for Italy. The first stage might be a customs union. Cobden and his free trade had aroused the interest of Italian politicians and economists: even Azeglio, who all his life really cared little and knew less about economics, had met Cobden and had learnt something—if only a catchphrase or two—about his theories. Sir Robert Peel's budgets, on which Azeglio was better informed than upon theories, had drawn further attention to the doctrine. Powerfully reinforcing the theory was the practical example of the Prussian Zollverein as a working model that might be imitated in Italy. Pius was willing to open discussions that might lead to such an organization: and at the same time he wished to explore the possibilities of establishing a league of Italian rulers. A commercial and fiscal common system, backed by a political alliance, would prepare the way for a closer co-operation, perhaps eventually a federation of Italian states. Tuscany and Piedmont-Sardinia were the ones most likely to be attracted into such a scheme: and so in October 1847 Pius had sent his confidential adviser, Monsignor Corboli-Bussi, on a mission to Florence and Turin.

In Florence he had an encouraging reception. The Grand Duke was perfectly willing to consider entering into a customs union and a league of princes. His benevolent authoritarian brand of liberalism made him favour such a progressive scheme, and like others in Tuscany and Rome he believed that such a step would be a salutary and effective rejoinder to Mazzini and the Young Italy movement. But disillusionment awaited Corboli-Bussi in Turin. Although he was warmly welcomed and although Lord Minto joined him to second his arguments, he found himself unable to make any progress. Only in November, a month after his arrival, was even a basis for discussion agreed upon and after that the negotiations dragged on until March 1848. This was one of the occasions when Charles Albert, according to most critics, displayed his characteristic indecision.[1] But it may be argued that he knew precisely what he was doing.[2] He was being offered a place in a customs union that might become a federation in which Sardinia would have a status no higher than Tuscany's, under Papal presidency. But a war with Austria had all along been a part of Charles Albert's secret plans. Should he emerge successful from this war he would be able to negotiate a settlement of the Italian question from a position of strength. It was not politic to refuse point-blank to negotiate: liberals desired a federation and merchants a customs union, so he temporized. On 24 March 1848, with the outbreak of war, he broke off the discussions and whilst asking Tuscany, Rome, and Naples to send armies to second his own he insisted that all consideration of the future political organization of Italy must be postponed until the end of hostilities. The other rulers had ample cause to suspect his motives—the King of Naples in particular, owing to the offer of a Sicilian throne to the Duke of Genoa.

Even before the battles of Custozza and Novara Charles Albert had effectively killed the scheme for a customs union or a Giobertian federation: to sacrifice the chance of such a union in favour of a possible later one on terms more favourable to Piedmont was a gamble: but during the war Durando and Azeglio, at the head of the Papal army, were working away towards the same end.

[1] E.g. King, op. cit., Vol. I, p. 188.
[2] See on this point C. Spellanzon in *Convegno di scienze morali ecc.*, Rome, 1949, pp. 214ff.

VII

AZEGLIO AND THE EVENTS OF 1848

AZEGLIO, like Piedmont, passed through three stages in 1848; from political intrigue both graduated to military action and showed conspicuous heroism in it, and both ended the year in a state of uneasy convalescence. Azeglio's first contribution to the events of 1848 was the publication in early January by Le Monnier of Florence of a pamphlet written at the very end of 1847 on a question that was apparently a side-issue at a moment when the future of the Italian people was likely to be changed by the outcome of a crisis that was becoming clearly imminent: yet this apparent side-issue was a matter of controversy that was to cause sordid and noble pages to be written into human history for long years to come. His concern was with the status of the Jews in Italy—a matter on which he and his brother Roberto felt deeply. Roberto, whose religious feelings, moral sense, and awareness of social wrongs and duties went much deeper than Massimo's, may have inspired his brother's writing: but this was not a transient interest: Massimo had been shocked by the humiliations that had been traditionally inflicted on Jews in Rome, and he was later to put himself into the charge of Jews when he escaped from the Austrians after the battle of Monte Berico with a serious wound in his leg. Obviously in no degree anti-Semitic, he was at the same time not being consciously pro-Semitic, or choosing Jewish doctors as a moral gesture, and thus behaving unnaturally even if honourably: he was simply choosing good doctors and was paying no heed to race or religion.

His pamphlet *On the Civil Emancipation of the Jews*,[1] like others of his writings, gave every sign of having been written with enthusiasm and in haste, and as a result was weakened by being too long. His case rested on two main arguments, complementary to each other. First, to oppress the Jews in any way or to any degree, however slight, was a denial of Christian principles. Secondly, to refuse them full civil rights was illogical in a nation that was itself striving for its own rights against a foreign oppressor.

[1] *S.D.P.*, I, pp. 343–402.

So on grounds of morality and of expediency their treatment as an inferior race was unjustifiable.

From this abstract argument he passed to a survey of the treatment of the Jews in modern times in the parts of Italy outside Piedmont. Their entry into the Kingdom of the Two Sicilies had, he asserted, been effectively prevented, and in the absence of Jews from that kingdom there was no 'Jewish problem' there; though it may be suggested perhaps that their absence was peculiar enough to constitute a grievance. In those parts of the peninsula under Austrian rule, or under the most effective Austrian influence, the status of the Jews had been more advantageous than anywhere else, a circumstance that harmonized with his earlier insistence that in many respects Austrian rule in Italy had often shown itself more civilized than that of the native princes. In Lombardy-Venetia, Parma, and Modena Jews had been eligible for state and municipal office and the legal and medical professions had been open to them. In Rome they had suffered from a long and evil tradition of ill-treatment. They had been confined to a ghetto and had been subject to ceremonial humiliations, though these had at last been commuted to exceptional payments to the Papal treasury. The accession of Pius IX had brought new hopes to his Jewish as to his Christian subjects. They had received permission to build and to occupy houses outside the ghetto, and they had even been accepted as eligible for membership of the Civic Guard. The statement of these facts gave Azeglio the opportunity to write yet another panegyric of the Pope. He concluded:

I, for my part, in expiation of the past and as a pledge for the future, can offer the Jews no more than these poor pages and my goodwill; may they accept this slight gift in the spirit in which it is offered; and if to this gesture that I believe to be the performance of an act of justice they wish to attach a greater value, and one worthy of reward, let it be that they forget the past and hold me and all of my faith, as we will hold them, in brotherhood: such will be the most acceptable and appreciable reward that I could imagine or desire.

The sympathies shown to the Jews by Roberto and Massimo were genuine and purely altruistic. But prejudice died hard and in Turin society there were plenty of those who considered this was a needless raising of a distasteful question. The Jews of Piedmont-Sardinia received their civil emancipation on 29 March 1848: but Costanza noted that their energetic political support of Roberto in the election of that year provoked unfavourable comment. It was also considered tactless of them in 1863 to plan a new synagogue (eventually completed by the municipality as a memorial to Victor Emmanuel II and now known as the Mole Antonelliana) on such a scale and, in particular, rising to such a height that its pinnacle dominates the skyline of modern Turin.

The only part of the pamphlet about which one might have legitimate reservations is the panegyric of Pius IX. What Azeglio said was factually correct but its emotive colouring made it part of the process of creating a myth of Pius the liberal whose zeal for reform was not exhausted and might be inexhaustible. The Pope himself knew, and any serious thinker should have known, that though social and administrative reforms were overdue and were being granted, the Pope would not abdicate any of his ecclesiastical authority and, being spiritually absolute, would be reluctant to share political power with his subjects. The later disappointment with and animosity against Pius arose from the discovery that he had all along been himself and not the legend that Azeglio and others had created.

The publication of the pamphlet at the beginning of January 1848 (apparently on the 10th) was overshadowed by events that involved not just a religious minority but the whole Italian people, the Tobacco Riots in Milan. Provocation there had led to minor disturbances and these to major ones and to massive retaliation by Radetzky's troops, despite the Viceroy's attempts to impose a conciliatory attitude. The news sent a wave of indignation surging over Italy and determined Azeglio to indict Austria not only before the jury of his fellow-Italians, whose verdict could never be in doubt, but also before the opinion of Europe and, in particular, that of Britain and of France. In late January and early February he was writing *I lutti di Lombardia*. As fast as he wrote it he sent instalments to Le Monnier so that publication might not be delayed. Much of the information that he was using came to him from his wife Luisa in Milan, who passed it on to him via the Marchesa Doria of Genoa. The Austrian Government suspected Luisa of some such activity, though the very fact of her being the wife of Azeglio was enough to cause her to be coldly regarded, and in February she was asked to leave Austrian territories. It was not until 10 March that *I lutti di Lombardia* came from the press. Azeglio had awaited his wife's safe arrival on Tuscan soil: and he had also had to await the abolition of censorship in Tuscany, for not even its relatively easy Government would have tolerated the publication of this diatribe. Luckily for Azeglio a seizure of power by the Left in Tuscany came in time for the pamphlet to be published freely before it had lost its topicality. An English translation by Fortunato Brandi, sensationally entitled *Austrian Assassinations in Lombardy*, was published by Newby in London without much delay.

I lutti di Lombardia,[1] 'The Griefs of Lombardy', was a fierce indictment of Austrian behaviour during and after the Tobacco Riots. It was not an attack on Austria's rule as Azeglio had observed it during normal times. It would have been hypocrisy for him to have assailed its general record, which he himself had already in print compared favourably with that of other rulers in Italy. On one important matter, nevertheless, he might have criticized Austrian rule as he had known it in a seriously damaging way without recanting his former expressed views: he could have accused Austria of financial exploitation of her Italian provinces. It is true that at one point[2] he spoke of Austria 'absorbing the gold created by sweat on Italian soil to the enrichment of the Imperial Treasury'. More might have been made of this, for it has been estimated[3] that on an average 60 million *lire* were transferred annually from these provinces to Vienna. But economic questions were never of great interest to Azeglio, and the precise figures were probably unprocurable in any case.

His pamphlet opened dramatically.

A great iniquity has been committed in Milan. The greatest iniquity that the mind of man can conceive, that of taking the lives of unarmed men . . . a vileness: of men taken unawares . . . a betrayal: of men neither called to, nor condemned by trial . . . a lawlessness, the lawlessness of anonymous hired assassins: the lives of men who could not have laid hands on their killers, who could not have wished to provoke them, who on the contrary were themselves studiously provoked until a hiss, a word, a shout was made the pretext of their slaughter. So we reach a climax—a vileness, a betrayal, a lawlessness, a conspiracy.

Azeglio went on to develop the contrast between Italy, the home of one nation seeking its independence, and the Austrian Empire, a congeries of people living together under constraint, and he rose to a climax of indignation in describing the woes of the Italians.

---

[1] *S.D.P.*, I, pp. 421–97.   [2] Ibid., p. 435, 'l'oro sudato sulla gleba italiana'.
[3] A. Solmi, *The Making of Modern Italy* (1925), p. 9.

Who were those whom you slaughtered? Who were these poor victims?
Were they fearsome and dangerous enemies? Were they such that you
had to choose whether you should perish or kill them? Did Vienna
tremble as long as they lived? These seventy-year-old men, these
women, these ten-year-old children—did they hold in their hands the
fate of the Empire, the destiny of Austria? Your proclamations have
told us who they were. You have uttered the famous, the sacramental,
the repeated phrase—'A seditious sect, the friends of disorder, enemies
of good government and the law . . . etc. etc.' After the events in Milan
twice you have thus defined them in your proclamations: but if you
twice say 'Sects', thrice will we repeat 'We are a Nation, a Nation, a
Nation!' A nation that, having tried short-sighted methods, fallacious
ways to regain our rights, has known for two years now what is the
right way, a way worthy, wise, and honourable to gain our great aim
—a nation that has arisen as one, open and single-minded: that moves
slowly but surely towards new destinies: a nation that has been the first
to beat down force without force, violence without violence, deceit
without deceit: without arms, to break your arms: to make mortal war
the most fearful war that can assail you, without shedding blood.

As for the Austrian Government, 'I know and believe that
Austria Upper and Lower, Bohemia, Galicia, Moravia, Silesia,
Styria, Carinthia, Tyrol, Lombardy, and Venetia, peoples so
discordant in race, language, customs, desires and hopes, agree
on one thing only—in hating you.' More penetratingly he concluded that the Austrian Empire was nothing but a bureaucracy.
'That monster of a thousand heads, a thousand arms, a huge
belly and no bowels—no bowels of mercy—that is termed a
Bureaucracy.'

From generalization Azeglio passed to a survey of facts, tracing
events in Lombardy from the first signs of trouble in September
1847, when the Austrians used disproportionate force to disperse
demonstrations greeting the entry of the new Archbishop,
Romilli, and cheering the Pope. He used eye-witness accounts of
events during and after the Tobacco Riots, and subsequent
incidents in Pavia. In conclusion he appealed to Great Britain
and France to see things as they really were in Italy under
Austrian rule.

I lutti di Lombardia was in effect the last of Azeglio's writings,
starting with his two novels, devoted to awakening and con-
solidating Italian national consciousness. Though *I casi di Romagna*
is still on the whole the most impressive, they amount to an
inspiring contribution to the advocacy of the national cause. Some

of the hopes of *I lutti di Lombardia* were to be dispelled during the years 1848 and 1849: the conviction of the solidarity of the Italian people was to prove illusory, and the divisions between their native rulers to be apparently unbridgeable. But the story of 1848-9, despite its ending in failure, was to be the worthy prelude to the later epic of Italian endeavour. Despite military and political ineptitude, to the latter of which Azeglio was to contribute his share, it was a story of heroism from the Tobacco Riots to the death of Anita Garibaldi and execution of Ugo Bassi, a story sullied on the Italian side by singularly few such crimes as the murder of Pellegrino Rossi.

Rapidly as Azeglio might write and Le Monnier print, events were galloping even more swiftly: not in the direction of national independence as yet, but towards constitutionalism. As for this ideal of limited monarchy, Azeglio had already formulated his views. To Luisa he defined them: 'I have always worked and written that Italy might become independent with as few constitutional monarchs as possible. One such, however, I have always desired'[1]—meaning the Pope. Observation of popular demonstration in Rome led him to state: 'As for the fear of a '93, the Civic Guard, Piedmont, and, as a last resort, Austria are there to prevent us from "dérailler".' So, the continuance of Austrian rule in Italy was preferable to republican revolution, though the prevention of this by the middle class or by Piedmont would be better still. Whether the constitutionalist movement was to remain bourgeois or to become radical, it was sweeping through Italy. Faced with the rising in Sicily, and hoping almost as much to embarrass his fellow-princes as to extricate himself, the King of Naples on 29 January granted the basis of a constitution for his dominions.

In Turin Roberto had presided over a meeting of newspaper editors from the capital and Genoa who had met to draft a petition for a Civic Guard but had ended under Camillo di Cavour's influence by deciding to ask for a constitution for the state. They forwarded their request to the city councils of Turin and Genoa and after a lengthy session, with excitement mounting in the streets as the people learnt what was under consideration, the Turin council endorsed it, as did that of Genoa soon afterwards. After hesitating and threatening to abdicate, the King on 8 February promised a constitution, which was issued on 5 March,

[1] Carcano, op. cit., p. 311.

though to make it look more respectable it was called a 'statute'. Charles Albert had had a long struggle with his conscience, fearing that he was breaking a promise given to Metternich.[1] But once he had taken his decision he was, according to Costanza d'Azeglio, unusually cheerful.[2]

Whilst Charles Albert was being inveigled in this way along the road towards a limited monarchy the Pope had made his own position clear. On 10 February he had issued a Motu Proprio[3] that was unambiguous, save to those who chose deliberately to misread it, in its restatement of the case for the maintenance of his temporal power and reminder that his subjects were not just those in Italy but all Roman Catholics throughout the world. 'A bare three million of our subjects have two hundred million brothers of every nation and every tongue. In times very different from these, when the whole Roman world was disordered, this fact remained the salvation of Rome. Owing to it the ruin of Italy was never complete. And this will always be her protection as long as the Apostolic See stands in her midst.' Zealots for Italian unification ought to have read the reference to the 200 million spiritual subjects in brotherhood with the three million temporal ones as a clear warning, as the Pope meant it to be. But His Holiness ended his proclamation with the prayer: 'Therefore, Lord God, bless Italy and preserve for her this most precious gift of all—the faith!' By a process of falsification in omitting all that was unpalatable in the Motu Proprio, and seizing on the words 'God bless Italy', then interpreting 'Italy' as though it were a political, and not, as Metternich had described it, a purely geographical term, the liberals read the Pope's utterance as an encouragement of their cause. In the case of some this interpretation was due to naïveté, but Azeglio and his like were willing to make use of this misinterpretation. In a letter to Rendu in April Azeglio quite explicitly described the process of myth-making. 'If the Pope wishes, if he consents to be what opinion is making him, the Papacy is definitely the guiding force of the world. If he refuses I do not know what will happen: Providence does not offer a chance like this a second time.'[4] 'If he consents to be what opinion is making him'—and it was Azeglio and his like who were making this opinion. It was a curious conception of the Papacy

---

[1] Prince Metternich, *Memoirs* (1880), Vol. IV, pp. 264–6.
[2] Schettini, op. cit., p. 210.   [3] Hales, op. cit., p. 70.
[4] Rendu, op. cit., p. 33.

to imagine it to be bound to follow in the wake of 'opinion'. It was also a total failure to understand the character of Pius IX to think he could be led by the nose in this way. To Minghetti Azeglio wrote about this time: 'Let him [Pius] make himself the head of the principle of concord in the name of God, come forth openly, speak, lift up his voice, be the *deus ex machina* who resolves this drama. . . .' This is less cynical, but also seems less self-assured, though still refusing, or perhaps failing, to realize that the Pope had in fact come forth as openly as he could be expected to do and had committed himself finally on the only basis that he ever could have accepted.

Azeglio was by this time with the Papal army. It had left Rome on 26 March under Durando's command and had marched to Bologna. The Pope's intention was that by taking up its station there it would defend the northern part of his dominions against Austrian encroachments, revolutionary incursions from outside, or uprisings within his dominions. Durando, Azeglio, and others of the Piedmontese faction hoped that their next move might be to cross the frontier to give active help either to Charles Albert or to the Republican Government that had been proclaimed in Venice, if this body was willing to bring itself to act in concert with the Piedmontese. On 26 March a second army left Rome, under the command of Ferrari: he was a veteran of the Napoleonic wars, now at the head of a force of some 9,000 volunteers mostly drawn from the Kingdom of the Two Sicilies. They were ill-equipped, if equipped at all, and proved, as might have been expected, to be ill-disciplined, but they were by no means lacking in courage and acquitted themselves better than Azeglio gave them credit for, when they found themselves in action. The Papal army might be willing to content itself with the limited aim of garrisoning the Papal States and watching events across the Po: but the volunteers had not enrolled for any such inglorious inactivity and, like Durando and Azeglio, fully intended to intervene in Venetia, though the commanders of the regular army would have to gain some measure of permission before doing this. Pius and his ministers had taken steps that might be considered encouraging. There had been the mission of Corboli-Bussi to Charles Albert, and at the end of March Azeglio in turn was with the King: in a letter to Minghetti of 7 April he spoke of this visit as having been made at the order of the Council of Ministers in Rome. Of the business discussed we have no information, but

Azeglio argued afterwards that the Pope, by stationing his army at Bologna and then by sanctioning this contact with Charles Albert, had initiated a course of action that logically could only lead to a crossing of the frontier. Azeglio and Durando were convinced that Aldobrandini, the Pope's Minister for War, was of their opinion, and that the Pope's instructions that they were to stay on their own side of the frontier were just a face-saving device. They were justified in assuming that Aldobrandini and Minghetti, also in a responsible position in the Papal Government, approved, for both had written letters committing them to this policy.[1] But none of them had any justification for pretending that this was the Pope's intention. Yet this is precisely what they now began to do, not merely in private letters but in public declarations. On 27 March Durando signalized his army's arrival at Bologna by the issue of an Order of the Day,[2] the first of a series written, like the later ones, by Azeglio and in his most flamboyant vein. Its peroration is a fair enough sample of his military rhetoric.

Militiamen and soldiers! The whole world fixes its gaze upon you, saying 'We see the armies of Italy at their task'. The glorious souls of those who fought at Legnano smile upon you from heaven: the great Pius gives you the blessing of the Almighty: Italy trusts in your courage and is confident that each of you will fulfil his duty as an Italian citizen and soldier. Long live Pius IX! Long live Italian independence!

Ferrari's volunteers, still trudging up to Bologna, ill-shod, ill-clothed, ill-armed, and ill-fed, might be cheered by the celestial smiles of the men of Legnano (whatever or wherever they might imagine Legnano to be), but the Pope could feel nothing but shock at this invocation of himself as the moving spirit of Italian independence. Worse was still to come. The entry of Piedmontese forces on to Austrian territory provoked a second Order of the Day by Azeglio, signed by Durando, dated 5 April.[3]

De Rubris, Azeglio's biographer and editor of his political writings, describes this as 'vibrant with enthusiasm'. Minghetti more cautiously opined that it 'showed the vivacity of a poet rather than the wisdom of a statesman'. Its literary style might be considered as no worse than inflatedly high-falutin. 'Italy is condemned by the Austrian Government to the pillage, rapes, and cruelties of a savage soldiery, to incendiarism, assassination,

---

[1] A. Jemolo, *Chiesa e stato in Italia negli ultimi cento anni* (1948), pp. 79–85.
[2] *S.D.P.*, I, pp. 546–7.   [3] Ibid., I, pp. 548–9.

and total ruin. She has seen Radetkzy carry war against the cross of Christ, throw down the doors of the sanctuary, stable his horses therein, profane its altars, violate the ashes of our fathers with the loathsome banners of his Croats.' On reading this Order, printed in the *Gazzetta di Roma* on 7 April, the Pope, according to Minghetti, 'went up in fury'. For the content of the Order was more shocking to his taste than the rhodomontade of its literary style. From it His Holiness learnt that he had been long-suffering, 'and on his august lips the word that would make them the instrument of divine punishment had remained suspended!' Apparently he was holding excommunication in reserve. But, goaded by Austrian iniquities, 'He has blessed your swords, which, united with those of Charles Albert, must act together for the extermination of the enemies of God and of Italy. . . . Such a war of civilization against barbarism is not merely a national but a supremely Christian one. . . . It is therefore fitting, and I [Durando] have ordered it, that we go forward wearing the Cross of Christ.' So Pius was informed that he had excommunication in reserve: that his army was to co-operate with that of Charles Albert in exterminating the Austrians, and that the war was a crusade since the causes of God and of Italy were identical. His fury was understandable, his reaction too guarded. In the long run it would have been better for his reputation had he dis-avowed his subordinates much more explicitly. As it was he made the *Gazzetta Ufficiale* announce simply that 'The Pope, when he wishes to make declaration of his opinions, speaks *ex se*, never through the mouth of any subordinate.' Azeglio's indiscretion was a deliberate one, part of the Piedmontese plan to compromise the Pope, and even after reading the disavowal in the *Gazzetta* he was impenitent. 'The official letter which disapproves of Durando in various matters must be a meddling of the old party, of those officials who have robbed till now and who are now standing idle in Rome instead of marching.'[1]

Azeglio went on with his eyes deliberately closed to the realities of the Pope's position, insisting that Pius was being deflected from his intended policy by the machinations of the reactionary priests around him, and deluding himself into the belief that the Pope could be manœuvred into declaring a holy war. Not until the Allocution of 29 April did Azeglio admit that he had been living in a fool's paradise, by his assumption that he knew the Pope's

[1] Minghetti, op. cit., Vol. I, p. 420.

mind better than the Pope himself. But even with the Allocution all was not lost, for Charles Albert would then be undisputed leader of the national cause. Until then he went on writing to Minghetti in the same self-deluded strain.

> Greet the ministers; see that Aldobrandini does not let himself be influenced by the clique of old robbers in the War Department.[1]

> The Pope and Charles Albert will only save us from the republicans by being the champions of independence.[2]

> If the best of Popes should decide, I do not say to proclaim a holy war, but to put himself openly at the head of the national idea and of the Lombard-Ligurian-Piedmontese alliance, he will lay a new cornerstone under his edifice and Italy will bless him and his ministers.[3]

Azeglio and Durando were not of course alone in urging Pius to take this lead. On 27 April Count Enrico Martini, Milanese representative with Charles Albert, wrote to Corboli-Bussi a letter intended for the Pope's eye urging Pius to break off diplomatic relations with Austria. How, he asked, could he have a representative at the camp of Charles Albert and one with the Austrians? Two days later the Pope issued his Allocution, making his position so clear that all false hopes in him were dissipated once and for ever. It was clear and it was emphatic: but it was not new in its *prise de position* and only the self-deluded could have been surprised by it. But it came when spirits were losing their exuberance in the north. The war was a month old and the situation discouraging. There was no feeling of political solidarity between monarchist Piedmont and republican Milan and Venice: the military situation was no more cheering than the political one. The Sardinian army had crossed the frontier on 25 March, three days after the declaration of war, and was slowly moving east through a terrain made none too easy by rice-fields and waterways; its supply lines were becoming overtaxed as they lengthened; and Radetzky had been able to concentrate his forces of no less than 60,000 men in the strongholds of the Quadrilateral.

Durando and the Papal army crossed the Po on to Venetian soil on 22 April: he had had no instructions to make this move but he argued that it had not been specifically forbidden and was a logical corollary of the ministers' instructions to him to co-operate with Charles Albert. But on 29 April, the day of his arrival at

---

[1] Minghetti, op. cit., Vol. I, p. 421.   [2] Ibid., p. 425.
[3] Ibid., p. 437.

Treviso, where Ferrari's volunteers joined him a week later, the Pope issued his Allocution.

His Holiness's ministers had requested him to consent to a declaration of war on 25 April 'as the best policy, required by the necessity of the times and the spirit of public opinion'. The Allocution, made in a secret consistory on the 29th and immediately published, was the Pope's reply. In it he defended the reforms made in the Papal system of government during his pontificate, pointing out that such reforms had been advised by Catholic sovereigns on previous occasions and especially in 1831. But the vitally important part of the Allocution was of course that which referred to the existing situation.

Since some desire that We with other peoples and rulers of Italy should undertake war against the Germans, We judge it our duty finally to profess here clearly and openly in this your solemn assembly that such a thing is in fact far from our thoughts. . . . We cannot refrain in the sight of all peoples from rejecting the deceitful counsels expressed in newspapers and various writings by those who would make the Roman Pontiff the president of some new republic to be constituted of all the peoples of Italy.[1]

The only surprising thing about the Allocution is that so many professed themselves surprised by it. It was fully in harmony with the Pope's earlier pronouncements and in truth said nothing that a Catholic should not have foreseen as inevitable. As Gustavo di Cavour, conservative elder brother of Camillo, wrote, 'The most determined sceptic must admit that the Pope can only be considered as vicar to the Prince of Peace. . . . As father of the faithful how could he forget how many of his children are numbered in the vast Austrian empire?' True, the Pope might well have made his position as clear as this on an earlier occasion; but it was not he who had killed the idea of 'some new republic to be constituted of all the peoples of Italy'. In its Giobertian form it had been killed by Charles Albert, yet it was seen in Rome that the Allocution closed an era: for whilst rehearsing the Pope's reforms it made no reference to the constitution for the Papal States on which a commission had been at work: it was evident that the Pope had abandoned this as he had abandoned the idea of a constitution for Italy. His ministers resigned *en masse*, only Antonelli staying in office, and Minghetti, who for so long had supported

[1] Jemolo, op. cit., p. 61.

the Piedmontese interest in Rome, left to take service under Charles Albert.

The military effect of the Allocution was not so easily assessed, but it could not have been other than demoralizing, for if the Pope was not at war against the Austrians what was the status of the soldiers in his army? If taken by the Austrians could they not be shot out of hand as outlaws or brigands? The question was of more than academic interest. Yet large-scale desertions were not mentioned until after military defeat, and when they did begin, it was the officers, according to Azeglio, who were the first to go. This was not altogether surprising, for if the Austrians should treat their prisoners as outside the rules of war they would be more likely to shoot officers than the rank and file.

Durando and Ferrari were now on the line of the Piave. At the beginning of May Nugent, with reinforcements for Radetzky, came westwards from Udine, passing in front of Durando, who lost contact with the enemy. Not knowing whether Nugent would turn south to attack him, or continue onwards towards Radetzky, Durando had made the classic mistake of dividing his forces. He left Ferrari at Montebelluna with some 4,000 men, mostly volunteers, whilst he himself with the great majority of the regular soldiers went west to Bassano. This division of his army was risky. Appallingly bad staff-work made it disastrous. On 8 May Ferrari learnt that Nugent was coming south towards him. He therefore took up a defensive position, and a very good one too, near Cornuda, and sent reliable information of the situation to Durando. Fighting was joined on the 8th, but was not heavy, and Ferrari held on to Cornuda, assured by Durando that he was coming. On the 9th the battle was resumed. In the morning Nugent had 2,700 men to Ferrari's 4,000, though it must be remembered that the Austrians were regulars and fully equipped, whilst the bulk of Ferrari's men were volunteers and ill-provided, especially in artillery, in which the Austrians had great superiority. By the afternoon Nugent had 6,000 men in the field. Durando had been told of the state of the battle and had sent word to Ferrari that he was coming at the double—'Vengo correndo', he had said. Encouraged by this, Ferrari held on and his men continued to fight an offensive action at heavy cost. But Durando had changed his mind. He had come to the conclusion that Ferrari was engaged only in a minor skirmish, presumably having arrived at this conclusion by discounting what he had been told of

Ferrari's situation as the kind of heroic exaggeration to be expected of volunteers. Worse, he did not inform Ferrari of the change in his plans. Having reverted to his first assumption that Nugent's main aim was to move immediately to the west, and that already the bulk of the Austrian army might have outflanked him (an assumption for which he had no justification), Durando, instead of 'coming running', was falling back. In the late afternoon Ferrari's men, exhausted and seeing no sign of relief, were withdrawn by their commander to Montebelluna and thence still farther back to the Treviso line. This was in effect the end of their existence as an army. Doubts about their status in consequence of the Allocution had to some quite immeasurable extent weakened their morale: for as irregulars drawn from outside the Papal States for the most part they were in a position even more questionable than Durando's men of the regular army: their relative ill-equipment had all along made it obvious to them that they were regarded as second-class soldiers. The realization that they had been badly let down by Durando on 9 May completed their demoralization. It seemed inescapable that either Durando was culpably incompetent or else he had regarded them as expendable.

Azeglio, as a member of Durando's staff, must have some measure of blame for the total breakdown of its intelligence service. One could forgive him this if one were not left with the impression that he had had a low opinion of the volunteers: it is true that they may have looked an unimpressive lot, but however they were dressed, armed, and grounded in paradeground drill their behaviour at Cornuda on the 8th and 9th of May was beyond praise. On the fourth of that month Azeglio had written: 'Men and money are lacking. Luckily Austria *dormivit cum patribus suis*, otherwise we were finished . . . you cannot imagine the nuisance that these volunteers, citizen-patriots, can be.'[1] On the 29th—three weeks after Cornuda—'This canaille of Neapolitans who ought to have relieved us here . . . they are the shame of Italy.'[2] His most scathing attack none the less was reserved for the Papal regular army.

You may now know what I have never yet told you, that the Papal army is worse than the Neapolitans, that at Treviso, at the first cannonade, the cavalry who were the vanguard turned back on the

[1] Minghetti, op. cit., Vol. I, p. 440.   [2] Rendu, op. cit., p. 41.

infantry and all ran like thieves: that the ambulances collected sixty men of whom only six were wounded: that two went mad and others died of fear: more than ten officers—of the Grenadiers, too— abandoned their posts in the face of the enemy . . . that on the day of the sortie a platoon of dragoons three hundred paces behind us was abandoned by its commanding officer, who took up his position another three hundred paces farther back: that one of their colonels on the evening when it was certain we should be attacked wrote that he was too dangerously exposed and gave in his resignation—and that in the face of the enemy.[1]

Thus he wrote to his wife on 2 June: his letter of 29 May already quoted is more out of character, not in its content as such, but in its destination. For as a rule when he was writing to Rendu he did not belittle his fellow-Italians as rancorously as he might do in correspondence meant for his fellow-countrymen: that at least may be counted in his favour. When he wrote to Luisa he was rather enjoying the fighting. He had already observed that it made him feel twenty-five years younger. There can be no doubt of his physical courage. It was to be shown at Monte Berico; but it was not a quality of which he had a monopoly and despite his strictures the irregulars had shown it at Cornuda when General Headquarters was showing nothing more ennobling than total inefficiency, and it was to be shown again at Monte Berico by the regulars at whom he had sneered. The real weakness had been in leadership. The Venetian Press had been severely critical and Azeglio at the end of May was engaged in disputation with Manin. It had been alleged in Venice that Durando was deliberately refraining from aiding the Republic until it should surrender itself to Charles Albert, and Manin himself was convinced that this charge was justified. In a letter of 29 May to Azeglio he reiterated what the Press had said and asserted that Charles Albert's agents were everywhere pushing his propaganda. Azeglio denied this, defended Durando's conduct of the campaign, and insisted that the strategy followed had been dictated by purely military considerations.[2]

Nugent had now entered Verona and joined Radetzky. The Piedmontese army under the King was to the west of him on the line of the Mincio—at some points not more than ten miles away. Durando and his forces were much farther away east of Radetzky.

[1] Carcano, op. cit., p. 351.
[2] G. Sforza (ed.), *M. d'A. alla guerra dell'independenza* (1911), pp. 33–39.

What mattered was who would take the initiative. If the Italians were to move against Radetzky in a well-timed double attack his position might be dangerous in the extreme: were he to use his central position to attack Durando or the King in turn he might score a couple of decisive knockouts. This was to be his strategy. The first forces, under Thurn, to test the defences of Vicenza on 22 and 23 May were beaten off. Durando, realizing the importance of Vicenza as a menace in the rear of the Austrian army, concentrated all the men he could muster, using the newly-opened railway that connected Vicenza with Padua and Venice. Radetzky had given him a breathing-space, for he had moved to attack the Sardinian army to the west. He met with a resistance severer than he had expected and, rather badly mauled, he withdrew southwards into Mantua. But not for long. He had decided to deliver a decisive blow at the weaker of the two armies arrayed against him, and moved towards Vicenza, not directly but south about, by way of Padua, thus cutting off Durando from any chance of withdrawing his forces into the Papal States should they be defeated in open battle. Charles Albert, it may be said, had shown a due sense of gratitude to providence by the solemnization of Te Deums for his victory at Goito: but he had not seen fit to follow Radetzky, whom for a time he believed to be still in Mantua when he was well on his way to Vicenza; nor did his intelligence service inform Durando of the movements of the Austrian army when they were known. Radetzky had some 30,000 men with 124 cannon (compared with Durando's estimated 11,000 with no more than thirty-six guns) and his forces were closing in on the city from five directions between north-north-east and south-south-west. To the south of the town was the high hill of Monte Berico and if the Austrians were to gain possession of this the city would be at their mercy. It took the form of a narrow spur in places barely wider than the roadway that ran along it. The defence of this key position was entrusted to Azeglio and Cialdini, to whom Durando assigned 2,000 men drawn about equally from the Papal army, including Swiss Guards, and from irregulars. The Austrians attacked along the crest of the hill, and simultaneously along its steep and wooded sides. The fight was cruelly fierce and raged for ten hours. All the defenders of the ridge acquitted themselves magnificently, both regulars, of whom the Swiss were in fact mercenaries, but who were fighting as for an ennobling cause, and the volunteers, who were by now veterans and who fought as such. Stage by stage the defenders were forced back. By four-thirty in the afternoon their ammunition was almost exhausted, though the Swiss were still capable of a desperate but vain bayonet counter-attack in which they were nearly annihilated. By seven o'clock the ridge was in Austrian hands and the remnants of Azeglio's force were falling back into Vicenza itself. About a hundred yards from the city gates Azeglio was hit in the knee by a bullet and had to be carried. For years to come he was to suffer from the effects of this wound, which for long obstinately refused to heal. At the time he spoke of it as 'a slight wound', though characteristically he was furious when he read it so described in the Turin newspapers. He was put to bed in Vicenza, which was under bombardment all night. The next day Durando had no alternative but to capitulate. Radetzky, whose harshness was so much attacked, gave the vanquished most surprisingly lenient terms, allowing them to leave with full military honours on condition that they returned to Papal territory and undertook not to fight again for three months.

For Azeglio this was the beginning of a long and painful journey, for not until December did he reach Turin. He was carried out of Vicenza but not for some days was he well enough to be taken across the Po. The delay fretted him, since he began now for the first time to feel fear: he was convinced that he might be made an example should he fall into Austrian hands. He was accompanied on this journey by his godson Stefano Pacetti, son of his old artist friend of Roman days. With them was an army doctor, a Roman and a Jew, the first of the series of Jewish doctors who were to care for him skilfully and devotedly in the months to come: no doubt they were motivated mainly by professional honour, but they could hardly have been unmindful of the championship of their race by the Azeglio brothers in Turin and in Rome.

Azeglio's first stop was in Ferrara, where he was received in the house of Cardinal Ciacchi, and where he was joined by his wife. Ferrara was still too near the Austrians for him to feel safe and at the beginning of July he had himself moved to Bologna. There he stayed for the rest of that month, but then even Bologna became unsafe, or so he was convinced, for the Austrians were entering the Papal States to suppress the revolutionary movements there. So in August he went on to Florence. He was still in a miserable condition, 'For with the wound cured it is now necessary to cure the cure that has reduced me to skin and bones.' In truth his wound was so far from cured that he could only get about on crutches. Almost exactly two months after leaving Vicenza he arrived in Florence, where Doctor Esdra placed him in charge of another Jewish doctor, Isaac Galligo, whilst he was to be the guest of yet a third such doctor, Giacomo Almansi, in his villa on the outskirts of Florence. His room there has been kept as a small museum, with a pair of his crutches as one of its principal exhibits. He had many friends in Florence and was far from feeling neglected and to pass the time he took up his brushes again as well as his pen. One painting done at this time was given to Almansi as a souvenir and is still in the villa. It is a 'Flight into Egypt', whose execution may have had therapeutic value though its artistic merit is not great. The Holy Family rest at the foot of a crag that falls from a wooded height almost into the sea: the place is definitely enough Egypt, as one would know not only from the colossal palm trees but also from the fountain by which the fugitives are resting, for its waters gush from the mouth of a sphinx.

From Villa 'le Scalere' letters flowed out. In some he looked back over the campaign and to Rendu he tried to do so philosophically. 'Despite all our disasters I am not at all discouraged. Frankly I was afraid for Italy's sake of a too easy victory, almost as much as of a disaster. If we had rid ourselves of the *straniero* in one campaign heaven alone knows where we should have been led by the violence of political passions and the excess of parties whose presumption would have known no limits.'[1] To Pantaleoni: 'all is to do over again . . . we have to think how Italy may develop strength to act on her own behalf, for nothing is to be hoped for from others';[2] to Persano: 'Our cause will win in the end, but this is an all too painful moment. Italy as a nation has done nothing. 25,000,000 inhabitants have not given 50,000 volunteers. Instead of action the parties have set about tearing each other apart.' 'Our greatest enemies are not the Austrian but the trouble-makers amongst the Italians; they are few but the inertia of the many makes them, if not dangerous, harmful.'[3] Azeglio told Persano that he was fighting them from his sofa with his pen. For besides letters to his

[1] Rendu, op. cit., p. 46.   [2] Pantaleoni, op. cit., p. 183.
[3] Persano, op. cit., pp. 24, 25.

friends he was writing for the public again. And a new destiny was opening up before him—that of a career of active politics as a Deputy, which he already was, and perhaps as a Minister, which in fact he was so soon to become.[1]

[1] In describing the military events of 1848 this chapter draws heavily, but could not mprove, upon the account given by the Berkeleys.

VIII

PRELUDE TO OFFICE

AZEGLIO, as already observed, had been busy during his period of physical immobilization at Bologna and Florence painting and writing an abundance of letters, a new series of political articles, and a couple of pamphlets, one of them of some length. It is to his credit that his public utterances of this time harmonize perfectly with the opinions expressed in his letters. Their expression may be less acid, but the actual ideas are quite as uncompromising. The theme that is most consistently repeated is the need for the abandonment of party disputes and class-warfare. Whilst still in Bologna he heard that extremists there were agitating for the overthrow of the Pope's temporal power, the establishment of a provisional government, and the eventual transfer of allegiance from the Pope to Charles Albert. All this he stigmatized as dangerous nonsense in a letter 'To the Bolognese', published as a flysheet supplement to the *Gazzetta di Bologna*.

Provisional government! To what future does this title of 'provisional' refer? There are whispers of a surrender to Charles Albert. In what kind of a brain could the idea ever have been born that King Charles Albert would be anyone's accomplice in robbing his ally, robbing the Pontiff, robbing PIUS IX! . . . Do you not see that Charles Albert is far away, occupied in war still . . . that you have an enemy at your gates, that of all the events that Austria might hope for, none could be more welcome than for her to be able to say that Pius IX has been ill-used by his subjects and that she has become the vindicator and liberator of the ill-used Pontiff?[1]

After the defeat of Charles Albert at Custozza and the subsequent 'Salasco' Armistice, Azeglio had privately deplored the passiveness of most Italians during the crisis, with less than 50,000 volunteers from a population of 25 million, and had blamed the divisions of the parties tearing each other apart. The terms of the armistice were as moderate as Radetzky could have made them: and 'had we not signed it was total ruin with incalculable results for the future'. His pamphlet, *The Honour of Austria*

[1] *S.D.P.*, II, pp. 3–5.

and the Honour of Italy,[1] written and published in Florence, is as blunt as any of his letters.

Italy has had the most magnificent chance to free herself that has been offered her for seven centuries. She has not known how to use it. All classes from princes down to the humblest of the populace have failed to produce anyone equal to the chance that was given; opportunity did not fail the men, but men failed the opportunity. . . .

Who is to be held responsible for this weakness? Knowing Azeglio's usual views one expects him to lay the blame for political divisions fairly and squarely on the radicals and members of Young Italy. But not this time.

For thirty-two years the Austro-jesuitical party, in part by threats, in part by corruption, by slow unwearying incessant deception, has set to work by every possible means to weaken Italy, to wear down all strong characters and sturdy intelligences, to eliminate all such from administrative posts, and to fill these with men base, ignorant, corrupt, or simply null. Governments and princes wishing to change their policies did not know, wish, or attempt to change men. They tried to do new things with the old agents and things went wrong.

The armistice as signed was for a period of six weeks, but was renewable. Azeglio was by no means sure that Austria would grant an extension, and foreseeing further fighting he called on his fellow-countrymen to be bold and resolute.

I see written on the walls, I read in the newspapers, I hear in the streets 'Out with the foreigners', 'Death to the Germans', 'The unspeakable Austrian'. All very well. But one good musket well sighted, held in a strong pair of arms, is of more worth than a mountain of 'Death to the Austrian'. . . . A little less fury in the press, a little more fighting. In the Chambers, less rhetoric, less longwindedness, more urgency.

In this essay and in another written soon after it[2] he also discussed the reaction of Germany, France, and Britain to the events in Lombardy. Germany especially had disappointed him. At Frankfurt a German Parliament was trying to achieve German liberalism, yet 'Germany that is all agog to gain her independence, to make herself a nation, at the very same time turns against Italy to deny her her independence and nationality. And what reason does she advance? Her HONOUR!' As for Britain, he considered

---

[1] *S.D.P.*, II, pp. 9–16. [2] Ibid., pp. 19–25.

that *The Times* was expressing governmental opinion when it was
pro-Austrian. 'It says in effect "Austria has by superior force
rendered herself once more mistress of Lombardy: her rights are
based on long possession and on treaties: diplomacy can do
nothing against the accomplished fact."' This view he contrasted
with the willingness shown by Britain to recognize the Sicilian
claim to independence in January 1848, an argument that was
unconvincing. When Britain was considering the Sicilian case it
was because independence seemed to have been gained *de facto*:
when the Bourbons reconquered the island their sovereignty over
it was recognized. The case in Lombardy was similar: the
Austrians had quite as evidently regained control, so no question
of recognizing Lombard independence arose. Azeglio therefore
admitted that by convention Britain and *The Times* had 'logic
on their side and not a word can be said in reply', but a new era
had opened, that of nationality, traditional international law
was now out of date, and the great new question now was: 'How
and when must force be used to compel the recognition of the new
law that is to be established on the great basis of nationality?'

'No despotism, either from the throne or from the streets':
this was the title of Azeglio's next article,[1] written at Villa Almansi
on 6 September, and it was to remain the dominant idea of many
future writings and speeches. There had been an uprising in
Leghorn against the Tuscan Government headed by Capponi.
Leghorn, as restless and radical as its rival Genoa, was under
the influence of Guerrazzi, the revolutionary lawyer-novelist
who was always a special object of Azeglio's dislike. He condemned
the timing of the rising, on the eve of the expiration of the
armistice, when national solidarity was essential; he ridiculed its
pretexts—the price of salt, the low pay of clerks; and whilst not
naming Guerrazzi he described the populace as 'used as the
instrument of base and secret ambitions, seduced by deceptions
and flatteries, scientifically corrupted so that it might be twisted
to serve as a tool for men who have not even the energy or daring
for crimes—for a castrated Catiline or an enervated Masaniello'.
Guerrazzi may not have known whether he was the Catiline or
the Masaniello, but he may be assumed to have resented Azeglio's
offensiveness, and he was to give his attacker a very narrow escape
soon afterwards. Without discussing the taste of the article one
must admit that it was a clear statement of what was to remain

[1] *S.D.P.*, II, pp. 29–36.

Azeglio's main determination, to fight radicalism and republicanism by word and deed, and at the same time to maintain as far
as circumstances permitted the balance of power between King,
Ministers, and Parliament. 'The paternalism of kings formerly
made me wish myself an orphan, but the fraternalism of certain
brotherhoods today makes me wish myself an only son.'[1]

There were many in Turin and Florence who shared these
views, who were opposed to royal despotism however paternal,
to anarchy from below (more hostile to this than to despotism
from above, it must be admitted), dedicated to the cause of
Italian liberation, but against premature attempts to make war
on Austria until assured of strength, unity, and preparedness at
home and of some measure of sympathy from abroad. What was
Azeglio's speciality was his outspoken expression of these views,
his willingness to speak his mind to kings or demagogues. This,
on top of his earlier reputation as a patriot-novelist and pamphleteer and his more recent one as patriot-soldier, gave him a new
potentiality as a man of action.

In early September serious efforts were made to persuade him
to take office in the Tuscan Government.

Since yesterday [2 September] I have sustained a siege by the ministry.
I have said I have not the simplest notion about the task they offer
me—the War Office—and that I must go to Turin. Honestly I should
not know how to set about being a minister. Today Lambruschini
came to persuade me, saying that if I did not accept others would
refuse to join, and that the times were serious for the salvation of Tuscany. I am genuinely perplexed. All this may be true, but as must be the
case with any man, what I cannot do, I cannot—these are matters of
fact.[2]

Azeglio had no wish to stay in Tuscany whether as minister
or as private citizen, intending to return to Turin as soon as his
wound would allow. Pantaleoni was begging him to go back to
Rome, but this did not attract him. 'As for Rome, NO! I have
had enough of priests. . . . Italian affairs are not being directed
from there any longer: the head of the house has seen to that. And
I must remind you that I am a deputy and ought to go to the
House to twaddle there.'[3]

In no part of Italy was the political scene to his liking. In
Tuscany the Grand Duke had been compelled to call Guerrazzi

[1] *S.D.P.*, II, p. 41.   [2] Carcano, op. cit., p. 356.
[3] Pantaleoni, op. cit., p. 185.

into office on 27 October. In Rome only Pellegrino Rossi seemed to stand between the Pope and the republicans, and on 13 November he was murdered as he entered the building for the opening of Parliament. The crime was shocking, but more disgusting to Azeglio was the behaviour of the Parliament that did not even suspend its sitting, and of some of the Roman mob who demonstrated their joy beneath the windows of Rossi's widow. No wonder that Azeglio became ever more confirmed in his detestation of the radicals, like Guerrazzi and Sterbini, who were on the scene, and of Mazzini, whom he considered to be their prompter in the wings. In Piedmont Alfieri di Sostegno, a reluctant Prime Minister, was striving to make a peace with Austria: the Governments of France and of Britain had offered to mediate, but only about the indemnity to be paid and the occupation by the Austrians of Piedmontese fortresses. Lombardy and Venetia were indisputably Austrian, though Palmerston saw fit to read Austria a lesson on how to govern them. The democrats were urging the repudiation of the Salasco Armistice and the resumption of war, and Gioberti, a member of the Chamber, was equally ardent for this whilst Austria-Hungary was still in turmoil.

Azeglio was already a member of the Chamber though he had never taken his seat. As far back as 3 April he had been nominated as one of the first Senators, but in June Cavour had arranged for him to be put forward as a candidate for election to the Chamber for Strambino, and on 26 June he had been duly returned. Now that Guerrazzi, mindful of the 'castrated Cataline or enervated Masaniello' gibe, was in office in Florence it might be prudent for Azeglio to withdraw himself. So his transfer to Turin and his taking of his seat in the Chamber were merely a question of time. 'A band of fools and rogues of the lowest rank has managed by intimidation to make themselves arbiters of this country',[1] of Tuscany: but the fact that he was still hobbling painfully about on crutches, as he would have to do intermittently for months to come, postponed his journey to Turin. Had he wished he might have arrived there as a minister of the Crown and not merely a deputy. As he told Luisa in a letter of 12 December written from Genoa,

I have had a letter from Pinelli, who on the King's behalf calls me to Turin to become President of the Council of Ministers. I have answered that I have no experience of practical politics and no knowledge of men

[1] Rendu, op. cit., p. 49.

K

or affairs in Piedmont and so cannot accept. All the same I am going to Turin so as not to fail in my duty and to give my reasons. My decision is to refuse to say 'Yes' but I believe it possible that my friends may present the situation in such a light that I may not be able to refuse. You can guess whether this idea amuses me.[1]

Two days later he wrote again to her.

I arrived in Turin and explained that I have neither the physical strength to do much work nor the mental capacity: nor yet the knowledge of personalities and policies in Piedmont. Further, in the present situation I do not believe it possible to renew the war, yet do not wish to be the one who must make the peace, above all to have my name attached to the treaty. I must go to the King, determined not to yield but to say the fateful '*I voeui nen ch'em secao*' [I do not want to be worried with it].

Charles Albert was in truth in a most difficult situation. The existing ministry under Perroni (who had replaced Alfieri di Sostegno), whose most influential member was Pinelli, had no effective support from the Chamber and its resignation could not be long delayed. The King, like his ministers, would have preferred Azeglio as Perroni's successor but there was a widespread desire inside the Chamber, and a very vociferous pleading outside it, for Gioberti to be called to office. A deputation from Genoa to demand a 'Constituent Assembly' and a 'democratic' ministry was known to be preparing to descend on Turin. After Azeglio's refusal it seemed advisable to forestall any such demonstration by calling on Gioberti at once. Charles Albert was reluctant to appoint this enthusiast for democracy and hammer of the Jesuits, but Azeglio's unwillingness to take on responsibility left him no alternative. 'I went to the King,' says Azeglio, 'who received me with great kindness, and as everything had been understood in advance we passed the time in chat. Leaving him I came face to face with Father Vincenzo [Gioberti], who was going in. "Out with the cold-, and in with the hot-heads", I said and made off, like a child that has managed to dodge school.'[2] To Pantaleoni he said much the same in a letter of 19 December.

Liberty with its follies has put the handle of the dagger into the grasp of despotism: . . . What scum we have around our feet! . . . I believe we are in the stage through which every revolution must pass, of fools and

[1] Carcano, op. cit., p. 362.   [1] Ibid., p. 363.

rogues, and that it is useless to fight against it. Like all convulsions, the stronger it is the shorter may be its duration. . . . I came here summoned by the King to form his new ministry but—*pas si bête*! I would not make war because we can do nothing alone against Austria, and if peace is to be made I had rather the Abbé signed it than I.

To refuse office because he felt incompetent for it was commendable enough. But to advance as further reasons that it would involve him in tasks that would be tedious, difficult, or unpopular was not to Azeglio's credit. Even if by analogy with the Salasco Armistice Piedmont were to have an 'Azeglio Peace', it would be nothing to its maker's discredit—unless the terms were utterly dishonourable. Luckily for Azeglio's reputation as a patriot he was to accept office in a far graver crisis of Piedmont's affairs and to undertake a treaty with Austria when the gaining of acceptable terms would be infinitely more difficult than it might have been at this date.

The Chamber of which he was a member had in fact only a short life left to it, for by the end of the year it was dissolved and a new election was ordered for January 1849. Azeglio was once more a candidate for Strambino though he had not found his experience as a legislator at all to his taste.

For me, the obligation of a fixed employment at a fixed time and in a fixed place is an impossibility. When I was in the Chamber I was on hot bricks. Yet wishing to stay there I managed to control my body, but my mind—never! I would resolve to pay heed to the discussion, but within ten minutes I was voyaging through space only to return after a more or less lengthy period. Of the discussion I would know nothing. So as a Deputy I am absolutely null.[1]

There is no reason to doubt this. Even as Prime Minister he found it wearisome to attend sessions and the only thing that irked him more than having to make speeches was the boredom of listening to other people making them.

Azeglio supported his candidature by publishing a *Letter to his Electors* dated 8 January 1849 and written within a week. He was well pleased with it. 'The book has made a furore here. . . . Balbo says it is the least bad one I have written.' Like others of Azeglio's political tracts it is needlessly long, running to some fifty pages that might have been halved had he not been writing in such haste. It is far from being a typical election manifesto as we know

[1] Carcano, op. cit., p. 373.

them, for it contains no promises of any definite political programme. Azeglio was simply not the man to be bothered with such minutiae, but he was always an adept at sketching an attractive and at times amusing outline of his general political philosophy. As in his other writings of this period he is concerned to explain why he is so much opposed to the current craze for 'the Constituent' and for 'democratic ministers'. A Constituent was the very newest shibboleth. It had begun in Leghorn as a demand for the election by universal manhood suffrage throughout all Italy of a body to make a constitution for the whole peninsula. Genoa had echoed Leghorn in what to Azeglio seemed so impractical as to be sheer buffoonery and in his *Letter* he poured scorn on it. How, in fact, could such an assembly ever get itself elected? How, if it managed this, could it draw up such a constitution? And even should it succeed, how could it ever put it into operation? Azeglio needed no arcane wisdom to see how unanswerable such questions as these must be. As for 'democratic ministers', he confessed himself equally nonplussed. He assumed it to mean ministers forced on to rulers, or on to elected chambers by popular demonstrations. As for these demonstrations, of which there certainly were plenty all over Italy, they were no more, he alleged, than a put-up job.

A company of stage extras and professors of riots and tumults is touring Italy from village to village with the mission of representing the people. Whoever has need of 'the people', of a demonstration to make him Minister or something, strikes a bargain with the leading comedian. The company arrives, is given its few shillings and its words to shout, and all is done. The next day one reads in the press that the people of heroic ———— (here follows the name of the town) have risen like one man against those who have trampled on the rights and betrayed the sacred cause of the people. . . .

Another paragraph was aimed clearly at both Montanelli in Tuscany and Gioberti in Piedmont.

It has been a sad business to see that men of irreproachable lives and reputations, men who in the past have consecrated their waking hours, their study, and their actions to the cause of their country, who have risked their very lives for it, should now be the ones to set the sorry example of power gained by ignoble means and by disloyalty, by the intimidation of a peaceful and honourable majority through the work of a few fomentors of discords. In a word, by the work of sectaries.[1]

[1] *S.D.P.*, II, pp. 121–4.

Azeglio was duly re-elected, but the general result gave a decisive overall majority to the 'Democrats', and they with Gioberti seemed firmly established in office, though whether Gioberti was leading them or they him was a moot point. To sit assiduously in a Chamber dominated by such a party was much too much for Azeglio and though he took his seat on 22 January he was impatient to go away to Tuscany again. The change was from bad to infinitely worse. He had not realized what was happening in Tuscany, where Guerrazzi, already in the ministry since the end of October, was now head of a Provisional Government: the Grand Duke Leopold had left Florence on 31 January, eventually to join the Pope at Gaeta. Tuscany became a Republic under a Provisional Government headed by Guerrazzi. Whatever Azeglio's opinion of him might have been, Guerrazzi made a reasonably good job of smoothing over the transition and preventing Tuscany from falling into utter chaos. In the Grand Duchy even the intervention of Austria and the re-establishment of the rule of the Grand Duke had a relative mildness that seems almost incredible when one considers the events in Rome, the Two Sicilies, and Lombardy-Venetia. One near-celebrity almost became a victim of the Provisional Government—Azeglio.

I arrived in Pisa and was going to go on to Florence to arrange to withdraw my daughter [Rina] from her convent. The day of my arrival the 'Provisional Government' was proclaimed. My friends believed that I, as an impenitent diehard, would be the object of a demonstration, but I did not undergo any. I did however receive a warning from a person in a position to know, that if I did not leave at once it might fare the worse for me. Knowing the tribe, I realized it was no matter for jest. I mounted my horse and rode with my batman as far as Spezia through the pine woods along the shore, avoiding the main roads. I was correct in my guess, for half an hour after my departure they came to arrest me and sought me everywhere except where I was. This is the reward for one who has given his time, spent his money, and had his hide pierced for that ——— called Italy. And despite all this I love her as much as ever. Tuscany is under an anarchical reign of terror and will fall to pieces unless saved by an intervention. The leaders know perfectly well that their government cannot last, but they are the kind who will always fall on their feet.[1]

So Azeglio returned to Piedmont and to observation at close quarters of the confusion of the political scene. Affairs had no

[1] Quoted by Ghisalberti, op. cit., p. 126.

run smoothly for Gioberti, who had made mistakes that a modicum of experience might have avoided. He had chosen ministers to the courts of the Pope and the King of Naples whom both those rulers found objectionable, and he had further offended the Pope by receiving in Turin representatives of the revolutionary government in Rome. Inept as he had appeared in these matters he ran into a crisis over relations with the Grand Duke of Tuscany. Foreseeing the likelihood of Austrian intervention to restore the Grand Duke to absolutism as well as to his Duchy, Gioberti had considered it preferable to forestall this by Piedmontese action, to overthrow the revolutionary government, but preserve a moderate constitutional government for Tuscany. On this basis he might begin to build his edifice of a federation. With or without the consent and approval of his colleagues (this became a matter of dispute afterwards) he offered Sardinian aid to the Grand Duke, who for a time considered accepting it. But in the end he fled to join the Pope and King of Naples in Gaeta, whilst Gioberti was forced to resign. The King refused to agree to intervene in Tuscany, intent solely on the chance of renewal of war with Austria, and the cabinet disavowed the scheme.

General Chiodo replaced Gioberti, but the real leader of the new ministry was Urbano Rattazzi. Convinced that all thought of federation or unification was in vain as long as Austrians were on Italian soil, Rattazzi and the King carried the ministry and the Chamber into the heroic if ill-fated renewal of the war against Austria. On 12 March they informed the Austrians that they no longer considered Sardinia bound by the armistice, and on the 23rd of the month the army crossed the frontier into Lombardy.

Azeglio was worried and despondent. He was still in Spezia receiving medical attention to his wound and there he tried to order his thoughts in a letter to Luisa.

As for this war here is my opinion. On the one side Piedmont—four and a half millions. On the other, Austria with Russia in reserve. Reckon up how many millions they make. Central Italy—nothing. Naples hostile. England concerned for the treaties of '15, with a strong internal party anxious only for administrative reforms and therefore for the avoidance of continental embroilments. France weakened by schisms, weary of her Republic and of its disorders, almost on the verge of accepting despotism for the sake of order. Germany weary also of demagogues and inclined to make her peace with her rulers. All that presages nothing good in my view. We may have advantages at the start but whether they will last I doubt, unless there is some new development in the non-Russian Slav areas of the Austrian Empire to occupy Austria. . . . As for the Republicans, either they are as imbecile as ever or I understand nothing. Either the King will win with his army (and it is not republican) and then with the glory of victory will hold the dagger by the handle: or he will lose and Austria will be the mistress of Italy, and I do not think she will have worked on behalf of Mazzini. Should Lombardy rise it will be something, but she will not do so. I hear that not one Lombard or Tuscan has come over to us. The news today is that the Austrians are trying to cross the Po below Pavia and our forces are opposing this. You see they are not thinking of standing still in their four fortresses. I do not see things in an auspicious light, and so . . . God help us.[1]

The following day in a letter to another friend he expressed no greater confidence.

This war will decide all. Having weighed up the forces and considered the state of Italy and of Europe, I cannot see things in a rosy light. True, the thousand possible combinations of so many diverse elements may bring unforeseen and unforeseeable results. But it is an unhappy condition to have no other hope than in the unforeseen.[2]

When brought face to face with situations that he did not like, Azeglio could be very short-sighted or wilfully blind. But a survey like the one in his letter to his wife shows how acute his judgement could be when he did not feel himself committed: he had foreseen what might be the outcome of the French Revolution, the insular preoccupations of England, and the probability of Russian intervention in the Austrian Empire to suppress revolution there. However sadly wrong he might often be about matters inside Italy, he would over and over again guess by intuition the attitude the great powers would take up.

The day after that on which he wrote the second of these two letters the Sardinian army was routed at Novara. Charles Albert sought death on the battle-field but though he took suicidal risks even this wish was denied him, and he was destined to die, and to die agonizingly, in exile a few months later. Costanza d'Azeglio, on hearing of his death, reflected: 'His end seems to me to have a sadness that is worthy to crown our sad adventure. For he belongs to history, which will probably make of him something quite

[1] Carcano, op. cit., p. 381.
[2] M. de Rubris (ed.), *Confidenze di M. d'Azeglio dal carteggio con Teresa Targione Tozzetti* (1930) (hereafter referred to as *Confidenze*), pp. 37–38.

unlike what he really was. What one can say with truth is that had all been as devoted as he, the cause would not have been lost.'

As she foresaw, writers have tried to explain Charles Albert: and it may be said that many have tried to explain away his son. A man coarse in speech, inordinate in his physical appetites and activities, Victor Emmanuel II has been portrayed as 'Il Re Galantuomo'. It was Azeglio who invented the term and began the creation of a legend that later he came to regret. The traditional conception of the King as bluff but honest, loyal to a constitution that he disliked but observed scrupulously, has come in for re-examination. Azeglio learnt from experience how much craft underlay the directness. Jemolo has a somewhat despairing page on the difficulty of coming at the truth about him.[1]

Victor Emmanuel, despite the great popularity of his person, is little known to those who are not content with narrative. In Italy even in the periods of greatest liberty of the press 'nihil de principe' was observed, extending even to the dead. Outside an apologetic, written to order, nothing might be written within three generations . . . of princes: . . . whilst other dynasties opened their archives here only a very limited number of letters placed at the disposition of court writers was published. . . .

Of a problem concerning the King's early life he asks: 'Which of these explanations is the more convincing? No one can say with certainty, and perhaps we shall never know.' Jemolo's despair may be unjustifiable. It may be that the secret archives, if they exist and come to be thrown open, may tell us no more than can be safely inferred without them. Victor Emmanuel's actions are on record; so too are many of his words, as for instance his assurance to the Papal Nuncio in November 1849 that he 'held the constitutional to be the worst of all systems: that it was not necessary to attack it from the front, but that it was necessary to await occasions opportune for causing it to fall'.[2]

On his first appearance as King in Turin Victor Emmanuel was greeted with enthusiasm by the people in the streets and by the garrison, but Azeglio heard that he was received coolly by the Chamber of Deputies. Genoa, rarely cool, rose in revolt: wild rumours had been circulating there—that the King had abolished

---

[1] Jemolo, op. cit., p. 131.

[2] Ibid., p. 131, quoted from Padre P. Pirri, *Pio IX e Vittorio Emanuele II dal loro carteggio privato* (*Miscellanea historiae pontificiae*, Vol. VIII, Bk. I) (Rome, 1944) (hereafter referred to as *Cart. priv.*), p. 48.

the constitution, that the Austrians had invaded Piedmont and were marching on Genoa. The rising was an impromptu one: many citizens who could not be suspected of any taint of republicanism or Mazzinianism had supported, even helped to lead it, and left alone it might have fizzled out when more reliable news arrived from Turin. But the capital had decided to humble Genoa. The radical ministry of Rattazzi had been compelled to resign on 26 March as a result of the catastrophic failure of the war they had undertaken and a new ministry of moderates and conservatives under de Launay had come into office. Weak in the Chamber, unsure of themselves in the country, and seemingly at the mercy of Austria, finding themselves faced with this rising the ministers decided on punitive action and sent La Marmora to execute it. On 10 April, after two days of artillery bombardment, street-fighting, and undisciplined looting by the forces of order, the city capitulated. To moderates and conservatives La Marmora was from now on a man of destiny. Azeglio approved the repression, laying the blame for the disorders on the 'democrats', who

claim that the war of kings is over and the war of peoples is to come, the 'War of God' as they call it. But I seem to have noticed that God has already had the bad taste to prefer Radetzky to Mazzini, and to love regular soldiers more than civic guards and volunteers, and any kind of soldier at all more than the civil population. . . . I have learnt in these two years that it is not enough to strike off the chains of slaves, but it is necessary to change the minds of slaves into the minds of free peoples. The people of Italy are twenty per cent. stupid, rascally, and bold, eighty per cent. stupid, honest, and timid, and such a people has the governments it deserves.[1]

Not for the first or last time Azeglio was wrong, even maliciously wrong, about the immediate situation under his very eyes, but tragically right about the real, deep-seated malady of Italy, the numbing effect on her people of long centuries of misgovernment, the lack of popular education and of political experience. This malady was not to be remedied by the creation of a united Italy (a political change that did not necessarily involve a social regeneration), and may be held responsible for the creeping paralysis from which parts of southern Italy in particular still suffer.

[1] T. Tommasoni (ed.), *Lettere inedite di M. d'A. e F. Gualterio a Tommaso Tommasoni* (1885), p. 151.

Despite this military triumph in Genoa, de Launay's administration was insecure. The moderates and conservatives had nothing like a majority in the Chamber nor were their sympathizers there in any sense organized as a political party or parties. Always there was a frantic looking around for enough supporters to carry any measure—and each measure was a new crisis for the Government. Every possible recruit had to be pressed into the service of the ministry, and Azeglio, resting in Spezia, received a summons to Turin with the offer of an official appointment. He was still a light-weight, of course, and only a light-weight post was offered him.

From Turin there has arrived my nomination as Director of the State Theatres! Minister Pinelli must be a wit! I have replied, with a million thanks, that at this moment my attention is entirely concentrated on the Theatre of Italy, so that it would be impossible for me to direct that of singers, comedians, ballerinas and puppeteers. . . . I begin to suspect that, as Balbo says, Pinelli is anxious to keep me to one side.[1]

He went to Turin nevertheless, and found himself in a family reunion, for Prospero had just arrived as an exile from Palermo. Though Massimo had seen him in Palermo in 1842, in 1845, and in Rome in 1848, it is apparent that Roberto and he had not set eyes on each other since boyhood, nor did they meet again after this occasion.

Now once more, on or about 22 April, Massimo was again asked to accept service. Precisely what office was offered him he did not explain but once more he declined, and once more on the pretext that he was not willing to give his name to an 'Azeglio Peace'. He conceded that he would support the Government as best he might by writing, though apparently he made no promises about speaking on its behalf in the Chamber. The ministers must have interpreted his refusal as no more genuine than the 'Nolo Episcopari' of a cleric already resigned to a mitre, for on 25 April another approach was made. This time he might choose between a ministerial portfolio or a diplomatic mission. Once again he refused, and yet again the ministers could not bring themselves to accept his refusal as definitive. The cynical observer might note that each offer was more attractive than the previous one. This could not have escaped Azeglio's notice, but it does not necessarily follow that he was intentionally being coy in order to

---

[1] Carcano, op. cit., p. 395.

raise the bidding. On 5 May he received the final offer, the ultimate in allurements—the Premiership itself. 'This morning whilst
still in bed I was awakened and saw Pinelli and Roberto before
me. They told me that the only remedy for the situation was that
I should accept. The King and the public apparently wish it. . . .
Now I must go out to investigate before I accept. I wish to make
pacts and to have things seen clearly.'[1] Two days later he accepted
office.

His reluctance to undertake ministerial office seems less in need
of explanation than the persistence of those already in office
to bring him in, first as a colleague and then as their leader. One
finds that one is asking one's self what can have been the minimum
requirements of a Prime Minister and what evidence there was
at that time for Azeglio's possession of them. He was most certainly not what one might term a 'good House of Commons man'.
Though a deputy since June 1848, he had been absent not only
from the Chamber but from Turin for almost all that time,
recuperating in Bologna and Florence, and more recently in
Spezia. Even when in Turin he had spent little time in the House,
and when there had made no apparent contribution to its debates.
If he made any speech it has not been preserved: and he made no
secret of his boredom at listening to the speeches of others. Nor,
as events were to prove, was he ever willing to sit, as a good Prime
Minister must, listening to debates of minimal interest in order
to be able at any moment to assess the temper of the House or to
know the potentialities of its members. Not only that, but to be
even moderately in control a Prime Minister, or someone on his
behalf, must be active at all times to ensure the support of an
organized and disciplined party in the House. But such a party
did not exist anywhere in the Sardinian Parliament. The so-called
'democrats' were not as amorphous or as fissiparous a group as the
centre or right-wing groups, yet Azeglio never tried to impose
on his own supporters even their modest degree of cohesion.
Still more seriously, he did not attempt to do this in his cabinets,
which in crises might reflect the divisions of their presumed
supporters. As for the routine work, drudgery perhaps, of planning
sustained and coherent policies for the future and watching their
translation stage by stage, act by act, and clause by clause into
practice, or of supervising the day-to-day activities of the civil
service at home and of diplomats abroad—of experience of such

[1] Carcano, op. cit., p. 398.

work Azeglio had none, nor did he ever develop a taste for it. Whole realms of governmental activity, especially in economic or commercial matters, were totally outside his ken. Why then was he so suddenly the man of the moment?

The answer lay of course in his known personal qualities. He was as evidently anti-Austrian and ardent for the liberation of Italy as anyone of his generation. Not only *Ettore Fieramosca* but Monte Berico had shown that not even Guerrazzi could outdo him there. His later writings showed his enthusiasms controlled by an awareness of the need to work within the limits of what was practicable. From *Degli ultimi casi di Romagna* onwards he had been urging the necessity of avoiding precipitate or exaggerated action in the national cause, since such action could only end in leaving Italy more than ever at the mercy of Austria. First Custozza, and then Novara had shown how real a danger this was, and no one knew as yet what Austria's mercy might be, for the treaty of peace was still to be negotiated. The time was ripe for a man of caution: even the peace treaty might be more lenient if the Sardinian negotiator were one with no responsibility for the second disastrous attack on Austria. There was much to be said, too, for his dedication to the idea of educating the people, not only in political concepts but in the humdrum three Rs as well. Azeglio, like every patriot, was anxious to be able to recognize the moment propitious for Italian action when it might come: but he was more anxious than most to prepare Italians for such action, and for the responsibilities that would follow if success were attained: he, too, more than anyone else, held views that might persuade western Europe that Italians were worthy of the cause. He had insisted continuously on the need not only for the geographical unity but for the social unity of class and class that to him seemed the basis of national regeneration. In this he seemed conservative—even '*codino*'—to many: but he had left no one in doubt as to his aversion from class-warfare, and this naturally gained him the suffrage of bourgeoisie and landowners rather than that of the working classes, though these were at a disadvantage politically in the Sardinian system of franchise. His political writings had given him the reputation of moral courage and of candour. He had not hesitated to say what he thought even though it might be unpopular. Everything he had signed, from *Gli ultimi casi* onwards, bore this out. The only exceptions one must make were the Orders of the Day written for Durando, for these fell a long way short of his normal standards of integrity.

That he was an amateur in politics was not necessarily a disadvantage, nor the caricature in *Fischietto* harmful. A man to whom politics was not a career or source of livelihood might have more integrity than one financially dependent on his parliamentary career: the lawyer or banker turned politician was always more suspect than the man of independent means, even though slight. To be a Taparelli d'Azeglio carried the further advantage in that it linked him with Roberto, a constitutionalist since 1821, champion of Waldensians and Jews, organizer of elementary schools, hero of the cholera epidemic in Turin: such a family connexion helped him as surely as Cavour was handicapped by being the son of the holder of an unpopular office, brother of a reactionary, and member of a family that had grown rich by trade in, amongst other things, corn. All in all, Azeglio was by conventional standards a gentleman; this Rattazzi never would be considered to be, though he might move to the Right, co-operate with Cavour, be in the confidence of the King, and marry a descendant of the Bonapartes.

Finally, as all who ever made contact with him realized, Azeglio had charm, unmistakably if not definably. 'Maxime est né séduisant,' Manzoni said: and it was a spell that he could cast on people of all classes, popes, kings, or brigands, on almost any man, and on most women. But how far these personal qualities would make him a successful Prime Minister was now to be seen.

IX

TOWARDS A STABLE EQUILIBRIUM

THE tasks that faced a Sardinian Prime Minister in May 1849 were daunting. A peace treaty with Austria had to be made, and it was to be feared that it would be draconian. Some kind of *modus vivendi* with the other Italian rulers had to be evolved—most urgently with the Pope after his restoration by the French in July. Internally the reorganizing of the army and the stabilizing of the kingdom's finances were urgently necessary. Of all the problems, however, the one of greatest importance to the future of the state was the necessity of preserving the constitutional system.

In this task Azeglio's difficulties were not with the Parliament alone: on the other side of him stood the King, whose inexperience was obvious, but whose attitude to the constitution was still unknown. He may have been sincere in his quoted statement to the Nuncio that 'in his view the worst of all systems was the constitutional one' but, whatever his opinions, there were in his court powerful influences, lay and ecclesiastical, hostile to the constitution, and the womenfolk of his family were the most irreconcilable and at times the most persuasive. The abrogation of the Statute, as it was termed, would have been pleasing to Austria and to all the other Italian rulers, and in times of crisis— most menacingly with the Moncalieri Proclamation—it was made clear that if the realization of a policy that seemed to the King and to Azeglio to be the only feasible one were to be frustrated by Parliament, it would be Parliament and not the policy that would be sacrificed, regretfully by Azeglio but cheerfully by the King.

The Chamber as Azeglio found it had a majority far too radical in its views on home affairs and too intransigent in its attitude towards Austria to offer easy hopes of co-operation with the ministry. It was an assembly of individuals and not of organized political parties and was not likely to guarantee stability to any ministry whether of left or right. Azeglio's handling of it was at times casual and off-handed, at others obstinate and heavy-handed. But despite crises the constitution, though infringed in the letter and in the spirit, was preserved. To achieve this when King, ministers, and members of the Chamber and of the Senate were equally inexperienced was no small achievement. The task would become cumulatively easier as time brought familiarity with parliamentary procedure and the evolution of organized parties in the Chamber, and as ministers and King also gained in finesse. That the constitution was preserved was of importance far beyond the boundaries of Piedmont-Sardinia, for her moral leadership of the Italian people was to be based in part on her having risked military action against Austria in 1848 and 1849 and in part on her being the only Italian state to have saved a parliamentary system out of the wreckage of those years of violent flux and reflux. For all his mistakes in tactics Azeglio's strategy should gain him credit as contributor to Piedmont's political maturation.

On 11 May, four days after accepting office, Azeglio issued a second letter to his electors, sub-titled *Programme of Government*.[1] Much of it rehearsed what he had already written more than once: his aim would be to maintain the constitution: to keep alive the ideal of nationality: to prevent a restoration of aristocratic influence whilst controlling the demagogy of Young Italy, 'whose principles and action have been our ruin'. The army was to be reduced and reformed. For Italy the ideal was a union of princes amongst themselves, and of peoples with their princes in constitutional rule. Each state in Italy should be guaranteed against 'disloyal schemes of aggrandizement', an obvious attempt to reassure those who believed that Piedmont's aim was the absorption of her neighbours.

Nine-tenths of this was unexceptionable, even admirable, but as always Azeglio lost all sense of balance when considering Mazzini and Young Italy. His tone then became shrill, his expression almost hysterical. His accusations against Mazzini made in private were even more distasteful than his public attacks: in August 1849, for example, he sneered that Mazzini was safely back in London 'fresh as a rose': he had had the chance 'to smell powder, to wash away the charge of cowardice and had not taken it'.[2] Considering Mazzini's part in the defence of the Roman Republic, this was monstrous. Towards Garibaldi at this time Azeglio behaved more considerately. After his escape from Rome and from the Austrians, and bereaved of Anita, the hero

[1] *S.D.P.*, II, p. 165.   [2] Tommasoni, op. cit., p. 165.

had arrived on Piedmontese soil. Azeglio was determined to be
rid of his presence and appealed to him to leave the country,
offering him at the same time a pension: this the hero refused for
himself, but accepted for his mother: he agreed to go, and was
taken as far as Nice on a warship commanded by Azeglio's friend
Persano.

For Azeglio to continue to insist as he did that all who sat
further to the Left in the Chamber than he did were double-dyed
republicans, and to allege that they and their like bore sole
responsibility for the defeat of the Italian cause in the first war of
liberation, was the negation of political sagacity. The Left included
men of various shades and it would have been wiser policy for
Azeglio to split them, as Cavour later did, and bring the moderate
element round to his side. But this, though it was advised, he
refused even to consider. His tactics were to dissolve the Parliament and to hope for the election of a more sympathetic one. But
he had no real strategy, for he made no serious effort to swing the
election in his own favour, nor had he foreseen the need to
organize his supporters effectively even if they should find themselves in a majority. The dissolution and the election were delayed
by a serious illness of the King, so serious that on 21 May his
brother Ferdinand, Duke of Genoa, was appointed regent, an
office that he held until the King was able to resume the exercise
of his powers at the beginning of July. Then, on 3 July, a royal
proclamation[1] was issued, signed by the King and countersigned
as the constitution required by Azeglio, who had, of course, written
it. It is simply Azeglio's election manifesto graced by a royal
signature and its only real significance lies in its close anticipation
of the later and more celebrated 'Moncalieri Proclamation'. This
second version should not have surprised anyone who had read
the first, issued also from the royal castle of Moncalieri.

Europe, threatened in its social order, is compelled to choose between
this and liberty. The one and the other could exist not merely together
but aiding each other if in men just action and temperate thought
went together: but that is not, or is all too rarely, the case. Compelled
to choose between the two, neither peoples nor governments hesitate.
If we look around we see numerous examples. In several countries
we can see society, shaken to its foundations by the excesses of liberty,
turn in fear to whoever can save it even at the price of losing the
benefits of a true and honest liberty.

[1] *S.D.P.*, II, pp. 173–5.

The reference was unmistakably to France, where the attempt at a social revolution had been defeated; but to Sardinia the warning was clear enough. Faced with the choice between the maintenance of the existing social order or 'liberty', the Government would support the former and would feel confident of the approval of 'men of just action and temperate thought'.

If Azeglio had regarded this as a master-stroke of electioneering he was to be disillusioned by the result of the polls. Voting took place from 15 July and the new Parliament assembled to hear the speech from the throne on the 30th of that month. Until the Chamber met and began its deliberations and its voting its precise composition was not known. Even in England at that date the effect of an election was in doubt until the session of a new Parliament was under way. But it was fairly obvious that the election had not given Azeglio the kind of returns that he had hoped for. Turin returned supporters of the Government, in part owing to the intense activity of Roberto d'Azeglio, whose personal popularity was universal, and who received so much support from Waldensians and Jews as to excite unfavourable comment from extreme reactionaries. The British acting-Minister in Turin thought that the constitutionalists had a majority, but he was under the impression that the new House was composed largely of lawyers, professional men, and comparatively few landowners. On 23 July Azeglio admitted to Pantaleoni that the election had gone unfavourably. He feared that the conservative element had been too inactive, leaving the initiative to Young Italy. But he added that the Government felt itself 'strong enough to dissolve not one but ten Chambers because the people know that it is working to save the constitution and not for despotism'.[1]

A most open rebuff came to Azeglio immediately the Parliament assembled in the election of the President of the Chamber of Deputies. This was always the occasion for a trial of strength and a prudent ministry prepared the ground for it meticulously, choosing its candidate carefully and then lobbying in his favour. This Azeglio neglected to do (and he was to make exactly the same mistake on a later occasion). The Government's nominee was the Marchese Santi, formerly Sardinian Minister in London, but the Chamber elected Lorenzo Pareto by seventy-six votes to forty-two. This was unforgivable, an outright slap in the face for King, ministers, and conservatives *en masse*. For Pareto

[1] Pantaleoni, op. cit., p. 203.

L

was the representative of the Government in Genoa who had allowed himself to be nominal leader of the patriotic but misguided rising there that La Marmora had so clumsily mishandled and so violently suppressed. Azeglio, then still out of office, had approved La Marmora's action. For the Chamber to elect Pareto its Speaker was as good as a vote of no confidence in Azeglio and of censure on La Marmora. Pareto's office in effect was much more influential than the reference to him as 'Speaker' would imply, for as President of the Chamber he had great control over the agenda of the House as well as over its procedure. Whether the nominee of Government or of Opposition, the President was regarded as a potential next Prime Minister. So Pareto would have to go, even if that meant that the Chamber also would have to go. The ministry was having difficulty enough with the negotiation of a peace treaty with Austria that the Parliament would in due course have to ratify without being harassed by sniping from the rear and the threat that ratification might be refused if the present Chamber were still in existence. Another dissolution and another election were therefore inevitable.

A correspondence of some importance was going on at this time between Azeglio and Galeotti, who was editing in Florence *Lo Statuto*. Azeglio's letters to him went by way of the Sardinian Foreign Office and Minister in Florence so as to evade censorship: they had originated because Galeotti had asked Azeglio to supply him with material, not so much for the sake of straightforward information but for suggestions as to how to 'orchestrate' the news. Azeglio's letters were therefore intended for indirect publication without implicating him personally. To Galeotti he described Pareto as a man who, as a minister of the crown, had had a hand in the rising in Genoa: amnestied later, he had been honoured by the Chamber: in view of his oath, and of the speech from the throne, his election had been an insult to the King, but Azeglio aimed at keeping the Chamber and working with it if he could, though 'they are so imbecile that I gravely doubt this'. If necessary he would dissolve as soon as he was constitutionally free to do so. 'I have demagogues and reactionaries on my back but the constitution has got to be saved.'[1] To Minghetti he said much the same. 'The present Chamber is "bestiale" [stupid] rather than ill-natured. The King and his ministers stand firm and when all attempts at conciliation have failed they will fall back on Prussian

[1] Tommasoni, op. cit., p. 165.

methods. . . . One could not without sinning let Piedmont and Italy slip again into the hands of men like Rattazzi and Valerio.'[1] There is nothing new in all this, nothing divergent from Azeglio's basic ideas; what he was saying in his letters had already been said more conventionally through the mouth of the King. If the constitution was going to bring the extreme Left into power unavoidably, then it would have to go: but if possible the constitution must be kept.

The difficulty of working with the Chamber and the doubts about the maintenance of the constitution were not Azeglio's only worries between May and November. There was the business of Ramorino, for one thing. During the Novara campaign this general had been in command of the 'Lombard Division', mainly composed, as its name implies, of volunteers whose services had been accepted by the Sardinian army chiefs. During the planning of the campaign specific instructions had been given to Ramorino, and these he had most deliberately broken. His disobedience had left the way open for Radetzky to march unhindered against Charles Albert's main position, and his unexpectedly early arrival had been set down as the chief cause of the defeat. For his breach of orders Ramorino had been court-martialled on the orders of de Launay, then Prime Minister: he had been found guilty, and sentenced to death. Azeglio had not been responsible for the initiation of the trial but he was Prime Minister when sentence was pronounced. He could have intervened to save him, but this he implacably refused to do, and Ramorino was shot on 29 May. Of Ramorino's guilt there is no doubt, but the execution of a Ramorino or of an Admiral Byng leaves behind it a nasty suspicion that he has been made a scapegoat for the shortcomings not merely of the fighting forces or of their command but of the political organization behind them. In Ramorino's case one cannot help suspecting that the general's career before the Novara campaign had led to his being prejudged. In youth he had been a Mazzinian—a fact that of itself would have prejudiced Azeglio against him—and he had been the appointed leader of the Mazzinian invasion of Savoy from Switzerland in 1833. His conduct then was so dilatory and incompetent as not merely to cause the affair to end in fiasco but to raise the suspicion that he might have been a double agent deliberately sabotaging the rising he was supposedly leading. Then, to add to the dubiousness of his

[1] Minghetti, op. cit., Vol. II, p. 453.

reputation, his name had been much bandied about during the rising in Genoa, when it had been rumoured that he was to come to take over the defence of the city. His general record suggested, at best, mediocrity of gifts and it is not surprising that Charles Albert was supposed to have been reluctant to grant him command of a division in 1849. Plainly, he seems to have been a political general, doomed now not merely by his incompetence as a soldier but also by his having been associated with, if not promoted to mollify, the political Left. On both counts he would have been distrusted by Azeglio: but there was no need to shoot him: the exercise of clemency would not have done irreparable damage to the safety of the state or the reputation of King and minister. And perhaps one is misinterpreting the affair in discussing it in purely personal terms. It may be that this was another case of the cry 'Nous sommes trahis' being raised by a state that had undertaken a task too big for it, that had been injured in its pride by a defeat that it had not thought possible, and had struck out vindictively at some individual to preserve the general illusion.

The court-martial was followed by a general inquest into the state of the Sardinian army. This task was entrusted to a commission under Chrzanowsky, the Polish exile who had been commander in the Novara campaign. His reputation had not suffered in this defeat and it was, in the eyes of Azeglio if of no one else, to his credit that there was written evidence that he had warned Charles Albert and his ministers that the army was not prepared either materially or morally for the war it was being ordered to undertake. His commission drew up a scheme for army reform in which the first step was a drastic reduction of its size. By July it was planned to cut the army back from 105,000 to 85,000. It was announced that this had been achieved, but the British acting-Minister, Bingham, reported home that he believed the new figure was unrealistic, including, he thought, considerable numbers of men who were unfit for general duties, some even hospitalized, and many probably non-existent save as names on a payroll. He thought 60,000 would be nearer the mark. In October the number under arms underwent a second revision and was cut down to what was now to constitute its peacetime strength of 35,000, capable of expansion to 78,000 in time of war.[1] No

---

[1] Public Record Office, London, *Reports of Her Majesty's Ministers in Turin*, F.O. 67, Vol. 165.

increase of officers would be needed to place it on a war footing. After this drastic, or perhaps, rather, realistic, reduction came the real job of turning this small army into a fighting force to be taken seriously. This was entrusted to La Marmora, and the extent of his success is demonstrated by the excellent reputation earned by the Sardinian forces who less than six years after Novara took part in the Crimean War.

The stabilization of Sardinia's finances proved a more difficult task and until Cavour entered it the ministry had little success in this. The state had a debt of around 400,000,000 francs when Azeglio took up office, and the deficit for that year added another 23,000,000. Attempts were made to secure loans and in October James Rothschild was in Turin to negotiate a loan of 120,000,000 francs. Sardinia was not able, to the Government's chagrin, to borrow on terms as advantageous as Tuscany had just secured in borrowing from Aubert et Cie. of Paris. Despite the growing prosperity of Piedmont not even Cavour's skill was able to close the gap between revenue and expenditure and the debt consequently continued to rise. But as against this, Piedmont was being modernized commercially and economically, her transport system was becoming efficient, and railway links with France and Switzerland on the one side and with the rest of the peninsula on the other were to make her an important artery of trade.

These internal affairs, preoccupying as they were to the ministry, were less urgent and less frightening a responsibility than the making of peace with Austria and the clarifying of relations with the other Italian states. On this second matter Azeglio attempted little save negotiations with the Papacy. Gioberti before him had initiated some, sending first Rosmini unofficially, and then Martini officially, to Gaeta to attempt to regularize relations: so in May 1849 Azeglio sent Balbo to Gaeta, where the Pope had been joined by the exiled Grand Duke of Tuscany.[1]

The express and unconvincing reason for Balbo's mission was to announce the accession of Victor Emmanuel. His secret instructions were to use his influence to neutralize the actions of the powers seeking to persuade Pius IX to abolish the Statute of the Papal States: to urge the Pope to continue the secularization of his Government to such a point that it might collaborate with

[1] For Balbo's mission see Pirri, *Cart. priv.*, Book I, pp. 26*–32*, and ibid., Document 6, pp. 8–10.

other Italian governments in developing a Federation of Italian states, and finally to persuade the Pope to nominate Aporti as Archbishop of Genoa. All three of these aims were to prove vain, but of them all the last was the most futile.

Negotiations over this appointment had been in progress since June 1848 and Balbo's intercessions were of no avail. Aporti was a Giobertian and hence politically suspect: but to support his recommendation he had been so misguided as to send the Pope a manuscript copy of his most ambitious theological work, and this had damned him for ever. Apart from any doctrinal errors that it may have had, its Biblical quotations had been taken from a prohibited Italian Protestant version. The Pope made it politely but firmly clear to Balbo that no preferment would ever come Aporti's way, so Genoa was left vacant to be a cause of continual bickering between Turin and Rome. The future system of government of the Papal States had been decided upon before Balbo left Turin: on 27 April the plenipotentiaries of the Pope, Spain, Austria, and Naples had agreed that full personal powers should be restored to the Pope, who patiently explained to Balbo his conviction that events of 1848 and 1849 had demonstrated the unpreparedness of the Italian people for self-government. However, should the Pope ever consider the issue of a constitution he would consult all the powers—and not just the Roman Catholic ones.[1]

Balbo had failed with Pius IX: and this was not his only failure. It had been a further part of his mission to persuade the rulers of Tuscany and of Naples to accept liberal policies after their restorations; in addition it was hoped that Gioberti's plan for concerted action to overthrow the extremists in Tuscany and make a constitutionalist sovereign of the Grand Duke might be revived. Sardinia was not prepared for unilateral action, but if the Grand Duke and the King of Naples would agree, Piedmontese forces would enter Tuscany. An invitation to them to do so had come from the Commission of Government in Tuscany, but the Duke had committed himself to reliance on Austria's sole aid, and on 25 May, three days after Balbo's arrival in Gaeta, the Austrians entered Florence.

Complete as the failure of Balbo's errand obviously had been, Azeglio still held to some hopes of regaining initiative for Sardinia

[1] See N. Bianchi, *La politica di M. d'A.* (1883) (hereafter referred to as Bianchi, *Politica*), pp. 68–78, for Balbo's reports.

in Central Italy. In July he was writing to Galeotti to explain this; Azeglio had hoped, he said, for a 'general intervention in Rome that would have softened the irritation that this foreign multiple intervention awakens'. But Pius was especially hostile to Piedmont's participation. It was inevitable that Austria would now continue to control Tuscany, and Modena also, in order to give her access to Tuscany: but it was equally vital to Piedmont to see that Parma retained her independence, as she was Piedmont's link with Central Italy. This somewhat new-found concern for the independence of Parma did not prevent Pius from going on to say that it was Sardinia's hope that Parma would eventually come into union with her.[1] This idea continued to be entertained in Turin: on 31 October Bingham reported that there were rumours of a scheme to be put forward for the occupation of the Duchies as a whole—i.e. Tuscany, Modena, and Parma—by Austria and Sardinia jointly. When Bingham asked Azeglio if such a scheme had been mooted Azeglio denied it, but despite this Bingham was certain that a proposal had been made to Austria through the Sardinian Minister in Paris by way of his Austrian colleague there.[2] It is not impossible that Bingham's information was substantially correct but, if so, the failure of the scheme, harebrained as it was, could only be beneficial to Piedmont in the long run. To have appeared anywhere in Italy as Austria's co-adjutor could have done nothing but harm to her chances of gaining and keeping moral leadership in Italy.

Within twelve years of Novara, as we now know, the whole of Italy with the exception of the Patrimony of St. Peter and Venetia had come under the rule of the house of Savoy: in the case of the Two Sicilies this may have been no more than the result of the acceptance of a military *fait accompli*, but in the Duchies, the Papal States, and Lombardy the accession to Piedmont did seem to be the result of an act of will on the part of the peoples. Immediately after Novara there might have been some hope of seeing the aspiration of Italians crystallize round a country and a dynasty that had gambled everything on war against Austria, yet the impression with which one is left is of distrust of that kingdom, its rulers and its politicians. Here and there were partisans for Sardinia like Minghetti and Pantaleoni, and in

---

[1] M. de Rubris (ed.), *Carteggio politico di M. d'A. e L. Galeotti* (1928) (hereafter referred to as *Galeotti*), p. 37.

[2] P.R.O., London, F.O. 67, Vol. 165.

Tuscany there was to be Ricasoli, but in 1848 they were few and uninfluential. That the princes should be suspicious of the house of Savoy was natural enough. There was all too obviously a connexion between Sardinia's zeal for Italy and a keen eye to the main chance. The luke-warmness shown by the Piedmontese towards a scheme for a federation of rulers whilst there was hope of her gaining decisive victories in the field against Austria, and the subsequent mooting of similar schemes by Gioberti and, less openly, by Azeglio when the recourse to arms had failed and diplomacy was her only hope, seemed to justify these doubts about her disinterestedness. So the princes were more willing to draw an Austrian *cordon sanitaire* round Piedmont than to merge with her. Nor was there any sign of a softening of the attitude of hostility shown by the sectaries. Mazzini, Garibaldi, Guerrazzi, and Manin all had visions of the Italy they hoped to create: but it was not of a Piedmontized Italy: rather of an Italy including a Piedmont at last Italianized: an Italy that would be republican, and the house of Savoy, like the Italian Bourbons and Habsburgs, only a historical memory, and that not a happy one. The failure in 1848 and 1849 of the King and his army to achieve any degree of confidence or of effective co-operation with insurgents in Milan or in Venice was not a local or temporary difficulty but was due to a profound difference and one that seemed as though it might be permanent. The one gesture of appeal to the house of Savoy, the Sicilian offer of the crown to the Duke of Genoa, had been no more than a gambler's decision to place a last bet, in the form of an I.O.U. that would probably be dishonoured, on a rank outsider. A wholly new climate of opinion had to be created inside and outside Piedmont if the house of Savoy was ever to move from Turin to Rome. Cavour was to be main agent in creating this new confidence, but Azeglio made his contribution, and one of the chief ways in which he achieved this was in his making of peace with Austria. Negotiations had been in progress for two months, with no agreement in sight.

On the day after the battle of Novara the new King had met Radetzky to open negotiations for an armistice: its terms were given to him and of necessity were accepted the following day, 25 March. Though they were considered to be severe it would be difficult to argue that they were in any degree vindictive. Of the armistice after Custozza Azeglio had said that had Radetzky signed on any other terms he would have deserved to be shot; he might have said the same of this second armistice. Sardinian forces were to be withdrawn across the Po-Sesia-Ticino line and the Duchies were to be evacuated. The Sardinian fleet, that had been sent to help Manin in Venice, was to be recalled from the Adriatic. So far there was nothing that a defeated country could legitimately complain about. Alessandria was to be jointly garrisoned by Austrian and Sardinian troops, an uncomfortable but not an unendurable prospect. An indemnity to recoup Austria for the expense of her war of self-defence was to be paid, its amount subject to negotiation. It would have been the height of hypocrisy for Sardinia to protest against this in principle and clearly everything would depend on the amount fixed. Finally, the division of Lombard and Venetian volunteers attached to the Sardinian army was to be disbanded. Radetzky was not so obdurate as to ask that these men should be handed over to the Austrian authorities to be proceeded against as rebels. Yet this disbandment was to be the condition that was to prove most unacceptable to the Sardinian deputies when it came before the Chamber.

Having signed the terms and left Radetzky's headquarters with his head held defiantly high, Victor Emmanuel went to Turin and found himself face to face with an insultingly cold reception from the Chamber when he appeared before it on 29 March to take the statutory oath to maintain the constitution. His action in signing the armistice had already been challenged as a breach of the constitution, since by Article 67 of the Statute 'Laws and Acts of government have no force unless accorded the signature of a minister'. But in cold fact Article 5 is irrefutable. 'The King commands the armed forces by land and sea, declares war, makes treaties of peace, of alliance, and of trade, giving notice of them to the Chambers as soon as the interest and security of the state permit, and adding such communications as may be opportune.' The Chambers were not merely hostile, but clearly in the wrong constitutionally—as well as lacking in commonsense and courtesy. As they were so unpractically bellicose the only thing to do was to dissolve (30 March) and see the effect of a new election. This was not held until 15 July and it returned a new Chamber of Deputies as recalcitrant as the old one, and it was evident that the ministers, by then under Azeglio's presidency, were going to have the utmost difficulty in securing the ratification of any terms of peace whatsoever.

When the negotiations for the treaty opened, the Austrians made clear at the very start that the severity or leniency of the terms would be largely dependent on the type of government established in Sardinia. If the Piedmontese were willing to give up (the more diplomatic term used was 'modify') their form of constitutional government they might expect favourable conditions. No indemnity would then be demanded and Piedmont would be recognized as having reversionary rights over Parma. It has been assumed that it was right and proper, even inevitable, that Sardinia should refuse to treat on this condition: but her refusal was an act of amazing courage at the time. Even had the King been in favour of constitutional rule as a matter of principle, the way in which the system had worked—or failed to work—and the personal humiliations to which he had been subjected by the Chamber would have made his acceptance of this suggestion a natural act. His ministers might well have been equally disillusioned by representative government. In addition, to escape the payment of an indemnity whose amount could prove crushing, and to have the reversion of Parma, whose geographical position was so important to Piedmont, might have made Austria's offer irresistibly tempting. By refusing it against their own self-interests the King and his ministers chose to go the hard way, and that at a time when no one could have dreamt that their way might ever be anything other than a dead end. A sense of honour had not been lost on the fields of Custozza and Novara: Austria's interest in Sardinia's internal affairs was derogatory to Sardinian pride. So negotiations began on Austria's alternative proposals. Though understandably severe, these were not vindictive. An indemnity of 230,000,000 francs was demanded—about £9,000,000. The 'Lombard Committee' in Turin was to be dissolved. De Launay counter-proposed that Austria should give a general amnesty, renounce all claims to suzerainty over the Duchies, and recognize Sardinia's reversionary rights in Parma. Such a reply was little short of impudent. Could it be that its makers had forgotten who had won the recent war? Austria naturally refused to discuss these proposals, even to accept them as a basis for discussion. Why in sober reflection had Sardinia made such egregious suggestions? Quite plainly and simply because for Austria, if not for her, the war was by no means over. De Launay was playing for time, hoping that the still continuing risings in Venice and in Hungary might turn to Austria's grave disadvantage, hoping also, perhaps, for eventual diplomatic assistance from France and Britain. To bring Sardinia to a sense of reality the Austrians took over the entire garrisoning of Alessandria and broke off negotiations. And that was the precise situation when Azeglio came into office on 7 May.

That Austria was seriously embarrassed by the situation in Hungary and by the continued resistance of Venice is clear enough: equally certain is it that Britain and France were urging her to come to terms with Sardinia. It is difficult nevertheless to avoid the conclusion that on Austria's part there was a quite genuine wish for a peace treaty. Her plight was not dangerous, for the reduction of Venice could not be long delayed: with Russian help order could be restored in Hungary: the arguments of Britain and France, though sincerely urged, were not likely to be backed by any form of sanctions. If the worst came to the worst she could easily move aggressively against Sardinia with impunity and compel her to accept a dictated treaty. Instead she withdrew her troops from Alessandria and agreed to reduce her indemnity claim from 230,000,000 to 75,000,000 francs, and thus secured the reopening of negotiations. Azeglio analysed the situation in a letter of 14 June to Luisa.[1]

Austria has made proposals for the reopening of negotiations. England and France insist on a peace. I have always replied that we also wish it, but an honourable and not a ruinous one, admitting all the same that 'the loser pays'. Now the Austrian claims have been lowered by more than two-thirds and I believe negotiations can be reopened. If I can insert one word into the treaty, however small a one, to save the principle and gain something for the Lombards to show we do not abandon those who fought with us, I will sign. If it cannot be inserted someone else will have to sign.

To Gallina, Sardinian Minister in London, he wrote two days later: 'It is certainly not my intention in making a treaty to break it when it suits us: but if a great European conflagration should occur I intend that Piedmont should be free to choose such allies as will be most likely to save her integrity and the just influence that she ought to maintain in the peninsula.'[2] And to Boncompagni, Sardinian representative at the peace conference, he wrote: 'Austria can yield without loss of dignity, not being under duress. But sacrifice of her dignity is something that the ministry

[1] Carcano, op. cit., p. 401.   [2] Bianchi, *Politica*, p. 27.

knows Piedmont-Sardinia will not even hear discussed: for us the question of dignity is a question of life. . . . Any amnesty conditions must be public: Piedmont would be dishonoured were they not so, no matter how generous they might be.'[1] (This letter also contains a characteristic Azeglianism: 'It is essential not to tell lies, even in Treaties'.) A letter of the same date to Pantaleoni traverses the same ground but also develops a line of thought that was as typical of Azeglio as his quip to Boncompagni, and of far greater significance, an idea that became almost an obsession with him. The real problem, he says, was not the Austrians but the Italians. 'Even if the Austrians went away of their own accord we should not be a nation as a result of that. . . . We have to give thought to forming Italians if we wish to have an Italy.'

Negotiations now slowed down to a near-deadlock. The indemnity was the least important cause of this impasse, though on 18 July Azeglio wrote to da Bormida, who had joined the Sardinian delegation, to say that Piedmont could not pay more than 70 millions. As for the Duchies, he went on, Austria was determined to keep her control over them—and perhaps to extend it to Sardinia: maybe she could not be stopped, but 'we must resist to the utmost'. This letter was not uniformly gloomy. It contained one *bon mot:* 'Austria's propositions and counter-propositions remind me of the chef who asked the chicken, "What sauce do you wish to be eaten with?" . . ." But I do not wish to be eaten!" . . . "Ah, now you are tergiversating!" '

The decisively important point at issue was the question of an amnesty. Sardinia was insistent that it should be complete and explicit in its inclusion of all citizens of Lombardy-Venetia who had fought with the Sardinians. Further, he was determined that it should also be extended to citizens of the Duchies. His nephew adds a further explanation: his uncle was so determined to gain this amnesty that he sought information as to how France would act should Piedmont renew the war. Inevitably he received no satisfactory answer, the French Foreign Minister making the obvious answer that the question was hypothetical, since the situation was not one that seemed likely to arise, and that France was clearly bound to preserve her liberty of action.[2]

Before the end of July two things had become clear. The first was that at home the elections had not gone favourably enough for Azeglio and the moderates, with the result that the treaty

[1] Bianchi, *Politica*, p. 27.   [2] Ibid., p. 58.

would not have an easy passage—if indeed it passed at all— through the Chamber of Deputies: the second was that the final conditions of the treaty were taking shape and they were such as Azeglio was willing and determined to stand by.

I became a minister in order to save Piedmont and the constitution, and so to maintain at least this corner of Italy independent. . . . I will sign it since I know that the public good demands it, and it is one's duty to sacrifice even one's name for that. But I will not take the 50,000 francs [that would by rule come to him on signature of the treaty] for myself, but will found an infants' school with them. I have no wish to gain money from the misfortunes of my country or to seem to have sold my signature. . . . Tomorrow the Chamber will open: to me it appears rather red [*rossa*]. If it will not see reason we will send it home again.[1]

The King's speech at the opening of the first session of the new Parliament informed its members that the negotiations with Austria were about to be concluded.[2] They would be communicated to Parliament, which would then 'deliberate on that part that the constitution calls them to examine'. It was not likely that Parliament would be interested in any business other than the treaty for quite some time to come, but the speech indicated a large number of topics for consideration, as though the ministry expected the Chamber to enjoy a long and fructuous life. The public finances called for thorough examination, whilst public works were so necessary that the need for economy must not be allowed to prevent their being undertaken. In particular it was essential to push ahead with the railway network already begun. Urgent measures were needed for the physical and moral welfare of 'the most numerous and least well-endowed class of the people'. All in all the speech has a familiar ring. The state of the country's economy is such that the most rigid economy is essential. But the welfare of the people demands a great increase in public expenditure at the same time. To reconcile these irreconcilables is the most elementary task of any statesman.

On 6 August the terms of peace were signed in Milan by Boncompagni and da Bormida on behalf of Sardinia and de Bruck for Austria. The indemnity had been fixed at 70 millions as against the original 230 millions and the later reduction to 73: but to offset the final reduction Sardinia had to agree to pay

---

[1] Carcano, op. cit., p. 407.   [2] *S.D.P.*, II, pp. 179–81.

within two years: earlier she had been given three. The amnesty dispute had been settled on terms far more favourable than might have been expected. Austria had agreed to a general amnesty, but with exceptions whose number eventually sank to eighty-five. It had been thought that the list might be around a hundred. There were some well-known names amongst those excepted, including two of the famous Borromeo family. Even at this reduced number the list is misleading in that practically all those excepted were outside Austrian jurisdiction. As Azeglio had said, the amnesty was a point of honour to Sardinia: it had to be written into the treaty as a condition of peace and not come as an independent gesture from Austria: and to satisfy Sardinia's punctiliousness the amnesty was published in advance of the signing of the treaty. There was no mention in the treaty of the King's reversionary rights to Parma, but those to Piacenza were recognized. Otherwise the terms of the treaty were exactly what those of the armistice had foreshadowed. Bingham, reporting to his Government, summed up his opinions: 'Forbearance so remarkable on the part of Austria can only be accounted for by a desire to conclude matters as speedily as possible. The check which Austria has just met with at Raab may not have been without its influence in the matter.' It may well be so: but had Austria been both in a hurry and in a vindictive mood she might have cut the negotiations much shorter and compelled Sardinia to sign under threat of duress.

Now the ministry had to pilot the treaty past the Chamber: the election of Pareto as its President had made clear that it was not going to be used as a rubber stamp and Chamber and ministry were soon petrified in a deadlock. Had the Chamber congratulated and thanked the negotiators who had gained such terms from Austria it would not have seemed obsequiousness: in fact it was more in the mood to impeach them. Cesare Balbo, as a compromise, proposed that the Chamber ratify the treaty without discussion in silent protest against the terms imposed by Austria (not, presumably, in protest against the signing of these terms). This plan was not accepted by a House that seemed determined to fight Azeglio all along the line. On some points he was willing to yield to it: in October he remodelled his ministry and left out Pinelli, who was particularly unpopular. He brought in Paleocapa, whose appointment was regarded by Bingham as a sop to the Left, to balance the appointment of La Marmora as Minister of

War. Bingham was already suggesting that Azeglio lacked 'that energy required to carry out efficiently the affairs of the country at this difficult crisis. . . . I may add that the Government as at present constituted does not possess the confidence of the country.'[1] This charge of lack of energy was to be heard often during Azeglio's period of office. Bingham approved the appointment of La Marmora, who ever since his suppression of the Genoa rising had had the reputation of resolution: but it was not a reputation that would endear him to the Left.

Besides remodelling his ministry Azeglio did make a further concession to the Chamber by the frankness with which he placed before it the documentary records of the negotiations that had led to the signature of the treaty. But the Chamber was not to be hurried. It discussed all manner of business, interrupting its deliberations on the treaty and finally deciding not to ratify it until the ministry agreed to give Sardinian nationality to all refugees who had entered from other parts of Italy and who desired it. This may not seem a condition so impossible as to justify a head-on collision between ministry and deputies, but Azeglio chose this as the occasion for a decisive trial of strength. His objection was presumably to the persons of many of the refugees, who naturally tended to be drawn from amongst the most hot-headed elements of the population of their native states. Amongst them there was, for instance, Sterbini, who had played so considerable a part in the revolutionary movement in Rome, and who was widely believed to be at least morally responsible for the murder of Pellegrino Rossi. So far Azeglio had let him stay in Piedmont on condition that he refrained from any political activity—not an exorbitant request to make, one might think, of a fugitive from his own state's Government. Sterbini had given, and had immediately begun to break, this undertaking. The irony of Azeglio's opposition to the granting of nationality to these people lay in the fact that after he had won the next election he himself piloted this very measure on to the statute book. As yet the motion supporting it, though passed by the Chamber, was defeated by the Senate, and so to the deadlock between ministry and Chamber was added a further one between the two Houses, though since the Senate, as a nominated House, would normally support the Government in power this was not a very significant

[1] Dispatch of 5 November, F.O. 67, Vol. 165. (Bingham soon afterwards handed over to the returning British Minister at Turin, Abercromby.)

complication. Tact or cleverness on Azeglio's part might now have split the opposition, for some of the more moderate members to his left in the Chamber made overtures to him, offering their support if he would give an explicit undertaking to preserve the Statute. But Azeglio was by now determined to fight it out. Parliament was prorogued and then on 20 November dissolved by royal decree issued from the royal castle of Moncalieri.[1] The decree was the work of Azeglio, as was constitutionally right and proper: but it was criticized then, and has been since, for its tone was needlessly provocative in expression. Its content was the more serious cause of objection. For in this proclamation the King was made to appear to be electioneering on behalf of his ministry. The following passages from it are the most significant ones.

Before the summoning of this Parliament I addressed frank words to the nation and in particular to the electors. In my proclamation of 3 July 1849 I urged them to keep to such methods as would not render the constitution impossible. But only one-third, or a little more, of them took part in the elections. The remainder neglected that right which is also a strict duty of each one in a free state. I had performed my duty: why did they not perform theirs? In the speech from the throne I made known, though it was scarcely necessary, the sad condition of the state. I showed the need for making a truce to all party passion, for promptly deciding vital questions that held public business in a state of uncertainty. My words were inspired by a profound love of my country and pure honesty. What fruit had they? The first acts of the Chamber were hostile to the crown . . . I say nothing of the unreasonable war waged by the opposition against *the policy that my ministers were loyally following and that was the only one possible.* . . . I signed a treaty with Austria, honourable and not ruinous. So the welfare of the state required. The honour of the country, the sacredness of my oath demanded that it should be faithfully executed without duplicity or cavilling. My ministers asked for its acceptance by the Chambers, which, adding a condition for this, stultified its acceptance, destroyed the reciprocal independence of the three powers, and so violated the constitution of the realm. . . . I have sworn to maintain justice and the enjoyment by every man of his rights. I have promised to save the nation from the tyranny of parties whatever be the name, aim, and rank of those who compose them. These promises, these oaths I fulfil, dissolving a Chamber that has become impossible, calling another immediately: but if the country, if its electors deny me their

[1] *S.D.P.*, II, pp. 195, 196.

co-operation, not upon me will fall the responsibility for the future: and in any disorders that may arise they will not have to complain of me, but of themselves.

The evident theme of the proclamation was that there was absolute identity of views between King and ministry, and consequently opposition to the ministry was opposition to the King. This was even clearer in the wording of the first draft of the proclamation and the circumstances in which that wording was changed are of interest. The proclamation originally read: 'I say nothing of the unreasonable war waged by the opposition on the policy that was mine and that was the only one possible.' When the draft reached Cavour's newspaper *Risorgimento* the editorial staff were reluctant to pass for the press a sentence that to them seemed contrary to the constitution in its implications, and they decided that it might not be printed until Azeglio had been consulted. He, however, was not easily found—not that that is altogether surprising. Only at midnight were they able to trace him. He admitted that he had not appreciated the full significance of the sentence and he accepted an amendment proposed by Castelli of the *Risorgimento*. So the statement appeared as 'a policy that my ministers were loyally following, and that was the only one possible'.[1]

The proclamation gave rise then, and has given rise later to much discussion. Was it altogether constitutional? But, apart from this, was it expedient? The latter point has been less thought about. Clearly the King and the ministry were gambling on winning the next election. The scarcely-veiled threats would then not need to be put into execution. But suppose the Left had won again? Presumably Victor Emmanuel would have to eat his words, dismiss Azeglio, but keep the constitution by calling Rattazzi or some other of his party into office. A stubborn conflict of wills might then follow, whose results would be unforeseeable. Alternatively he might act as he threatened, dissolve the Chamber once again, and, abandoning or emasculating the Statute, become virtually absolute. Whichever of these two alternatives he adopted in case of a radical victory a major political crisis was certain. So everything did depend on the moderates winning the election, and, it was to be hoped, successive elections until any controversy over the proclamation should have died down. The

[1] *S.D.P.*, II, p. 194, note by de Rubris.

M

gamble in the event came off but Azeglio had risked more than his own future on it.

Whether or not it was expedient, was it lawful? There were many even amongst the uncommitted who thought it had gone too far. Bingham approved it in general and sent a copy to Palmerston, who, he believed, would also approve: but he admitted that he did not altogether like the undertones of menace. Bolton King[1] expresses what on the whole is the accepted view.

The language in which it vehemently attacked the majority and threatened stronger measures unless a compliant chamber was returned was a breach, if not of the letter at least of the spirit of the Statute. . . . It was felt that not only did the Proclamation of Moncalieri weaken the chances of parliamentary rule in the other states, but that by bringing down the king into the field of party conflict, it made the future more difficult in Piedmont itself. Still, ill-judged as it was, the Proclamation deserved little of the extravagant praise and blame that were given to it. If it was a coup d'état it was one of a mildness worthy of its author, and the constitutional march of Piedmont went on almost unaffected by it.

Such condemnation is so mild that to cavil at it may seem trivial: it amounts to saying that the constitution was bent, but that the bending, though noticeable, prevented its breaking completely. But in all this discussion there is the latent danger of seeing constitutional monarchy through British, if not also twentieth-century, eyes. It is not really easy to see how the letter of the Statute had been broken. It must be remembered that at this time the constitution was not three years old: it had not aged enough to have been modified by unwritten conventions: it was still taken to mean what it said. And it said that 'The King appoints and dismisses his ministers' (Art. 65); 'To the King alone belongs the executive power' (Art. 5); . . . 'The King appoints to all offices of state and makes the decrees and regulations necessary for the execution of the laws, without suspending or dispensing their observance' (Art. 6). Though this was not laid down in the Statute the King might, and in fact very regularly did, preside over the meetings of the cabinet. Quite explicitly the Statute seems to be making clear that the King governs as well as reigns. To expect otherwise in a state like Piedmont with its long traditions of personal loyalty to the crown and of heroic royal leadership in crisis and in war would have been utopian. The

[1] King, op. cit., Vol. I, p. 359.

whole history of the state and of its dynasty was on the side of the proclamation. If it was not 'un-Piedmontese', was it somehow un-British'? Not, surely, so very much so by the standards of its day. The only great power that set Sardinia an example of limited monarchy was Britain. Admittedly the sovereign there did not descend into the electoral arena as publicly as Victor Emmanuel had now done: yet every British statesman of the century would have known how real none the less was the influence of the crown in British affairs. To expect of the King of Sardinia in 1849 an impartiality that had not then been accepted by the British monarch was a little unreasonable. If then the Statute had been infringed in letter or in spirit the valid comment might be that that showed that it was a little too doctrinaire for its day and generation. But, legality apart, the question of the expediency of Azeglio's use of the crown on this occasion remains, and on this one may be less inclined to acquit him.

What has not come in for the same amount of criticism but much more thoroughly deserves it by purist standards was the conduct of the next election, although here too a due measure of historical perspective must be kept. If this election was managed in such a way as to cause a student of twentieth-century British elections to raise a shocked eyebrow, it was not so heinous when compared with a mid-nineteenth-century election, with its narrow franchise, public hustings, and open voting. Nothing so odd in Sardinia that could not have been outdone in Ireland of that date—or later: or in Andrew Jackson's America if it comes to that.

As the King, or Azeglio in his name, had pointed out, only about a third of the electors had voted in July. Now every effort was to be made to get as many as possible to the polls in the hope that this would lead to the defeat of the 'Democrats'. The rural element was to be whipped in to out-balance the more radical town voters, though Turin itself from Azeglio's point of view was airly reliable—much more so than her erring sister Genoa. Aristocracy and squirearchy were to take an active part, not only by voting themselves but by marching their dependents to the polls. Costanza d'Azeglio had no doubts as to their competence to exercise this duty. She described them in November 1849 as not being absentees but accessible to their tenants: active in stimulating education and even teaching in schools despite opposition 'from the Jesuits and from the lawless elements'.[1] The picture is

[1] *Souv. hist.*, p. 376.

too roseate, as though all of them were Azeglios, with not a Squire Western to be seen: but enlightened or not they did their duty. Massimo was as satisfied as his sister-in-law. 'The die-hards have bestirred themselves this time and have gone hither and thither to their colleges [their electoral districts].' Others too besides the landed gentry had had their hints. All state employees had been instructed not only to vote, but whom to vote for. 'To the officials we have put it clearly, and to some we have enforced it most clearly—we have dismissed them. Each day in the Council [of ministers] I demand someone's head. In my ministry, where I command, I have dismissed three in one day.'[1] The spoils system can be a powerful incentive to orthodox political thinking, if those who make the ministry can make the election. Roberto corroborated much of what Massimo had said when he wrote to his son, and incidentally implied that in all there had been some 87,000 electors at the polls. After all these somewhat unsubtle manœuvres the result of the election was most gratifying. On 18 January 1850 Azeglio was able to write: 'The Piedmontese people has genuinely shown that "genius is but commonsense": and I would not have thought it had this genius so widely shared. The King is the first to give proof of it. It is impossible to have more honest good sense than he, and it is a great joy to us to work together. On New Year's Day he sent me his portrait.'[2] The gift was especially touching to Azeglio, for this portrait had been intended for the King's father.

This was a time when political relations between Azeglio and the King were idyllic. Despite the obvious contrasts between the rough-spoken, rough-mannered, philistine King and his polished, artistic minister they had much in common. Both were womanizers, the King in a more brutally direct way, and both could enjoy a salty conversation in their native Piedmontese: both had a reputation for frankness—the quality that was summed up in the term 'Re Galantuomo', applied whether justly or not to the King. And both were intolerably bored by routine business. As early as May 1849 an observer had commented: 'Here everything moves with a measure of somnolence. The King is bored by being King, the new President of his Council by being its President.' Azeglio, in October, could say: 'The King is good and true, firm as a tower, fearing nothing, not even the devil himself.' Or 'The King is frank and honourable and has as much taste for being

---

[1] Carcano, op. cit., p. 423.   [2] Ibid., p. 425.

King as I have for being a minister, having in fact not a trace of despotism in his blood; so as long as things keep going he is content with his position and seeks no other.' Later Azeglio's attitude was to change and towards the end of his life he would refer to the King as 'Uncle Victor' (barba Vittorio), or 'the Boss', or even 'Rosina's friend',[1] an allusion to Victor Emmanuel's second, morganatic wife Rosina, a woman of very humble origins, ennobled as Countess Mirafiori.

Azeglio's distaste for regular work was no secret and he felt called upon to defend himself against that charge. 'They [the opposition] say that La Marmora steers the boat and that I leave it to him; but for one thing I know him to be a gentleman, and for another, I read all the dispatches. From morning to night I am at the shop and often write confidentially to the ambassadors.'[2] Not all were convinced of Azeglio's unremitting industry, even within his own family, and the King on at least one occasion felt it necessary to reproach him as gently as might be. 'Tell me, my dear friend, if you do not think that your presence and the help of your potent oratory may not be necessary in the Chamber these days?' It was probably true that La Marmora was as influential inside the cabinet as he was active there and outside it. But the most dominant personality in the Chamber, Cavour, was still a free-lance supporter. In December 1849 Siccardi became a minister, and was recognized to be Cavour's Trojan horse in the cabinet. The entry of Cavour himself would be the logical next step.

[1] E.g. in a letter of 24 March to Emanuele d'Azeglio. Original in O.P.T.
[2] Carcano, op. cit., p. 241.

X

CHURCH AND STATE

THE new Chamber to which Victor Emmanuel read his speech from the throne on 20 December 1849 was much stronger in deputies of the centre than the previous one, thanks in part to the Moncalieri Proclamation and in part to the careful management of the election. On the extreme right sat a group of some seventeen who included Gustavo Benso di Cavour, brother of Camillo. Most of them came from Savoy and tended to use French in debates, as specially permitted by Article 62 of the Statute, in preference to Italian. They were unquestioning in their acceptance of the guidance of the Church, hostile to anything that savoured of liberalism whether in Church or State, and further united by so strong a feeling of being Savoyard and not Italian as to permit one of them at least to declare in the Chamber' that they would seek union with France should Italy be extended to the Alps: ten years later they were to accept just such a union. On the extreme left were about twenty who took their lead from Valerio and Brofferio, with whom Azeglio could never consider allying, though on occasion they supported some aspects of his policy, especially in regard to the Church.

The rest of the 204 members formed loose groups. To the right of centre were those who accepted the lead of the moderate conservatives (who might tend to speak of themselves as 'liberal') like Azeglio and Balbo: slightly further to the right in their views were Pinelli and Revel, who was so extreme as to be barely distinguishable from Gustavo di Cavour, but was, like him, genuinely Piedmontese and not a hypothetical secessionist. The left-centre was led by Rattazzi, cold, unimaginative, Piedmontese of the Piedmontese, with little sympathy for and little knowledge of the rest of Italy. His career was typical enough in its slow migration from left to right in politics. He had ceased to be the Rattazzi of the period of Novara, though Azeglio could never bring himself to realize this, and he was to become a dextrous, almost obsequious courtier later, high in the confidences of the King. Azeglio's hatred of him was now due less to fundamental difference of political opinion than to a clash of personalities. By the time of the 'Connubio' Rattazzi had come alongside Cavour in policy, and had Azeglio wished he could have forestalled this alliance by attaching Rattazzi to himself. However, in his view Rattazzi was very definitely not a gentleman and that was that.

The King's speech was in Azeglio's vaguest strain of well-intentioned generalizations. It gave no precise information at all about the programme for the session: that was cleared off in one casual paragraph. 'It is not opportune to indicate the questions whose urgency demands an immediate solution. They are well enough known. It only remains to me to recommend them to your prudence and prompt judgement.' The more significant part of the speech was an expression of gratitude for the attention paid to the Moncalieri Proclamation. 'There arises in my heart a new and stronger faith in the future of our country and of our institutions. The electors heard my voice. They took part in great numbers in the election. I am happy on this occasion to express my gratitude to them. The consideration they have devoted to public affairs I consider to have been paid to myself. I hold it therefore the more dearly, anxious as I am for the public welfare rather than for my own.'[1] By this tribute Azeglio showed clearly not only that he believed that the Moncalieri Proclamation had been successful, but that he still believed that it had been justifiable.

The most urgent need was the ratifying of the peace with Austria. Debates over this had threatened to become endless, or even to end with an outright rejection. Now Azeglio was confident that it would be passed; and determined that it should be passed quickly. To ensure this he changed his tactics and introduced the treaty in the form of a project for a law. The significance of this astute move lay in the fact that in this form debate on it could be controlled by the customary rules of parliamentary procedure: for a treaty under discussion far more extreme latitude could be claimed. The argument in the Chamber was heated enough at times, and there were still radicals to be found to stigmatize the treaty as dishonourable—an accusation that stung Azeglio to make his only recorded contribution to the debate, for on no point would he rise more readily than to defend his honour or that of the state. The speech is not a very significant one: it could not have taken more than about three minutes of the Chamber's time, and it is a rather empty piece of rhetoric into the bargain.

[1] *S.D.P.*, II, pp. 199–200.

'Piedmont is an ancient home of honour, an ancient warrior country, and had we made a dishonourable treaty the Piedmontese, for their betrayed national honour, would have stoned us, and not sent their elected representatives to give us their staunch support . . . a dishonourable treaty would never have the signature of Massimo d'Azeglio.'[1] On the day of this intervention by Azeglio, 9 January 1850, the Chamber passed the treaty-law by 112 votes to 17, figures that indicate some seventy absentees or abstentions. On the 18th of the same month it was approved by the Senate and at last the legislature could concentrate on other business. The next big question was to be the relations between Church and State. That this would cause acrimonious disputes was certain, but not alarming to Azeglio, who had something of a reputation of being a 'priest-eater'.

Fortuitous circumstances had led him to order his thoughts about the Papacy and, incidentally, central Italy. He had been asked to write a memorandum for Palmerston to inform him of his views, and about the same time he sent a letter to de Tocqueville discussing the character of Pius IX. His memorandum on the state of affairs in central Italy was forwarded by Abercromby on 2 January. In this, as in his letters to Rendu, Azeglio was very anxious to make a good impression abroad, for Rendu had access to the circle immediately surrounding Prince Louis Napoleon: and direct access to Palmerston was even more important. Azeglio argued that there were three possible prospects for the Papal States: foreign occupation for an indefinite period in order to maintain the unpopular government of the Pope's advisers: or partition of the States: or a change in their form of government. The prolongation of clerical despotism backed by foreign troops might provoke red revolutionary uprisings and the only insurance against this would be the granting of constitutional government. Such reform would be in the interests of Britain and France, for it would swing the Italian states into the orbit of the western powers. As it was, central Italy was part of a bloc extending from the Baltic to Ancona. Abercromby approved the views of the memorandum and his covering letter expressed his regard for Azeglio's personality and policy, a regard that was to cool somewhat before he left Turin. A fortnight later he received, and similarly forwarded to Palmerston, a memorandum that he had requested at the end of 1848 on specifically Roman affairs. Azeglio had been

[1] *S.D.P.*, II, p. 201.

asked to write it but had deputed the task to Pantaleoni. Abercromby did not name the author but summarized his career for Palmerston. This document also found favour with Abercromby: Azeglio was most enthusiastic about it. 'I have received the magnificent work on Italian and Roman affairs that is now at the Foreign Office. . . . The west of Europe has no plan like the east's, and the characteristic of our epoch is lack of foresight. . . .'[1]

Azeglio's letter to de Tocqueville about Pius IX contains some balanced judgements that even a century later seem acute and just. 'Pius IX has an instinct for what is good but not for what is true or generous. . . . His mind has no profound convictions except on religious matters, no stable plans. Pius IX was the "Amnesty", all the rest was the result of passing influences. . . . Attacked on his weak side he had not the firmness that a high intelligence gives to let him distinguish sophisms from truth.'[2]

On 27 January, with the treaty no longer on his mind, Azeglio gave one of his very rare official receptions. Costanza acted as hostess, 'upholding the family dignity in the family diamonds'; fourteen or fifteen rooms were in use, one of them given up to a display of Azeglio's collection of caricatures of himself. Refreshments were abundant, with cards for the elderly and dancing for the young. There was a short musical recital during the evening, which ended with such guests as were still there coaxing Azeglio to the piano-stool, where he sang to his own accompaniment. One feels sure that his performance pleased them: and in retrospect it amused him to wonder how many of his contemporary Prime Ministers in Europe could have rounded off an official reception in the same way.

But, however amusing, that was only an interlude. The ministry now turned its attentions to the relations between State and Church. In other Catholic states of Europe the Church had for three-quarters of a century been fighting a rearguard action against secularization. The reformist activities of the Emperor Joseph II had led to the limitation of the Church's privileges in the Holy Roman Empire and to the expulsion (not eventually to *Austrian* prove permanent) of the Jesuits. In France there had been the persecutions of the Revolutionary era and then a Concordat between Papacy and Empire that had brought comfort to neither. The Restoration of 1814-15 had brought back the Pope and old dynasties to their capitals but could not universally set back the

---

[1] Pantaleoni, op. cit., p. 253.   [2] Bianchi, *Politica*, p. 201.

clock so far as to restore all the privileges the Church had enjoyed before the Enlightenment.

Piedmont-Sardinia was one state in which the powers of the Church still survived in ways that had come to seem not merely unenlightened but even ludicrous. Under Charles Albert some gains had been made at its expense. The Waldensians and Jews had gained the right of worship and civil rights: a system for school-teachers to be trained by the State had been initiated despite frantic opposition from Fransoni, the Archbishop of Turin. The gains were slight compared with the powers still retained by the Church. Alongside state control of the Press there was still a religious censorship and the Church could hinder the circulation of the Bible in the vernacular and prevent the dissemination of theological and devotional works of which it disapproved. The University of Turin was completely under its control, as were most of such schools as there were for elementary education. Of secondary education it had a virtual monopoly, most of it being conducted by members of religious orders. The church law-courts not only still existed but were active and powerful. In Piedmont the controversy between England's Henry II and Becket was still to come, for the courts of the Church had sole control over all matrimonial cases, and all matters concerning tithes, heresy, and blasphemy came before them, so that in all these cases prosecution and judge were in effect the same person. Clerics accused of indictable offences came before the church courts, and it was notorious that the penalties imposed by these courts were much lighter where a priest was concerned than would have been pronounced by a state court against a layman for the same offence. There was no form of civil marriage in Piedmont, and in conse-quence no possibility of civil divorce. Saints' Days were numerous and were strictly observed as enforced holidays as well as holy days. It was even the case that some churches still possessed at this date the right of asylum, and criminals who had taken refuge there were inviolate. What Azeglio had observed in the Castelli Romani thirty years earlier was still practised in his own supposedly more advanced country.

In all these ways it could be argued that the Church had an influence that was deleterious to liberty of thought and to effici-ency and equity in the administration of law: whilst the holy days, trivial as this grievance might seem, militated against the eco-nomic progress of the State. The survival of so many ecclesiastical privileges in Piedmont at that time must have seemed extraordinary not only to a foreign Protestant but to a Roman Catholic from any of the greater European states. But that was not all. Besides these cultural rights and juridical privileges the Church enjoyed the control of great and ever increasing wealth. Piedmont-Sardinia had never had its Statute of Mortmain and as a result the Church had accumulated great landed possessions that were still increasing from the bequests of the faithful. Such lands were not subject to all the fiscal obligations of estates in lay ownership: so the State suffered in its revenues, whilst at the same time the vast army of ecclesiastics, secular and regular, were outside the productive labour force of the country. It was not the case that the churchmen were all equally privileged. In this kingdom as elsewhere the parish priests, though they might be woefully under-educated, were as woefully under-rewarded: they were cut off for the most part by an unbridgeable gulf between themselves and the far more highly endowed higher clergy. Nor can it be argued that the Church was totally obscurantist. There were in Piedmont, as in Lombardy-Venetia, ecclesiastics as well as laymen who were regarded as near-heretical or Jansenist in their views, and, as has been noted, Cesare d'Azeglio had founded his 'Gli Amici d'Italia' to combat such tendencies. There were also priests carrying on magnificent works to help the physically, mentally, and economically afflicted, the most notable being Canon Cottolengo with his Ricovero in Turin, then and to this day one of the most remarkable institutions anywhere in its willingness to accept all who need its help, and in its reliance on charity, for its founder forbade it ever to accumulate property or investments. Cottolengo himself was a victim of the typhus outbreak in Turin in 1842. The existence of such individuals could still not justify an ecclesiastical system of privilege inside the Church and between Church and State. If Piedmont was to develop a reasonably good educational system at all levels, an atmosphere of intellectual activity, a judicial system that was not only equitable but manifestly so, a soundly-based fiscal system, and economic development such as her hard-working population was capable of giving her, the immemorial privileges and powers of the Church had to be modified. If this could be done by agreement with the Church so much the better. But there were many, now in positions of political influence, who were determined that with or without the Church's consent these barriers to progress must go down.

By such arguments the introduction of what came to be known as the 'Siccardi Laws' might be defended; but these arguments were not the whole story. If the Piedmontese Government were to restrict drastically the influence of the Church, and especially if the intransigence of the Church compelled it to do this by unilateral action, it would emphasize the importance of the gulf between the policy of that state and the reactionary policies of the other Italian governments. It would be an act of defiance not only of the Papacy but of those states that were the Papacy's temporal protectors. It would be regarded as a guarantee of the constitution, for a government that had gone to this length against the Church could never slip back into despotism. Conversely, the refusal of the Pope to grant any concessions to Sardinia could only be judged as an attempt to discredit her constitutional system. Much of what her Government was asking had been conceded explicitly or had not been opposed explicitly in the case of Austria, France, Bavaria, and Belgium. But by 1850 the Pope had committed himself so finally to political reaction that he could not permit himself to make concessions to a representative form of government in Piedmont. In this way Gioberti saw it at the time: Rome's opposition to the Siccardi Laws was motivated mainly by 'the intention to weaken the constitution, to render this province odious to the reactionary governments, to offer Austria a hypocritical pretext for meddling, inflaming discord and civil strife. So displeasing is it to Rome that in one corner of Italy a spark of liberty should survive and shine forth.'[1]

As soon as Sardinia was granted the Statute the question whether this was reconcilable with the privileges of the Church was bound to arise. The only solution seemed to be to negotiate a new Concordat and Rosmini, sent by Charles Albert to the Holy See in 1848, had discussed this amongst other matters. Pius IX had not at that time seemed unsympathetic but Rosmini had no official status and could only seek and give information. Then the onrush of events of the revolutionary period caused these secondary questions to be left aside. Balbo's mission had been mainly concerned with the attempt to persuade the Pope to maintain some form of representative government and to appoint Aporti to the Archdiocese of Genoa, and in both these aims he had failed. The wider questions were now to be asked, and the King himself was one of the first to ask them. In his first interview with

[1] Quoted by Jemolo, op. cit., p. 203, from Gioberti's *Rinnovamento*.

the Papal Nunzio to his court he had said 'the times were very critical, and in his kingdom there were many evil priests who had done great harm'. The allegation was not without substance. On the one hand there were ecclesiastics like Fransoni, Archbishop of Turin, whose only offence was political, a flat refusal to come to terms with the new constitutional tendencies, and who were using the pulpit as 'the safe and sacred organ', if not of sedition, of reaction. But there were more extraordinary cases. There was appalling controversy over Monsignor Artico, Bishop of Asti.

This prelate had been accused by one of his clergy of criminal sexual perversions. One inquiry had cleared him of the charge and Charles Albert had done what he could to re-establish his reputation by inviting him to pay a visit to him at one of the royal castles. But mud was still being thrown, and as always some of it was sticking. Even if he was totally innocent it was thought that his usefulness at Asti was at an end. Victor Emmanuel, who privately doubted the bishop's innocence, and who had all a natural sinner's horror of unnatural sin, was anxious to see him transferred to some other appointment. Of the actuality of some other very odd happenings in this very same diocese there could be no possible doubt. The King himself was aware of what he termed 'the wicked and mad heresy of Viarigi' and when in September 1849 Siccardi went to Rome on the Government's behalf, the King in his letter of recommendation explained that his messenger would give His Holiness details. An unfrocked priest had arrived in Viarigi and had begun to preach there despite an episcopal ban. His sermons attracted a growing following, which included some priests of the neighbourhood, and their content grew steadily wilder until he proclaimed himself the Messiah come to earth again. He prophesied his own crucifixion, to take place in the parish from which he had been expelled. Pius IX would be assassinated, Rome destroyed, the Holy See transferred to the parish of his martyrdom, and his former curate elected Pope. Great numbers were converted to this fantasy and priests from parishes around had been bringing their flocks to take part in regular evening processions and acts of worship. The new Messiah eventually ended his days in a state prison, but for a time there was mass-hysteria in and around Viarigi.

The purpose of Siccardi's mission to Rome was to show the Pope 'the urgent need for essential modifications in the

Concordats then in force, especially in the parts concerning ecclesi-astical jurisdiction'—so ran the wording of the letter he carried from the King. He had also the task of finding a solution to the unsatisfactory tenure of office by the prelates of Turin and Asti. In his first interview Siccardi made it plain that the two digni-taries must be removed, and his attitude seemed to confirm the report already sent to the Pope that the satisfaction of this demand was to the Sardinian Government an essential preliminary to discussion of the Concordat. It was left to be understood that although the removal of the two bishops could only be accom-plished by the Pope, the modification of the Concordat would if necessary be carried out by the Sardinian Government with or without the agreement of the Holy See. Siccardi had therefore come to Rome with requests to urge but with nothing to offer in return, and with the threat of unilateral action in the last resort. To describe this as negotiation, as Azeglio did, is something of a euphemism.

As regards Fransoni, the Pope was inflexible. He had done nothing uncanonical and the removal of a prelate was not within the limits of civil authority. As for Artico, his conduct was being investigated once more and whilst this was *sub judice* any action against him would be an inexcusable interference with the course of justice. It was made clear all the same that if he were to be exculpated he would be translated to some other appointment. As for the Concordat, the Holy See was prepared to discuss modifications, and suggested that the one that had been made with Tuscany might serve as basis for discussion. To this proposal Siccardi replied that he had no authority to continue conversation 'as the basis was unacceptable and the times were not ripe for such negotiations', i.e. without the dismissal of the bishops, there could be no bilateral modification of the Concordat. It was widely believed in Piedmont afterwards, and the ministry made no effort to scotch the rumour, that it was the Papacy that had refused to discuss the Concordat, a view that has been generally accepted, but one that seems difficult to uphold. Siccardi himself went further and accused the Papacy not merely of refusing to negotiate, but of doing so for extraneous reasons, moved by ill-will towards the form of government established in Sardinia and hop-ing to see the abolition of the Statute. Victor Emmanuel, as has been seen, told the Nunzio that that seemed to be the aim of the Pope, but that though he thought the constitutional form of government the worst of all and wished to abolish it, 'he wanted to arrive at that end by other ways, and thus prevent the danger of any tremendous reaction'.

No matter who was to blame, Siccardi had come to a deadlock in his mission. The Pope now sought to break it by sending an emissary of his own to Turin. The man chosen was Monsignor Charvaz, Bishop of Pinerolo from 1834 to 1848, and formerly tutor to the King, who had formed and never lost a very high regard for him.[1] It had been hoped that Charvaz would reach Turin and meet the King before Siccardi returned, but an illness of Charvaz and then an absence of the King from his capital prevented this. Charvaz was to convince the King that the Pope could not possibly yield on the question of Fransoni, that Artico's case was under consideration, and his removal practically a certainty when he was cleared, but that as regards the Concordat the prevailing spirit shown by Turin made negotiation at that time extremely difficult. When Charvaz saw the King he found him in a mood of distinct irritation against the Church. But he agreed that Fransoni must be allowed to return to take up his duties in Turin: he agreed that much as he desired to see the powers of the church courts limited by new conditions it would be as well to postpone the discussions for the time being; but he was convinced that Artico was guilty and must go. The measures proposed for the reform of elementary education would, the King believed, leave the powers of the bishops to supervise it unmodified, and 'one of his most influential ministers had assured him it would be so'. Finally the scheme for a new press-law had his approval, and could not offend the Church since its aim was to control the wilder excesses of the Press.[2]

One other question was no nearer to a solution. There was still no Archbishop of Genoa. The candidate proposed by the ministry had been totally unacceptable to the Pope, who had submitted for the ministry's consideration another candidate of whom Charvaz thoroughly approved. But when it seemed that agreement was in sight Siccardi proposed yet another name, that of Fantini, newly appointed Bishop of Fossano and Senator of the realm. The thing that was best known about him was the unmeasured loyalty towards the Government that he had developed since gaining his mitre and his seat in the Senate: he

---

[1] Pirri, *Cart. priv.*, I, pp. 45*–49* of Introduction, pp. 50–74 of text.
[2] Ibid., Document 13, pp. 57–61.

too was unwelcome to higher authority in the Church. So Genoa was vacant and was to remain so until in 1853 Charvaz himself was accepted by all parties as the obvious man for it.

Looking back on the failure of his mission Charvaz wrote in February: 'I see the King is completely dependent on his ministers, who render all his good intentions abortive: he makes promises and means them, but his hands are tied and he could only carry them out by some extraordinary measure, through something like a *coup d'état*. Now he finds such a step repugnant after the oath he has given to the constitution, though this might be the only way to save it, after having modified it, of course.'[1]

Azeglio's ministry had made its obeisance to the idea of negotiating a change in State and Church relations in amicable agreement with the Holy See. In effect they had said 'Dismiss the two bishops and then let us discuss the Concordat'. The Papacy had found the prior condition totally impossible of acceptance. But the ministry might now argue that it had tried to negotiate and had found the Pope intransigent. Such an argument, the Papacy being what it was and must be, seemed convincing. So far the King had followed in the train of his ministers, however reluctantly. Though he personally thought Artico must go, and that it would have been a tactful step to move Fransoni as well, he was not so convinced that the new measures were so necessary. His immediate family circle, and above all his mother and his wife, were always there to warn him against laying his hand sacrilegiously on the ark of the covenant, by any act of betrayal of the Church.[2] Yet despite one collision between himself and Azeglio he did not attempt to sabotage the Siccardi laws as he did the anti-clerical legislation of Cavour's ministry. Azeglio himself accepted the idea that the laws were necessary but did not show any fanatical zeal for them, and the collection of his political speeches and writings includes only one speech in their support. Cavour has more generally been considered responsible for all the laws on Church and State relations. It is true that Siccardi was his ally, ambassador almost, in Azeglio's cabinet, and he himself made one decisive speech in their defence. The last laws of the series, the one on civil marriage, and the still more disputed one for the dissolution of some houses of religious orders, were introduced during his premiership: but despite this it is unjust to

---

[1] Pirri, *Cart. priv.*, I, p. 65.
[2] Ibid., pp. 83–84, for a letter of the Queen to Pius IX.

assign to Cavour all credit, if such it was and for what it matters, for the Siccardi Laws. Whatever may have been Azeglio's personal attitude, whatever the degree of his zeal or his lukewarmness for the laws, he had adopted them as part of his ministerial programme. Should the Chamber reject them his resignation would be inevitable: and he had the other less public but by no means less difficult task of steering them past the King as well as the Parliament. Whilst one must be on one's guard against exaggerating Azeglio's activity or effectiveness, one must not fall into the conventional attitude of regarding the period of his ministry as simply a vapid curtain-raiser to the great drama whose central character is Cavour.

On 20 February Siccardi invited three of the Piedmontese bishops most favourable to the ministry to hear a statement of policy: he explained that attempts to negotiate a new Concordat had failed, though the Pope had not been hostile to the idea of a revision of the status of the church courts. As some action about them was urgently necessary the Government was going to present to the Chamber the project of a law as soon as the King had given it his signature. They were asked not to report this to the Nunzio, as Azeglio himself was going to do this. Why Siccardi had summoned them was not clear, for their views were not asked for: Pirri conjectures[1] that the interview was a blind and that one of them, almost certainly Fantini, was being used to persuade the King to consent to the 'project of law'.[2] After hesitating, the King signed the project, which could then be laid before the Chamber. But after signing he changed his mind. The Nunzio gave an accurate account of what happened. 'After having signed the said project the King, on the better advice of wise persons, sent a courier from Moncalieri, where he was staying, to the Cabinet to let them know that he was withdrawing his signature from the project, not wishing it to be presented to the Chambers. The Ministers went that same day in a body to the King and answered that in that case they would all resign. The King took fright and yielded.'[3]

As promised, Azeglio informed the Nunzio in person of the content of the project, and the Sardinian Minister to the Holy See,

[1] Pirri, *Cart. Priv.*, I, pp. 49–50.
[2] Royal assent to such a 'project' or draft was essential before its presentation to Parliament.
[3] Pirri, *Cart. priv.*, I, p. 51* of Introduction, and Document 13 L, pp. 65–66.

N

Spinola, similarly officially informed the Cardinal Secretary of State. But the note he passed on from Azeglio contained another gesture of an offer to treat with the Papacy—a gesture that was bound to be rejected: 'There was nothing', his note said, 'to prevent the Holy See from treating with the Government of His Majesty: but any such discussions must be opened in Turin and not elsewhere.' And the decisions of the Sardinian Parliament were not to be subject to negotiation. The Papal reply, published officially, insisted that the various missions sent to the Pope had never actually broached the questions of the Concordat and of ecclesiastical immunities.[1] Although this was disbelieved, it seems to have been true enough from what is known of the Balbo and Siccardi missions.

Now that the King's signature was committed to the project it could be brought before the Chamber, and this was not delayed. On 25 February Siccardi presented it in nine clauses. Five dealt with church and civil jurisdiction, one with the right of asylum, the seventh with religious holidays, the eighth with acquisition and acceptance of property by religious orders, and the last one foreshadowed legislation 'to regulate the contract of matrimony in its relations with civil law'. Not without effrontery the Government informed Antonelli that it was acting 'for the sake of order and justice and in the best interest, rightly understood, of religion itself'. There is much power in that 'rightly understood'!

Separate from but parallel to the Siccardi Laws the Government had another reform on foot. It proposed to abolish the payment of tithes on the island of Sardinia and to make the State responsible for the basic stipend of the priests. To initiate this change it had sent (11 January 1850) a circular letter to the bishops of the island requesting them to suspend the filling of vacant livings 'in so far as the service of the Church and decorum of worship allow'. The statute dealing with this question was not promulgated until the following year: it was to pass eventually on 15 April 1851, to come into force on 1 January 1852.

At the wish of the Chamber the Siccardi project was recast in the form of three projects, one on the law courts and the right of asylum, one to abolish the penalties for non-observance of festivals, and the third concerning the property-holdings of religious corporations. The question of civil marriage was to be held back for later consideration. Discussion of the first law began on

[1] Pirri, *Cart. priv.*, p. 52* of Introduction.

6 March and was opened by Siccardi himself. The project at once sent some of Azeglio's supporters from the right-centre into opposition, and as they moved away from him his Government found itself receiving greater numerical support from the left, and coming more and more to rely on the votes of this group, thus beginning the move whose logical conclusion, utterly repugnant to Azeglio, was the Cavour-Rattazzi alliance. One of those who went into opposition, Revel, argued that the plan was inopportune, and that it had been mismanaged: for the aim in view, of which he declared himself in support in principle, ought to have been achieved by negotiation. It was inopportune in that it would divide the country into irreconcilable factions. Balbo opposed because he approved the existing system of church law and church courts, and believed that their infringement was contrary to the letter as well as to the spirit of the constitution of the State. The Bill was supported by speakers from the left, and by Cavour, who on this occasion made his first major speech to the Chamber. His argument was that the State as a matter of courtesy had sought a revision of the Concordat by consent: but this courtesy did not concede the right of the Church to dictate in these matters. On the failure of these overtures by the State, the Government was compelled to follow its present course in order to keep a middle course between revolutionary and reactionary extremes. If these laws should drive the ultra-clericals into open opposition, that would be less dangerous than their underground scheming. Finally he urged the precedents of Wellington, Peel, and Grey, who had forestalled revolutions in Britain by reforms.[1] The following day Azeglio, in a very short speech, wound up the debate. He denied that there was any division in his ministry over the law: he suggested that the only argument against it was that 'the negotiations with Rome were not carried on long enough, and consequently ought to be re-opened. . . . We may be wrong, but we believe in all conscience that we have done all that was possible, that nothing more was to be expected from negotiations. I repeat that in this we may be wrong, but such is our profound conviction. And now to whom do we turn for a decision? To Parliament.'[2] The vote was taken the next day and the Bill was through the Chamber by 130 votes to 26.

[1] Full reports of debates were given by Abercromby (British Minister in Turin), F.O. 67, Vols. 169, 170, 171.

[2] *S.D.P.*, II, pp. 219–20.

The next public battle would be in the Senate. But a more dramatic one was being fought out in private with the conscience of the King as battle-ground. The Nunzio had tried to win him over to a firm stand against the Bill, but the King, though protesting that he was determined to favour the Catholic religion, blamed the Papacy for its intransigence. The Nunzio warned him that should he give his consent to the Bill, in the event of its passing the Senate he must ask for his passport and leave the kingdom. Though the Nunzio might feel compelled to leave, Charvaz returned to Turin, sent by Antonelli to use his influence with the King. Charvaz had no great hopes. Could the King replace his ministers by others more favourable to the Church? With the existing Chamber that seemed impossible. Could he dissolve the Chamber and trust to a conservative victory in an election? That too seemed out of the question. 'They have misled public opinion in Piedmont and have inculcated the idea that it is essential to take action against the Pope and Austria in order to win Italy over to themselves and protect their chance of success in the question of Italian independence whose achievement they hope for sooner or later. It seems there is no resource other than the suspension, at least temporarily, of the constitution and the reform of some of our fundamental laws to restore order and justice to this unhappy country.'[1]

Charvaz arrived in Turin on 29 March and saw the King the next day. He told him frankly what he thought of the ministry's policy and the King seemed deeply distressed. To Charvaz it seemed that there were three possible courses of action. To have the project withdrawn by cancellation of the royal signature: to have discussion in the Senate postponed pending agreement with Rome: or to let the law pass on condition that it should not enter into force without agreement with Rome. The first seemed out of the question: the second the King was prepared to consider, though he wished to consult members of the Piedmontese hierarchy first of all to be quite sure of their support. But the King proceeded to inform some member of the cabinet that such an interview was being considered. The ministry as a whole learnt of it and, resentful of these plans being made behind its back, informed him that 'if the project of law should be withdrawn or discussion in the Senate suspended they would not be answerable should revolution break out and the King be in danger of losing

[1] Charvaz to Antonelli, 13 March. Pirri, *Cart. priv.*, I, p. 68.

his crown'.[1] The King gave way: and the ministers sent a message to Charvaz suggesting that he use his influence to reconcile the King to the situation. Charvaz still had some hope that the measure might be defeated in the Senate, though whether that would have any permanent effect could not be foreseen. In the end the measure was passed. Abercromby forecast a two to one majority and was not far wrong. On 8 April the Senate approved the Bill by fifty-one votes to twenty-nine. Roberto d'Azeglio had been amongst its supporters and had spoken twice in its favour. The next day it received the royal assent. By its terms the courts of the State became the only ones to try all civil cases between ecclesiastics and laymen or between ecclesiastics: all cases concerning church benefices and property and rights of nomination were also to go before the same courts. All criminal cases, including those involving clerics, were to be tried by the criminal courts of the State. That would leave canon law cases—heresy, matrimonial cases, and so on—still in the jurisdiction of the church courts: but already their competence on the latter group of causes was threatened by the hint of legislation to come on civil marriage.

The 'projects' of the second and third Siccardi Laws, on holy days and on the acquisition of property by religious corporations, were voted upon in the Chamber on 13 March. The first proposed that the holy days whose observance would be compelled by law should be limited to Sundays and the major holy days. This law, seemingly the least controversial of all, provoked so heated a discussion in the Chamber that Cavour proposed a motion, approved by the Chamber, that the law should not come into force until the following year. Azeglio was quite willing to compromise on this law. The law on church property seems to us to have far more significance but apparently aroused less animosity. And it was opposed by a much smaller minority: the voting on festivals was 107 to 42, that on property 128 to 7. The rise in absentees and abstentions, fourteen, does not seem very significant, and the voting would indicate that there was a general feeling, even amongst the most orthodox, that the measure had some justification. It was not a drastic law, requiring that acquisitions of property should be subject to state authorization. A subsequent proposition of the Cavour ministry on church property was to be much more punitive to the Church.

[1] Pirri, *Cart. priv.*, I, p. 54* of Introduction: Document 13 K, p. 65.

These measures of a ministry presided over by his brother were a source of deep anguish to Prospero d'Azeglio. He had not yet arrived back in Sicily, where the events had in his view little importance in the end except to those unfortunates who had lost their heads. From Naples he wrote to Costanza:

Grievous news reaches me which almost makes me despair of poor Piedmont. They write to tell me that the minister Siccardi has already proposed to the Chamber a first law against the Church and has three others ready in his portfolio to abolish monks, confiscate their property, take away the jurisdiction of the Church, etc. etc.—in short to undertake an absolute persecution. And this is called 'liberalism'! . . . and as a height of shame I am assured that these proposals have been received by a 'moderate' Chamber with applause and their discussion voted to be a matter of urgency, I still have some hopes that Balbo, Lisi, Provana, and other similar men will let Europe know that amongst the Piedmontese liberals there are still some Catholics, or at least men of honour who hate bureaucratic as much as monarchical tyranny. I was talking of this with a French naval officer who could not reconcile himself to Massimo as Prime Minister. How could a man with his brain make so false a move? To violate property in Piedmont whilst Proudhon is convulsing France![1]

Prospero was better informed on matters in general than most Italian priests—and especially Southern Italian ones. If he was convinced that the measures proposed included the abolition of monks, confiscation of their property, an absolute persecution, one can imagine the exaggerations that were current outside Piedmont. But however shocked the pious might be, there were not lacking those whose anti-clericalism might make them think that what was happening in Piedmont must benefit someone, for what was being lost on the clerical roundabouts must be being gained on the lay swings.

The closing stages of the passing of the Siccardi Laws saw tempers beginning to rise. When rumours circulated in Turin that the Senate might reject the laws there were demonstrations in the street, and crowds began to gather ominously in front of the Palazzo Madama, in which the Senate met. Azeglio on this occasion made perhaps the silliest gesture of his career, coming down to the Senate on horseback in full military uniform. *Fischietto* deservedly caricatured this in a cartoon depicting 'Ettore

[1] Letter of 8 March 1850. Original in O.P.T.

Fieramosca pigeon-hunting in Piazza Castello'. The military cleared the streets, the proceedings in the Senate ended satisfactorily, and Azeglio finished the evening by a visit to a house of ill-fame in Via Po—'una casa sospetta'. What is surprising about this is not so much his visit there as the fact that he quite calmly told his high-minded sister-in-law about it.

Obedient to instructions, the Nunzio had asked for his passport: he wrote a last letter of protest against the laws to Azeglio and left Turin on 12 April. A few days later the King gave an audience to Falloux, the French statesman, who was passing through Turin. According to him, 'the King stated how displeasing to him had been the departure of the Nunzio: as regards the Siccardi Laws he was in a very embarrassing position, but from that moment onwards he would not take a single step in such affairs without a prior agreement with the Holy See'.[1] Falloux was convinced by the King's tone that his embarrassment was genuine and his situation painful to him, that his actions had been totally controlled by his ministers, and that he would like to regain freedom of action.

Now that the laws were on the statute book the question was how they were going to be implemented and what measure of acceptance or defiance they would receive from the clergy. The Piedmontese bishops sought instructions from Rome: but this was not to be expected by return of post, as the question had been submitted to the Congregation of Extraordinary Ecclesiastical Affairs. In the meantime Fransoni saw it as his duty to issue interim instructions. How one judges these depends on one's preconceptions. To Bolton King[2] it seemed that 'Fransoni issued a pastoral ordering his clergy to defy the new laws and appear before the lay courts only on compulsion'. Jemolo, in marked contrast, argued that 'these instructions were aimed at facilitating the carrying out of the law, saving the question of principle'.[3] Without going as far as Jemolo one is tempted to modify Bolton King's interpretation. Fransoni's circular instructed the clergy, if summoned before a lay court, to protest against the violation of clerical immunity before obeying. Eventually Rome might order disobedience, or might come to terms with the Government: but for the time being Fransoni's instructions seem wise enough —to safeguard the principle by a protest, but to obey the

---

[1] Pirri, *Cart. priv.*, I, p. 75. [2] Op. cit., Vol. I, p. 395.
[3] Jemolo, op. cit., p. 213.

summons. His words were restrained: but his own actions showed him to be inflexible. The police seized copies of his circulars at the printers, and the ministry ordered Fransoni to withdraw from Turin, where his presence was a menace to public order. This the Archbishop refused to do. He was thereupon summoned before the courts on a charge of 'incitement to insubordination to the law'. He sent in reply a protest that such a summons was beyond the powers of the civil authority, and that he would only obey it when instructions should have arrived from Rome. So, though he himself had counselled obedience to the law after due protest, he refused to follow his own instructions. The ministry, as he guessed, had wanted a test case, and what better one than this involving the Archbishop himself? His refusal to appear brought the ministry for the first time face to face with a situation of their own creating, and plainly they did not like it at all. Azeglio himself, Santa Rosa, and Paleocapa were believed to be in favour of making a prudent retreat. But Siccardi and others, apparently not a majority of the cabinet and not all of them senior members, were for making an example of Fransoni. They carried the day. On 4 May the Archbishop was arrested in his palace, removed to the citadel, accused of breach of laws, and sentenced on 23 May to a month's imprisonment and a fine of 500 francs. It was not insignificant that one judge refused to take part in the trial, and was consequently dismissed from the bench. When a group of senators interpellated the ministry Siccardi told them that a mission was being sent to Rome, and that negotiations were being opened with hopes of a settlement. In fact no mission was being sent, for all whom he had approached had declined to take part. Fransoni had barely been disposed of when the Archbishop of Sassari, Varesini, was sentenced for the same offence. It was reported that the King, who had agreed to the proceedings against Fransoni, had not been informed about the Varesini case, and was furious at not having been consulted.

Whatever the King might have felt, there was no sign of public excitement over the arrest of Fransoni and Azeglio was confirmed in his guess that the people, if not the two-thirds of the clergy whom he was counting on, were in favour of the Siccardi Laws. Though they had imprisoned him, it was essential to the ministers that they should not make too evident a martyr of the Archbishop and in his case imprisonment in the citadel was interpreted as lodging with the commandant in his house there. Abercromby had imagined that the ministry would be satisfied by a gesture of imprisonment and would let him out within twenty-four hours, but the Archbishop refused bail and stayed: the period of his incarceration awaiting sentence was counted as part of his month, so he was set at liberty quite soon. Once he had seen how quietly everything had passed off, Azeglio was reassured, even jocular, though he might have been frivolous about the prelate even if there had been popular disapproval. 'I have had enough of that blessed Archbishop. I have so managed it that he has ended up in the Citadel. As his aim was to play the victim he has got what he wanted, but the affair is passing off with no one worrying about it, and as he is well lodged in the house of the commander, the impression of martyrdom has been avoided. I feel regret for this incident, but it was not the Government's job to prevent it. The law was passed by Parliament by a large majority. It was received with great pleasure by the country, and a law of the State must be the same law for all.'[1] 'Parliament has passed a law and we are having it kept. True we have on our backs a certain number of rogues and fools who wish to impede us . . . but on the other hand the King is firm as a rock. I am trying feebly not to be frightened and so are my colleagues. The public is quiet and more than happy.'[2] As one would hope, his public utterances were more guarded and more sensible, and Abercromby commented on the moderation and correctness of his communications with the Holy See (a couple of virtues less apparent to Rome).

Tempers had in any case been embittered by an adventitious incident that was to presage a much more serious one. In mid-May Pietro di Santa Rosa, Minister for Agriculture, fell gravely ill and when he believed himself about to die desired the last sacraments. His parish priest duly came to see him, but made it a condition of his administering the sacraments that Santa Rosa should retract his approval of the Siccardi Laws, in support of which he had spoken influentially in the Chamber. Santa Rosa refused to retract and the priest, realizing that he had perhaps gone too far, gave way. Santa Rosa recovered and wrote a full account of the matter for *Risorgimento*.

But the bridges were by no means down as yet, and both sides were still manœuvring for position. In March Spinola, Sardinian Minister to the Holy See, had had an interview with Antonelli to inform him of the proposed legislation and to express the hope

[1] Carcano, op. cit., p. 426.   [2] *Confidenze*, p. 65.

that it was still not too late for negotiation. Through the Nunzio Rome protested in this same month against the threat of unilateral action, and on 14 May Antonelli handed to Spinola a formal note of protest. Though Spinola may not have known it he had nearly been replaced: Azeglio had seriously considered that he was too uncompromising and he had been trying to persuade his brother Roberto to accept the mission in Rome. Roberto had supported the Siccardi Laws already introduced, but he was later to be a most determined opponent of the proposed law on civil marriage. His general reputation might have made him moderately acceptable in Rome, but he declined to undertake the task.[1] Antonelli expressed his full support of Fransoni in his note and denied the right of the Government to modify existing Concordats by unilateral action. He implied a threat to appeal to the Powers, but since many of them had already negotiated terms similar to those Sardinia was now imposing it was not likely that he would risk a diplomatic rebuff from them. Azeglio's reply, given on 3 June, was an insistence on a state's right to legislate regardless of undertakings previously entered upon, since these must be considered as 'dependent on such modifications as with the passage of time and change of circumstances every state must judge necessary to its peace and internal prosperity'.[2] The matter, according to Azeglio, was not international but a domestic one over which Sardinia had full sovereignty. Equality before the law, of which the first Siccardi Law was a corollary, was part of the Statute: so was the independence of the judiciary. The arrest and condemnation of Fransoni were in accordance with a constitutionally made law and were not the action of legislature or cabinet. Abercromby, it may be noted, thought Azeglio's note was courteous while firm. So too was Antonelli's reply. For, as neither would yield on substance, each was anxious to make to the world the more favourable impression of sweet reasonableness in manner. A further note from Azeglio on 24 July carried the argument into a new channel and one may be forgiven for wondering who had written this one, so different was it in its arguments. Any treaties such as those being invoked by the Holy See always contained a 'rebus sic stantibus' clause. A change in the form of government might, it argued, void a treaty containing such a clause. Such a change had occurred in Sardinia with the promulgation of the Statute: hence, treaties of earlier date than

[1] *Souv. hist.*, p. 398.   [2] Pirri, *Cart. priv.*, p. 64* of Introduction.

the Statute might be void.[1] The argument might have strange consequences if accepted. But stranger than this was a rumour going round Rome that the Sardinian Government had in its possession a document whose publication would thoroughly wreck the Pope's personal reputation. Azeglio, when told of this report, warmly denied that such a document existed and said that in any case his ministry would not have used it for blackmail. But as a sign that each side felt compelled to appear to be more reasonable than the other the ministry accepted Antonelli's invitation to them to send yet another mission to Rome.

Azeglio made it clear that, whether or not the envoys would act *suaviter in modo*, they would act *fortiter in re* by choosing as their leader Pinelli, a former President of the Chamber and one of the most outspoken champions of the Siccardi Laws. Members of the Church in Piedmont took action parallel to that of the State, for a number of clergy sent to Rome an appeal for a compromise settlement: but this too was suspect since its organizer was the Bishop of Fossano, whose appointment the Holy See had regretted ever since the discovery that he was an out-and-out supporter of the Sardinian State and that this had been the main reason for his having been recommended for promotion.

Any hope that bitterness might be eradicated or that should it continue the State might be clearly seen to be its instigator was destroyed by the events surrounding the death of Santa Rosa in August. As in May, he had again refused to retract, and once more the priest called to his bedside refused to administer the viaticum: but whereas in May the priest had relented, this time Santa Rosa was allowed to die without extreme unction. He had accepted this deprivation courageously but so serious was it to a devout Catholic that the news raised a tremendous storm. Fransoni was held personally responsible for this intransigence. He had certainly approved it but the blame was not his: the case had been considered since May by a committee of canonists first, and later by a synod of priests of Turin, and all had agreed that extreme unction could not be administered to him without this recantation. It is further alleged[2] that the Bishop of Fossano had urged Santa Rosa not to yield on this point: if so, he too was

---

[1] Bianchi, *Politica*, p. 210. Thayer believed that this interpretation was in accordance with Wheaton's *Elements of International Law* (1836).

[2] Pirri, *Cart. priv.*, p. 65* (Introduction).

prepared to make political capital out of a most sacred rite. At first it was decided that Santa Rosa could not even be given Christian burial: but this was accorded to him: he had been in receipt of the sacraments even though he had not been accorded the viaticum and extreme unction: and he had, it was said, admitted that had he known he was contravening the laws of the Church he would not have done what he had done. His funeral was the occasion of a violent demonstration of sympathy for him and of disapproval of the clergy who had been so unyielding. Government at this moment happened to be in the hands of La Marmora. Azeglio was at Acqui having medical treatment at the spa there for his wound. The King was based on Courmayeur but was away in the mountains for some days, chamois-hunting. So La Marmora, with the encouragement of Siccardi, took action. Azeglio thought he went a little too far, but stayed in Acqui: the King, according to Siccardi, approved thoroughly. Fransoni, being considered mainly responsible, was arrested again and imprisoned, not this time in the citadel of Turin but in the much more remote and forbidding fortress of Fenestrelle, nor was he in the governor's house, and his release was conditional on his leaving the kingdom, as he did, never to return. He went into exile in Lyons: his possessions were sequestrated, but he was supported in his banishment by voluntary offerings of the faithful. The priest who had refused the sacraments belonged to the Servite Order, which served the parish in which Santa Rosa lived and died. The house of the order was likewise sequestrated and its members dispersed to other houses, except for the luckless one who had been called in. He was imprisoned in the citadel.

Another one to feel the weight of governmental displeasure at this time was the Archbishop of Cagliari, Monsignor Marongiu-Nurra. He had been affronted by the law dealing with tithes in the island of Sardinia and had refused to co-operate with the agents of the Government: further, he had instructed the clergy to withhold their co-operation, and had excommunicated the civil servants who were executing the law. For his pains he was arrested and deported to the Papal States, being set ashore at Civita Vecchia. Azeglio had not ordered this step and was still apprehensive that his ministry was acting too precipitately and much too harshly: but he none the less wrote frivolously about it to his nephew from Genoa on 29 September.

You will receive a circular and documents about the round-up of Archbishops we have been making. Those two at least will trouble us no more. The important thing is to make clear to the press that all we have done is legal, ultra-legal. I am very proud of the Cagliari expedition, for which I award myself a large part of the honour. Once the Archbishop had been found guilty and, a ship by chance being there, he was embarked, shipped off, and landed at Civita Vecchia and the ship was back in Genoa all in 48 hours. And there we are. To think that in Rome they hoped the mob [*sic*] would take the part of the priests. Had the police not been there they would have been drubbed like Haynau, or at least hooted.[1]

These measures against the prelates were, as Azeglio says, taken calmly by the people in general: the news that the faithful were collecting for Fransoni led some of the anti-clericals to propose a public subscription for the erection of a monument in Turin to commemorate the Siccardi Laws.

It is no wonder, then, that Pinelli was making little headway in Rome. He was still insisting that in adopting the Siccardi Laws the Government had exercised its rights, and going on from that he now requested that the Holy See should accommodate the Sardinian Government by removing Fransoni from his arch-diocese in Turin, and transferring him to some appointment elsewhere, in Rome itself perhaps. All these points emerged when Pinelli first went to present his credentials to Antonelli, but as his claims were so clearly totally unacceptable he was informed that so also were his credentials: his visit must be regarded as officious rather than official and his own interview with the Pope was to be considered as a private conference. Not an inch of progress was made and Pinelli had to ask Azeglio what he should do. He was told that if he saw fit he should return, informing the ministers of other states, especially of Spain and France, of the futility of his staying longer. In fact he stayed in Rome for some time afterwards.

In Turin the legislative machine was still grinding slowly away at the church laws. The project for the third Siccardi Law, for the compulsory registration of accessions of property to religious corporations, had already been approved: the law itself then had to be drafted and presented to the Chamber as a Bill: this had been done, it had been debated, and at long last in January 1851 it was accepted by the Chamber and could go to the Senate. But

[1] Bianchi, *Lettere*, p. 93.

it had received less support than the two previous Acts, passing by 98 votes out of only 129. The Right of course voted against it: but the Left saw little good in it: Brofferio had urged that the State should confiscate church property outright and pay the priests a salary. Petitions in this sense had been coming to Azeglio from various districts, but such a scheme was far too radical for his taste: confiscation of property and closing of monasteries was no part of his policy nor did Cavour, who had by now joined the ministry, wish to go to such lengths, though later he was to be responsible for legislation much more drastic than Azeglio's.

Siccardi himself resigned his post as Keeper of the Seals, i.e., Minister of Justice, in February 1851 on the pretext of ill-health, but in reality, Abercromby believed, in protest against a cut in the estimates for his department. The last of the church laws to be passed through its final stages in the Azeglio ministry was accepted in the following month, that for the abolition of tithes in the island of Sardinia: the State had already surveyed the working of the tithes system there, despite the resistance of the Archbishop and the bulk of the prelates. The clergy of this desperately poor island, unlike their colleagues on the richer mainland, were to be compensated by a modest salary to be paid by the State, a change apparently as acceptable to the parish clergy as it was to the tithe-payers.

One of the greatest criticisms that can be made of Azeglio and of his successors is that of failure to do anything effective for this island. Even minor measures like this one were few. The shocking state of Sicily was notorious: Sardinia was little if any better off, though she had no Mafia: neither had she the bustling if slum-ridden cities of Sicily. She remained entirely agricultural, her roads almost non-existent, her railways late in developing and limited, illiteracy scarcely challenged, and deforestation the one thriving activity, to the eventual ruin of her agriculture. But in all matters economic or commercial Azeglio had virtually no policy, and even Cavour was more skilful in assisting healthily growing industries than in large-scale rescue operations such as Sardinia needed.

For all his jauntiness Azeglio was not really so sure of himself as he would make out. The royal family were not to be overlooked, and their influence was not in his favour. In January he had an audience of the Queen and tried to convince her of the reasonableness of Government's policy. How effective he might have been he doubted, but he believed the discussion had cleared the air somewhat. As before he was convinced that the King was standing firm and would continue to do so. 'Things here are going full-sail. The King is firm in his attitude: the court-war under you-know-whom has given us a short truce. . . . I gave a little ultimatum: "If you want war you can have war, but remember that some of you will be in despair at losing your jobs whilst I don't give a damn. . . ." After this he-courtiers and she-courtiers have come to my dances and their smiles are a delight.'[1]

[1] Bianchi, *Lettere*, p. 107.

Siccardi Laws

1) Restricting the jurisdiction of the ecclesiastical courts and making ecclesiastical persons justiciable by the civil courts

2) Restricting the number of holy days & Sundays & Christmas, Easter, Whitsun, Corpus Christi (these church festivals)

3) Obliging religious corporations to register accession of property (p. 193)

4) abolishing tithes in the island of Sardinia; so that clerical stipends in the island were henceforward payed by the state.

5) Establishing civil marriage (p. 190)

6) Dissolving some houses of religious orders

XI

AZEGLIO AND CAVOUR

Azeglio had now dealt highly successfully, he believed, with three major problems. He had made peace with Austria on terms that were far better than might ever have seemed likely: the difficulties created by the left-wing domination of the Chamber had been overcome by the Moncalieri Proclamation and by the management of the subsequent elections, and he had seen three of the Siccardi Laws pass on to the statute book and a couple of Archbishops exiled. As against these achievements he had had his troubles. The King had been restive and critical on occasions. His ministers were mediocrities and the finances of the country, even though in the hands of a successful banker, were in an unsatisfactory condition. Outside the Chambers there were deep rumblings of discontent from the clerical Right and sharp savage peals of thunder from the Left, with the Press enfilading his ministry from both flanks. Abercromby criticized him for being too harsh in his treatment of the Right, others accused him of persecuting the progressive children of the light who were to be found on the Left. These accusations are, as they stand, too generalized and it is as well to look at a specific example that caused considerable stir at the time.

This was the case of Bianchi Giovini, victim of proceedings in 1850. He was a Lombard refugee in Piedmont, an extreme republican who had taken to journalism. To Azeglio it seemed at the mildest to be bad taste for a Lombard to be so illogical as to preach republicanism after having taken refuge and found safety in a monarchy, even if his tenets were preached in sober terms. But Bianchi Giovini had been grossly offensive in his expressions. In one article he had made a venomous personal attack on the Austrian Minister in Turin, Baron Metzburg. A second article criticized equally offensively certain Austrian generals and the Archduke Maximilian. After the publication of this he was warned by the Sardinian Ministry of the Interior to desist from these vituperations. They had shocked quite a large number of people: Pantaleoni in Rome was pointing out to Azeglio that even the *Gazzetta Ufficiale* was excessively anti-Austrian in tone: how, he asked, would Azeglio or his countrymen relish equally anti-Sardinian articles in an Austrian *Official Gazette*? Despite the warning Bianchi Giovini wrote yet a third article, but changing his target: this time it was not an Austrian but the Pope himself who was his victim. And it was not Pius IX's politics that he attacked but his morals, for he accused him of being the lover of Countess Spaur. This was intolerable and Azeglio had him expelled from Piedmont. He found refuge in Switzerland, and there were some who considered that he had been ill-used. What is unsatisfactory is not the sentence against him but the manner of his deprivation. A sound press law, with a just and efficacious law of libel, would surely have permitted a government to keep extremists like him in check by due process of law instead of by executive action. But it is unrealistic to expect a workable yet liberal press law in a state newly become constitutional in the mid-nineteenth century; even the twentieth century has not always seen emergent countries make this adjustment successfully. Azeglio was untroubled by any doubts. 'If I am not afraid to send to gaol an archbishop I am no more afraid to send to the devil a journalist.'[1] 'The action of the ministry is not only not an act of weakness but rather one of vigour against the more or less revolutionary party that in fact has unleashed itself through the press against the expulsion of Giovini. The ministry has seized this opportunity to show that it dominates the sects and is not dominated by them.'[2] In short, Azeglio maintained, 'The press must either learn its responsibilities or risk severe censorship.'[3]

The finances of the country were not so easily dealt with. The mainland provinces were prosperous enough, but little revenue came or seemed ever likely to come from Sardinia. Communications between the island and the mainland had been left completely to the navy, whose ships were unsuitable for the transport of either goods or passengers and whose officers were innocent of commercial or logistic skills. In 1850 the navy was relieved of this function and special commercial vessels were supplied by private enterprise. A subsidy from government funds had to be given to them, but on balance the Government gained financially from the change. Once better communications with the island had been established it was hoped that travel and trade would develop inside the island and from it to the mainland. Progress was bound

<hr>

[1] *Galeotti*, p. 35.   [2] *S.D.P.*, II, p. 365.   [3] *Galeotti*, p. 35.

to be slow and in fact Sardinia remained, like Sicily, neglected and underdeveloped. Even had there been greater determination to do something for it, funds were lacking. The Government had had to rack its credit to pay the indemnity to Austria and it was now committed inescapably to essential expenditure on railways into which huge sums would have to go before any considerable returns began to come in: Piedmont, placed in the gateway to Italy, simply had to have railways, and to have them she had to borrow and to go on borrowing. The Government failed to balance the budget in 1850 and though in November of that year the ministry was sanguine that a balanced budget might be achieved in 1851, the hope proved illusory. Even after Cavour assumed the Ministries of Commerce, Agriculture, and eventually Finance the deficit for 1851 reached fifty million *lire*.

The difficulties confronting the ministry were intimidating, but the most serious feature was its unawareness of their gravity. The cabinet was a collection of second-raters and the only excuse for Azeglio surrounding himself with such mediocrities was that few better were available. Only one man in the Chamber was of more conspicuous ability—Cavour. Nigra, the Finance Minister, was successful as a banker in private life but he was no parliamentarian and never attempted to become one. He avoided the Chamber and was content when a financial statement had to be made to arrange for a deputy, specially briefed by him, to make it. La Marmora was considered the strong man of the ministry: he acted as deputy Prime Minister during Azeglio's too frequent absences, and he had shown more determination than discretion in dealing with republicanism in Genoa and recalcitrance in the Church. But for much of the time he was occupied with the reform and reorganization of the Sardinian army and his seat on the ministerial bench was normally empty. The system of allowing the active heads of the army and navy to sit in Parliament and to act as members of the cabinet responsible for their departments was thoroughly bad. If they were doing a full-time job with the armed forces they could not serve adequately in the Chamber or the cabinet: at the same time their commitment to a political party might lead to the embroilment of the forces in political controversy or to political influence in promotions or in the placing of contracts. Azeglio's friend Persano was for a time a member of the Parliament and of the bloc that supported Azeglio and he was all too apt to involve Azeglio in his very frequent imbroglios within the service. Paleocapa, the Minister for Public Works, was a scholar and a talker, but as a man of action he was negligible. Siccardi had shown himself active, effective, and not too scrupulous in his control of religious affairs, but he was in poor health and anxious to retire from politics. In any case he had never been an originator of policy, for all believed that he drew his ideas and his moral courage (if such it always was) from Cavour.

Though individually unimpressive the ministers would have been less ineffectual had they formed a genuine cabinet; but this they never did as long as Azeglio was in charge. He was quite content to have ministers rather than a ministry. The cabinet met spasmodically and, unless the King presided, informally. No solidarity was demanded of them and, as will be seen, Azeglio and his ministers were continually being taken by complete surprise by crises that were perfectly foreseeable. The fault for this rests on Azeglio himself, though the general inexperience of King, ministers, and parliamentarians may be pleaded in mitigation. It is unrealistic to expect too high a standard of parliamentary skill where constitutional government was still so new. Despite this excuse one must say that Azeglio did not try hard enough. He had not the patience or the industry to attend the Chamber regularly enough to feel the temper of the House. He was absent when he should have been present, silent when he should have spoken; and when he should have spoken precisely he all too often contented himself with brief and vague appeals for the confidence of the House. He cannot have been unaware of his shortcomings, for his friends were as assiduous as his enemies in pointing them out to him frequently and insistently.

Abercromby, happy in his assumption that it was part of his duty as Her Britannic Majesty's Minister to the Court of Sardinia to advise Azeglio how to run his cabinet and his country, was lavish with advice. In June 1850, when the Government had been defeated on a Finance Bill and had withdrawn it, Abercromby reported an interview he had had with Azeglio, having found a 'good opportunity' for speaking seriously to the Chevalier d'Azeglio on the subject of the evils arising from the careless and listless manner in which government business was carried on. 'People inside Sardinia', he told Azeglio, 'may know that such defeats are due to the casualness of the government: but to people outside they appear as signs of Sardinian instability as well as of governmental weakness.' Azeglio did not deny this accusation nor did he seek seriously 'to defend the want of management that evidently exists on the ministerial side of the chamber'.[1] In the following November Abercromby warned him that 'his government must convince the country that they are seriously intent on establishing the financial administration of the country on a solid and permanent basis or they will diminish the majority that at present support them'. Azeglio does not seem to have resented Abercromby's plain-spoken tutorials: but then neither does he seem to have profited by them. A year later Pantaleoni was giving him the same advice. Fresh from a visit to London he urged Azeglio to organize his supporters on English party lines, with whips and party discipline; but he also advised in vain. His advice might not have been entirely wasted at Westminster, for a simple, classic two-party system was not very obvious when Whig shaded off into liberal or radical, when a Tory was either a Peelite or a Disraelian protectionist, and when a flying squad of Irish members could be relied on to keep things moving.

Despite his criticism of Azeglio's lack of control and a sense of urgency, Abercromby in July 1850 made a very favourable report on the ministry's record. Fifty-one projects had been passed into law, some of them of considerable importance.

It is probable that many legislative omissions may be discovered . . . but when it is considered how completely the country had been wanting in anything like public discussion . . . , how limited the number of persons engaged in the administration of public affairs, how ignorant the public had been kept . . . , the industry, the application, the generally calm, decorous and earnest conduct of the deputies afford the most encouraging grounds for the assurance that the representatives of this nation will not for the future be unmindful of the serious nature of their duties. . . .

It was typical that though he might criticize the Sardinian politicians to themselves he defended them to the outside world, since as an Englishman he had to demonstrate that the parliamentary machine was working in this part of Italy and was therefore a viable British export. But the locals had to be taught how to assemble and use the machine.

On the whole, then, the Sardinian political drama was being acted by a weak cast, too loosely directed by a bored producer,

[1] F.O. 67, Vol. 171, 20 June 1850.

whilst in the wings a theatrical genius was waiting to come on to
the stage as an 'extra' who, before the fall of the curtain, would
have taken over the parts of the King of Denmark, Hamlet,
Laertes, and Fortinbras. Little noticed by some of the audience,
Cavour had already had a hand in the drama that was being
performed, having written some of the speeches and acted as
prompter to some of the actors. Siccardi had relied greatly on his
assistance: but he had also been a close friend of the late Santa
Rosa, and Nigra had often consulted him: their co-operation was
to continue for quite a time. But his name still did not figure
amongst the cast as printed. In September 1850 Azeglio began to
make overtures to him and in an undated letter of that month
Cavour declined the invitation.

I am still convinced that I cannot become a colleague of Mamelli. If
you think a major cabinet reshuffle inopportune I beg you not to hold
yourself in the least committed to me, and to seek without delay a
successor to poor Santa Rosa. You and your colleagues may rest
assured that in Parliament I shall be an open and decided defender
of the cabinet you preside over, and will do all in my power to avoid
whatever might shake a ministry whose existence is of importance not
to Piedmont alone but to all Italy.[1]

The possibility of Cavour's entry into the ministry and the
importance such a step would have were being discussed by
political observers. A week before Cavour accepted office Pallavicino, who was somewhat to the left of Azeglio, wrote to Montanelli: 'It is believed that Monsieur de Cavour is most anxious
to replace Monsieur d'Azeglio, and with this aim has approached
M. Rattazzi. We know M. Rattazzi: he is openly democratic. But
what are Monsieur de Cavour's political principles? That
problem has not yet been solved.'[2]

Cavour's success in business affairs was evident to all: his
interventions in debates on public finance had shown his flair for
that: he had had his own newspaper to expound his political
views: why then the 'problem not yet solved'? At its simplest, the
members of his own class found it hard to forgive either his
commercial activities or his political alignment, whilst the
liberals could not easily believe that the son of Michele and brother
of Gustavo di Cavour could really be in sympathy with them. He

[1] L. Chiala, *Lettere di Camillo Benso di Cavour* (1883), Vol. I, p. 167.
[2] Quoted by Chiala, op. cit., Vol. V, p. ccclxxxviii.

had been ousted from the committee of the Agricultural Association that he had helped to found, and from the treasurership of
the Infant Asylum Committee. He had been defeated in four
colleges at the election of the first Piedmontese Parliament:
entering at the next election he had been put out at the third,
returning in July 1849. Since then he had been active behind the
scenes, co-operating with Nigra, advising Santa Rosa, and briefing
Siccardi. Now on 10 October 1850 he was at last brought into the
cabinet as Minister of Marine, Commerce, and Agriculture.
Despite its triple-barrelled title this ministry was not considered
to be of major importance, and to give it to him Azeglio had had
to overcome not only his own scruples but those, more resistant,
of the King, who distrusted Cavour and foresaw that he would
come to dominate the ministry, then Parliament, and finally
perhaps the King himself. 'I warn you', he told Azeglio, 'that this
man who is coming in by the back door will soon turn you all out.'
Azeglio wrote reassuringly to his friends explaining what a good
colleague Cavour was. 'Cavour is genuinely most useful in the
Chamber. We needed a fighter and he has filled this role with
great verve and talent. He has refuted his reputation as a man
difficult to live with, and the most profound peace reigns in the
ministerial household.'[1]

The peace was not to be profound for long. But that the
ministry had enlisted a fighter possessed of verve and talent was
undeniable; his willingness to accept the drudgery that is normal,
and his joy in the cut-and-thrust excitement that is occasional in
politics marked him out as plainly as did his greater practical
knowledge of economic affairs, of the European scene, and of the
strengths and weaknesses of human nature.

The Parliament reassembled for its new session in November.
The Chamber as a whole was sympathetic to the ministry and,
as Abercromby could see, there was a general desire not to
endanger the constitutional experiment by embarrassing the
Government, whilst the Government in its turn seemed likely to
avoid any further dangerous controversial measures. To Azeglio
it was a good omen when the Chamber elected Pinelli as its
President, for he was now of Azeglio's own school of moderate and
constitutional conservatives. More comforting still to him was the
devastating rebuff given at this election to Rattazzi, who was
awarded only nineteen votes out of 110, of which sixty-six went

[1] Azeglio to Abercromby, 20 December 1850. Chiala, op. cit., Vol. V, p. 215.

to Pinelli. The closing debate of the previous, 1849–50, session had been concerned mainly with finance, and this preoccupation was reflected in the speech from the throne at the opening of the new session. This was a short and highly generalized statement of policy whose vagueness of thought was proclaimed rather than concealed by Azeglio's elegant and for once not too flamboyant phraseology. Senators and deputies were congratulated on their prudence and the King's subjects on their confident tranquillity: thanks to these qualities Piedmontese institutions were continuing to be an enviable example to the rest of Italy. The hope was expressed that relations with Rome might improve, and financial reforms were promised. 'First and foremost our finances must be set in order; the growing prosperity of the country and the proven willingness of the peoples of Piedmont to accept sacrifices will serve to facilitate this.'[1] In the subsequent debate on the speech ministers explained quite cogently that the payment of the indemnity and the beginnings of heavy state investment in railways had caused the great rise in expenditure. But when they undertook to bring a balance within sight of achievement, if not to achieve it, they were promising more than they were to be able to fulfil. Despite a rise of thirty per cent. in revenue from taxation, a year later they had to admit to a deficit of sixty million *lire*. Cavour was much more effective in these debates than Azeglio, whose only interventions in this session on finance were on matters arising out of expenditure on the diplomatic and consular services. His most original and successful speech was one on literary copyright negotiations between Piedmont and France.[2] The main weight of all exposition of financial policy had to be borne by Cavour, and Azeglio was enchanted with him. It was in the fight over the last of the state-church laws, that on ecclesiastical property, that Cavour was of most assistance, defending the law not only against the ultra-clerical Right, but also against the Left under Brofferio. With the passage in April of the law about tithes in Sardinia Azeglio's main programme of church reforms was completed.

Azeglio's only private worries during these early months of 1851 had been caused by his friend Persano. The peppery seaman had been given the job of taking Sardinia's contributions to the Great Exhibition from Genoa to London in his warship. At the very beginning of the voyage Persano, whose navigation does not

---

[1] *S.D.P.*, II, pp. 233–4.   [2] Ibid., pp. 243, 251.

always seem to have been of the best, though it could be excellent on occasion, had the misfortune to run his ship aground when barely out of harbour: she did not stick and he continued the journey, even going as far up the Thames as Chatham before taking a pilot on board, to his great satisfaction. In London he then foolishly involved himself in a dispute with the British Customs officials, for which Palmerston soundly berated him in a letter. Azeglio in Turin and his nephew in London had to straighten that matter out. Then the admiral-commanding sought to know why Persano had sent in no official report on his mishap at Genoa. His reply to this was not such as could be considered an official report and court-martial proceedings were instituted. He was acquitted, but was moved to a different command. All this had given Azeglio a good deal of trouble, trying to make Persano behave reasonably, and the Admiralty leniently. No sooner was that all settled than Persano, as if in appreciation of his good offices, asked Azeglio to arrange for him to be given a surreptitious passport in an assumed name. He was planning a romantic foray into Lombardy but did not wish the Austrian Government to be aware of his presence: still less would he have liked them or anyone else to know the purpose of his trip. This service Azeglio flatly refused to perform for him. It was undignified of Persano to be chasing a ballerina to Milan and stupid of him to think that he could go there secretly. All Milan, including the Austrians, would have recognized him at once and in no time at all have learnt why he was there: he would become the laughing-stock of all north Italy, especially if the Austrians should ask him to leave. Persano had the sense to accept this reproof, and did not conceal the occasion of it too effectively when he came to publish Azeglio's letters to himself.[1]

In public affairs it was Austrian policy that was giving Azeglio most apprehension. The most disquieting rumours were in circulation. As early as January 1851 it was being reported that Austria was going to seek the approval of the German confederation for the inclusion of her non-Germanic possessions in the confederation. Hitherto they had been excluded. It had not mattered vitally in some ways, for the actual powers exercised by the confederation over its members were not great: the Austrian

---

[1] Persano, op. cit., pp. 54–55, Azeglio's letters of 22 and 26 June printed in part. Persano did not print any part of Azeglio's letter of 21 March about the grounding of his ship and treatment of the court of inquiry.

presidency had prestige value, but the Emperor's importance stemmed from his dynastic possessions rather than from his leadership in Germany. Apart from this it was by no means certain that such a request would necessarily be accepted and honorary Germanism conferred on Magyars, Italians, and assorted Slavs who were living under Habsburg rule. Yet if it should come about it would widen and deepen the chasm between Lombardy-Venetia and the rest of Italy not merely in political matters but also in tariffs. By March the rumours were even more alarming. Schwarzenberg, it was said, had been talking about 'finishing once and for all with Sardinia and Switzerland'. It was believed that France would not consider an attack on Piedmont as a *casus belli*, but would content herself with occupying Nice and Savoy.[1] A little later Austria was credited with a more modest and therefore more practicable and alarming intention of trying to form a customs union of all Italian states except Piedmont under her own presidency. Such a customs union had been discussed before and the idea was not such an unlikely one, since if it were to be formed it would give Austria some compensation for her exclusion from the Prussian customs union that was achieving a growing importance in German affairs, to Austria's serious detriment. An anonymous English agent in Lombardy informed the Foreign Office through Abercromby that Austria was strengthening her defences in Lombardy-Venetia: work on a big scale was in progress in Mantua, Verona, and Peschiera. At Milan the new works were so sited as to overawe the city rather than to defend it from outside attack.[2]

Despite these reports Sardinia took no new defence measures. But the Government, urged on mainly by Cavour, initiated a commercial policy intended to counterbalance the threatened Austro-Italian customs union. One aspect of this plan was the improvement of communications between Piedmont and the states beyond the Alps. Such schemes were not new in 1851, but their scope was expanding. Now a railway was being planned from Genoa, whose shipping might gain in importance as a result, via Turin, the Grimsel, Constance, and the Rhine valley to western Germany, Holland, and Prussia. The benefit that this would bring to Piedmont's economy was as evident as its potential political

---

[1] Reports of Abercromby to Palmerston, especially of 3 and 20 March. F.O. 67, Vol. 177.
[2] F.O. 67., Vol. 177, 21 April 1851.

and military value. Abercromby pressed upon Palmerston the advisability of the British Government helping Sardinia to float loans in London to finance the project. The Government in Turin sought technical advice from Britain and engineers, including Brassey, went out to examine the scheme and to view the actual terrain. In November 1851 they reported against the Grimsel route, and against the first proposal of an alternative way by the Lukmanier. Instead they recommended a line from Turin to France by way of Susa, thence via Chambery through Savoy— virtually the line that now exists as the main way from the Channel ports and Paris to Turin by the Mont Cenis.

Besides transport links Sardinia was seeking treaties. Cavour negotiated arrangements for the reciprocal lowering of tariffs. A trade treaty with France in 1850 was followed by others, with Belgium and with Britain early in 1851, with the Prussian customs union at the beginning of June, and, shortly afterwards, with Switzerland, a treaty that also settled further details about the proposed railway between the two countries. In this way Cavour replied in advance to the possible threat of the exclusion of Sardinia from Italian markets should the Austrian customs union eventuate, by gaining what might be much more valuable outlets for her trade in the markets beyond the Alps, richer by far than those in the peninsula. He was Europeanizing Piedmont if he could not yet Piedmontize Italy. He would probably have wished for a more radical free trade policy but for that the time was not yet ripe.

A revision of the treaty with France encountered opposition in the Chamber in June and July 1851. The Left made the ratification of the new treaty the occasion for attacks on the general policy of France, and especially on her continued maintenance of a garrison in Rome. Azeglio intervened in the debate with a speech that was much admired, explaining the political importance of the treaty:[1] Cavour defended its commercial aspects and he made the question into one of confidence, leaving it quite certain that a rejection of the treaty would allow him no alternative to resignation. It was not assumed that his resignation would involve that of his colleagues.

Political overtures to Britain were less successful. Azeglio proposed to Palmerston[2] that Her Majesty's Government should instruct her ambassadors in small countries to consult and co-

[1] S.D.P., II, pp. 303–9.   [2] Bianchi, Politica, p. 169.

OXFORD UNIVERSITY PRESS *send with
compliments a review copy of*

MASSIMO D'AZEGLIO
An Artist in Politics, 1798-1866,
by Ronald Marshall

PRICE in
United Kingdom:

50/- net

NO REVIEW *should appear before publication
of the book on:*

14 April 1966

THE SOURCE *of the book should be stated
as follows:*

Oxford University Press

*The publishers would be grateful for a clipping
of your review, which should be sent to them at*

ELY HOUSE,
37 DOVER STREET, LONDON W1

operate with Sardinia's representatives on matters affecting both countries: parallel instructions had been given to Sardinian ministers. To this Palmerston agreed; but an additional request for a British guarantee of Sardinia's independence was declined, Palmerston explaining that it was not in accordance with British policy to give such guarantees. Palmerston was confident, he said, that should Austria attack Sardinia France would intervene. To this Azeglio made the sensible reply that intervention would be equally unwelcome whether from Austria or from France: the one would seek to compel the abrogation of the Sardinian constitution, the other, once established in Savoy and Nice, might be difficult to dislodge. It is interesting to see how apprehensive Piedmont was about French hopes of gaining these territories as early as 1851, even though there was no more than rumour to go upon. Apart from this slight rebuff Azeglio had every reason to be well pleased by the trend of English official policy and English public opinion. Gladstone's famous letters indicting the treatment of political prisoners in the Kingdom of the Two Sicilies were translated and published in Cavour's *Risorgimento* and then issued in pamphlet form: they were widely circulated and read, by no one more enthusiastically than Azeglio. As he observed to Abercromby, they were especially valuable as coming from someone not too closely associated with Palmerston. References to Sardinia and the moderation of her Government in a House of Commons speech by Palmerston were also appreciated, whilst Abercromby was busily sending dispatches from Turin intended to furnish his Prime Minister with more ammunition. In August he wrote: 'The oppressions and degradations that they [the Italian people] have been made to suffer have roused a spirit which I feel satisfied will only be allayed by the complete withdrawal of the Austrians from Italy.'[1]

To balance this feeling that Britain's attitude towards Sardinia was friendly and likely to remain so, there was apprehension about the position of France. All parties in Piedmont, even those of the Right, regretted the presence of the French garrison in Rome, where the Government of Pius IX was growing more and more self-confident and more and more repressive. Naturally the politicians of the Left were the more hostile to this aspect of the foreign policy of the Prince-President Louis Napoleon Bonaparte. But when the situation inside France was under consideration the

[1] F.O. 67, Vol. 178, August 1851.

Right was more apprehensive than the Left. To them it seemed that the Revolution that had broken out violently in February 1848 was only temporarily being held in check, and another major crisis might be impending. The news of the *coup d'état* by Louis Napoleon on 2 December 1851 therefore came as a reassurance to many in Piedmont: an autocratic government in France was less to be feared than the anarchy that, according to inspired sources, had been impending. When news of the seizure of power by the President came to Turin Azeglio was unwell and it was Cavour's task to report to the Chamber the attitude of the Government. This he did cautiously but approvingly. Roberto d'Azeglio was less restrained. He was delighted to see Louis Napoleon firmly in power, and, strangely enough in a man of such integrity, he was as pleased as he was excited by the skill with which this thoroughly unscrupulous seizure of power had been carried out.

A less spectacular 'take-over' was preparing in Piedmont also. Cavour was becoming more and more obviously the source of energy in Azeglio's ministry. As far back as April 1851 he had replaced Nigra at the Ministry of Finance, adding this to his other offices. Nigra's total lack of interest in the parliamentary side of his duties had not been compensated by any success in managing the state's finances, a task for which as a banker he ought to have had some flair. There was no prospect of ending the run of deficits, and expenditure was continuing to mount. Railways were eating capital: army reforms led to seemingly insatiable demands for money. Even education was expanding and funds had to be found for the building of public schools. The ministry's methods of book-keeping did not make things easier, for they were antiquated and incomprehensible except to those trained in their arcane mysteries. Some seventy-five million *lire* were needed and the only way to get them quickly was by borrowing. Previous loans had been negotiated by Hambro's, but Cavour preferred to turn to Rothschilds', since he wished to prevent Hambro's gaining a monopoly of Sardinian banking business. When this loan was being finally arranged in January 1852 there was some suspicion in diplomatic circles that the ostensible reasons for it were no more than pretexts, and that the ministry was going to place the money in a secret reserve only to be tapped in case of war. In this as in all matters since he entered the ministry Cavour had done a good job: Azeglio was aware of that, and so was Cavour. Relations between them were becoming more and more strained. In April 1851 Azeglio had written to Emanuele: 'Cavour is as despotic as the devil, and I who do not like despots nearly walked out a few days ago over the Persano business.' A few days later Roberto told his son: 'Cavour lords it more exaltedly every day . . . I am afraid the ministry will change its name, and I am doing all I can to persuade Massimo that they have two specializations, two positions each of his own kind and equally necessary to the conduct of public affairs, but it seems he is getting to the limit. He has an awkward bedfellow. . . .'[1]

As 1851 drew to its end the omens for Azeglio were less and less auspicious. Although he had been cheerful about his health in the autumn, holidaying at Sestri Ponente, swimming and doing gymnastics on the sands, confident that his wound was at last healing completely, this proved to be a delusion. On his return to Turin he was even less active than usual in the Chamber, but now with good reason. Parliament reopened in November and the budget was its first major task. The Left were probing hard to find any weak spot in the ministry's actions, criticizing appointments as being too exclusively made to the advantage of the men on the right, and querying expenditure item by item, as any opposition should be expected to do. Azeglio's illness left the burden to be shouldered by Cavour, but despite his skill the debates on the budget made slow progress. Abercromby, who had been appointed to The Hague and was soon to leave Turin, was pessimistic.

The tactics of members composing the left-centre have been to profit by the want of union amongst the supporters of the government and to usurp for themselves the power of influencing the decisions of the chamber by giving their votes sometimes in favour of the government sometimes in support of the opposition. The consequence of this is that the action of the government may be crippled in the chamber and they may be forced to yield greater compliance to the wishes of the left than they would otherwise feel inclined to do.[2]

Two days after writing this he had an interview with Azeglio and warned him of the rising influence of the Left, and yet again urged a more active policy.

Activity might have its virtues, but it only served to widen the growing breach between Azeglio and Cavour. This became serious

[1] Letter in O.P.T.   [2] F.O. 67, Vol. 179, 3 December 1851.

again over the question of controlling the Press. Bianchi Giovini was back after his expulsion in August 1850: Azeglio was anxious to see him expelled again but Cavour opposed this step: he was in general more disposed than Azeglio to allow liberty to the Press, and, according to the British chargé d'affaires, threatened to resign should Bianchi Giovini be expelled again. The French *coup d'état* seemed about to cause a crisis over the Press. Journals of the Left had published articles that were either critical or downright offensive on the subject of Louis Napoleon and urgent representations had been made to Azeglio to take action about them. He was anxious to avoid giving any offence to the head of state in France, for he knew well enough that despite the French presence in Rome only France would be in the least likely to help Sardinia in case of war: England might be sympathetic, Palmerston certainly would be: but Palmerston was looking like a spent force, and in fact went out of office over the matter of the *coup d'état*— out for ever, some believed and others, including Queen Victoria and the Prince Consort, hoped. So it was necessary for Azeglio to appease Louis Napoleon. But he did so very cheaply by a press law that was reasonable enough.[1] It is never easy to say where freedom of the Press shades off into intolerable licence, or criticism into libel. This law, introduced by de Foresta and consequently known by his name, laid it down that when proceedings against a journal were undertaken on behalf of a foreign ruler the prosecution need not produce the demand of the insulted party for a prosecution: and the case was to be taken out of the competence of a jury and tried by a judge. Inevitably the Right thought that the measure did not go by any means far enough: the Left, though opposing it, were not unreasonable. Cavour disliked it but accepted it, and though the measure was criticized from both sides it eventually passed very easily, by 100 votes to 44 in the Chamber and by 49 to 3 in the Senate on 10 and 24 February respectively. The law in itself had little importance: but Cavour wished to ensure that it was not used to oppress the Left more heavily than the Right, and began to consider the possibility of making an alliance between the ministry and Rattazzi.

[1] King, for instance, not usually too favourable to Azeglio, takes this view, op. cit., Vol. I, p. 408.

XII

AZEGLIO'S RESIGNATION

THE debates on the Press Law compelled Cavour to look critically at the basis of support that the ministry relied on in the Chamber. The Right Centre that should have been its mainstay was unorganized, uncontrolled, and whimsical in its views. The Right, whose votes were necessary to guarantee a majority, was too reactionary in its opinions, though its leaders such as Balbo, Revel, and Menabrea were men of integrity. Cavour was anxious to free the ministry from its dependence on the Right and to gain the support of the Left Centre under Rattazzi, although to Azeglio Rattazzi was still the man of 1849. In all that now followed it was Cavour's argument that he and his party had not moved to the left, but that Rattazzi had come far enough to the right to have obliterated the gap between them. The Press Law, disliked by both Cavour and Rattazzi, seemed certain to pass, but its enforcement would not be dangerous to civil liberties if the Ministry, after buying or accepting the support of Rattazzi, should have broken with the Right. Cavour was now in contact with Rattazzi, his friend Castelli, in whose house they met, acting as intermediary. They were able to agree on a skeleton programme. Rattazzi and his friends would accept the monarchical principle and the existing constitution: both sides would further a policy of 'civil and political progress', and would maintain the independence of Sardinia from foreign (meaning essentially Austrian) influence.

That some measure of *rapprochement* had been agreed was immediately made clear; during the debate on the Press Law Rattazzi reaffirmed his opposition to the Bill but offered his support to the ministry on general policy. Cavour in reply acknowledged the offer and hoped that it would come into effect at once: then he explicitly broke with the Right. 'The ministry must expect to lose once and for all the feeble support it has received in the past from the Honourable Menabrea and his political associates.' The Right was taken completely by surprise. Menabrea replied that Cavour was free if he wished to set sail for new parliamentary shores, but the Right would hold to their

convictions. Revel declared himself astonished, not so much at
the ministry's divorcing itself from its customary partner, as at its
having made a 'connubial alliance' with the other party. From
that moment the new alliance was known as the 'Connubio'.

The initiative in this realignment had been taken by Cavour: that
this was so was evident to all in the Chamber—from which Azeglio
was absent at the time. The propriety of a subordinate member of
the cabinet thus committing his party and his ministry to such a
change of allies is obviously open to question; but in fairness to
Cavour it must be noted that Azeglio had had plenty of warning
of what was in Cavour's mind, however little he might like it and
however little he might have expected that Cavour would nail his
colours to the mast in this way. At a lunch party Cavour had done
his best to explain what he was intending, and why. Ricci,
Azeglio's son-in-law, had been present, to his embarrassment, and
later described what had happened.[1]

Azeglio, troubled still by his wound, had been lunching from
his couch. Cavour and Ricci were sharing his meal. La Marmora,
the man who had originally talked both Azeglio and the King
into accepting Cavour in the cabinet, had dropped in but was not
lunching; he was standing, his long legs crossed, leaning against
a bureau. At first the conversation was light and gay. Azeglio
was full of talk about a play by Dumas fils being presented at the
Théâtre d'Angennes in Turin by the Meynadier company from
Paris, with a Mademoiselle Fargueil in the leading role. He was
loud in her praise, and seemed to Ricci to be keeping the conversation deliberately on this subject, in which Cavour had no
interest. Seizing an opportunity in a pause between one mouthful
of *frittura* and the next, Cavour spoke as if jestingly of Azeglio's
antipathy to Rattazzi and his party. Azeglio answered, not
jestingly but tartly: Cavour began to become heated. Ricci, much
younger and not involved in politics, hardly dared look up: he
could see La Marmora changing his weight from one foot to
another. Finally Azeglio raised himself on his elbow and in his
broadest Piedmontese said: 'To end this, I wish to hear no more
of Signor Rattazzi!' Red with rage, Cavour rose with his plate of
frittura, flung it on to the floor, ran his fingers through his hair,
and rushed from the room. La Marmora bestirred his long legs
and raced from the room after him to pacify him and bring
him back: but ran in vain.

[1] *Rassegna Nazionale*, 1 April 1882, quoted by Chiala, op. cit., Vol. I, p. 338.

Azeglio's own account of the incident, given in a letter to Rendu on 24 May, differed in a vital respect from Ricci's.

After the famous sitting of 5 February, the 'sitting of the Connubio', I was on cool enough terms with Cavour. Imagine that my dear colleague, without a word said, had arranged this affair with Rattazzi and made his speech committing the ministry without consulting me. That day, like so many others, since this wearisome wound, I was in bed with a fever and the council of ministers was held at my house. Cavour, at the foot of my bed, took one of my ministers into the bay-window and said something like this. . . . 'This Menabrea wearies me and I am tempted to forgo his support.' . . . I knew nothing more: After leaving me they made the explosion in the Chamber.[1]

The difference in the two accounts between a small lunch party and a cabinet meeting does not matter much: but Azeglio is denying having been warned of Cavour's intentions. Ricci's account, which was that of a disinterested person, and carries conviction by its precision of detail, does not confute Azeglio, since it does not say that Cavour had explained his intentions: but it does show that Cavour had done all he could to warn Azeglio: and if Azeglio had not been told it was because he had refused to listen to what Cavour was trying to say, and this refusal implies that he must have guessed what he was in danger of having to hear. Still, admitting that Azeglio had not been left totally unwarned, Cavour had none the less exceeded his authority in giving his rebuff to Menabrea and his welcome to Rattazzi. His excuse must be that a time inevitably comes when, if the higher authority refuses to take action, the subordinate must do so of his own initiative. The successful pursuit of government policy demanded a stable majority of supporters in the Chamber. As the Right had not provided it, the Centre was bound to turn to the Left. Azeglio's procrastination, his incapacity for hard political thought, and his personal aversion from Rattazzi had let the crisis develop.

Once it became patent Azeglio made the best of a bad job and in public defended the Connubio without hinting that it had been concerted behind his back and against his own prejudices. To Rendu he wrote: 'We were in the midst of serious business [i.e. at the time of the Connubio] and I did not wish the public to be made aware of internal divisions: and wishing to see what

[1] Rendu, op. cit., p. 74.

P

would develop I acted like the general who, disobeyed by his troops, puts himself at their head to hide their treachery from the enemy.' In a speech to the Senate on 5 April he cast the cloak of his approbation over the Connubio: but he skilfully planted a few darts in some of his cabinet colleagues. For years, he argued, he and his ministry had been accused, inside and outside Parliament, of reactionary tendencies. Now they stood accused of having thrown in their lot with the party of revolution. In fact he had followed a straight line—the active defence of the constitution. At first this had been menaced from the left: the ministry had therefore seemed to stand on the right. But the *coup d'état* of Louis Napoleon had given encouragement to reactionaries throughout Europe, and in Piedmont-Sardinia the constitution was now under attack from the right. During the debates on the Press Law the Right had urged modification of the very basis of the constitution: the Left 'supported the ministry in its determination not to touch it [i.e. the constitution]: and as this support was not the result of any pact, as there was no bargaining, no demands or imposed conditions, the ministry accepted the support as any ministry would'.[1]

Thus Azeglio covered up the way in which he had been taken by surprise, saving his own reputation as well as Cavour's. But his speech went on to reiterate his argument that his ministry was anything but revolutionary, and ironically reminded the Senate that Cavour had been hissed in the Chamber (though he did not find it necessary to point out that this was by Cavour's new-found friends), that Farini, whilst still in his native Rome, had been associated with Pius IX rather than with the murderers of Rossi, and that La Marmora was the general who had suppressed the republican movement in Genoa in 1849. This might well have cleared them all of any charge of being on the extreme left: but it could not have been very pleasant listening—for them or for their new friends.

The experience he had undergone with the Connubio ought to have taught Azeglio that he needed to keep his ear somewhat nearer to the ground to find out what was happening even in so small a circle as his own cabinet, and to exercise some much more decisive control. This he failed to do. No doubt ill-health was to some extent responsible: he was still spending much time either on his couch or in his bed: yet even had he been in the

[1] *S.D.P.*, II, pp. 337ff.

rudest physical health he might still have drifted on, leaving cabinet and Parliament to make their own policy or to lie, if they so wished, becalmed between conflicting winds of change.

But on 9 March he received a shock serious enough in itself and the precursor of a really paralysing one to follow. On that day the Chamber proceeded to the election of a President for the session. By eighty-six votes out of 123 Azeglio's candidate was elected: but with seventy-one votes out of the same total Rattazzi was elected one of the Chamber's Vice-Presidents. This was a clear indication that the Connubio was becoming an active co-operation and not merely an exchange of civilities across the floor of the House. The Right could not ignore this, and from now on Revel and his party voted consistently against the Government, which thus lost some fifteen to twenty votes in the Chamber. As against this, the Left brought it the support of some thirty to thirty-five votes, a net gain of about fifteen if the Left should prove more consistent in its support than the Right had been. This support it did not give with any alacrity, and within a week the ministry escaped defeat by only two votes on a motion to sanction expenditure on defence works at Casale. As usual the danger had been due to sheer carelessness. No attempt had been made to whip in the Government's supporters and most of the ministers were themselves absent from the House when the vote was taken. As a solatium, a vote approving La Marmora's actions in suppressing disturbances in Sardinia was passed almost unanimously five days later, having been made a vote of confidence by the ministry. Whether or not Casale would be a nuisance to an invader, it was nuisance enough to Azeglio. For after its narrow passage in the Chamber the Bill to sanction the military works there had a rough passage in the Senate. This time Azeglio tried to prepare the ground, and lobbied senators in advance: but it proved a close-run thing. The vote was in effect one of confidence. The opposition sought to turn it into a vote of censure on the Government's recent veering to the left with the Connubio. Whatever Azeglio might think about the Connubio, he had to defend it in the speech already quoted: and the money for Casale was finally voted: but only by thirty-six votes to thirty-two.

Roberto d'Azeglio explained the underlying situation to his son in London. The ministry had gone ahead with expenditure at Casale in anticipation of Parliament voting the grant. It had then made as good a case as it could to the Chamber, and had been voted three or four hundred thousand francs. But it had made no attempt to justify itself to the Senate. 'And the senators have already complained on numerous occasions of being cavalierly treated by the ministers, accusing them of expecting the Senate's support as a ministerial fief.' Also, a tactless article in *Risorgimento*, regarded as a semi-official paper, 'summoned the Senate to give a favourable vote, and contained menacing phrases. I myself was angry at reading it and thought the effect it was bound to have would be bad. . . . The ministry has preserved some of the customs of absolute monarchy, the habit of posing as head of the state alongside the King, and forgets that in a constitutional system it is first of all the King who counts, then the Upper House, next the elected Chamber which completes the hierarchy, the ministry following behind.'[1]

For this narrow escape in the Senate the ministry found consolation a few days later in a vote of confidence in the Chamber of 137 to 23. But Roberto had noted his brother's political failing, his tendency to go ahead without consulting Parliament, though this was due not so much, as he suggested, to high-handedness as to lack of political flair. On the question of fiscal policy the new British Minister at Turin, Sir James Hudson, reported a curious piece of information. The ministry had expressed a determination to finance its policy as far as possible from taxation rather than from loans, though in the end, especially after Cavour had become Premier, it became regular custom to budget for a deficit and to rely on loans to cover expenditure. At this juncture, according to Hudson, the deputies from Savoy had objected to this policy and had threatened to withdraw from the Chamber in protest if the ministry should insist on such drastic financial measures. This was not totally unlikely, for Savoy, next to the island of Sardinia, was the poorest part of the King's dominions and would find itself hard hit by any increases in taxation.[2]

Hudson, who had taken over the post in Turin after Abercromby's appointment to The Hague at the end of 1851, was to regard this mission as his life's work. Like Abercromby, though for a longer period and with much more enthusiasm, he was to consider himself not just as the channel of official communications, but also as unofficial adviser to Sardinian Governments. And into the bargain he was their most sedulous advocate to the British Foreign Office. After Palmerston's dismissal in December 1851

[1] From a letter in O.P.T.   [2] F.O. 67, Vol. 184.

Malmesbury had come to the Foreign Office, and Hudson's dispatches to him are often extraordinary reading. At times he mustered up sufficient patience to explain the Piedmontese situation to Malmesbury in the simplest possible terms as to a willing if not very bright pupil: but some of his letters are written in a vein of scarcely veiled insolence, treating the minister as the veriest tyro, pretending to know more than his professional servants.[1] Hudson's opinion of Azeglio was never very high, yet as long as Azeglio was Prime Minister, Hudson would defend him in his dispatches. But from the very beginning of his mission in Turin Hudson was Cavour's man and in his eyes Cavour could do no wrong.

In April it was known that Pinelli, the President of the Chamber, was dying. This circumstance caused, first of all, a flutter in ecclesiastical circles. For Pinelli had supported the Siccardi Laws. Could the clergy give him extreme unction, or was he to be allowed to die unshriven like Santa Rosa, and thus bring down another storm upon the Church? The Chapter of Turin Cathedral deliberated the matter and decided, by a majority of one vote, to administer the last rites of the Church. So one kind of crisis was averted. But the political one was to shake the ministry to its foundations.

Having already blundered once by not arranging the election of a Vice-President in advance, Azeglio repeated his mistake now that the presidency fell vacant. Cavour, determined to bind Rattazzi and his party inescapably to the support of the Right Centre, was discreetly promoting Rattazzi's candidacy for the presidency. The ministry as a whole had again neglected to select and insist on a candidate of its own and left the matter to the free vote of the Chamber. Such a vote may be the best way of selecting a Speaker of the British House of Commons, since he is politically impartial: but the President of the Sardinian Chamber, like his counterpart in other continental assemblies, acted as a one-man 'steering committee' on behalf of the Government, and his election was therefore far too important to be left to the vagaries of the members any more than the choice of a Lord Chancellor is to be left to the free vote of the British House of Lords. When the Chamber proceeded to the election Azeglio himself was once again absent. For this he might have had some excuse, for his

---

[1] See, for example, dispatches of 21 April 1852 (F.O. 67, Vol. 184) and 14 June 1852 (F.O. 67, Vol. 185).

wound was still giving him pain: but most of the cabinet seem
also to have been absent—with no such collective excuse. As a
result Rattazzi gained a majority, though only on a third ballot.
His election should have completed the Connubio. But the scheme
misfired, at least for the time being: for as Rattazzi came in,
Cavour had to go out. Azeglio gave a curious explanation of the
event to his nephew in a letter whose light-heartedness was
somewhat artificial. 'Some busybodies gave many deputies to
understand that the King was favourable, or at least indifferent,
to Rattazzi's nomination, and they, being so endowed as to
understand damn-all, found the idea most attractive.'[1] That
Victor Emmanuel should have favoured such a candidate seems
at first glance improbable, even though they drew together later:
but after his election to the presidency Rattazzi placed himself at
the King's command, whether to accept or decline the office.
The King was firm. 'Tell Monsieur Rattazzi that I desire him to
keep it. To decline would be an act of weakness.'[2]

Azeglio had shown himself long-suffering. But the election of
Rattazzi and the notoriety of Cavour's arrangement of it were
too much for his self-esteem. The cabinet was divided and he
realized that he could no longer postpone its remodelling. Four
days after the election of Rattazzi he saw the King, and the next
day, 17 May, it was made known that the cabinet's resignation
had been accepted by His Majesty. By the 19th a new cabinet
had been formed. Cibrario, always a close confidant of the King,
came in as Minister of Finance. Cavour, as was expected, was
out. His exclusion created no sensation. He was recognized to
be a man of ability, but was still distrusted. Costanza d'Azeglio
spoke of his 'frivolous behaviour, his sulks', but she was acute
enough to add: 'He is believed to be the only man who can guide
us out of the financial embarrassment that threatens us.' From
Paris Collegno reported that the French Press spoke highly of
Azeglio and hoped he would continue to guide Sardinia: Pantaleoni in Rome saw the situation in a light more menacing to
Azeglio. 'I always regretted the lack of any organization in the
Chamber and the absence of discipline in the cabinet. Now you
have had an experience of it. How did your Government ever
come to appear before the Chamber without a candidate? Why
did you never make sure of a majority? . . . Now you have Cavour

[1] Bianchi, *Lettere*, p. 191.
[2] As reported by Hudson, 12 May 1852, F.O. 67, Vol. 185.

in opposition, and he will have the Left Centre with him. He is a passionate and ambitious man and will be followed by those wild democrats. . . .'[1] Pallavicino (24 May) struck a balance. 'Cavour is as good as d'Azeglio. In politics, a man of dubious reputation, but active and intelligent, is often preferable to a man who is honest but stupid, sick, or lazy. Monsieur d'Azeglio is not stupid —far from it—but for some time now he has had neither health of body nor energy of mind. He is worn out.'[2] A few days later he was more subtle in his judgement. 'Cavour is now the man for Piedmont: Massimo d'Azeglio is still just the man of Moncalieri.' This was utterly true. Azeglio was living on his past reputation, on one decisive political action, but an action that was now an historic event: his political eclipse was certain. Cavour had the future to offset Azeglio's past. Oldofreddi summed it up. 'The present Azeglio ministry cannot last, but the moment to overthrow it has not yet come, for in his place we could only have Revel.'

Cavour wisely and tactfully withdrew for a time from public activity in politics, making a trip to Paris and London. In these capitals he learnt how highly Azeglio was regarded as a democrat who was also a bulwark against revolutionary excesses. Perhaps it would be better to treat him with a little more show of deference, to let his ministry subside quietly rather than assail it violently. The King had already warned him that he for one was not going to be rushed. 'Monsieur le Comte, you have an income of a hunddred and fifty thousand *livres*, and whatever happens you will be all right. But understand that I do not want to end up where my father finished.'[3]

Whether Azeglio had learnt anything from the May crisis is very doubtful. Margherita Provana di Collegno, admittedly an enemy with a bitter tongue and pen, thought not. Her husband's letters from the Sardinian ministry in Paris were never answered: he suspected they were never read. Instead of letters to him, Azeglio sent special messengers. Turgot asked Collegno for information about a proposed treaty of commerce between the two countries: Collegno had been told nothing of it. 'It seems that they keep things from you in Turin.' Azeglio, she said, was an anachronism, a blend of the Chevalier Bayard and Salvator Rosa. He saw everything as an artist would, conspiring, fighting, and even giving an artistic colour to the job of being Prime Minister. He was an artist even in his marriages, the matrimonial role not being one in which he had shone. He and Charles Albert were two very curious figures for the nineteenth century anywhere and for Sardinia at any time.[1]

If Azeglio was still dilatory he did not lack friends who were urging him to action. Hudson warned him that Austria was reported to be trying to force Prussia to admit her into the Prussian customs union along with her non-German territories. Should Prussia yield to Austria, the results to Sardinia might be serious, as transit trade might well be diverted from Genoa to Trieste. To counteract this Hudson argued that Sardinia must press on as fast as possible with the development of her rail communications from Genoa to Susa and thence via the Mont Cenis. To tunnel through the mountains would, he thought, be impossibly costly and passengers and goods would have to go over the pass by road: on the other side the railway should run to Geneva and, less importantly, he thought, to Lyons. Action on this railway scheme was in fact going ahead and Hudson's promptings were not of great originality: as for the tunnel and for Geneva as the major objective he was to be proved quite wrong.

The King also was asking for more signs of activity. On 23 June it became known that he had sent a personal letter to the President of the Senate urging him to see that affairs were transacted in a less dilatory and more systematic way in his House. Some of the Senate had been shown the letter and had taken umbrage, not so much because of its perhaps embarrassing good sense but because it seemed an excessive intervention by the King in their private business. It seemed for a time that they might show their pique by rejecting some of the essential measures then before them. Quite a considerable quarrel flared up. In a Senate debate on 23 July it was revealed that the letter had come quite unconstitutionally, over the King's own signature alone with no ministerial counter-signature, and that the President of the Senate had been unconstitutional, therefore, in submitting it to a committee of the Senate for consideration. The House went into secret session to discuss the letter: and as far as anyone outside was concerned there the matter ended. But the King made it extremely clear to the President that he was angry with him for disclosing what was

---

[1] A. Malvezzi (ed.), *Diario politico di Margherita Provana di Collegno* (1926), (hereafter referred to as *Diario politico*), pp. 20, 26.

meant to be a completely private letter. Perhaps there was more to it than this. Is it possible that Azeglio had approved verbally of the letter? It chimed well with what must have been his personal view, and he might have talked to the King about the need to give some kind of goad to the Senate: but for this there is not a particle of evidence, and the King took full responsibility.

Amidst political worries Azeglio had some cause for domestic satisfaction in June 1852 when his daughter Rina became engaged to Marchese Ricci. They planned to live in Florence, to her father's delight, for then they would be not too far from Turin and in the Tuscany that he loved as much as he detested the Papal States, where Ricci's family was established. This was to prove a happy marriage, though for a time it was to give Azeglio a certain amount of worry and of ribald amusement.

In the wearisome tale of ministerial manœuvres and rather squalid caballings against a background of somewhat trivial parliamentary debates, it is almost refreshing to find a major political question once more dividing Parliament, royal family, and country in 1852, with the revival of controversy over relations between State and Church.

Since the autumn of 1851 there had been renewed contacts between Sardinia and the Holy See. The King had been in correspondence with the Pope and though on the whole his letters had shown loyalty to the constitution, there had been some passages in them to which his ministers might well have taken objection. In a letter of 13 February 1852 he wrote: 'May Your Holiness take note that in the present form of government I cannot take this initiative, and so I see the termination of this most unhappy affair retarded . . . but you must also know that if in any matter my policy displeases you it is my duty to follow it in this way, and for the present I cannot change it.' The references to 'the present form of government' and the repetition of 'for the present' show his reluctance to accept his constitutional position as necessarily permanent.

The Government for its part had been going through the motions of negotiating with the Pope, who had taken the initiative by making known his willingness to reopen discussion. Sambuy had been sent to Rome as Sardinian Envoy-Extraordinary and Minister-Plenipotentiary, arriving there on 11 November. But he had been most dilatory: only on 16 December did he announce that he had received the full powers to make final agreements (and Pius was still under the impression that his name was 'Sembury'). But when the Vatican made it clear that there could be no discussion on future measures until there had been agreement about past ones—meaning the Concordat—Sambuy could go no further. A note to him from the plenipotentiary of the Holy See dated 28 February, offering a basis for further discussion, went unanswered for eight months. And in the meantime the Civil Marriage Bill had become a vital issue in Turin.[1]

In effect Azeglio's Government had sent to Rome a negotiator who could not negotiate, since he could not discuss the past, and the Vatican would not discuss the future. The only explanation must be that the mere presence in Rome of an emissary gave some verisimilitude to the assertion made in the speech from the throne of 4 March 1852. In it the Government referred to the impending presentation of a Bill concerning 'the civil status of the family', a matter affecting religion and morals, both of which should be under Parliament's care. 'And for this very purpose the negotiations opened up with Rome have been intended. Sincere and reverent in guiding them, we are confident that they will end in reconciling the rights of the State with the true interests of religion and the Church.' It is well as a general rule to be on guard against the politician who is so devoted to the 'true interests' of his opponent, and Azeglio's professed, and in lay matters usually genuine, regard for honour in public and in his own personal affairs is hardly enhanced by this double-talk.

A commission had been engaged in drafting this law since November 1850. Its first draft had undergone modification after modification and in the end a civil ceremony had become optional instead of compulsory, being retained for those to whom a religious ceremony might be denied (divorcees or people outside the Church). But a marriage was only to be recognized by the State if it had been registered by the state registrars. A Bill to this effect passed the Chamber by ninety-four votes to thirty-five on 5 July 1852. To get it through the Senate was going to be a far more difficult task.

The Church, as was to be expected, demanded the outright rejection of the Bill, and made it clear that anyone who married by civil ceremony without religious rites would be excommunicated. The Bill, it was said, was a direct imitation of French Law,

---

[1] For Sambuy's mission to Rome see Pirri, *Cart. priv.*, pp. 71*–79* of Introduction to Vol. I.

and would lead to as high a rate of bastardy in Sardinia as prevailed in France. This argument was a godsend to the journals supporting the Bill, and relevant statistics were gleefully quoted by them. France, where civil marriage was compulsory, had a rate of 92·8 per cent. legitimate, and 7·2 per cent. illegitimate births: Austria and Bavaria, without civil marriage, had respectively 88·6 and 79·4 per cent. legitimate and 11·4 and 20·6 per cent. illegitimate births. Controversy over morality and statistics raged on in public and the Bill made no progress in the Senate. It was still under discussion when Cavour became Prime Minister. But bit by bit it was being made meaningless. The Senate sub-committee in its wisdom finally so modified the Bill as to make the validity of the civil marriage dependent on that of the religious one, should the contracting couple so wish, the civil marriage to be automatically dissolved if the Church should nullify the religious one. In this way the Bill was made to stand upon its own head. But ultimately, in November 1852, the vitally important first article was defeated in the Senate and the future of the Bill was hopeless. In all this the Church had been actively making clear its views. In a long letter of 2 July the Pope had informed the King of the utter inacceptability of the measure. 'The voice of conscience and the esteem and affection I feel for Your Majesty impose on me the duty of warning you that the projected law on marriage published in Turin is not Catholic.'[1] This letter, arriving at a time when feeling in Piedmont was running especially high, with protests against the Bill pouring in from the clergy throughout the kingdom, popular demonstrations in villages and small towns organized by parish priests and banned by the police, and with right-wing journals harried by the censorship, upset the King and convinced him that he must take action, even if it had to be surreptitious and unconstitutional.

Azeglio chose this moment to go on holiday, leaving La Marmora, his War Minister, in charge of affairs: so it was to him that the King showed the Pope's letter. La Marmora passed it on to Boncompagni and Cibrario, two other cabinet ministers, whom he asked to draft a reply. This took the form of an exposition of the unsatisfactory state of existing legislation, a defence of the proposed law, and a protest against the motives and methods of some of the Bill's opponents. This letter, for which the cabinet had to accept responsibility, though it was not signed by any

[1] Pirri, *Cart. priv.*, Vol. I, Document 24, p. 103.

minister and had not been seen by the Prime Minister, was sent
to the Piedmontese representative in Rome, Sambuy, for trans-
mission to the Pope. And this was, we may assume, the letter that
Victor Emmanuel had in mind when he later told Cavour that his
reply had been read and approved by the cabinet. Margherita
Provana di Collegno made the same assertion as though it were a
matter of common knowledge.[1]

But the most dangerous enemy of truth may be the half-truth.
And with this letter went another, signed by the King, that
could not conceivably have been seen, still less approved, by his
ministers before it was sent.[2] This began unexceptionably by
repeating that he had not seen anything anti-Catholic in the Bill,
which he said he had been led to believe would be acceptable to
the Church, for similar legislation had been introduced into other
Catholic states. Towards the end of the letter he regretted that
the Holy See had been intransigent on other matters. 'If Your
Holiness believes that the obstacles to the clearing up of this affair
come from one side, may he observe that there are some also from
another side. . . . I do not consider it to be religion to call a state
to revolt against its head and its laws whether by writings or by
base deception such as are anything but Christian or Catholic.'
To the content of all this Azeglio would have said 'Bravo', though
he would have disapproved its being sent without his foreknow-
ledge. But in the middle of the letter was a statement that would
have struck him as ominous. For the King wrote: 'Now may I
observe to Your Holiness that the law has still not gone for the
approval of the Senate, in which body are gathered the leading
virtues and abilities of the kingdom.' This could only be interpreted as meaning that the Senate, wiser and less demagogic than
the Chamber, might modify or even reject the Bill. It was in fact
the King's firm intention now to kill it outright, either by com-
pelling his ministry to abandon it, or by organizing sufficient
opposition in the Senate to out-vote it. A little over two years
later he was to remind the Pope of the success of his personal
policy, and to promise to defeat Cavour's schemes as decisively
as he had defeated Azeglio's. 'May Your Holiness realize that it
was I who did not permit the passing by the Senate of the law on
matrimony: and that it is I who will now do all in my power to
prevent the passing of this law on the convents. . . . I for my part

---

[1] *Diario politico*, p. 87.
[2] Pirri, *Cart. priv.*, Vol. I, pp. 104ff. Jemolo, op. cit., p. 133.

have always done all I can. . . . I will see that this law does not pass: but help me now.'[1] (He naïvely asked the Pope to burn this note after reading it.)

Having thus acted on his own by sending his personal letter, the King sought to regularize his position by sending copies to Azeglio.

I send you the letter the Pope wrote to me, and the one that I, poor devil, sent him in reply with a franked return so that it could be sent back to me: along with my own I sent a dignified unsigned letter written by the ministry summarizing the motives for the introduction of the Bill. . . . As you know, a most bitter campaign has been opened by the priestly party, hoping to turn the scales in their favour and rejecting no means of gaining their ends. I am having to bear the consequences, and if you do not show a little elasticity and solicitude towards Rome it is I who will end by having to skip, and not just my worthy ministers. . . . You will see the outline of my ideas from the letter I have sent the Pope, and you will give me your views. Above all it is essential to set to work, since the others are working hard.[2]

Massimo's reply has not been preserved—or has not been found. But it stung the King to a sharp reprimand. 'When I do something I know what it is I am doing, and, to speak plainly, I am not fond of receiving advice. . . . When I need it I will ask for it. For all that, do not bear me a grudge, my dear Massimo. I know well that you wrote me that splendid letter in order that I might say "Bravo" to it. And "Bravo" I say if you wish. But it is still true that with your comments you gave me a certificate of asininity. All the same I still do not think I am a total fool.'[3] A jesting tone was resumed at the end of this letter, and continued in the later ones. But the close personal tie between King and minister was breaking. The King's dislike of ministerial policy became steadily deeper: he resented its unpopularity amongst large and vocal sections of the people, an unpopularity that extended not only to the policy and to the ministers but, he feared, to himself also: and he resented the casualness of Azeglio, who, apart from one brief visit, stayed away from Turin throughout this difficult period. 'It seems to me that the grief the Grand Vizier must feel at his remoteness from the tyrant is mitigated by the pleasures found elsewhere: it is the way of the world: whilst I am in torments he enjoys the delights of Spezia.'[4]

[1] Pirri, *Cart. priv.*, Vol. I, Document 37, p. 157.   [2] Ibid., pp. 107–8.

[3] Vaccaluzzo first published this and cognate letters (see op. cit., pp. 395–8) but I have followed Pirri in assigning them to this date.

[4] Pirri, *Cart. priv.*, Vol. I, p. 107.

On 17 September the Pope replied to the King's letter of 25 July. The attitude of the Church towards the matters in dispute was stated with moderation and clarity, and the Pope made a most solemn appeal to the King. 'Your Majesty, we speak to you in the name of Jesus Christ, whose Vicar, however unworthy, we are, and in his most holy name tell you not to sanction this law that is fertile of so many disorders. We beg you also to seek to have some restraint placed upon the press, that overflows continuously with blasphemies and immorality.'[1] Both tone and content of the letter affected the King and deepened his determination to prevent the passing of the Bill. On 21 October he informed the cabinet that his conscience would not permit him to assent to a law that would displease the Pope, and that he was prepared to sacrifice anything for his country save only his conscience.

Only an inner circle of politicians and courtiers may have known how deeply the King was committed to opposition to this Bill, and how decisively he would use his influence to defeat it. But it was evident to all that the ministry was tottering to its fall. Even Malmesbury at the Foreign Office had heard so, and wrote in perturbation to Hudson, fearing lest Azeglio's overthrow should bring the 'democrat' party into power. Hudson replied with one of his typical dispatches, carefully spelling out the situation in a Chamber of Deputies where the extreme Left could muster twenty-one votes, the extreme Right, seventeen and the various Centre groups at present supporting the ministry seventy-four. Simple arithmetic seemed to make the accession to power of the 'democrats' somewhat unlikely: and though Azeglio might soon go, his successor was much more likely to come from the same centre grouping, with perhaps support from the right. On this last point Hudson was wrong: the Connubio was still potent enough to beget a ministry. That Cavour would be Azeglio's heir seemed most probable. Thiers in Paris told the Collegnos that 'Cavour will come to be in charge sooner or later, for he is the ablest man in Sardinia'.[2]

Cavour himself, then in London, was not so sanguine that the change was to come soon.

If the King stands by Azeglio I think we shall have to put up with the present ministry. Furthermore I have to admit to the conviction that the name Azeglio still exercises a great influence here. Ninety per cent. of English politicians know of absolutely no one else: to him alone do

[1] Pirri, *Cart. priv.*, Vol. I, pp. 116ff.   [2] *Diario politico*, p. 31.

May - Oct. 1852

Cavour out

9 8/he

they attribute whatever has been done well in Piedmont. You will tell me that this is an error or an injustice: so be it. But it is so, and it will be impossible to correct it without harming the reputation of our country. Palmerston, who has been infinitely pleasant to me, said straight out: 'In England we value Azeglio, we have great confidence in him.' To convince yourself how Azeglio is judged here read the article on Piedmont that has just come out in the *Edinburgh Review*. This is anything but hostile to me—on the contrary it says many agreeable things on my behalf: yet despite that, it judges the recent ministerial crisis [over the Connubio] one-sidedly, putting Azeglio completely in the right.[1]

Malmesbury was still kinder to Cavour, assuring him that not only Her Majesty's but the French Government too would be pleased to see him back in office: and Emanuele d'Azeglio also told him that his uncle would be happy to see Cavour return to the cabinet. Cavour's unwillingness to do so was not due to political reasons: as he assured Malmesbury, the ministry was now relying on the support of the Left Centre brought to it by the Connubio, even though the creators of that alliance were out of office: the only obstacle to his return was purely personal—a feeling that he and his friends had been treated cavalierly.[2] To Cavour it seemed clear that in England the Tories were less attached to Azeglio than were the Whigs. This was partly because they were less unsympathetic to Rome than the Whigs: but it was to some extent due to their suspicion of the personal influence of Emanuele d'Azeglio with the Whig leaders.

Cavour felt certain that time was on his side, so certain that he knew he need not rush things. 'I do not consider Azeglio indispensable. I even believe him more harmful than useful. But I maintain that we must not overthrow him, or allow him to be overthrown, by violent means. If he should fall, or, better, resign, it would be a great blessing to our country. But should he stay on, by his own or some higher will, I think we shall have to remain patient.'

If Azeglio's ministry was on the verge of being discredited by its failure to cope with a major question, small-scale oddities could still distract attention from the greater issue. In August both Azeglio and Hudson were put to some trouble by the writings in a Turin newspaper of a journalist named Ivan Golovine. His

[1] Chiala, op. cit., Vol. I, p. 259. The article referred to appeared, unsigned, in the *Edinburgh Review*, Vol. XCVI, July 1852, pp. 36–54.

[2] Chiala, op. cit., Vol. I, pp. 270–3.

criticisms of Azeglio were distasteful: but the anti-clerical tone of some of his articles went beyond what was tolerable. The complication for Hudson was that despite his name and his domicile Golovine was a British subject, who appealed to Hudson for protection. For Azeglio the complication was that some of the more damaging sentences or paragraphs were acknowledged extracts from Azeglio's own earlier writings, quoted out of context, perhaps, but nevertheless his words, not Golovine's.[1]

Less worrying, but a matter of concern to him, was the future of the Sardinian Picture Gallery. Formerly the royal collection, kept in the palace, it had been given to the state by Charles Albert, and had been transferred to rooms on the first floor of the Palazzo Madama. In this palace the Senate sat, and the rooms in which the pictures hung were wanted by the Senate as committee rooms. It was therefore proposed to remove the collection from the Palazzo to the Academy of Fine Arts: Roberto d'Azeglio, as Director of the National Gallery, was opposed to this, and wished instead to move the Senate. For some time to come senators were to be interposed between paintings and public.

In October the Parliament reassembled. Azeglio had prolonged the recess as much as he could, but the day of reckoning was come upon him. Cavour had seen its imminence and was back in Piedmont. As early as 6 September he had written:

It is time the comedy that Azeglio is playing should end. If he wishes to stay in power let him say so and he will have sincere allies in us. But if he is tired of power, let him depart and desist from making governmental problems insoluble by his continual hesitations. I have my own personal grievance against Azeglio, who has offended me, and offended me gravely. But I have no spite against him. I think that after his behaviour towards me he himself would cease to respect me if I agreed to return to office as long as our foreign policy continues to be directed as it has been in the past.[2]

Three weeks later, having heard that Azeglio had decided to resign, he approved the decision as the best 'for him, for us, and, what matters most, for our country'. It is odd and unconvincing to imagine Cavour as the injured party as a result of the Connubio crisis; almost more odd for him to have been misinformed, since Azeglio's decision was only made a month later.

But such a decision was inevitable. Cavour was in touch with

[1] Hudson's dispatches of August 1852, F.O. 67, Vol. 185.
[2] Letter to Ponza di San Martino, Chiala, op. cit., Vol. I, pp. 282–4.

Rattazzi through the latter's brother, and when the showdown finally came Rattazzi went out to join Cavour at his country house at Leri. The Left-Centre was moving away from Azeglio, their pretext being his 'weakness' over the anti-clerical laws. With his parliamentary majority slipping away, his cabinet as divided and unorganized as ever, and his rival waiting to inherit his office, Azeglio had to go. But his departure was not a dignified one and in the last few days he talked and acted in an unusually silly way.

For one thing he had quarrelled with Butenval, the French Minister to Turin, who had made a protest over a refugee in such terms that Azeglio had refused to receive it. To some extent Azeglio was in the right and the French Government disavowed Butenval's expression, but Azeglio seems to have become over-excited. In Paris Margherita Collegno even heard that Azeglio had challenged Butenval to a duel!

More seriously, he had been talking nonsense about Britain. On 18 October the King sent for Cavour, just back from London, and told him a strange tale that Cavour recounted to Hudson, who reported it to London. According to Azeglio, 'England had abandoned Piedmont'. He had told one of the Santa Rosa family, whom he had met in the street, that 'Piedmont was in a most critical position, menaced by France and abandoned by Britain', and that 'censorship of the press and modification of the constitution were becoming inevitable'. Hudson assured the King that all this was nonsense, a 'pure figment of Monsieur d'Azeglio's brain'. The following day he went to see Azeglio, who could only quote the vaguest justification for his accusations, which Hudson rebutted, and charged Azeglio with the duty of reporting his rebuttals to the King.[1]

Azeglio resigned on 22 October, and the arguments about his reasons for doing so at that moment continued for a little while. The essential cause was the King's announcement to the cabinet on 21 October that he could not in conscience give consent to a law 'that might displease the Pope', that he 'was ready for any sacrifice for his country saving only that of his conscience'. The next day Azeglio held his last cabinet meeting and announced his decision to resign. Cibrario went with him to see the King at the royal castle at Stupinigi, and later told Cavour that Azeglio had said to him that his resignation had been made necessary by the opposition of Cavour and of a majority, adding, 'Let Cavour come

---

[1] Hudson's dispatches of 25, 26, 28 October, F.O. 67, Vol. 186.

and take over now. But there have been other reasons not to be mentioned.'

Azeglio's sister-in-law blamed 'an incautious and foolish remark offensive to England, made by Azeglio to the Senate commission of foreign affairs', and also thought that the King and others believed that Azeglio stood in the way of a settlement with Rome. The fact that the King offered the premiership to Cesare Balbo suggests his anxiety for such a settlement.

To his wife Azeglio explained nobly enough: 'I cannot enter into explanations of the motive that caused the crisis, but I can tell you that whatever has happened was brought about by circumstances, and all tends to the welfare of the King and of the country.'[1]

Emanuele in London received a fuller explanation.

My ministry was not strong. Little determination in me and in Pernati[2] to be ministers: I because I was weary, he worn out by the attacks of newspapers and plotters. These, powerful in the Chamber, were hoping for Cavour. When he came back from Paris I was willing (and it gave me little enough pleasure!) to receive him as a colleague to keep the boat afloat. He was unwilling. It had come to the point where in the Chamber I could do no more and no less than he wished. That did not suit your humble signatory. . . . Greet my friends, and if anyone plays the Jeremiah over the ministerial change tell him that it was like smallpox; it had to come at one time or another.[3]

[1] Carcano, op. cit., p. 345.
[2] Name supplied from original manuscript in O.P.T.   [3] Bianchi, *Lettere*, p. 213.

XIII
AZEGLIO AS AN EX-PRIME MINISTER

WHATEVER else he might be, for the rest of his life Azeglio was to be an ex-Prime Minister, never again at the centre of public affairs, but never again the completely apolitical creature he had been before writing *Gli ultimi casi*. He would look on from the shore at those still swimming in the sea from which he had emerged, and sometimes he would wade in to give a helping hand: but he would never be a swimmer again. For most of his life he would be *l'homme moyen sensuel*, making a living by such talents as he had, enjoying a life of controlled hedonism, having some family ties but no family responsibilities; from the ordinary bourgeois point of view homeless: living in the present and the past, scarcely at all in the future; an ex-husband, ex-novelist, as well as an ex-Prime Minister: not, however, an ex-painter or ex-social figure.

On his resignation he made a brave show of professing his pleasure at being free of office.

I am liberated and I utter the cry of a man who finds himself freed of a weight with which his chest had been loaded—OUF! I accepted the steering-wheel when it had been shown that I could manœuvre more successfully for my country than anyone else. . . . Now the ship is refitted and I dare say the sails are spread to the wind: I leave the quarter-deck to another. . . . This other, as you know, is of diabolic energy, strong of physique and of mind: and then—he finds such pleasure in all this! As for me, apart from the fact that I am not devoured by ambition, I could physically endure no more.[1]

It is a gallant show of indifference, but one cannot believe that his relief was as heartfelt as he made it out to be.

From now on he would have to earn his living, for he was determined to stand on his own feet financially: although entitled to a pension, as a former minister of the crown, he declined to accept it. 'I have not accepted the kind offers of the King since, firstly, as long as one can rely on one's self for one's dinner one should not owe it to someone else: secondly, to show that our party is not like the old ones—La Margherita [*sic*] and others— who, it is true, served altar and throne, but at so much an hour.'[2]

[1] Rendu, op. cit., p. 78.   [2] Carcano, op. cit., p. 437.

The eight thousand *lire* due to him on his retirement and the small pension given to him along with his medal for military valour he gave to the church near Azeglio, according to Persano, to pay for masses, and later he was to settle an endowment on the school.

The King offered him honorary rank as General, and this also he declined. 'The epaulettes of a colonel I will wear, since even if I do not deserve them, at least I wore them under fire.' Finally he declined the Collar of the Order of the Annunziata, carrying with it the privilege of addressing the King as 'cousin'. 'They wish to give me the Collar, to make me a cousin of the King! I said to him that it did not seem fitting to me that his cousin should sell paintings. So I ended up as aide-de-camp, which gives me great pleasure as it keeps me close to Uncle Victor, and, as I said to him, "If ever war comes I shall dine with you daily".'[1]

He had to find a new home now, so he moved into Trombetta's hotel in Turin. This was to be his home-from-home when in Turin for the rest of his life, the kind of home-from-home that makes a man realize how homeless he is. Money was another problem and the receipt from Roberto of the 5,000 francs that had been in dispute so welcome that 'I doubt whether Xenophon's ten thousand were more joyously received on their return'.[2] Painting would have to be the main source of his income from now on, and his letters to Emanuele were full of references to commissions. He was hopeful of selling well in England and proposed a visit to London. In January 1853 he had two paintings commissioned for 3,800 francs, and hoped to sell 10,000-francs-worth in London to pay for his journey there.

The thought of making this visit to London, of spending some time with his nephew, of making the acquaintance of men like Palmerston whom he had never met, and of renewing his friendships with those like Minto whom he knew already was one of the major consolations for being out of office. Emanuele had become Sardinian Minister to the Court of St. James's in August 1850, and was to remain there serving under eighteen or twenty different Foreign Ministers at Turin and later at Florence for the next sixteen years. In 1852, whilst on a visit to Paris, where his cousin Villamarina was at the legation, he heard of the death of Gioberti in his humble lodging there. The two cousins took charge of the funeral arrangements, and even found a priest willing to officiate.

[1] Carcano, op. cit., p. 437.   [2] Unpublished letter to Emanuele in O.P.T.

A more difficult situation still had been created for him by the arrival in London of Luisa, Massimo's wife. A letter from his uncle shows just how awkward the situation was.

I must thank you for what you have done for Luisa. Like all women she has a passion for appearing as a victim, and this calls for patience. She wrote to me to ask for an introduction to you lest, she said, you should feel obliged out of regard for me to refuse to see her. I did not answer this, and she will have realized that this supposition was one of the least intelligent things she has ever uttered in all her life. As for her escort, that is a matter that a well-brought-up husband should ignore. It is comical that she wanted a medal given him for having been at Novara: but I was afraid all Tuscany would mock, and consider that this was a governmental reward for purely private services.[1]

Massimo was, of course, in no position to take a high moral tone about Luisa. Neither was Emanuele. Very shortly afterwards the uncle was telling his nephew that a ballet-dancer was on her way to London . . . 'pretty, young, and, as I think, a good dancer. She has besought me to find some way of arranging for her to dance in Paris and London. I promised that I would write to find out how to go about it. You who have the Jockey Club at your beck and call, do me the pleasure of letting me know something I may tell her. And if she comes your way I think you will not find it difficult to arrange a performance for yourself.'[2]

More ribald and at times distasteful were some of Azeglio's letters to his nephew about his son-in-law. It was on 8 June 1852 that he wrote: 'I have found a husband for Rina. A fine young man of twenty-six, a scholar and a man of talent, with a papa of my own age whom I have known for thirty years, a very decent man called Marchese Ricci of Macerata.' If this was his sincere opinion of the father he was soon to change it: and honestly as he might respect the intelligence of the son he was sarcastic about his lack of sexual experience. Rina herself remains a shadowy figure. She had spent more time with her stepmother than with her father: but we know that she was physically active and, like her father, passionately fond of riding. We also know that she was already becoming deaf, for as early as 1850 Massimo was trying to get a good ear-trumpet for her. He had heard of excellent ones being made in Aachen, but as it would take a long time to get one from there he wrote to his doctor-friend Pantaleoni to ask him to buy one in Rome.

[1] Unpublished letters in O.P.T.   [2] Ibid.

Ricci, unlike his father-in-law, was a genuine scholar. He had published a translation of Aristotle's *Politics* and planned a course of lectures on the philosophy of law to be given in the University of Macerata. But the Papal Government had its suspicions about this subject: even though the lectures might be unexceptionable they could lead to dangerous speculation, and the course was never given. Azeglio's hopes of a grandchild seemed doomed to frustration. The Riccis were fanatically Catholic and he had visions of such money as he might leave Rina eventually going to the Church. To forestall this he drew up a will in favour of his nephew, with reversion to his sister's children should Emanuele be childless, as seemed likely, Emanuele showing no intention of marrying. The cause of the barrenness of Rina's marriage was discussed at a family council at Livorno in September 1854, successfully diagnosed, and overcome in due course. But the conference led to a head-on collision between Azeglio and Ricci's father. Though Massimo had at first spoken of him as a 'very decent man', soon after the wedding he was referring to him as an 'Ostrogoth', even as an 'ultra-Ostrogoth', or as 'the most damned rogue I know, a perfect example of a Roman priest or Jesuit, always breaking his word, lying—in fact an animal of the lowest kind'. Worse even—a 'stinking Croat': and in view of the behaviour of the Slavonic members of the Austro-Hungarian army in Lombardy-Venetia the term 'Croat' was the most unpardonable of all the names Azeglio used. However, as an immediate result of the Livorno meeting the young couple were released from parental control, given an allowance of 15,000 francs by the Marchese, and 'disembarrassed of the "real presence" '. They were allowed to leave Macerata for Turin and later Florence, to the delight of Azeglio, who would not have been allowed to enter the Papal States, even had he wished to visit them there, but who welcomed any reason for going to Florence.[1]

But London, not Florence, gave him his most vivid experience in 1853. As long as he was Prime Minister he could not visit his nephew informally, yet he had longed to do so, to see him and also the city and country in which he had become so much at home. Emanuele was urging him to come, and to make the journey feasible, perhaps even profitable, there was the chance of selling some pictures. As his leg was still painful he did not hurry over the journey, but allowed himself ten days for it, spending five of them

[1] Details from unpublished letters to Emanuele preserved in O.P.T.

in Paris. Here he saw Victor Cousin, with whom he had occasional correspondence.[1] He had a terrible crossing of the Channel and felt unwell for some days afterwards. This did not prevent his dining at Buckingham Palace. He admired the building, but was taken aback when at the end of the meal a Scotsman 'senza calzoni' marched twice round the table playing on a bagpipe a melody that 'seemed to me charming, especially in its shortness'. Thanks to Emanuele's social success as well as to his own reputation, he enjoyed a considerable amount of lionizing. A whole procession of peeresses marches across the pages of his letters from London, Ladies Russell, Alderley, Dufferin, Ashburton, Granville, and the Duchess of Sutherland: he had meetings with politicians, especially with Clarendon, with whom he talked business at Cavour's request. For a dispute had arisen between Sardinia and Austria, whose Government had decreed the confiscation of the property of all Italians who had left Lombardy-Venetia—even of those who had left with the consent of the Royal and Imperial Government. Cavour was willing to break off relations with Austria if she refused to modify the decrees, and Hudson and Minto, who was then in Turin, had approved his stand. Since Azeglio was in London, and well-received there, Cavour had written to ask him to use his influence with the British Government to gain its support for a protest against Austrian policy. But as for any threat of war Cavour was quite explicit. 'We have no intention of risking a third encounter: the time of follies is past.'[2]

How well Azeglio may have presented Cavour's case we cannot tell, but Cavour was satisfied. 'You have borne yourself like a consummate diplomat,' he wrote: but Margherita Provana di Collegno had as usual the inside story: and, as usual, probably had it wrong. According to her, though how she knew this is something else we do not know, 'Azeglio had shown himself surprised that Clarendon would not give any hope that England would go to war for Piedmont and for the dispossessed Lombards. He [Azeglio] is a real amateur in politics.'[3] That Azeglio took a

---

[1] It has been suggested that Cousin and Azeglio were on terms of fairly close friendship, but this is not borne out by the few letters from Azeglio to Cousin that have been published (by Barthelemy-Sainte Hilaire in his *Victor Cousin, sa vie et sa correspondance* (Paris, Alcan, 1895). They had met at Manzoni's house at the time of Azeglio's marriage to Giulietta: but Azeglio's letters to him, dating only from the time of his ministry, are formal in tone.

[2] Chiala, op. cit., Vol. II, p. 257.   [3] *Diario politico*, p. 113.

simple view of foreign policy is credible; but not that he was as naïve as all that.

Besides business there was relaxation. With Emanuele he went to Greenwich to see the Whitsuntide Fair, quite a lively outing, apparently; and he was a guest at a military review at Woolwich, a less happy experience, for his horse took fright and though he had been a skilled rider from boyhood he was thrown. He was able to remount, so that he did not feel humiliated: nor was he so badly shaken as to be unable to go to a party at the Palmerstons that same evening.

But his main occupation in London was painting—and selling—some pictures. His friend Baron Marochetti, who modelled a bust of him (and whose best-known work in England is the statue of Richard Lionheart at Westminster) lent him a room to use as a studio: and there, 'shut in his studio as in a fortress', he worked, as he said, 'like a black'—despite which he received a train of visitors to see him at work in his painter's blouse, though his full social round did not begin until seven-thirty in the evening. Not only did he produce a fair number of paintings, some of which, though not all, pleased Emanuele, but he also sold them well. This he had not felt sure of doing, for early in his stay he had gone to see paintings by Turner, 'a painter who made one million two hundred thousand *lire* with his brush: his works frightened me, for I must confess I would not give a shilling for them, and if they give pleasure, mine are roasted. Enough, we shall see. . . .'[1] His sales disappointed him a little, but left him convinced that if he had stayed longer he would have gauged English taste better; 'but in a few months one cannot expect fruit to appear: and here nothing is improvised'. Still, he had made his expenses: and he had had a most flattering reception: it had its climax when Prince Albert came unannounced to visit him in his studio. Azeglio was so taken by surprise that, forgetting etiquette, he received him with a demonstrative handshake. A second highlight had been a dinner at Buckingham Palace in honour of the Duke of Genoa, the King's brother, at which he had been a guest. He had been impressed by the manifest wealth of London, and by the civic spirit of the English. 'The organization of English civilization is the finest that man has so far managed to evolve so as to live in society.'

[1] Carcano, op. cit., p. 445. Most of the information about his London visit is from letters of Emanuele to his mother, preserved in O.P.T.

After three and a half months he went back to Turin, determined to return to London as soon as possible. In Paris he had an audience of the Emperor, and was received by the Princess Mathilde. Here for the first time he began to sense that though there was talk of the stability of European peace the Czar was showing signs of aggressiveness. This was a passing observation and Azeglio gave it little thought. He did not linger in Paris, and by mid-June he was back in Turin.

Cesare Balbo died soon after his return. They had been closely associated in the eighteen-forties, when similarity of political opinion had given more strength to their blood-relationship. But the measures against the Church of Azeglio's ministry had hurt Balbo, who had moved away to the right as a result, and their friendship had died. 'His death has been a great grief; though for so many years I had no longer been seeing him, and the almost daily communion in life had ceased, I feel I have lost a companion, have had a habit broken, and am left more than ever alone. Curious how, in battle, seeing a friend fall can seem meaningless, yet quiet and normal deaths can leave one so downcast.'

Another friend, Persano, was causing him some perturbation also. Again he had run his ship aground going out of Genoa harbour, and this incident was made serious by the presence on board of the King and Queen. The vessel had not been much damaged, and had gone on to Toulon, repairs having been effected during the voyage, and Persano had defended himself by arguing that the rock he had brushed against had not been marked on Italian or French charts. All the same, such a misadventure in sight of one of Europe's great ports scarcely raised the prestige of the royal navy or of its admiral, who had to submit to a court of enquiry: the Admiralty had called him back from Toulon and placed him under arrest until the outcome of the council of war. He had been reduced in rank: but the opinion of Azeglio was that the procedure of the court had been distinctly irregular, and its motives influenced by malice. On the whole Persano does not seem to have been uniformly competent as a sailor, and as a man he was clearly totally lacking in discretion and self-control: it is hard to imagine anyone more unlike Azeglio than the peppery, hare-brained, red-faced sailor, yet they remained good friends to the end despite Azeglio's sermons to him, and despite Azeglio's friendship for the Countess Persano, about which some tongues wagged.

To complete this catalogue of misfortunes, within a year Azeglio lost his faithful servant Gaetano, who had been his batman during the 1848 campaign and had stayed with him afterwards. Left alone during the summer of 1854 to look after Azeglio's apartment he got the accounts into a muddle; he embezzled the trifling sum of 400 francs to gamble with in the hope of recouping his defalcations, lost it, and shot himself: one of those stupidly unnecessary tragedies, for had he been less conscience-stricken he would have had a pardon from his master, at the price probably of a thorough wigging in the most unprintable Piedmontese.

In autumn Azeglio went to Florence. His chief reason for going was to see Rina and her husband, but one can be sure he found other than family pleasures there. Margherita Provana di Collegno was as interested in his doings as ever and was able to report: 'Massimo d'Azeglio comes back from Tuscany with marvels to tell. It seems that the Florentine ladies have received him most kindly, as though he were still young.'[1] That may well have been so, for Massimo's charm did not depend on his youthfulness, and he was attractive to women all his life. But on the politicians of Tuscany he left a less favourable impression: he was critical of Cavour's policy and of Sardinian politics as a whole, and he seemed like a man who had had his day—a good enough day, too —in politics, but who had become embittered afterwards, an impression that was in fact well based.

On his return to Turin Azeglio took his seat in the Senate, as he had for some months been entitled to do. To Roberto he confided that he was bored with politics—quite credibly: he had been bored often enough when he was in responsible office and was hardly likely to find excitement in politics without power. Besides taking a seat in the Senate he entered into occupation of a new apartment and could leave Trombetta's Hôtel de l'Europe. The King had given him a kind of 'grace and favour' residence in the building of the Academy of Fine Arts. This was one large and unpromising room, though it was on the first floor and had windows large enough to give him plenty of light for painting. He called in an architect friend and, 'since space like matter is divisible to infinity', out of the one room they carved a studio, a drawing-room, a *chambre de toilette*, an ante-room, a corridor, a wardrobe room, a kitchen, a manservant's room, and a store-room for wood and coal. 'Since this is a stronghold in which,

[1] *Diario politico*, p. 145.

in all likelihood, I shall go to sleep with my fathers, I am making unheard-of efforts to make it comfortable and in good taste. There, in any case, I shall not be restricted as at Trombetta's to little pictures.'[1] As Emanuele pointed out when his uncle's letters were being edited for the press, Massimo's prevision was correct, for in this apartment he died twelve years later.[2]

Close on the gift of the apartment came a new appointment as director of the Royal Picture Gallery. This post had been occupied by Roberto, who had taken it most seriously. He had prepared an edition of engravings of the more important pictures in the gallery and had done much solid work on its catalogue. He had also carried on a long, and so far unavailing, battle to gain better premises for its exhibition. A minor crisis had arisen when it had been proposed to move the collection from the Palazzo Madama to the Academy. Roberto had opposed this move, publicly describing the offered accommodation as an attic, and making it clear that he really wished to move the Senate, not the pictures, from the Palazzo, not unjustifiably, as the building was later to become an art gallery, and quite a satisfactory one. It had been thought by many that Roberto had been too intemperate and too demagogic in appealing to public opinion instead of trying to influence the King through some such intermediary as Cibrario, though the idea of Victor Emmanuel becoming deeply concerned about a collection of paintings is hard to accept. In the end Roberto resigned his appointment as a protest. It had never been a source of income to him, for as one sees from his correspondence with his son he had consistently applied his stipend to charitable works, and in particular to endowing elementary schools. As he explained, he did not believe in charity *d'outre tombe* at the expense of one's heirs. The directorship was offered to Massimo, who accepted it, to Roberto's slight pique: for Roberto felt that Massimo had rather let him down by accepting what he had resigned on a matter of principle. Also, Massimo had no qualifications for such a post—as was true enough; and he was also to show that he had only a sporadic interest in it. But, as Roberto could not deny, Massimo was in no position to refuse a salaried appointment, however slight its emoluments might be. So, as director of the national collection of pictures, Massimo entered on yet another phase of his career. His lack of interest was clear enough, and understandable, for the collection was mainly of primitives, not then widely appreciated: and Massimo was never much interested in any paintings of a period earlier than his own, whereas Roberto, like his son, was genuinely enthusiastic not only about pictures but also about other branches of the arts, and especially ceramics. He and Emanuele were forever exchanging information about their acquisitions, and between them they built up a very comprehensive collection that Emanuele eventually bequeathed to the State: it came to rest in the Palazzo Madama, cause of such controversy to Roberto.

In his new home Massimo set to work on an exceptionally large canvas: his subject was the introduction of Tasso to the court of Emmanuel Philibert I of Savoy in the grounds of the Palais du Parc. This was to prove to be one of his finest works and Roberto was enthusiastic about it from the moment of seeing the first sketches. 'What I have seen gives me the most brilliant hopes for the new work: it seems to me one of his finest pictures and the costumes of that splendid period will help to give style and character to his composition.' Even Margherita Provana di Collegno was impressed by it. She considered, correctly, that the figures had greater importance than in most of Massimo's paintings, for as a rule they were very inconspicuous in the landscape: all were based, she said, on contemporary portraits, and the lake 'is of insuperable realism'. She had said many hard things about Massimo as a politician, but to give her her due she had always maintained that the artist in him was more gifted than the politician. The picture was intended for the Duke of Genoa, and it is still in the possession of his descendants. As in London Azeglio worked each day until the evening: 'I go to play the Senator in moments of recreation. . . . As it is for me an article of faith to live in society I go to the theatres, balls (even until midnight, note you), and so keep abreast of current affairs. Politics is a matter from which I willingly hold myself a long way off, now.'[1]

At this time, too, a new acquaintance came into his life, Stefano Stampa, a stepson of Manzoni, from whom he brought a letter of introduction. Little by little he was to become second only to Emanuele in Massimo's affections.

Emanuele would have liked to see his uncle back in London in 1854, but this was not convenient. The remodelling of his apartment was absorbing not only all his attention but all the money

---

[1] *Confidenze*, p. 106.

he could spare. Before going to London he would have to paint
and sell enough pictures to meet his expenses for the visit. 'When
I come to London I am determined to do so with my own money
—money I have brought with me. . . . To work in one's studio
six hours a day in order to be a man of the world in the evening is
all right once but I assure you it is an 'Uncle Tom's' existence. If
I come it will be to play the gentleman, and, my purse empty, I
shall vanish.' His state of health as well as his lack of money
discouraged this visit. After six years his Monte Berico wound was
still hurting him, and from early June it was seriously painful. In
Florence the doctors assured him that the pain in his knee was
due to rheumatism, and treated him accordingly. By November
he was scarcely able to walk, and spent a week indoors fearing
that he was going to be immured for the whole winter. But during
this week he began to give his knee a treatment of his own invention, frequent cold-water baths, and from then onwards it
began to improve until a final cure was achieved.

Despite all these preoccupations and interests politics could not
be ignored. It would have been difficult, however bored by them
one might be, never to mention them when writing to a nephew
who was a minister: but Azeglio's references to them are not
numerous, and show a considerable amount of restraint, especially
when discussing Cavour's management of internal affairs. His
financial policy puzzled many: his reorganization of the system
of taxation had led to a deficit that was to prove permanent, and,
to some extent, deliberate. But Azeglio was loath to be too
critical of Cavour's fiscal policy either privately or publicly since
he knew as little about financial affairs as, he suspected, some of
Cavour's most outspoken critics.

Another law on religious matters, on seditious utterances by
priests from their pulpits, was under discussion in the Senate.

As it involves theology, all the Generals in the Senate are in the front
line, beginning with Count de la Tour, as is always the case when
sacristy matters are in dispute. It is a real comedy. I shall vote for the
law because I do not wish to create opposition, and because I see
nothing in it to object to. But I don't like its being done at this moment,
since it is the usual courtship of the *Gazzetta del Popolo*, of the Connubio
and all that coterie.[1]

Azeglio could at times feel and write bitterly about Cavour, but
this was his more usual tone—to refrain from criticism of him in

[1] Bianchi, *Lettere*, p. 249.

matters like public finance that Azeglio did not claim to understand: to dislike the timing of some of his measures, yet to vote for them nevertheless because of their intrinsic merits. But the main reason for his support was given in an earlier letter to Emanuele. 'The ministry has the most important and the most genuine source of strength—there is no other to put in its place.'[1]

During this year, 1854, and for some time to come, foreign affairs overshadowed home affairs: this was the case even before Sardinia's decision to enter into the Crimean War. As early as January 1854 Azeglio was sure that a war was inevitable and that Aberdeen's policy of peace at all costs would prove too costly.[2] But he was sarcastic about the wild ideas held by some in Turin, who believed that Austria would enter into a war in support of Russia, that Sardinia would gain Lombardy-Venetia as a result of coming in on the side of Britain and France. He could see no sign of realism in such hopes, since he could not conceive Austria fighting against the western powers for the sake of Russia. But to Rendu he wrote in a different vein, for he always knew that what he wrote to Rendu was likely to be passed on to Napoleon III. So to him he expressed the hope that if a European war should come the peace might be the occasion of a radical revision of the map of Europe to satisfy the aspirations of the Italians, the Magyars, and the Poles. To end the war by a return to something like the *status quo* would be sheer waste of all the effort expended.[3]

[1] Bianchi, *Lettere*, p. 247.   [2] Ibid., p. 242.   [3] Rendu, op. cit., p. 81.

XIV
POLITICAL ACTIVITY RENEWED

THE year 1855 opened surprisingly with overtures from Cavour to Azeglio, who, although he had supported the ministry over its church laws and its foreign policy, had seemed to Minghetti to be disillusioned with politics and depressed, contemptuous of Rattazzi and sceptical about Cavour—'too pliable because of his personal ambition'. On 6 January Cavour saw Azeglio and made his unexpected offer. He would dismiss da Bormida, who had been in disagreement with him over the terms on which Sardinia should enter into active alliance with France and Britain in the war against Russia: he was also prepared to sacrifice Rattazzi, whom he knew to be still Azeglio's *bête noire*. More importantly, he was prepared to take a secondary place himself, according to Azeglio's account of the offer: for Cavour would content himself with the ministry of finance and Azeglio might have the presidency of the council with the ministry of foreign affairs into the bargain. There is some difference of views about the precise schemes for reconstituting the ministry. The account given here comes from Azeglio himself by two separate routes: on 9 January he consulted Giacinto Collegno on the proposal, and Margherita Provana records the offer in the terms quoted.[1] Her husband advised Azeglio not to accept, reminding him that Cavour had betrayed him once already and was not to be trusted. The ministry was tottering because of a law on church property that Azeglio himself had always opposed in principle: and Cavour was trying to use Azeglio to prop up his shaky edifice. Azeglio was convinced by Collegno and wrote then and there to Cavour declining his offer. To Emanuele, on 29 January, Azeglio gave an account that differs from this only in making no reference to consultation with Collegno. 'He [Cavour] came to me one evening to offer me the presidency and the Foreign Office. But apart from anything else I am not fully enough recovered to harness myself to such a waggon. Then, all those trouble-makers of the Connubio and I are scarcely created to progress together: so I thanked him for the high honour, placing myself at the cabinet's disposal for any other

[1] *Diario politico*, pp. 223–4.

purpose.'[1] According to Persano, Azeglio in refusing told Cavour:
'The ministry is safe in your hands: and I will be a foot-soldier
not a cavalryman. Make use of me as you wish.'

Cavour, writing also to Emanuele, gave a slightly different
version. He says that he had taken over the Foreign Office from
da Bormida, a heavy commitment along with the premiership;
that he had hoped Azeglio would enter the cabinet, but that he
had declined because his health was not good enough.[2] One must
assume that the premiership was in fact offered to Azeglio, but
one cannot imagine that this offer was anything more than a
manœuvre, that Cavour could seriously consider serving under
Azeglio, or that Azeglio would accept this office in a time of
crisis. It may be that Cavour counted on Azeglio declining the
premiership but offering to take over foreign affairs, thus lighten-
ing Cavour's burden whilst maintaining his control. It would
have given him a minister willing to sign the treaty with France
and Britain that da Bormida had boggled at,[3] and one who still
had a prestige outside Sardinia denied to all others of cabinet
rank.

Cavour's need of support was genuine enough. The country
was going to enter into the Crimean War: that had been certain
for some time. But on what terms? Cavour was willing to accept
an unconditional alliance, relying on the goodwill of France and
Britain to see Sardinia adequately rewarded somehow, sometime.
Da Bormida, whose view was shared, it was believed, by most of
the cabinet, held that the treaty should specify conditions for
Sardinia's intervention. This idea was only superficially reasonable. The great powers were not likely to bid very high for the aid
of Sardinia, to which they would have preferred that of Austria.
At the end of the war the allies would not have at their disposal
any territory desired by Sardinia, since Austria, who alone had
what Sardinia desired, had not been fighting on Russia's side.
Any suggestion of a cash compensation to Sardinia would have
been an unequivocal insult. In this matter Cavour had, and the
lesser men had not, the courage to make a supreme act of faith.
Azeglio, to his credit, despite his personal doubts about Cavour,
was willing to support him in this.

You ask me about the treaty [he wrote to his wife]. I have been one
of its keenest champions. It is an ancient tradition of our policy to seek

---

[1] Bianchi, *Lettere*, p. 259.   [2] Chiala, op. cit., Vol. II, p. 319.
[3] The treaty was signed by Cavour on 9 January 1855.

to be involved in anything of importance that is happening in Europe. And further, we must remember that at the end of all this the Eastern Question will be cleared up: and on that day it will be better to be admitted to the conference than to be left outside the door. When a state has a new constitution and a new flag she must give a reputation to both: and that means to act like men and not to sleep like moles: and lastly as long as France and England remain on the map there shall we be also.[1]

Azeglio had made his offer to serve in all sincerity: and in the same spirit Cavour accepted it. There was very soon a scheme on foot to send Azeglio on a diplomatic mission to Paris and London. The plan was extremely vague and it was not clear when or why he was to go. As early as 2 February Margherita Provana di Collegno had heard of it, but Azeglio himself did not mention it until April, when he told Emanuele: 'Cavour wishes to give me another mission that I can scarcely understand. That would be to visit you and Salvatore [Salvatore Pes di Villamarina, in Paris]. For what purpose? I do not know. I can imagine that for another combination of his chessmen it might be imagined that my profound knowledge of Italy could be useful. But in the present circumstances?'[2] In May it was still under discussion: Azeglio told Costanza that he would go only with a clear title of 'Minister Extraordinary'. This surprised her, as she believed that only the Chamber could sanction this, and she doubted if it looked with favour on such appointments.[3]

Gradually Cavour's motive for sending someone on such a mission became clearer. The Sardinian Government had believed that it had a right to send a representative to the forthcoming conference at Vienna. The British and French representatives at Turin had both questioned this: so it was decided to send Azeglio on a tour 'to perform his good offices'. Such, according to Pes di Villamarina, was Cavour's explanation. He had reasoned with Cavour and in the end it was agreed that if the war continued (i.e. continued long enough for Sardinian troops to play an active part) there was no doubt 'we should be found along with the others when peace was to be settled: and so the whole idea was given up. But [Villamarina went on] . . . most secret—Massimo will probably be asked to accompany the King on his forthcoming state journey to Paris and London. Cavour wishes it and Azeglio

[1] Bianchi, *Lettere*, p. 261.   [2] Letter in O.P.T.
[3] Costanza to Emanuele, 7 May 1855.

R

agrees.'[1] It was also being reported as early as this that Azeglio would be a Sardinian envoy to the peace conference. But by June the idea of a special journey to Paris and London had been definitely abandoned. It had really had little to recommend it and the practice of doing business through special envoys instead of through ordinary diplomatic channels was one of the things for which Azeglio himself had been most criticized.

Though he had not been used by Cavour on this occasion Azeglio was soon able to give him very real help. The anti-clerical laws were hanging fire somewhat: the one to institute civil marriage had not yet received its *coup de grâce*: there were others under consideration to control clerical political utterances from the pulpit and to control or reduce the Church's acquisition of property: too much, it was thought by many, being done too quickly. Even the moderate anti-clericals were apprehensive, and the King was being secretly busy on his work of sabotage.

Azeglio disliked the headlong course, but would not try to put a brake on it. On 10 April he wrote: 'The law about the monks will appear on the scene within a week. A badly drafted and inopportune law, and, in my view, scarcely a liberal one. But even so it is almost essential to make it pass.'[2] He was infuriated by criticisms that Antonelli was reported to have made of Sardinian treatment of the Church since 1848. Azeglio still maintained that he had done all he could to arrange for modification of the Church's judicial system by negotiation with Rome: he himself had seen to it that law and order were kept in the passing of the law; whereas for centuries the Curia, endowed with spiritual as well as temporal power, had governed her three million subjects to such effect that 'it needs four armies and two foreign powers to maintain itself'.[3] He was convinced that he had shown himself moderate and honest and that Antonelli had been and still was neither. In this latter belief few would quarrel with him. The Cardinal Secretary of State was politically much too devious to be able to claim much rectitude. So Azeglio launched a personal attack on him in February in the *Gazzetta Piemontese*. And, having published, he saw no cause to repent.

As for my admonition to Cardinal Antonelli, I regretted having to make it, but after having used him and his court with all respect, having

---

[1] Letter in O.P.T.   [2] *Confidenze*, p. 127.
[3] Letter to Spinola, 12 February 1855, in Bianchi, *Politica*, pp. 223-4.

stayed quietly at home disturbing no one, to be treated as a rogue,—
and that by one who like his brotherhood has done nothing but fill
his pockets for five years . . . that was too much. So a few words were
needed, and he has had them.[1]

If he had called just me a fool or a rogue, all right, one could pass
it off as only concerning one's self: but me, my colleagues, the King,
our country . . . no! One could not stay silent. Now a wasp's nest has
been stirred up in all the priestly journals.[2]

Not everyone was as satisfied by the diatribe as its author.
Margherita Provana thought such a 'fictional-novelistic tone'
lacking in dignity and in the decorum appropriate to speech with
the court of Rome, and in her view the inner history of Azeglio's
negotiations with Rome was not so immaculate as to justify his
admonitions.[3] More serious than this journalistic skirmishing was
the battle of wills between Cavour and the King over the new
church laws. Victor Emmanuel, who so often seemed to have a
peasant bluntness and scepticism, also had a very deep streak of
peasant superstition and he was at this time deeply affected by
the deaths in rapid succession of the two Queens, his mother, his
wife, and her new-born baby all dying within ten days. It was not
difficult to suggest to him that these deaths were signs of divine
displeasure: and his mind was worked upon so effectively that
he used all his influence to secure the rejection by the Senate of
measures to which as projects of law he had already given his
consent. Cavour had foreseen that this might occur and had done
all he could to whip up his supporters: he wrote to Azeglio, as to
others, to urge him to attend the Senate and to vote for the law
on the Friars, which he was going to make into a vote of confidence.[4] And Azeglio, putting aside all his personal and insignificant grievances against Cavour (the Cavour who in the
Azeglio private correspondence was 'the wicked rival'—'l'empio
rivale', or simply 'l'empio'), was cast into black depression at the
situation he saw developing. According to Margherita Provana,
Azeglio was speaking of the King as 'lost', as being in the position
of his father, Charles Albert, in 1821: of the soldiers as above
themselves, the bishops making impossible demands, the provinces
discontented, and many prefects on the verge of resignation.[5]

Azeglio was in fact taking the situation seriously enough to risk
a violent personal breach with the King by sending him a letter

---

[1] *Confidenze*, p. 125. [2] Carcano, op. cit., p. 462. [3] *Diario politico*, p. 237.
[4] Chiala, op. cit., Vol. II, p. 323. [5] *Diario politico*, 1 May 1855.

known since as the 'Spagna' letter.[1] It seems definitely to have been written at Cavour's request. But the wording is unmistakably Azeglio's and the ideas were as much his as Cavour's. Before writing the letter he had tried (on 30 April) to reach the King's ear through Nigra, in the hope of convincing him how dangerous to the throne was his opposition to the policy of his ministry, to which policy he had already assented. On the failure of this *démarche* he sent the 'Spagna' letter.

Your Majesty,

In Sparta it was forbidden to touch the king under pain of death. It happened to one that his garments took fire: no one would risk touching him and he burnt to death. But I, though I should risk my head or lose all your favour, would think myself the meanest of men if at a time like this I did not direct to you a word in writing since Your Majesty has denied me the chance to speak.

Majesty, believe an old and loyal servant who in serving you thought of nothing save your welfare, reputation, and the good of your country. With tears in my eyes, kneeling at your feet, I beg you not to go further in the path you have chosen. There is still time. Return to the former ways. An intrigue of friars has succeeded in one day in destroying all the work of your reign, in upsetting the country, and in weakening the constitution and obscuring the honour of your reputation. There is not a moment to lose. . . . Piedmont tolerates much, but to be placed once more under the yoke of the priesthood—by heavens, NO! Look at the intrigues of the Spanish friars against their queen to make her sign a shameful concordat, and to what end these have led her! Such intrigues ruined James Stuart, Charles X, and many others. . . . Amedeo II resisted Rome for thirty years and won. Let Your Majesty stand firm and you will win likewise.

Do not be angry with me. My action is the action of an honest man, a faithful subject and true friend.

Azeglio.

Azeglio sent a copy of this letter to Persano, amongst others, asking him to keep it in his most secret archive: but so many had seen copies that eventually Persano published it in 1878 after the King's death.

The letter was effective in that it helped to prevent further unconstitutional action by the King. But it must have been unpleasant reading—especially in its references to previous kings

---

[1] Inaccurately, from the substitution of 'Spain' for 'Sparta' in the opening sentence. Text in *S.D.P.*, III, p. 43.

who had suffered deposition for their reactionary ecclesiastical policies. It caused a coolness to be the normal relation between the King and Azeglio from then onwards. There were short honeymoon periods of cordiality: but on the whole Azeglio's influence with his monarch had ended.

Luckily life for Azeglio could never be serious all the time. In March 1855 he was asked to speak at the distribution of prizes to pupils who had qualified for entry to the *corps de ballet* of the Turin Opera, and to confer the 'premio della virtù'. He took this invitation seriously enough to ask his friends to come to hear him. But his speech scandalized the more circumspect of Torinese society: for it looked forward to the girls' future careers; it did not exactly preach puritanical rectitude (how could Azeglio of all men do that?) but it counselled prudence in awarding their favours as the best policy in the long run. Needless to say no one was more shocked than Margherita Provana. In June Azeglio had an accident that might have had appalling consequences for him. He was staying with friends whose son decided one evening to play the ghost, wrapping himself in a sheet and carrying underneath it some burning mixture in a dish. The sheet took fire and Massimo, tearing the blazing sheet off the boy, got all the burning contents of the dish full in the face. His hair, eyebrows, and whiskers were burnt as well as his skin, and it was only by sheer good luck that his eyes were not damaged.

Before he had fully recovered he received an invitation from Cavour to undertake a very tricky assignment. It was considered necessary that Victor Emmanuel should make the acquaintance of the other allied sovereigns, and the moment seemed auspicious, since Sardinian troops were not merely in the Crimea alongside the French, British, and Turks, but were already distinguishing themselves in action. The only cause for hesitation was Victor Emmanuel himself. No one could possibly foresee what he might say or do: the phrasing of his ideas might shock the Tuileries: the substance of them might shock Windsor even more than the mode of expression. Yet that was a calculated risk that had to be taken sooner or later, and the presence of Azeglio at his side would show that it was possible to be both Piedmontese and polished. Azeglio described his function as that of a 'lightning conductor'. A serious, almost fatal, illness of the King caused the visit to be postponed. 'If the doctors', said Azeglio, 'had cared to follow my system, leaving all to God, the illness would not have lasted so long: with the added advantage that the Lord does not charge for his visits.' The party left Turin in early November. At the last moment Cavour decided that he would go along with them—a decision that was not totally pleasing to Azeglio, who was thus relegated to second place. Cavour kept all important diplomatic negotiations in his own hands, as was right and proper once he had joined the party: but in London Azeglio figured more obviously than Cavour as royal bear-leader on social occasions.

On the whole the visit was very successful. The King was well received by the crowds in London when he drove in an open carriage through the streets. At Windsor he made a reasonably good impression on the Queen and Prince Consort. According to Clarendon he had no 'protocol', was rather plain-spoken, and had no small-talk. The Queen felt sympathy for him in the apparent loneliness of his life, and his devotion to duty. He must have made some of his notorious gaffes: Azeglio referred to an evening when 'he scared us by his speech': but the Queen may not have understood all his French: or perhaps she had heard worse things from some of her German relations. Clarendon found their conversations 'on the whole satisfactory, though the King did not much like my shrug of the shoulders when he asked me what he was going to gain by all this [i.e. participation in the Crimean War] and whether we could not manage for him "une petite extension de territoire". He is shrewd and, I am sure, truthful and honourable.' Windsor hospitality enchanted them: according to Azeglio the servants of the Sardinian delegation found themselves eating from silver plates below stairs, with Bordeaux as *vin ordinaire* and champagne with dessert: two carriages were at their disposal for excursions.[1]

The climax of the visit was a dinner in the King's honour at Guildhall. He replied to the toast in a speech that Azeglio had written for him overnight. The King had had his doubts about its suitability but Azeglio had arranged for the Queen and the Prince Consort to see it in advance. They had approved it, and knowing this the King read it with conviction and feeling.

For Azeglio the consequence was an anti-climax. He had caught a cold on the drive through the City in an open coach: this developed into toothache and he stayed in Paris for a fortnight to have it treated by the fashionable American dentist Evans, who was to earn the gratitude of the French Imperial

[1] *Galeotti*, pp. 308–9.

Lightning Conductor during the royal visit to Paris & London

family fifteen years later by helping the Empress Eugénie to escape from Paris after the débâcle of 1870.

The trip to London had been a pleasant parade for the King and for Azeglio. But the really important business had been transacted in Paris between Cavour and the Emperor, obviously more important to Italy than Queen Victoria or her ministers because, unlike them, he was capable of initiating action on behalf of Sardinia. Already he was considering some form of intervention in Italian affairs. On 8 December Cavour wrote to tell Azeglio of a surprise move by Napoleon.

Yesterday evening the Emperor said to me point-blank 'Write confidentially to Walewski what you think I can do for Piedmont and Italy'. I would like to plan this task with you, or, better still, ask you to undertake it whilst you are doing nothing here in Paris. On your return to Turin we will look at it together and I will send it to Walewski. With the Emperor it is essential to be as concrete as possible, considering every possibility except that of war against Austria, which at present does not enter into his ideas. The cession of the Principalities to Austria in exchange for Lombardy and the Duchies, or the giving of the Duchies to the Duke of Modena, are ideas that were not ill-received. All the same he did not reject the idea of taking the Romagnas from the Pope —but less explicitly. With these data you can prepare an essay that will be very useful to us sooner or later.[1]

Azeglio set to work on the memorandum and by 20 January 1856 it was in the hands of Cavour, who wrote 'I wish to say that thinking again of your most attractive memorandum it came into my mind that it would be inopportune to speak of the establishment of a British legation in Rome. This advice from me would seem suspect since, as you know, I am considered Anglophile at the Tuileries.'[2] Attractive the memorandum might be: but Cavour decided that it was not what he wanted, or could use.[3] To La Marmora in London he wrote the next day: 'Azeglio has finished his memorandum: it is a magnificent job, but it is of inordinate length, and has in addition the disadvantage of not arriving at clear and precise conclusions. If I had sent it to Walewski he would not have read it, or at least would not have paid any attention to it.' Cavour therefore sent Walewski a memorandum of his own, about one-eighth the length of Azeglio's, and much more specific, explaining that he had a longer essay in

[1] Chiala, op. cit., Vol. II, p. 376.   [2] Ibid., p. 382.
[3] Azeglio's Memorandum in *S.D.P.*, III, pp. 77–120.

course of preparation and would send it when completed. This was a mere gesture, for he had no intention of sending him Azeglio's essay, of which he did send a copy at this very moment to La Marmora, who was just going to Paris in readiness for the Congress. Azeglio's discarded essay contained many excellent points used by Cavour: but it was not in his nature to produce the clear and succinct type of communication that Cavour wanted. Cavour should have realized this and not led Azeglio to suffer the disappointment that the rejection of his work caused him.

The next divergence between Azeglio and Cavour, and one that left a deeper scar on Azeglio, was over the representation of Sardinia at the Congress that was to make peace after the Crimean War. This was to be held in Paris, and not, as at first proposed, in Vienna. As early as January 1856 it was believed that Azeglio would lead the Sardinian delegation: before the end of that month he told Emanuele: 'They wish to send me to the conference. . . . Imagine! I, the little lap-dog amongst the bull-dogs—and all of them at Austria's feet! But though my ambition is not to be a minister, yet to be a man who is willing to go ahead in unpleasant circumstances, I have agreed.'[1]

The suggestion that Azeglio rather than Cavour should go to Paris seemed an odd one—to send an amateur who was out of office rather than the professional, who was in. An explanation might have been the simple one that Azeglio was widely known and as widely trusted: but this is not totally convincing and another possibility may be worthy of consideration. This depends on the possible status of Sardinia's representatives at the Congress: was he to be there at all discussions with powers equal to those of the other delegates or was he only to be present when Italian affairs were being discussed? Were it to be the former status, then Cavour would obviously wish to go, and equally obviously would be the right man for the mission. But in the second case a secondary figure might be sent: this would save Cavour's pride and might at the same time be a good insurance policy. For it was quite possible that despite Sardinia's sacrifice of men and money in a war that had been essentially Cavour's, undertaken by him as an act of faith with no material rewards promised, his country might go uncompensated at the peace settlement. Better that someone else should run the risk of an empty-handed return from Paris.

[1] Bianchi, *Lettere*, p. 270.

Azeglio was at first convinced that he would be present at the Congress on the same footing as the other representatives, though he was resolved to act with discretion, even with self-effacement. He informed Emanuele thus:

I have been to Cibrario[1] and told him that I thought it would be well if he wrote to get Palmerston's unofficial ideas on the *modus tenendi* of the Sardinian delegate at this cursed conference. Arrange for the English envoy to take me under his wing and do not imagine that I shall go with the intention of asking for a Kingdom of North Italy: my scheme is to keep a noble silence on all questions save our own and to be as modest as a Carlo Dolci Madonnina. In this affair you will remember that at the start they told us we should take part, but only on Italian questions. Then next we were to be admitted without reservations. In any case it would be as well to know from Palmerston if he does not think it would be in good taste to let the big fellows talk a little amongst themselves before joining in. One can announce that one is indisposed, and with that excuse hold back. My idea is to arrive after business has begun.[2]

Yet despite Azeglio's confidence it had not at that date been decided that the Sardinian envoy should have equal status at the conference. Austria was definitely against it: Britain was unwilling to offend her in this matter and France might well fall in with their views. Shortly before he was due to leave for Paris Azeglio was told by Cavour that Sardinia would only be admitted when the agenda concerned Italy, and, again according to Azeglio, Cavour instructed him to demand what Azeglio believed impossible, the cession to Sardinia of Lombardy and the Duchies.[3] That Cavour should seriously have made such a proposition is hard to credit: either he was misunderstood by Azeglio or he was determined to put Azeglio in so difficult a position that he would withdraw his acceptance of the mission. In fact on 5 February Azeglio wrote to Cavour asking to be relieved of his undertaking. Cavour thereupon determined to go himself. 'In the difficult situation in which Massimo d'Azeglio's refusal places us I have not hesitated, despite the countless affairs that demand my presence here in Turin, to announce to the King that I am willing to leave for the Congress, asking him to associate you with me on this mission' (Cavour to La Marmora).[4] So instead of going to Paris Massimo

---

[1] Cibrario was at this time Foreign Minister.   [2] Bianchi, *Lettere*, p. 270.
[3] So Azeglio told Margherita Provana di Collegno. *Diario politico*, p. 316.
[4] Chiala, op. cit., Vol. II, p. 393.

went to Genoa, putting as good a face on the matter as he could. 'I am not going to the Paris conference: Cavour goes instead and I do not envy him that pleasure.'[1] But he was deeply mortified at having been misled so definitely and so long: when he wrote to tell Emanuele the whole story he wrote in the Piedmontese dialect, as though to baffle someone's secret service. . . . 'So they will leave us outside the door for as long as they wish. If they had said so at the start, well and good. But now, when the country has believed their falsehoods! Had I gone to wait in an anteroom they would have stoned me on my return and I should be a discredited man. I have told Cibrario to find someone else.'[2]

Few things would be harder to believe than that Cavour was going to Paris in a spirit of noble self-sacrifice. For some time he had been certain that Azeglio was not the man for the job and he had thought of nominating an additional delegate to strengthen him. On 21 January he had told La Marmora: 'I have for a time thought of asking you to go to represent us at the conference, but we are already pledged to Azeglio.'[3] And on the 29th of that month, also to La Marmora, 'Here it is felt that Azeglio may not be positive enough. I have thought, if it does not offend you, of joining you with him. What do you say?'[4]

Why had Cavour played out this comedy, bound in the end to be hurtful to Azeglio? One is inclined to believe that, despite his assurances to Azeglio, Cavour had known all along that the Sardinian delegate was not going to be accepted as an equal at the Congress, and had thought that for such a status Azeglio was good enough—as well as expendable, should public opinion condemn the result. In the end, it is true, Cavour went to Paris with no certainty that his status would be that of a full member: one assumes that he had developed a new confidence that once there he would be granted a fullness of recognition that would have been withheld from anyone holding a minor office in the Sardinian Government—or, like Azeglio, no office at all. This is in fact the way it worked out: Cavour took a risk, since it was still not clear what his status would be when he left Turin on 13 February, arriving in Paris on the 15th. The proposal that he should be admitted to the Congress was speedily accepted. Clarendon's advice to him was important for its last sentence. 'You have too much tact to take part in affairs that in no way

---

[1] *Confidenze*, p. 146.   [2] Bianchi, *Lettere*, p. 273.
[3] Chiala, op. cit., Vol. II, p. 389.   [4] Ibid., p. 392.

concern you. You will be present at the discussion—and you will think of something else. But in truth I cannot imagine what the question might be which would not interest you.'[1]

One cannot doubt that Cavour achieved, and by sheer force of personality and diplomatic skill was certain to achieve, far more at Paris than Azeglio could ever have done. Contemporary observers were sure, even before the results were known, that the replacement of Azeglio was all to the good. Hudson and Collegno, talking it over whilst the Congress was still in session, were agreed that Azeglio had not been the right man to send, since he had been rather silly, chattering to all and sundry his criticisms of the ministry, saying things he should have kept silent about. Collegno said as much to Emanuele. 'For a long time I have thought he was going astray: he should either set ambition aside or be more prudent. I do not understand his claim to represent a system that is not his own and that he criticizes endlessly.'[2] That Azeglio had been chattering wildly in this way is extremely credible: and the criticism on which Collegno and Hudson were agreed is justified by the known fact that though Azeglio had until the last moment been considering going to Paris he had done no work in advance and had not even asked to see the relevant papers.

As was rather his custom when hurt, Azeglio took refuge in the consolation that his conduct had been morally superior. 'As for the "wicked one" [i.e. Cavour], I believe we wish the same thing in the end, but as regards the means we cannot agree. I do not speak of the progression by fits and starts, often even by lies, that I maintain to be a false method especially for today and one that does not accord with my character. But even in the course of action to achieve the great aim of improving conditions in Italy I cannot agree with him.'[3] All the same, once over his initial disappointment Azeglio as usual could acknowledge Cavour's superior skill. 'It was better that he should go. He is a man of economics, stock exchanges, railways, all matters of first importance. And in action he proved himself an able man immediately. He is younger, stronger, and more active than I could be. And he has that petulance which in Paris especially is essential.'[4] Later, on more mature reflection, Azeglio saw more profoundly into

---

[1] Quoted by A. J. Whyte, *The Political Life and Letters of Cavour* (1930), p. 196
[2] Letter from Collegno to Emanuele, 26 February 1856, in O.P.T.
[3] Bianchi, *Lettere*, p. 276.   [4] Ibid., p. 280.

the situation than this rather superficial, even grudging first impression. In correspondence with Minghetti, whose learning and sincerity seem always to have drawn out the best in Azeglio, he concluded that Cavour at Paris had done all that had been possible for Italy, and that all Italy appreciated his work. The Crimean War and the Peace of Paris seemed to Azeglio to mark the end of an epoch, the first major break in the Vienna settlement. An old order had died in Europe, though the new one had not yet been born. As for Italy, Azeglio had by now reached conclusions from which he was never to swerve: in 1856 they might seem common sense, but by holding to them Azeglio within five years would seem a reactionary. All Italy, he thought, should concentrate on limited and practicable aims. 'The mouse was more successful in escaping from the net than the lion, according to the fable. The important thing is to be prepared: and a reform that raises the moral and material worth of the people by one rung is worth more than spectacular but ill-founded events.'[1] One should not underestimate the sincerity with which Azeglio refers to 'moral and material worth'—in his consistent opinion the making of Italians was more important than the making of Italy, for given the right Italians the rest would follow, and would be securely enough based to be durable.

The Azeglian view of progress laid down here in what was to be its final form is surely in the tradition of English conservatism— that of Peel as expressed in the Tamworth Manifesto of 1834 rather than that of Disraeli and his 'leap in the dark' with the Reform Bill of 1867. The great Garibaldian epic of 1860 would to Azeglio be a 'spectacular but ill-founded event'. As for Italy's eventual political future, Azeglio, according to Minghetti, was now convinced that unity and not federation was the only possible solution for her. But he envisaged this as something that might take fifty years to accomplish. As we with hindsight know, it was to take less than fifteen years: and the nearer it came the less Azeglio liked the prospect. Yet in 1856, in advocating 'limited and practicable aims', Azeglio's seemed to be the voice of common sense. Mazzini, Garibaldi, *et hoc genus omne*—even Cavour—to Azeglio were chasers of will-o'-the-wisps. Common sense, apparently, is not enough.

After this check to his diplomatic career, 1856 passed quietly for Azeglio. He finished his 'Tasso' painting, which others besides

[1] Minghetti, op. cit., Vol. III, p. 134.

himself considered his finest work up to that date. And at the end
of the year he was somehow involved in an outburst of scandal in
Turin arising out of a quarrel between two ladies: it reached the
newspapers with a reference to 'the person who is building a villa
on Lake Maggiore'. This villa was to be Azeglio's great hobby
from now onwards. In May he had told Emanuele: 'I have bought
myself a little house to be a port in time of storm. It is not to be a
"cottage orné" but an Italian-style "casetta" between Cannero and
Oggebbio, facing Luino . . . half an hour from Switzerland. . . .
Two hundred and twenty-five metres along the shore, eighty
metres in depth, planted with large trees, with three springs.
I am building a neat little house with two storeys and eight
bedrooms.'

The next two years, 1857 and 1858, Azeglio spent in a tranquillity that he must have assumed was to be his lot for the rest of
his life. In 1857 he was at first in Turin, then at Cannero: in
July in Florence, and from there he went to Evian to take the
cure. His knee had ceased to trouble him but he was suffering
now from gout. Evian bored him to death and he hated the hotel
where he was staying, 'full of the Torinese with whom I have the
pleasure of dealing all the year round'. In late August he arrived
back in Cannero. His daughter Bice, who from this time was to be
with or near him frequently, was there also, and Emanuele came
to visit him. Although he presumably did not know it, Emanuele
had been near to demotion from his post in London. Malmesbury
had already complained to Cavour about a minister being so
closely allied with one particular English political party and its
leader, Palmerston. There was substance in the complaint: the
most foolish demonstration of this partisanship was still to come
when, on the defeat of Lord Derby's ministry on 11 June 1859,
Emanuele and a French attaché joined in the cheering in the
public lobby of the House of Commons. In 1858 Malmesbury
went so far as to ask Cavour to remove Emanuele from London:
this request Cavour declined to accede to, since it would seem to
be an act of weakness on the part of the Sardinian Government,
and though Emanuele's breach of manners was regretted he was
too useful in London to be sacrificed.[1] In July 1858 Massimo was
in Siena and saw the Palio, which enchanted him by the beauty of
its setting in the Piazza del Campo, by the splendour of the
costumes worn by the representatives of the 'contrade', and by the

[1] Chiala, op. cit., Vol. VI, p. 198.

custom of taking the winning horse into the Duomo for a Te
Deum. From Siena he went back to Cannero, thence to Turin and
to Genoa. At the end of the year he moved to Florence, 'to escape
from our Siberia, which really surpasses all moderation'.
Despite these journeyings Cannero was becoming more and more
his permanent home. He had, amongst other tasks, enlisted
Persano's expert aid in having a flag made in the Taparelli
colours for his boat on the lake, and a uniform for his boatman',
also in the Taparelli red and white. He asked Galeotti to buy him
fifty dessert-grape stocks for his garden: and amongst other guests
he had entertained Minghetti there in August 1857.

As for politics, Azeglio was a not very keenly interested spectator
during these two years. June 1857 saw a Mazzinian uprising
attempted in Genoa, suppressed as usual with somewhat excessive
zeal. Azeglio was made still more bitterly hostile not only towards
Mazzini but also to Rattazzi. 'This silly and wicked scrimmage
in Genoa has made everyone lose patience with those who made
it and with those who should have foreseen it and prevented it.
It is said that Rattazzi will resign, and by right he should.'[1]
Rattazzi felt no such obligation, and Cavour's ministry was
relying more than ever on support from the Left. In July Minghetti wrote to tell Azeglio of a long discussion he had had with
the Pope.[2] Pius had spoken severely of Azeglio: Minghetti
suspected that the Pope had been hearing gossip about what
Azeglio was said to have been saying in private conversations. It
was possible, for Azeglio was as apt in conversation as in his
letters to say too much too indiscreetly.

Elections in December 1857 came near to overthrowing
Cavour's ministry. Heavy taxation had made it unpopular: its
anti-clerical laws had offended the faithful, and the priests, of
whom it was estimated that some ten thousand were now en-
franchised, had done all they could to muster their flocks to the
polls to do their duty as Christians. Cavour himself was returned,
but by a marginal vote. On the other hand della Margarita, a
typical honest reactionary, was returned by four constituencies. The
ministry had to use all possible influence to win those seats where
a second ballot was needed. According to Azeglio this led them
to support the extreme Left and 'carry—can one believe it?—
Brofferio against Revel!' As a result of this election Cavour would

---

[1] C. Tommasi (ed.), *Lettere inedite di M. d'A. a Matteo Ricci* (1878), p. 57.
[2] Minghetti, op. cit., Vol. III, p. 177.

have to placate the Left in order to stay in office, and even then his majority was so slight that 'an epidemic of colds might unseat the ministry'. Another criticism of Cavour made by Azeglio in the same letter, and one not altogether devoid of truth, was that Cavour had not found men of sufficient ability or independence of mind to act as colleagues, 'wanting none but the most humble servants'.[1] Perhaps this was an occasion when all good men and true—like Azeglio himself—should have rallied to the support of the party: but Azeglio was wandering around north Italy and can have been of little support to Cavour in the Senate. He was given to picturing himself as an outworn, half-forgotten onlooker. 'As for politics, I cast my mind back several centuries and console myself for the present world by seeing that history is only a tissue of more or less lame transactions that have always dragged the poor posterity of Adam in conflicting ways without ever letting him reach his goal. . . . If I were young I could and should take part in this struggle, but it is now too late. The goal of my life has been missed.'[2] 'I think that when a man has had one aim in life, as I have had, to seek to lead a nation to independence, and when he misses this aim, there is nothing to do except leave the stage. I do not much like what some do, to change parts to suit the occasion as is the custom of companies of actors. For one individual, one role is enough. Mine is over. Do not imagine that I am playing the victim. The role I had was one I would never have hoped for.'[3] Even the weariest Cincinnatus ought at that time, the end of 1858, to have noticed that there was a smell of gunpowder in the air. But this Azeglio failed to notice. On 7 December he wrote: 'You ask if I expect the war, whether it seems to me that it will be proclaimed like the First Crusade in the days of Peter the Hermit. . . . I must say that I believe in a war that will be the fifth act of the drama, and have as much importance in the political field as the Thirty Years' War in the religious one—but not yet.'[4]

The portents unseen by Azeglio were visible to many another long before Napoleon III's famous hint to the Austrian Ambassador. In April 1858 the Prince Consort wrote to Stockmar: 'I fear he [Napoleon] is at this moment meditating some Italian development which is to serve as a lightning conductor, and ever since Orsini's letter he has been all for Italian independence, only

---

[1] *Galeotti*, pp. 114–15. [2] Rendu, op. cit., p. 87.
[3] *Confidenze*, p. 173. [4] Ibid., p. 174.

the Pope and his compact with the Church standing in his way.' In November Palmerston and Clarendon were invited to Compiegne, an invitation that was awkward to accept since they were then in opposition, but more difficult to refuse. The Emperor told them of his intention to withdraw his troops from Rome, though it passed his wit to see how it could be done. 'The dearest wish of his heart was the regeneration of Italy, to accomplish which France had become the ally of Russia and of Sardinia against Austria.' Clarendon warned him that 'Austria would spend her last florin and sacrifice her last man in defence of her Italian possessions', and that 'the danger of disturbing the peace of Europe was very serious'. In December and again in January the Prince Consort told Malmesbury of his fears that France intended war, but Malmesbury in December was still assuring the Queen: 'It appears impossible that Napoleon can make a *casus belli* with Austria. Besides this, Your Majesty may be assured that no such warlike preparations are making in France such as must precede a war.'

The speed of events was accelerating and the dangers of the situation becoming evident even to those least willing to realize it. Cavour and the Emperor had met at Plombières and the result of the meeting could only be some form of concerted action by France and Sardinia. On 1 January, at his reception to the diplomatic corps, Napoleon had expressed to the Austrian Ambassador his regret that the relations between their two countries were not more satisfactory: in his speech from the throne on 7 January the King of Sardinia had announced that he could not be insensible to the 'cry of grief' arising from so many parts of Italy. The phrase about the cry of grief was Napoleon's. Cavour's draft of the speech, considered too outspoken by his ministerial colleagues and submitted to Napoleon for emendation, had referred to the prospects for the new year as being 'not entirely serene'.[1] By mid-January Malmesbury had to admit that it was now his view that war was inevitable, and he wrote to Her Majesty's Ambassador in Paris a letter to be shown to the Emperor, urging him to maintain the peace. But in the early days of February it seemed as though the atmosphere had cleared. The British Ambassador in Paris, Cowley, was sent to Vienna to try to persuade Austria to join with France in a simultaneous withdrawal of troops from the Papal States and in a recommendation

[1] King, op. cit., Vol. II, p. 56.

to the Pope that he should reform his system of government. As Napoleon had neither requested this mediation nor agreed to any such proposal, Cowley's mission was a quite futile one. Despite its failure optimism survived.

Azeglio had reacted like most others, at first believing that war was imminent and soon afterwards breathing freely again. On 17 January, when war seemed likely, he wrote admirably and unselfishly to Cavour, to whom he was always willing to rally in crisis. 'If in the past I have had objections to your policy it is now essential not to discuss it but to make it succeed. With all the frankness of which you may believe me capable I ask you to count on such little help as I can give you, old and worn-out as I am. There is no point in telling you that I desire no dignities, for it is my chief wish, when I can no longer be useful, to retire into private life. So there is no task, no position that I shall consider beneath me.'[1] Cavour, in replying, asked Azeglio to come back to Turin from Florence. On his way, Azeglio wrote to a friend: 'I do not know if it will be war or peace, for as usual I know nothing: but in any case I do not see any urgency now. I feel that before cannonades there will be diplomatic business. Will it succeed or not? There's the question: the best answer to it is "We shall see".'[2] Within ten days, thinking the crisis over, he was planning to go back to Tuscany. 'I had set out deeply worried, thinking to arrive in Turin to find the last days of Pompeii. Instead I found it calmer than ever. As for all this fuss about a war that was to happen, I humbly confess that I understand nothing.'[3]

Within a fortnight of this letter Azeglio was on his way to Rome. Ostensibly he was going to present the Collar of the Annunziata to the Prince of Wales. The Prince's mother had planned his tour of Italy and had very deliberately excluded Turin from his itinerary. She knew Victor Emmanuel's reputation, and was not going to risk her son being led astray by him. The Pope and Rome were safe: so the Collar had to be taken to Rome. That much the Pope could appreciate: but he could equally appreciate that Turin had some ulterior motive in entrusting the delivery of the Collar to the 'Marchese Ciceruacchio', as Azeglio was called by some who thought him not very different from the demagogue of 1848, with whom for a time he had been associated. Azeglio himself admitted in confidence that his mission was to renew contact with the Roman liberals. This was not difficult:

[1] *Confidenze*, p. 178.   [2] Ibid., p. 179.   [3] Carcano, op. cit., p. 492.

S

they in fact contacted him, large numbers of them calling to leave
their cards on him.[1] But a still greater importance might attach
to his mission. Even before 1848 Sardinia had always liked to
have agents planted ready for action in other states in expectation
of crises: and on 27 February Cavour sent a message to Azeglio
explaining his role. A new diplomatic situation had arisen. The
Pope had himself asked both the French and the Austrians to
withdraw their troops from his territories: should they go—and
Napoleon was considering withdrawing them—grave events
might follow in central Italy and in Rome. Azeglio was therefore
to linger in Rome as long as possible, and should he still be there
when a crisis arose he was to do all he could to prevent disorders
in Rome itself. As for the Romagna—it would be as well if it
should revolt, but 'as little irregularly as possible'. Funds would
be sent to him should he need them. Boncompagni was in Florence
with similar instructions.[2]

It would be hard to find a better example of Cavourian
preparedness for the occasion: and it was clever as well as lucky
to have as a screen someone like Azeglio, of unusually widespread
reputation for honesty, to help him in a policy that, in Cavour
by himself, would have seemed openly immoral.

On 16 March Azeglio had an audience of the Pope: it was a
guarded and for him perhaps not a happy one. He had been
trying to secure the release from prison of Count Adolfo Spada,
who had been arrested on 9 February. His name must have recalled memories of Azeglio's first venture into politics, for Spada
was one of those (Amadori the other) who had sent Azeglio off on
his journey through the Trafila in 1845: and if Pius did not know
of this he would at least be all too aware of Azeglio's *Ultimi casi
di Romagna* that had followed. But had Azeglio known what letter
Cavour was writing that very same day he would have been deeply
mortified: for Cavour was explaining to Prince Napoleon, for the
information of the Emperor, just why Azeglio, whom they had
suggested as a favoured candidate for the Sardinian ministry in
Paris, was unsuitable for such a post. 'Sa nature d'artiste, sa
santé ébranlée, ses habitudes d'une vie dégagée d'entraves et de
gêne le rendent peu propre à la lutte.' To be rejected as both
physically as well as temperamentally unsuited for such a desir-

---

[1] See Ghisalberti, op. cit., pp. 206–23, for an account of Azeglio's activities in Rome,
and for reports of the secret police on his movements.

[2] Chiala, op. cit., Vol. III, p. 377.

able post had an absolute finality: and what Cavour said was all fairly true. At the same time he did not mean to regard Azeglio as of no further use: he was to have other missions for him: but none of them would have the glamour that the Paris mission would have had. Azeglio was lucky not to have known how he had been sought after and how he had been rejected.

The diplomatic activity that Azeglio had foreseen as something that would happen before cannonades, began to increase from mid-March. On the 18th Napoleon suggested a congress of the five great powers to discuss the Italian question. Wrangling at once began as to what Italian states if any were to be represented, and on what status. Onlookers became more and more convinced that France, Sardinia, and Austria were playing for time, and that war was a certainty. Spring in any case was not a suitable season for moving troops from either Austria or France into Italy. In early April the idea of a congress was gaining some acceptance, and the disagreement was now over the preliminary measures of disarmament. Austria insisted that Sardinia must demobilize prior to the meeting of the congress: France maintained that this must be part of a general demobilization to be arranged at the congress. Cavour at this stage decided to call on Azeglio for help, and asked him to go to London as a special representative. Malmesbury was told of this mission on the 10th and Azeglio set out from Turin on the 14th of April. For Cavour the situation was becoming critical. London was advising him to yield to Austria's demand for demobilization: on 15 April France gave him the same advice. It was impossible for him to flout their advice, yet to accept it outright would mean the collapse of his whole policy. He had thus to give way and at the same time to delay as far as he dared. He therefore made an offer: if Austria would cease to send reinforcements into Italy Sardinia would not call up her reserves, would maintain her army on a peace-time footing, and would not go beyond her defensive positions. It was a risky decision, and was taken only in the hope that Austria would refuse: yet the terms were such as she could well have accepted without loss of face. If she did accept, the Pact of Plombières and all the hopes that had been built on it went up in smoke. But Cavour was certain that Austria would consider Sardinia's offer as a rejection of her demands. Malmesbury was informed of Sardinia's offer on the 17th: Austria was to receive it on the 18th, and Cavour believed that she might invade Piedmont as a reply.

Azeglio, already in Paris, was told to urge the Emperor to hasten his military preparations.

But on the 17th Malmesbury heard that Austria had already made a unilateral demand for Sardinia's disarmament. If France stood firm Austria had thus played right into Cavour's hands at the last moment. But France drew back—or tried to do so. London, believing that Europe was rushing headlong down to destruction, proposed that all three powers, Austria, France, and Sardinia, should disarm simultaneously, and that in compensation Sardinia and the other Italian states should be admitted to the conference on a basis of equality. Napoleon III supported the offer. This counsel from Britain and France reached Cavour at one a.m. on 19 April. His entire policy had collapsed. The war was not going to happen: Plombières had been expunged: Lombardy and Venetia were going to remain under Austrian rule until some totally unforeseeable future miracle should occur. He had wasted money that Sardinia could not afford on staging what had now proved to be no more than a glorified military review of ridiculous length and expense to purchase a resounding diplomatic defeat. Lafitte told Malmesbury that no French bank would undertake a loan to Sardinia. 'London would not take even £2,000.' Not merely bankruptcy but even disorder might be Sardinia's future, for the volunteers who had been flocking into Piedmont in earnest expectation of war might rise in revolt. 'There is nothing for me now but to blow out my brains,' said Cavour, and his friends believed that he might do so. He spent the night burning his papers. At ten in the morning he wired to Napoleon his acceptance of the terms. To him, in his desperate state of mind, it was no consolation to be told that Britain admired his moderation. Azeglio telegraphed from Windsor that day: 'The Queen has been greatly pleased by our conduct. My tone has been that we asked only for justice . . . Malmesbury said to me: "Now that the matter has been brought under discussion I become again, as I always have been, a friend of Italy. At this congress I shall put myself into the hands of your, and Italy's, plenipotentiaries." '[1] The Prince Consort made it clear that all along it had been Napoleon's policy, not the Italian cause, that had been distrusted.

Only Austria could now save Cavour, force the Emperor back

[1] Chiala, op. cit., Vol. VI, p. 391, and *Cavour e l'Inghilterra: Carteggio con V. E. d'Azeglio* (1961) (hereafter referred to as *Cavour e l'Inghilterra*), Vol. II, Book I, p. 311.

on to his Plombières undertakings, and swing England decisively over to approval of Franco-Sardinian policy. In Vienna a tug of war had been in progress between the war- and the peace-parties, and the former had been gaining the upper hand. Why not do as Cowley, the British Ambassador to Paris, was said to have advised the Austrian Minister, Hubner—'settle with Piedmont once and for all, invade, and then declare that you are ready to negotiate in the congress when and as the powers desire?'[1]

On the 21st Malmesbury told Azeglio that Austria was going to refuse the terms offered by Sardinia and that Giulay had been given power to demand that Sardinia disarm within three days. 'Malmesbury est furieux contre l'Autriche.' The next day Azeglio wired to Cavour that Britain had offered to mediate instead of waiting for a congress and had protested most strongly to Austria. Cavour in reply was able to tell him of Austria's ultimatum demanding that the Sardinian army be placed on a peace-time footing and that the volunteers be disbanded: three days' grace had been given. Malmesbury, according to Azeglio, 'still lulls himself with the idea that hostilities may be averted by riper reflection and as a result of our reply'. On the 26th Austria received Sardinia's answer—a rejection of the ultimatum—and from that moment a state of war existed.

Azeglio summed up his own reflections. 'Austria's demand at the very moment when we had become England's Benjamin has been one of those pieces of gambler's luck that happen only once in a century. Whether we are prepared or not, the moral victory is ours and more than half our enemies have become our friends, seeing us now as victims and not as provokers. . . . It has been a terrifying bit of navigation, a shoal every moment: but one does not go to heaven in a carriage. Prudence, urgency at times, patience—and with God's will we will come out the winners.'[2] As for Napoleon III—'He has not realized that in arousing everyone's distrust he has made an enemy of everyone: and I think that his first concern now must be to win back confidence— *if he can.*'

With the breakdown of schemes for a congress, and the beginning of hostilities, Azeglio's presence in London was no longer necessary. He left on 30 April and, after a channel crossing 'fit to make one reject one's faith along with everything else', reached

---

[1] Quoted by W. R. Thayer, *The Life and Times of Cavour* (1911), Vol. I, p. 596.
[2] Chiala, op. cit., Vol. VI, p. 395, and *Cavour e l'Inghilterra*, Vol. II, Book I, p. 319.

Paris and, on 10 May, Turin. There 'Cavour is everything. The King and Cavour—no one else exists.'

What importance can be attached to Azeglio's work in London? Clearly he had not in any degree influenced the course of events. This was being decided in Paris and Vienna, not in Turin, nor even in London. Insomuch as the dispute was between powers of such magnitude as France and Austria, Sardinia, despite Cavour's guile and finesse, was shuttlecock. When a decision had to be made on Sardinia's behalf it was Cavour who made it in Turin, not Azeglio in London. At no time had Azeglio exercised any freedom of action. Cavour kept in touch with Paris perfectly well by telegraph: why then send a special envoy to London? Presumably because he wanted the benevolent neutrality of the British Government. Had Palmerston been in office this could have been taken for granted: but Malmesbury had confidence in neither Napoleon III nor Cavour (a 'Piedmontese attorney', he had once called him), since both were suspected of duplicity. But Azeglio, as Cavour reminded the King, 'is so to speak author and father of the Italian question. His name exercises great prestige. . . . In England Massimo is considered, in practical matters, infinitely superior to me.'[1] Cavour might well know that the English were hopelessly wrong in their judgement, but what mattered was Azeglio's presence: Queen, Prince Consort, Malmesbury—all found it easier to condone a Sardinian policy that was supported by Massimo d'Azeglio.

[1] Chiala, op. cit., Vol. III, p. 57.

XV

AZEGLIO AND ITALIAN UNIFICATION

On his return to Turin from London Azeglio was for a little while unoccupied. War had been declared on 19 April and fighting had begun on the 29th: on 4 June the allies gained a major victory at Magenta and on the 24th of that month, by a narrower margin, were victorious at Solferino and San Martino. But there had been no need for Azeglio in a Sardinian army that was now much more professional than any he had served in earlier. Only in politics could he be used, and there a task was soon found for him. Excited by the war, the Duchies and the Romagna had risen against their rulers at the end of April. On 10 June the Austrians had to withdraw from Bologna in the Papal States. Thereupon, in Azeglio's vivid if not entirely accurate account, 'Cardinal Millesi sent for the city council. "Gentlemen, can you guarantee tranquillity?" "Your Eminence, no." "Then I should go away?" "Your Eminence, yes." After the Cardinal's departure the dictatorship of Victor Emmanuel was proclaimed. Now there were only two courses to follow—either to say to the delegation from the Romagna "I know you not", and then within a month Mazzini and his assassins will reign, or to accept the delegation.'[1] Cavour had already decided to use Azeglio as Sardinian agent in the Papal States, as Boncompagni was acting in Tuscany: Costanza had told Emanuele this as early as 22 May: for a time in fact Cavour had thought of placing Massimo in charge of Tuscany as well as of the Romagna. 'Boncompagni is finished. He is far too weak.'[2] But in the end Azeglio was made military commissioner for the Romagna only. His instructions were given to him by Cavour on 5 July. 'The objects of your mission are twofold: participation in the war and internal order. Every other question, and specially those referring to the future territorial arrangements of the peninsula, will be inopportune. Nevertheless I authorize Your Excellency to declare if necessary that His Majesty's Government will use all its authority, and not we hope in vain, in order that the Romagna shall not fall again under the

---

[1] Rendu, op. cit., p. 104.   [2] Chiala, op. cit., Vol. III, p. 99.

misgovernment of Rome.' Cavour went on to make clear that Azeglio's authority was limited to the legations, the Papal forces having recaptured Perugia on 20 June. The city was subjected to barbaric treatment, commemorated by the striking of a special Papal medal for conferment on the victorious soldiery. By 24 June all Umbria and the Marches were again under Papal rule: but the Pope's army had stopped short at the frontier of the Romagna. Cavour went on: 'Had the peoples of these regions [Umbria and the Marches] succeeded in freeing themselves, well and good. But Piedmont-Sardinia is not at war against the Papacy and cannot invade them: yet it *is* the duty of the Piedmontese-Sardinian forces in the Romagna to resist and expel any Papal invasion to reconquer.'[1]

Under his command Azeglio had only companies of volunteers from outside Piedmont—his 'chenapans' (blackguards), Costanza called them. He asked for some Sardinian regulars to reinforce them, but for reasons that were diplomatic rather than military these were refused. Cavour was anxious to make it appear that the events in the Romagna were a purely spontaneous rising. 'If the Romagna puts a reliable military force in the field and has learnt to govern itself peacefully during the war, no European congress will be able to force it to submit itself to the Papal yoke again.'

After Solferino, worried by the diplomatic situation, apprehensive of the form the solution of the Italian question seemed likely to take, unsure of his ability to conquer Venetia with its powerful fortresses, Napoleon sought to withdraw from the war. A cease-fire was arranged and, having sought in vain first of all to gain the mediation of England and then her moral support for his proposed terms, Napoleon negotiated an armistice at Villafranca. Though this envisaged the cession by Austria of Lombardy, it assumed the restoration of the former rulers in central Italy and the establishment of an Italian federation over which the Pope would preside and in which Austria as ruler of Venetia would be represented.

In protest against what he considered a betrayal by the Emperor, Cavour resigned, but one of his last acts was to recall the Sardinians from the Duchies and the Romagna lest their presence should be held to invalidate the terms of the armistice. Azeglio afterwards described what he then did.

[1] Chiala, op. cit., Vol. III, p. clxxxii.

On my arrival [in Bologna] I found the place in a ferment, and *against orders* I assumed full powers, formed an administration, and set up a government. All that in three days after my arrival. On the fourth I received the order to remove my troops, about eleven thousand men, and leave the country. I believed that the King would not have wished to dishonour himself and me, leaving those provinces to anarchy, and I disobeyed. Instead of moving my forces to Turin I sent nine thousand men to the frontiers of the Romagna to defend those who had trusted me against the Swiss Guard of Perugia. So there was no disorder: and on the fifth day I arrived in Turin to tell the King he could send me before a court-martial. He said I had done the best thing possible. So the Romagna will be given a chance to organize and act for itself.[1]

On Cavour's resignation the immediate and vital question was of his successor. Cavour saw only two possibilities. To La Marmora he wrote: 'It is necessary to form a government with authority not only in this country but also in Europe, which, according to the Emperor, is to unite in a congress. Now in Europe only three Piedmontese names are known—Azeglio's, yours, and mine. A ministry in which not one of these three is included will be considered as having neither strength nor consistency.'[2] Azeglio says that 'the King did not call me or seek my opinion on Cavour's resignation', but he was asked if he would accept the portfolio of foreign affairs when cabinet-making had begun. Cavour urged him to accept, but Azeglio declined. 'To serve Cavour, to serve La Marmora well and good: others—*NO*. I am off to Cannero and am going to think no more of politics: it seems to me that I have played out my part.'[3]

It was by this time clear that France and Austria at Zurich would make peace on the basis of the Villafranca armistice terms: but Napoleon desired a European congress to settle outstanding questions about the Italian peninsula as a whole, and also to make the treaty a European, and as a result perhaps a more permanent, one. England refused to agree to supporting a conference with such aims. As Russell argued, an Italian confederation that included Austria for the sake of Venetia, and in which the restored dukes, the Pope, and perhaps the King of Naples would side with Austria, would be an Austrian and not an Italian confederation. He also protested in July against any attempt to restore the dukes by force. It did not by that time seem

---

[1] Carcano, op. cit., p. 449.   [2] Chiala, op. cit., Vol. III, p. 109.
[3] Bianchi, *Lettere*, p. 296.

probable that Austria had any desire to take such action. It had seemed more likely to come from Napoleon, who, in the hope of winning belated approval from England for his scheme of a congress, now denied that he had any intention of intervening in the Duchies, and agreed to press for a modified confederation that would exclude Venetia, and thus Austria. After this clarification, and after the conclusion of the peace negotiations at Zurich, invitations to a congress were sent out, England now agreeing to be represented. At this juncture Azeglio was asked to go to the conference as Sardinian representative—yet again.

When the ministry had been formed the King called me one day to tell me they might send me to the congress. I told him in reply that I would never serve any ministry that included Rattazzi. I served Cavour because he is a man of talent and a gentleman: but Rattazzi. . . ! The King asked why not. 'Because he is a rogue.' To the King's 'soft accents' I did not know what to answer and we spoke of it no more. I know perfectly well I have not 'fait mon cour'. But you know as well as I how much that matters to me. Rattazzi's high favour is a story you will know or guess at . . . but it is a motive for me to have nothing to do with him. . . .[1]

Rattazzi's villainy was still an *idée fixe* with Azeglio: a little later he was still fulminating against him. 'We are in Rattazzi's hands, whom I have known and weighed up since 1849 and about whom I have never changed my opinion. I believe him the most dangerous man amongst us to be in office, for his character as well as for his opinions.' But Rattazzi, as Azeglio could plainly see, was in high favour with the King, and it was not surprising in any case that Victor Emmanuel should have little patience with one whose objections to Rattazzi were based on judgements passed on a Rattazzi of ten years earlier, and on prejudice against one who was 'not a gentleman', for the King was less snobbish, and less of a gentleman, too, than Azeglio.

The elected Governments of the Duchies, and soon afterwards of the Romagna, declared in favour of union with Piedmont-Sardinia. But the King and his ministers hesitated to accept their decision lest it cause a crisis between Sardinia and France. Russell was consulted and he advised that Victor Emmanuel should declare that the creation of a large kingdom in north Italy was a matter so much affecting the balance of power in Europe that

---

[1] Unpublished letter to Emanuele of 28 August 1859, in O.P.T.

he could not make a decision without European consent; but that in the meantime he would be prepared to defend Tuscany against internal disorder.[1] The King proposed to send his cousin, the Prince of Carignano, to Florence as regent, but this Napoleon vetoed: so Boncompagni, who was already there, acted as Sardinian agent. By now Austria had let it be inferred that she had no intention of intervening by force in central Italy.

Azeglio guessed that this was the case, and was scornful of Sardinian reluctance to take immediate advantage of it.

Now, if there is no intervention—and I believe it to be impossible—the affair is finished. I hope England will not oppose our enlargement: with her fear of France she must desire us not to be in the least degree dependent on that country.[2]

They say the magnificent votes in Tuscany and Modena, quickly followed by Bologna, have cast our ministers into perplexity. Madame Potiphar had only one Joseph: central Italy has six! . . . It is not Austria that frightens me now, nor the Jesuits, nor diplomacy. I am frightened at seeing our Honourable Blockheads masters in one of the most glorious but most difficult situations we have lived through. The other day in your letter you told me not to stand aside. But do you realize that these local bosses dealing with Italian affairs—the one thing I know really well—have never asked me my opinions?[3]

This was Azeglio at his now all too frequent worst, sulking yet grumbling at not being consulted, still convinced that his knowledge of Italy was unrivalled, yet unable to understand his fellow-Piedmontese: desiring influence yet refusing to accept responsibility—perhaps luckily for Italy.

In September, in an essay *Il Piemonte e l'Italia centrale*, he implied that the situation needed 'great characters who may save the state'. La Marmora, as Prime Minister, was not unnaturally somewhat nettled at what he considered a reflection on himself and on 17 September wrote to Azeglio offering to resign if Azeglio wished to take his place. 'After your memorable article you will be carried in triumph.' He was not the only one who read the essay as a criticism of the ministry, but Cavour, who had seen and approved it in advance, believed that outside Italy it would be favourably received as a call from a moderate for moderates to take up their responsibilities: but when La Marmora made his offer to Azeglio it was Azeglio who played the part of Joseph.

[1] Spencer Walpole, *The Life of Lord John Russell* (1889), Vol. II, pp. 313ff.
[2] Bianchi, *Lettere*, p. 297.   [3] Ibid., p. 208.

Cavour would not be so coy: he had determined already that it was time for him to return to office.

Azeglio's evasion of responsibility was not due solely to lack of fibre or of ambition: the fact was that his views about the future of Italy had undergone a change, and though they had taken what was to be their final form they had not become second nature to Azeglio: and they were not likely to become popular with anyone else.

Before the war he had analysed them in a letter to Rendu: but, as we have seen, he believed that what he told Rendu would reach the Emperor and was apt to let what he thought Napoleon wished to hear colour what he was saying. He had then been in favour of an Italian federation, as was the Emperor, with Rome as its capital, and he was even prepared to accept the Pope as its President. It is hard to credit that Azeglio really desired this, and harder still to imagine him or anyone else popularizing the idea. Now he could take a fresh look at the Italian question, for the Emperor had come to Italy and gone, and it was not benevolent military intervention by the French that had to be encouraged but a European congress that had to be educated. And his chief aim was to kill any idea of an Italian federation to include Austrian-controlled Venetia and the Papal States before a congress could fall for such a scheme. To this end, in November at Cannero, he wrote an eighty-page pamphlet, *La Politique et le droit chrétien*, published in Paris on 22 December through the good offices of Rendu. The two great grievances of Italy were foreign domination and the temporal power of the Papacy. Both were supposedly justified by the principle of legitimism: but this meant nothing more than 'force legalized by time'. Foreign domination imposed by force was a flagrant negation of Christian right, and it was of the very essence of such government to oppress and to corrupt. Azeglio quoted a political catechism that had to be learnt by all children in elementary schools in Venetia containing such stupidities as 'Does God himself not reign on earth?' 'God being invisible has placed in his stead emperors and other monarchs at the head of nations.' 'What is our fatherland?' 'Our fatherland is not only the land in which we were born but that also that into which we find ourselves incorporated.'

More controversial than foreign domination, that few could defend except by ineptitudes such as these, was the question of the temporal power. But this also Azeglio insisted was based on military conquest alone. All documentary justifications in the form of title-deeds, like the Donation of Constantine, were forgeries. The Pope's dominions had been acquired since the return from Avignon by acts of war under the leadership of *condottieri* like Hawkwood. Unjustifiable by moral argument, the temporal power was unjustifiable equally in practice, as a barrier between the Pope and the faithful. 'If instead of having to fight against three million subjects who reject him as their temporal prince, the august head of the Church reigned in majestic calm in a Rome become a free city,[1] what other guarantee would one need to find for the independence of the spiritual power? Are these three millions at present a fortress between the Pope and Europe? Far from it—it is against them that the Pope has to be defended.'[2]

The pamphlet sold well in Paris, and an unauthorized Italian translation came out early in 1860 in Florence under Le Monnier's imprint. But in Paris Azeglio's thunder had been stolen two days after the appearance of his essay by the publication of another pamphlet, *Le Pape et le congrès*, by La Guerronnière: for it was well known that the real author, or at least inspirer, of this essay was none other than the Emperor. Azeglio's *Droit chrétien*, which had been known to Rendu and others before its publication, almost certainly served as pretext for this new indication of the way the Emperor's mind was working: for *Le Pape et le congrès* argued that a European congress had become pointless: and it also accepted the idea that the Romagna should be permanently separated from the Papal States.

As long as there had been any likelihood of the congress actually meeting it had seemed almost certain that Azeglio would go as delegate, not from Sardinia, but from Tuscany, to defend its right to unite itself with Sardinia. As late as 25 December he was assuring Rendu that he would be there, if the congress did ever meet. That he should go in this capacity had been Cavour's idea and it had been he who had written to his friends in Tuscany to say of Azeglio: 'His voice is the most influential in the business that will come before the congress, and on public opinion in Europe.'[3] But as the publication of *Le Pape et le congrès* showed, the Emperor had by that date accepted the fact that no one in Europe

---

[1] This seems to be the first reference to the idea of Rome as a free city that was to become Azeglio's favoured solution of the Roman problem.
[2] *S.D.P.*, III, pp. 222ff.   [3] Vaccaluzzo, op. cit., p. 246.

wanted his congress. Few in fact shared his enthusiasm for proposing congresses, though he could quickly console himself for the failure of his projects.

Azeglio was not at all disappointed by this check once he saw that the Emperor was sound on the Romagna. So he could concentrate on another ploy, and that was to work behind the scenes to try to make a caucus against the ministry then in office in Turin under La Marmora: and in this he succeeded. To his joy Cavour returned to power. 'The Government was invaded and surrounded by such scum! However, Cavour has been called in. We are awaiting the composition of the new cabinet. But at least we shall have to deal with men who wash their hands and face in the morning.'[1] Cavour warned Azeglio that he would rely on him for active support. Posts at Paris and Milan would fall vacant: he hoped that Azeglio would accept one or other. Though he hinted at offering it, we know that Cavour had already decided that Azeglio was unsuitable for an important diplomatic post like that in Paris, and it was Milan that came to be offered to him on 27 January. To be Governor of Milan was not likely to be a sinecure. Although Lombardy had voted for union with Sardinia it was not easy for the province to accept what might seem subordination to Piedmont: and the city of Milan certainly could not like taking a rank lower than that of Turin. Roberto, in November, had foreseen trouble. 'Milan in truth will always be the most ungovernable city in the Kingdom of Upper Italy, for there is no populace more "frondeur" and harder to satisfy.'[2] Milan had been promised the Court of Cassation, but its people would want more than this.

Azeglio was pleased to hear that his nomination had been well received in Milan, and his wife Luisa tactfully left the city before his arrival. His setting out had been delayed by a severe cold, 'and I fear that between balls, dinners, and theatres it will return: but the faithful subjects are so impatient that one must have patience one's self'. Once in Milan, Azeglio found life stimulating, as he had done long years ago, and in addition he was convinced that he was doing something important that perhaps he alone could do. 'Every day I am more convinced that had I refused to come here I would have had it on my conscience. It is true that all wish me well, especially in Milan itself: but one has to know them, and to know how to deal with them: and in the lower

---

[1] *Confidenze*, p. 209.   [2] Letter to Emanuele in O.P.T.

classes there *is* something unruly: so it needs tact, cajolery, and force in turn: without mentioning that all the hotheads in Italy pour down upon us here.'[1]

His first task as Governor was to arrange the plebiscite that would decide the future of Lombardy. He had not been enthusiastic about the prospect of a complete merging of the province into the kingdom. 'I entirely share your [Rendu's] opinion that we should centralize as little as possible, and Cavour is of that opinion. The unforeseen and improbable have become the only thing possible.'[2] The vote went in favour of annexation to Sardinia, and this was proclaimed in March on the anniversary of Milan's glorious Five Days of 1848. To Azeglio's horror, 'Now there are people who talk of the rest, and who, God forgive us, would swallow down Naples.'[3] But on the other side of Italy it was France that was swallowing down, for at this same time, after a singularly well-managed plebiscite, Savoy and Nice had voted for annexation to France. The transfer of Savoy and Nice was ratified by votes of the Parliament of the Kingdom of Upper Italy, and amongst those who voted for it was the aged Manzoni, a senator now, who went specially to Turin to cast his vote for the various territorial changes. Whilst there he saw Roberto again, but apparently Massimo when in Milan saw little if anything of his former father-in-law.

The handing over of Savoy and Nice was a squalid incident reflecting little credit on Cavour, much less on Napoleon III, and exemplifying the falsity that could be masked by plebiscites. By contrast the same year saw the epic triumphs of Garibaldi in Sicily and Naples, as morally justifiable (except to the legalistically-minded) as they were heroic. This was the Italy that 'farà da se', the Italy of romantic individual action in a cause that could fetch Englishmen and Irishmen from their professional careers to join with enthusiasts from so many other European countries as a significant if small contingent in Garibaldi's army.

To Roberto and Massimo d'Azeglio, as to all moderate conservatives, the expedition raised more questions than it was solving. Would Garibaldi set up a Mazzinian republic in Sicily or would Cavour's emissaries to him — la Farina, de Pretis, Persano — manage to swing him over to the monarchist side: could the invasion of the mainland be justified when its recently acceded King, Francis, had given his people a constitution: whether

---

[1] *Confidenze*, p. 215.   [2] Rendu, op. cit., p. 150.   [3] Ibid., p. 158.

justifiable or not, would it succeed, even were Austria to remain
neutral: if it succeeded and if Naples and Sicily were brought
under the rule of the House of Savoy, would the new kingdom
be strengthened or weakened by the acquisition of this poor,
backward, overpopulated realm: and, finally, how could the
hotheads be kept clear of Rome or of Venetia after such intoxi-
cating success?

Roberto's changing reactions can be followed in his letters to
Emanuele. In May, 'Great deeds are being done, a veritable epic
fit for a great poet to celebrate or for a great writer to inscribe
on the pages of history! Garibaldi's noble temerity, that cannot
be sufficiently deplored or admired, has left us amazed.' By July,
'We are passing through a sorry quarter of an hour faced with
this phantasmagoria whose beginning dazzled us. I believe the
man set out with the unswerving resolution to republicanize us,
despite ourselves and despite Europe. That shows his political
sense, and how much can one count on his control of his enterprise from the governmental point of view?' By September, 'If
Garibaldi is great as a soldier, as a politician and organizer he
is null, dominated by an evil faction' (of which Roberto believed
Bertani to be the worst by far). Yet in November, after the King's
entry into Naples, 'We have not really understood Garibaldi,
a character so unusual, so moulded on the ancient Greek or
Roman that one could not judge him by the ordinary scale of
modern social conduct.' Roberto still thought him a mixture of
'military brilliance, and political imbecility', but admired his
refusal of titles and honours. 'He was not made for such childish-
ness.'[1]

Massimo in Milan was not above the mêlée, as was Roberto:
he had to take action, and what he did was typical of him. He
made public his opinion that 'one might declare war on Naples,
but one might not keep a representative there and yet send guns
to the Sicilians'. He dismissed a councillor who was enrolling
volunteers for Sicily, and he prevented the Milanese from sending
a collection of rifles to Garibaldi. Azeglio's attitude was not
dictated solely by his conviction that the invasion of Sicily was a
defiance of international codes: he was really much more
influenced by his certainty that Garibaldi was republican. 'What
maddens one is that now as in 1849 the Mazzinian republican
party and suchlike are putting our country in danger, covering

[1] Extracts from Colombo, op. cit.; originals in O.P.T.

themselves with the mantle of Garibaldi. Men who for their sect or for themselves have always ruined the work of our people; who in 1849 caused the return of the Austrians to Lombardy, Tuscany, the Duchies, and only by a hair's breadth missed bringing them to Turin. Men who to gain office in their republic would walk over their father's body. Luckily the majority are not with them and as we beat them in '49 so we shall beat them in '60.'[1] By July he had revised his opinion. By then Sicily had been won, and 'unless it has changed totally it will be no terrain for Mazzini . . . I do not know Garibaldi, but for some time I have wished him well, for he is the opposite of these [i.e. the sectaries], and I have never known him think of himself. He is of a generous nature and men like him always believe others to be honest: heaven save him from his friends, for against his enemies he protects himself well.'[2] That was to Persano: but a letter of the next day to Rendu contained ideas more typical of him: 'Francis gives a constitution: Austria prepares for invasion: we maintain diplomatic relations with Naples, yet send convoys to Sicily: and the Garibaldians, until they have got their republic, sing hymns to Vittorio Re Provvisorio [Victor, provisional king].'[3] Others of his friends received letters with similar expressions. 'I hope God will save Italy from further annexations: another Novara would frighten me less.'[4] 'We are steering blindly: what use is logic? I pray God that for now he spare us from our Neapolitan brothers, and grant us time to put our house in order.'[5] To Ricci he argued that there was a chance of the Neapolitans putting their own house in order if their liberal element could take over the government; this would be better for Naples than to be brought under the control of Turin: true, they must expect treachery from the King —'bombino' (little bomb, son of 'Bomba')—and some would go to prison as Poerio had done: but if a man warned is a man half-saved, they should be three-quarters saved already.

Hostile as he was to Italian unification as an end to be sought, and doubly hostile to the means being employed in its pursuit, Azeglio could not bring himself to believe that Cavour could really wish it either—as later he was to refuse to believe in Ricasoli's sincerity in desiring it. It was to become a monomania

---

[1] *Confidenze*, p. 221.   [2] Persano, op. cit., p. 116.   [3] Rendu, op. cit., p. 166.
[4] C. Paoli (ed.), *Lettere a Giuseppe Torelli* (1870), p. 69.
[5] Bianchi, *Lettere*, p. 305.

T

with Azeglio, and as tiresome to his contemporaries as it is to a present-day reader of his letters and articles; but there were parts of Italy that he was pleased to see annexed—most of the Papal States for example, and he would probably have welcomed Venetia had he lived long enough. In truth it was Rome and any region south of Rome that was repugnant to him.

With these views it was illogical of him to continue to associate himself with Cavour's policy by retaining the governorship of Milan. A circular letter in Farini's name had gone out publicly from Turin to the governors of the newly acquired provinces, enjoining them to ensure non-intervention in Neapolitan affairs. 'I executed it strictly, yet saw that in the neighbouring province volunteers were still being sent. I quickly understood the tune that was being played, and if I had not, a private letter from the police chief in Genoa to one of my staff would have made it clear. It appears, said the letter, that people in Milan are not in the swim as regards the real intention of the present ministry. So I saw it was to be my business to be the servant of the agents of Mazzini. I therefore said "Enough!"'[1]

He did not wish to make his differences from Cavour public, so he gave ill-health as a reason for asking to be put in 'disponability', not altogether untruthfully, as he was really not well. There was a genuine streak of high-mindedness in Azeglio's actions as Governor of Milan and his disapproval of the hypocrisy of Sardinian policy at this time was completely in character. But his constant belittlement of Garibaldi, not only as a politician but even sometimes as a soldier, is small-minded. After the conquest of Sicily, a superb military achievement if ever there was one, Azeglio would still think: 'To set off for Marsala with two steamers, that, God knows, needed guts [*fegato*]. But for the rest—it was an affair that went on its own impetus: when one sees a kingdom of six millions with an army of a hundred thousand defeated with the loss of only eight killed and eighteen wounded —well, whoever wishes can understand.' Even to Rendu he could write: 'Garibaldi and his men have triumphed as long as no one fought them.'

At the same time he fully approved the Piedmontese invasion and subsequent annexation of all the Papal States except the Patrimony of St. Peter. 'The fusion with the Neapolitans frightens

[1] Letter to Emanuele, partly printed by Bianchi, *Lettere*, pp. 307–8. Original in O.P.T.

me: it is like sharing a bed with someone who has smallpox.'[1] But to liberate the Papal States was another story. So he wrote to Rendu:

I understand your irritation about all that has come to pass and about the entry of our troops into the States of the Church. It is not a question of estates or buildings, but of a people that belongs to itself and to no one else, that has its rights like any other people. It is today no longer a question of Piedmont, Tuscany, Naples, or Papal States, but of Italy: all that aside, I say in conclusion: 'When for centuries a nation has been trampled under foot, when kings, governments, neighbouring states by guile and arms have constantly united against it to exploit it in their interests, divide, share, sell, re-sell, torture, and annihilate it—can one expect that on the day of its awakening it will respect the laws, pacts, and treaties made without it, with the aim of striking its name from the roll of the nations? If one sows the wind one reaps the whirlwind.'[2]

A page like this, seeming to come from the pen that wrote the best passages of the novels and the *Ultimi casi di Romagna*, a passage that is one of the finest justifications of the great Italian upsurge towards liberation, goes far to make one forgive the pettiness disfiguring so much of Azeglio's letters of this period. But it must not be forgotten that this generous enthusiasm so finely expressed was for Italy's liberation—liberation from bad government within or foreign yoke from without. For unification he cared less. When he did mention it to Rendu it was to express his doubts and fears. 'It is not Austria that frightens me most; I am more afraid of the difficulty of restoring order and organization, especially in the Kingdom of Naples. God—what people! And what can one think of governments that have corrupted their peoples to such a point? For my part I would not have wanted their annexation so soon: but God may show me to have been wrong—I hope!'[3]

Yet already men, even men in responsible positions or of general good sense, were thinking of Rome. 'Do not talk to me of Naples —it is my *bête noire*—and now they even want to climb up to the Capitol.'[4] Cavour was amongst those who had burnt incense at the altar of Rome. Speaking in defence of the Law of Annexation of the Papal States in October 1860, he had said it still remained 'to bring it about that the Eternal City on which twenty-five

[1] Pantaleoni, op. cit., p. 429.
[2] Printed partially by Rendu, op. cit., fully in Chiala, op. cit., Vol. VI, p. 612.
[3] Rendu, op. cit., p. 172.   [4] Ibid., p. 174.

centuries have bestowed glories of every kind shall become the
splendid capital of the kingdom of Italy'. This, if Cavour really
meant it, brought Azeglio to a final repudiation of his policy: but
that Cavour, Piedmontese in every word and instinct, good
European though he might be at the same time, could really mean
this seemed incredible to many besides Azeglio. Cavour had
assured Costanza, and she fully believed him, that he would never
leave Piedmont if the seat of government came to be transferred
elsewhere: that he would prefer to stay, live, and die there though
he might be no more than Governor of Turin. With justice, then,
the Cambio restaurant in Turin, where he would eat looking
across to the Carignano Palace in which the Chamber of Deputies
met, still keeps his table reserved and his place laid.

At times Azeglio suspected that in his prejudice he might
perhaps be wrong—as with his 'God may show me to have been
wrong—I hope!'—as regards Naples at least. Pantaleoni now
invited him to visit him in Rome. 'You ask me to come to Rome
for my health's sake, but do you know if the Director of your
Establishment of Hygiene has a room for me? I imagine that at
the frontier (and in parenthesis I do not know where this is) they
will stone me on hearing my name. Yet, curiously, I have an idea
that not much time will pass before we find ourselves strolling on
the Pincio or dining with your wife as my hostess.'[1]

Politics apart, 1860 had had its consolations. It had been
stimulating to live in Milan again—'the joy, the life, the gusto
animating Milan at this moment'. The villa at Cannero was
steadily developing into the home he wished it to become, and
with the Papal States liberated, Macerata, the home of Rina
and her husband, was no longer like 'the realm of Queen Pomare',
and in England a new edition of the translation of *Niccolò de' Lapi*
had come out—the second in five years. 'It seems they had a great
capacity for it!' It was amusing to hear from Roberto that Verdi's
Il Trovatore had been banned in Rome because during the
Miserere scene some wags in the audience had shouted 'The scene
is Gaeta!', where Francis of Naples was holding out, and that the
clergy of Rome had been embarrassed during Nativity services
by the fervour with which their congregations had joined in at
'O Emmanuel, Rex et Legifer noster, expectatio gentium,
salvator earum, veni ad salvandum nos, Domine Deus noster'.

[1] Pantaleoni, op. cit., p. 434.

XVI

POLITICAL OBSESSIONS

DURING 1861 Azeglio continued to be obsessed by his dread of Rome becoming the capital of the Kingdom of Italy. Month after month in his letters, and in March in one of his ablest pamphlets, he wrote about it—about its undesirability, about its practical impossibility. The following quotations from letters between March and August show what was almost a pathological *idée fixe*. 'I count on France that we may be saved from the Capitol. . . . The only thing that disgusts me is all the artifice to be found in the pretended furore of the Italians for Rome. . . . People in general look towards Rome as though the main question were there: I would give more thought to the Quadrilateral: two Romes would matter less than these four fortresses. Let us hope Austria's internal ills may free us from them.'[1]

He was unshakable in his conviction that Cavour's determination to see Rome incorporated in the Kingdom of Italy was sheer play-acting. In March Cavour again 'promised the Capitol in a speech to the Chamber: yet I spoke with a member of it yesterday who had just arrived here [i.e. in Florence] and according to him Cavour has neither the idea nor the wish to go to Rome. . . . As for Cavour's affirmations, no one takes him seriously. The dear man has arrived at such a point that when he speaks the only thing to be held impossible is that which he asserts to be possible. . . . If France should have the ill-luck to have to leave Rome unoccupied now, certainly it would be difficult to avoid accepting it. But I hope the Emperor will spare us this danger.'[2] Cavour had publicly stigmatized Azeglio's arguments against Rome as capital as 'futile': 'If he, finding them futile, had had the confidence to put forth the "non-futile", my conversion would be more complete.'[3] When Ricasoli in turn as Prime Minister declared in favour of Rome, Azeglio went on making believe that he too (a man so incapable of compromise as to have been nicknamed 'the iron baron') was play-acting like his predecessor.

[1] *Confidenze*, p. 240. [2] Rendu, op. cit., pp. 183, 188.
[3] Paoli, op. cit., p. 108.

Yet Azeglio's views about Rome were not as negative or as superficial, even dotty, as this catena of quotations would suggest. To him, 'Rome as capital' was a piece of electioneering, a catch-penny slogan, whose proponents had refused or failed to realize that Rome was not just another city: it was the seat of the Papacy and as such it simply could not be absorbed as Florence, Naples, Milan, or Venice could be. Events were to prove him right, for the solution of the 'Roman Question', by the entry of Victor Emmanuel into the city and the assertion of Garibaldi that 'Rome now comes to Italy and Italy goes to Rome', only veneered over the rough, unmalleable fact that a new Roman Question had thus been created. Azeglio expressed this complication succinctly and clearly to Rendu. 'The head of the Church must have the name, independence, great and exceptional position of a sovereign: he must reside in Rome—nowhere else . . . and Rome must be in direct and free communication with the rest of the world: but Rome must be Italian like any other Italian city.' As one knows, the ultimate solution was to be the virtual partition of Rome, with the creation of the sovereign state of the Vatican City. This solution did not occur to Azeglio, and had it done so would probably not have pleased the politicians nor would it have been considered for one moment by Pius IX.

Azeglio did not confine his views about Rome to his letters and conversation. In March he published a brochure, *Questioni urgenti*,[1] to disseminate them publicly. Like others of his political writings this was too diffuse, and he discharged his artillery against too many targets. He began by praising the Italian people for their practical good sense. 'Wisdom in seeking after the possible rather than the ideal, knowing how to wait, and practical common sense, all at one time the attributes of the chosen few, have now been conferred on the multitudes.' And from that he went on to show the multitudes how they might still be misled by the few. The first offender was Garibaldi, whose primary offence was his captious opposition to Cavour, 'excusable up to a certain point as a result of the cession of Nice, but no longer justifiable, especially in the form it has assumed'. He attacked Garibaldi's record as dictator of Sicily, and especially his 'so-called national recompense to the memory of Agesilaos Milano that caused public opinion to stop short and ask "Who are these that reward assassination?"' He ridiculed Garibaldi's announcement of a forthcoming campaign

[1] *S.D.P.*, III, pp. 335–96.

against Rome: 'who rules this state—King, cabinet, and elected Parliament, or republicans and volunteers?'

The unsuitability of Rome as capital had been demonstrated by recent history. 'Cases like those of Rossi are impossible in Turin. If a minister had fallen in the corridor of the Carignano Palace, stabbed in his jugular vein, deputies would have rushed forth from the Chamber and crowds from the streets, so that the authors of such a deed would not have had the joy of spending the night in merry-making and insulting the family of their victim as they did in Rome. . . .' The superior morale of the Torinese was shown when, 'after the battle of Novara, with Radetzky at the river Sesia, and again in the recent war with the Austrians only fourteen miles away, the people of Turin were, as usual, perfectly tranquil and government could deliberate and act without a trace of pressure. . . . I feel profound bitterness in saying this: but Italy and one's duty come first: I do not consider Rome as yet to be a suitable place for our new government.' The arguments in favour of Florence were rehearsed: its cultural prestige, central position, equable climate, purity of Italian speech, defensible site, and its general acceptability to citizens of other Italian cities. In any case, at the end of all arguments, there was the fact that the Pope and the French were still in Rome.

Some 3,000 copies of the pamphlet were sold, a moderate number, and probably to people anxious to be annoyed rather than convinced by it. Roberto wrote: 'It has aroused much irritation and in general has had no success. The question is too inflamed for prudence and reason to be heard. I find all the same that his advice deserved a different reception and, especially, to be maturely examined.'[1] It had no more success abroad. When, three years later, Persigny published a brochure on the same question and Emanuele pointed out to him that it contained ideas that Massimo had been putting forward in speeches and writings, Persigny disclaimed ever having read a word of them. 'But he is precisely one who having spent a fortnight in Italy believes he understands questions better than those who have devoted all their lives to them.'

Convinced that Cavour's speeches in favour of Rome as capital were insincere, Azeglio was equally certain that, despite his public statements, Cavour was practical enough to do nothing rash himself and influential enough to restrain others. Cavour's death at

[1] Colombo, op. cit., Vol. II, p. 298.

this juncture seemed catastrophic, and as unnecessary as it was momentous. For his illness, his friends thought, need not have been fatal had he called in a good doctor instead of relying on a very mediocre one, a mere quack as some said: according to Roberto d'Azeglio he had preferred such a one because he could dictate his treatment to him rather than take orders. This was fatal, for Cavour believed in bleeding, and his doctor was willing to administer this. Besides lowering his own powers of resistance in this way he showed equal obstinacy in refusing to rest. Even at his weakest he would have Nigra with him for a couple of hours on end to discuss state affairs. When a good doctor was eventually called in his condition was hopeless.

Azeglio grieved for Cavour the man even more than for the statesman, and was surprised by the intensity of his grief. 'We have all been thunderstruck by the death of poor Cavour . . . I have wept for him as for a brother, and God knows whether I regarded him as such on many occasions or whether I was always enthusiastic on his behalf: yet I am surprised that I cannot think of him without a tightening of my throat.'[1] 'The fate of poor Cavour has afflicted me profoundly.' As to the seriousness to Italy of this loss, Azeglio was somewhat confused. At one moment he wondered: 'Who now is going to be the counterweight to Mazzini and Garibaldi? Who now can keep the revolution safe indoors like some domesticated hyena?'[2] At other times he was inclined to think that an individual, however brilliant, was less important than the generality of the people. 'Though deeply grieved by the fate of Cavour I am far from losing heart—and even believe the future to be reassuring. Remember, my friend, that after Villafranca what saved Italy was the general good sense that held in leash even Garibaldi and all his phantasmagoria.'[3] Of one other thing he was certain—he himself was not going to be involved in politics on any account. So he stayed in Cannero whilst the new cabinet was being formed in Turin. 'And then I am a fossil, and in revolutions the actors who appear in Act One never come back on to the scene in Act Five.'[4] 'I am at Cannero and do not intend to leave. Every day I bless the hour and the moment when I resolved to leave the governmental world.'[5]

He had once been betrayed, as he believed, by Cavour: he had often opposed his policy: but in crises he had come gallantly

[1] Rendu, op. cit., p. 196.   [2] Paoli, op. cit., p. 130.
[3] Pantaleoni, op. cit., p. 437.   [4] Ibid.   [5] Bianchi, *Lettere*, p. 311.

to his assistance, to drift away afterwards into isolation and distaste. Now that Cavour was dead there was no other politician who mattered to him. Ricasoli had more of his approval than any other but he could never be a replacement of Cavour, never call forth Azeglio's co-operation or provoke him to such waspishness as Cavour had done. Azeglio had called himself a fossil and though he was apt to feel bitterly about this the fault lay in himself. He was not prepared to undertake any regular political activity: his appearances in the Senate were infrequent and his speeches there were becoming rarer than ever before: he was not willing to go into politics, yet grumbled because politics did not come to him. From time to time he would make a speech or publish a pamphlet: but even then the effect might only be to show how uninfluential he had become.

I have neither the parliamentary talent (I speak badly) nor the physical strength for this dog's life . . . and they have filled the administration with revolutionaries or, worse, imbeciles. . . .[1]

I have tried to serve Italy, or rather the Italians, as best I could: and they, except for a few honourable individuals, have served me precisely as was to be expected. But I have consoled myself by ignoring their judgements, injustices, and calumnies. Now I hear neither their applause nor their catcalls: between 1845 and today I have been stoned a dozen times as a hothead or as a reactionary. One must take things as they are: and a people that is fickle by nature is what many centuries of misgovernment have made it.[2]

His tendency to regard all practising, full-time politicians as rogues if not ignoramuses was becoming more and more marked. To Emanuele he wrote on 13 April 1863 a bitter letter on this theme, only extracts of it being published by his nephew.

For me, ever from my youth, Italy, her independence, and her dignity have been my chief passion. Once I lamented that one should have to feel ashamed to be Italian. Then for some years one could be proud: now I begin to blush again and, worse, to doubt our future. 'What— you will say—now that Italy may be said to have been created, and a success, you have doubts?' I, who am a realist, do not believe that any human association whatever can be founded on a series of tricks, perfidies, and lies. The Government inspires neither esteem nor affection. And never was Italy as divided as she is now. It is my nature to admire the beautiful, the pure, and the elevated in moral as in

[1] Rendu, op. cit., p. 249.   [2] *Confidenze*, p. 260.

material things. . . . Now from here I see the court become a brothel where one meets only the fine flower of roguery: I see the Government fallen into the hands of whoever can be found in this world corrupt enough: I meet face to face with such dirtiness—how can I who know it fail to fly into a passion?[1]

Emanuele accused him of being biased: but this he denied. Take Farini, for instance. 'I persuaded a minister to give him his first appointment. I made it possible for him to gain his daily bread in Turin. I made him a minister. Then he betrayed me in the Connubio affair. Yet in '60 I agreed to put myself under his command—such is my mania for being biased. . . .'[2] He accused politicians of corruption and petty-mindedness: sneered, as in the passage quoted above, at the King for his association with la Rosina: blamed him for accepting the co-operation of Garibaldi: yet with all that he still complained, as in January 1864, that no one consulted him. Only on three occasions had the Government sought his opinions, and each time on some question of public works. Beneath his intemperate, petulant language there lay one real and justifiable criticism. Cavour had introduced a double standard of morality into politics, with his 'If we did for ourselves what we do for our country, what rogues we should be', and his notion that it is permissible to do things in politics provided they are not talked about. Azeglio believed that to teach a young nation such ideas was unforgivable. 'The greatest of human events, the rebirth of a people, cannot be the work of low characters or degenerate hearts.'[3] By contrast it is good to see one almost incredible revision of one of his fixed ideas—a willingness to change his opinion of Rattazzi, who since 1849 had been the object of so many of his bitterest remarks. In 1862 he was able to find him preferable to Ricasoli, because more realistic on the Roman question. 'I am happy to tell you that I, Rattazzi's old enemy, hope they will support him [i.e. in the Chamber] because in the first place it is essential to have someone who will govern: and next because he has changed, having had experience of practical affairs, and is not trying to follow the Arcadian politics of his predecessor.'[4]

Azeglio's views on public morality found expression in his last

---

[1] Letter to Emanuele in O.P.T., 13 April 1863.
[2] Ibid., 6 May 1863, printed in part in Bianchi, *Lettere*, but misdated to 6 March.
[3] Carcano, op. cit., p. 526.   [4] Tommasi, op. cit., p. 83.

pamphlet, *A Letter to the Electorate*.[1] As usual his writing for
publication contained much common sense, with some points of
keen penetration, and without the petulance or acidity of his
private utterances. This work was written between March and
June 1865, less than a year before his death: but its publication
was held up until mid-August whilst he waited for the suitable
opportunity that a dissolution and a general election would give.
Ten thousand copies were printed and quickly sold, and for once
the author was congratulated from all sides. The pamphlet runs
to fifty pages, and is as usual too long. It has an improvised effect
and better planning and ruthless abridgement would have
increased its effectiveness. To a reader today it may seem somewhat elementary, but it was written for an inexperienced
electorate for whom its tone and general level were very suitable.
Azeglio's obsessive objection to the idea of Rome as capital of
Italy makes only a fleeting appearance early on in the pamphlet,
when he says that the liberation of Venetia, a more important
question than the site of the capital, must be left undiscussed, for
it could only be achieved by a European war, and Azeglio in 1865
(within, that is to say, a year of the Austro-Prussian war that was
to give Venetia to Italy) saw no likelihood of that. One will not
think any the worse of him for not foreseeing the war of 1866: he
still thought that the Crimea had taught Europe a permanent
lesson about the futility of war.

He was luckier in his argument that parliamentary government
works best with a two-party system. Where there is only government and opposition there is more realism in politics, and more
stability. The opposition, since it may become the government of
tomorrow, learns responsibility: government and opposition
formulate and offer two clear policies: this obviates the dangerous
situation where each of an excessive number of candidates in
every constituency in effect holds out local bribes to his electorate
to buy their votes.

An elector's first and foremost duty is to vote: then next to vote
for such a candidate as he believes the most honourable in
character. Ideally the elected members would be a cross-section
of society, not drawn too exclusively from the land-owning class,
nor, as often happened in the parliaments of new states, too
exclusively from lawyers. The duties of the elected candidate were
to attend regularly (a piece of advice little short of impudence

[1] *S.D.P.*, III, pp. 443ff.

from an almost permanently absent senator) and to vote in a disciplined way with his party. The making of speeches was of less importance: the Italian Parliament, he held, had far too many orators and would-be orators. This was partly due to the custom of electors valuing their member according to the number of speeches he was recorded as having made.

Azeglio ended his admonitions on a topic of which he never grew weary—the need in Italy not only for much more public instruction but also for much more education.

This extreme concern for what was open and above-board in politics and an ever-increasing detestation of any advocacy of a social revolution explain his fanatical hatred of Garibaldi and Mazzini. He could respect Garibaldi's personal courage and contempt for conventional honours, but he regarded his political views with horror, whilst trying to persuade himself if no one else that these views had been foisted on to a naïve hero by evil followers out to exploit him.

Garibaldi's unsuccessful attack on Rome in 1862 provoked his most bitter comments. To Persano he wrote: 'According to me, if you took Garibaldi you should make him face a council of war like any other and, since you know my maxim not to make any martyrs, after sentence pardon him.'[1] More mockingly he wrote to Rendu: 'The programme "Rome or death" has been carried to its latter alternative by some thirty individuals: others to the number of two thousand laid down their arms and a thousand more decamped.'[2] He believed that this fiasco had deflated the whole legend of Garibaldi and Mazzini but he wished for stronger measures to be taken against the revolutionary parties. Two years later he was shocked by the rapturous reception given to Garibaldi by the English. 'Garibaldi has left Caprera: for London, they say. It would not surprise me if he turned up somewhere else—in Hungary. And who knows if there is not in this some sublime invention of Rosina's friend [i.e. the King], who loves to meddle in these mix-ups.'[3] It was incredible that not only members of the British aristocracy but even the Prince of Wales should have paid homage at a banquet to one who proclaimed himself the friend and disciple of Mazzini, Louis Blanc, and Ledru-Rollin: he had made a fool of himself by ascribing his Neapolitan victories to English help without mentioning the aid given him by the

[1] Persano, op. cit., p. 157.   [2] Rendu, op. cit., p. 293.
[3] In part in Bianchi, *Lettere*, p. 338, the rest in O.P.T.

King, the army, and Cavour. Luckily his star in Italy was setting —or so Azeglio thought. 'Before Aspromonte the Neapolitans elected him for I do not know how many places! But at the election after it, when he had brought Italy into the imminent danger of splitting into two camps, he was elected only after a ballot, and with difficulty. In Pisa he went unnoticed except by his companions and some English dowagers.'[1] As for the Mazzinians, 'Why is the Government so supine? If the Kingdom of Italy is to take her place amongst the great nations it is necessary once and for all to finish with this government by Mazzinian clubs. In Milan in 1860 I had them closed and their members proceeded against for the sake of public order. Why do they not close those in Genoa?'[2]

His opposition to Garibaldi's social and political views might have been less bitter had Azeglio been more appreciative of his achievement in gaining the Kingdom of Naples for Italy. That Azeglio held that this had given Italy a liability rather than an asset had become known to the public through an indiscretion. A fellow-senator had asked him his opinion about southern Italy and he had written a pungent couple of pages in all confidence. To his anger this letter had appeared in print, and, to make matters worse, in a French newspaper first of all. It was easy to be annoyed by Azeglio's views, less easy to controvert them. 'In Naples we have chased out the sovereign in order to set up a government based upon consent. But to hold that kingdom sixty battalions are needed, and it seems that they are not enough. . . . It is time we found out from the Neapolitans once and for all whether they want us there or not.'[3]

His figure of sixty battalions may or may not have been correct: the guerrilla warfare being carried on by 'bandits' encouraged and paid by the Bourbon King, and, it was believed, the Papacy, was real enough: but to assume that this opposition was more than a temporary squalid nuisance and that the battalions were going to be there for an indefinite period to hold down a hostile majority was too pessimistic.

There was a southern problem and it was greater than that of the disorder then prevailing. One aspect of it, frightening to Azeglio, was the vote in the hands of a people who were mostly illiterate. 'The Italian electors are formed one-third of people in

[1] Bianchi, *Lettere*, p. 340, and O.P.T.   [2] Persano, op. cit., p. 158.
[3] *S.D.P.*, III, pp. 399, 400.

patent-leather boots: another third with no boots at all: the other third—troglodytes, more or less.'[1] 'As in a nation of twenty-two million Italians seventeen millions do not know how to read, write, or behave like civilized men, whilst the other five are as ignorant as turnips, one has to begin for them with the basic ideas of right and wrong.' This problem of the poverty and ignorance of the Italians was most acute then, as now, in the south. His conviction that the south was a political danger and an economic liability led Azeglio to play with the hope that it might secede. This, it should be remembered, was at the time of the American War of Secession, when many in Europe, and in England the governing class as a whole, tended to consider the southern states to be justified. So Azeglio could write: 'As for Naples, it is an ulcer devouring us. Imagine—the increased duty on stamps and the registration [of documents] in the north has brought in two or three millions: in Naples, 46—FORTY-SIX—francs! If one could reduce ours to a personal union, sending there a son of the King . . . who knows?'[2]

Even if some measure of autonomy for Naples and Sicily might seem a desirable solution, Azeglio was compelled to admit that he could not see how this could ever be brought about.

I do not see the probability of Naples escaping us on its own initiative: when has it ever escaped without someone else's aid? To undo present-day Italy would need a revolt of the masses of the Neapolitans who have always belonged to whoever has taken them and who have never claimed any rights. Or it would need the decision of a European congress. If a congress were to unmake Italy, who would be charged with its execution? For at Turin and at Messina there would be a large party, the party of national dignity, which would rise in defence of unity. And as you may guess, I would rise with it. How could one silently undergo such a humiliation? I see no way to cut Italy again into pieces. Who knows, though? If one found a way to annex Venetia in the north, perhaps one might negotiate. But all this is hardly, perhaps not at all, possible.[3]

Italians of Azeglio's and later generations have seen the Risorgimento not just as something to be explained by determinism but as a righteous and inspiring moral cause. That Azeglio, a Piedmontese who had made himself a 'complete Italian', should not merely be unwilling to see unification completed, but should consider it desirable though regrettably impractical to effect a

---

[1] Rendu, op. cit., p. 317.   [2] Ibid., p. 251.   [3] Ibid., pp. 222 and 243.

partial undoing of what had been accomplished, seems wildly eccentric. Yet his eccentricity grew from his conviction, a correct enough one, that by taking over the Kingdom of the Two Sicilies the Kingdom of Italy had gained not only territory but also a vast problem: and the acquisition of Rome would create still another. On this matter also, though aware that few could share his views, he maintained them steadily: and they were by no means foolish: what was foolish was to deny the sincerity of those who did not share them.

'I also wish to see Rome an Italian city, freed from priestly government, but I do not believe we can or must chase out the Pope in order to take our government there. Knowing Rome as you and I know her, I cannot think it practicable or useful to place a new Parliament, needing to raise its moral level, into such a sewer. I know that the Rome of the Middle Ages is gone, but the death agonies of these monsters, Rome, Austria, and Constantinople, drag on for many years.'[1] Azeglio's solution, and it was a more sensible one than one might expect from him in his excited state, was for Rome to remain under the Pope's suzerainty, as a free city, its citizens having dual nationality as Romans and as Italians. But this was a solution that no one but himself desired. Pantaleoni argued that all Italian opinion was for Rome as capital, as did Minghetti, Ricasoli, and other parliamentarians: Naples and other cities would accept Rome, but would not submit to Turin indefinitely. The Papacy, freed from its temporal power, would be able to reform itself. Azeglio could not accept any of this. Naples, for instance, 'did not want us with or without Rome': as for Cavour, he had, he said, been told that whilst demanding Rome as capital he had privately been urging Napoleon not to withdraw his troops. Pantaleoni, who had in fact been the very last messenger to go between Cavour and the Emperor, indignantly and categorically denied this: he had been sent expressly to state that Cavour and Italy were unable to accept any permanent alternative to Rome. Azeglio would not concede that Ricasoli could wish to go to Rome—was he not a Tuscan and a man of sound common sense? 'If I have called Ricasoli a poet it is because he does not speak the language of business affairs . . . he promises a coronation on the Capitol in March. . . . Is that prose?'[2] Later, 'At least we no longer have our blessed Bettino [Ricasoli] at the helm, who gave me goose flesh

---

[1] Pantaleoni, op. cit., p. 446.   [2] Carcano, op. cit., p. 510.

with his sapient politico-administrative lucubrations.'[1] There was
some consolation. . . . 'As for Rome, every day our politicians find
some new road that does not lead to it.'[2]

If not to Rome, the road had led, as Azeglio had hoped it
would, to Florence, as a full stop, he hoped: as a half-way house
to everyone else in Italy. Yet, though he had propounded this
move himself, when it became practical politics he could hardly
bring himself to accept it.

The transfer was a consequence of the Franco-Italian convention signed in Paris on 15 September 1864 by Drouyn de Lhuys
on the one part and by Nigra and Pepoli on the other. The
principal clauses of the convention concerned the Papal States:
Italy guaranteed not to attack, and to prevent any external
attack on the existing territories of the Pope: the French would
progressively withdraw their forces as an effective Papal army
became organized. In an attached Protocol it was agreed that the
convention signed that day should come into effect only when His
Majesty the King of Italy should have decreed the transfer of his
capital to such a place as should be decided by him, this transfer
to take place within six months.

Turin had not been warned in advance, as it should have been,
that such a move was imminent. When the news was broken the
pride of its people was deeply hurt and on 21 and 22 September
the city saw violent riots. The troops were called out to restore
order, and did so with needless severity. The casualties were
heavy: no fewer than 197 were reported as having been killed
when the Commission of Inquiry published its findings the following February. 'The events of September were atrocious: the
Austrians never did worse. The Commission has decided that
there was no provocation, yet all these were killed,' wrote Azeglio.[3]
He believed that the only gainers were the republicans, since
Turin for the first time in its history turned against the House of
Savoy. Guests going to the state ball on 30 January, even the King
himself, it was said, were booed. There was tumult beneath the
palace windows during the ball: and when the entertainment was
over the King left at once for Florence, where he received an
enthusiastic welcome.

Even if the transfer meant the end of the dream of Rome as
capital, as Azeglio hoped, the way in which it had been mismanaged made him bitter.

---

[1] Tommasi, op. cit., p. 83.   [2] Paoli, op. cit., p. 153.   [3] Bianchi, *Lettere*, p. 304.

For some time Turin has known that one day or another she must fall, but what she neither knew nor wished was that her fall would cause as much rejoicing as a victory; that no courtesy would be shown her and that so many of her citizens would be killed without motive. We do not have pictures or statues to show, but we have a gallery of battles, some of them won, some lost, but the only ones that prevented the occupation of Italy by the foreigner. The evil is that Italian hatreds have been revived, and that the people are intoxicated with madness and illusions, to the advantage of the ambitious and the trouble-makers —and that in all this no one really gives a fig for Italy.[1]

This transfer to Florence having been made, we may perhaps hope that the Italians will pardon us for 1848, 1859, and the years of anxieties, dangers, and cost that kept the flag flying and finally planted it from Trapani to Susa. Since this zeal for the Capitol is made up in equal parts of hatred of the Pope and jealousy of Piedmont, it is perhaps also to be hoped that now that Turin has been paid off this zeal may cool down by one half, and for once politics and the affairs of the country may be taken seriously.[2]

Though he was resentful that no one in authority sought his opinion, rank-and-file politicians had asked him for his views on the riots and on the transfer of the capital.

As for me, I gave up the governorship of Milan in order not to be associated with F—— [Farini]. Since then no one has suggested that I should return to active affairs. . . . Since I left the ministry in '52 NEVER ONCE has the King sought my advice on anything: since Cavour, who sometimes consulted me, died, no other minister has EVER done so, save Minghetti twice: once about the painted canvas [temporary] façade of the Palazzo Carignano, the second time about the decoration of the Bargello in Florence. When I have sought to publish my ideas uninvited you know the succession of jeers I had . . . so with 'Rome or Death' in full song what the devil do they wish me to do? I will go to vote—and then—amen. Believe me, to make an Italy out of Italians one must not be in a hurry: there will be worse to come, but we shall not see the end.[3]

I will go to the Senate simply because there have been these riots and one cannot appear to be dodging them if they should be repeated. But I am sure they will not be.[4]

So to Turin he went. He was suffering from a loss of voice (not an unusual affliction when he was due to make a speech, but clearly due to psychological causes) and his speech had to be

[1] *Confidenze*, pp. 303–5. [2] Carcano, op. cit., p. 523.
[3] Ibid. [4] *Confidenze*, p. 300.

U

read for him in his presence. It contained nothing that could have been new to anyone who had read his recent pamphlets. He maintained that the question of Rome as capital had diverted attention from urgent social questions, had stirred up discord when concord was most needed, and had overshadowed the fact that Italy's great need was of sound, honest, and efficient administration no matter where the capital might be. The transfer to Rome could only come about through the consent of the Papacy and of the French: and were its citizens to have no say in the matter? The idea of Rome as a free city was still, in his view, the better solution, but he made it clear that he stood by his earlier acceptance of Florence as seat of government.[1]

Of all his speeches it was probably the one of which the main decision had been accepted by him with the most reluctance, but it was his greatest parliamentary triumph. 'I thought to be hissed —at least from the galleries. Instead, frantic applause, embraces, tears of consolation for having said what a few months ago seemed heresy. What dear lunatics men are! One must take them as God made them. . . . The gain now is that this nonsense of Rome seems about to end. Now the public wish to be told the truth clearly.' As a mark of honour the day's sitting was suspended. But Azeglio was not sure of the permanence of the effects of his speech. 'One of those visitors whom the good wind is forever blowing on to one exclaimed "But, my God, who now thinks of Rome?", like the courtier who said to Louis XIV "But, Sire, who *does* have teeth?" '[2]

In a brief statement to the Press Azeglio summed up his opinion pungently.

I believe there is much to discuss in the convention [of 15 September] but, given the present circumstances. . . .
    Since it is acclaimed by the nation
    Since we Piedmontese are the ones particularly to suffer by it
    Since for Italy the supreme question is not the capital but unity, I judge that we should be the first to resign ourselves to accepting this convention.
    But I would not hear talk of compensation. For sacrifice I am prepared.
    But to present a bill. . . . NO!

That he and other Piedmontese should vote to move the capital

---

[1] *S.D.P.*, III, pp. 423ff.   [2] Bianchi, *Lettere*, p. 360.

from Turin to Florence was a noble gesture: for deputies from other parts of Italy to vote the same way was galling. The aged Manzoni, a senator of the realm, let it be known that he would brave the journey from Milan to Turin to give his vote for the move. According to report Azeglio, learning this, wrote to Manzoni's confessor to urge him to dissuade the old man: the priest gave the letter to Manzoni, who put it in his pocket, saying nothing. Whilst he was in Turin Azeglio and others ignored his presence: but he went with a friend to call on his former son-in-law. They were together for an hour, but Azeglio talked all the time of his new craze—spiritualism. Perhaps he was more anxious to avoid politics than to discuss the supernatural. This strained and disappointing meeting was their last—though the older man outlived the younger.

XVII

TWILIGHT

ANY satisfactions that Azeglio had from politics during these final years 1861–6 were slight and evanescent. But the bitternesses, though more deeply felt at the time, seem to have left no scar and he passed through disappointments and bereavements to serenity, even to happiness.

A succession of deaths deprived him of his closest associates of his own generation within two years. First to go had been Cavour in June 1861, but after this death Azeglio was spared further bereavement until April 1862. Then his sister-in-law Costanza died. She had regularly overtaxed herself in co-operating with her husband in his philanthropic and educational work, yet had found time for little acts of kindness: a school-mistress arriving at Lagnasco might find her school-house freshly decorated by her patroness and furnished from the big house. And amidst all her activity and despite ill-health she had found time to write her long, informative letters to Emanuele wherever he might be posted, letters that were his best source of information about what was happening in Piedmont before and behind the scenes, letters that were as entertaining as they were helpful to him in his diplomatic career.

Three months later, on 21 September, Prospero died in Rome. Though Massimo had seen little of him since their boyhood, 'It was with him that I got on best, though we never agreed about ideas. We saw each other at long intervals and always found each other unchanged. Talk, recollections, fun, arguments, dissertations: always with two different opinions and always each one of us as enchanted with the other as if we had agreed in everything. Such interchange between two minds is a treasure beyond price: and now he has been taken away from me for ever.'[1]

And then in December it was Roberto who died. He had known he was dying and was quite serene, even being privately amused by his doctor's attempts to convince him that he was improving.

These deaths caused Azeglio to draw closer to his nephew, to

[1] *Confidenze*, p. 262, from a letter to an unnamed correspondent.

his daughter Rina, and especially to his illegitimate daughter Bice. And there was always the anodyne of work to be done. There was, for instance, the Gallery of which he was still Director. It kept him busy during the winter of 1861–2, arranging its removal to the rooms vacated by the Ministry of Finance. 'I had to be busy, getting the idea accepted, finding the new premises obtained from the Ministry of Finance, which had kept its records there, sketching a scheme for their restoration, making the plans . . . and now I hope the law to grant the funds will be presented and will not be rejected.'[1] Persuading Parliament to vote the funds was not easy: two months later, 'I have not managed to make all the ministers understand at one and the same time that when one has a collection worth four millions it should not be allowed to decay. . . . When one minister comes to understand, the one who had understood it before him has now forgotten, and so it goes on endlessly.'[2] After a few months his grumbles ceased: whether he was fully satisfied one may doubt, but he stopped asking for more. For some thirty years this gallery, based on the royal collection of paintings, had been in the keeping of the Azeglios, first of Roberto and now of Massimo. And both had had more than their fair share of frustrations over it. But both had felt it was worth worrying about. 'For Italy's good fortune Piedmont in past centuries wielded the sword rather than the brush . . . yet there are two or three painters of the fifteenth and sixteenth centuries who will stand up to the best of the secondary painters of any other school.'[3]

He was also consulted about public works, as we have already noted. Once it was about a temporary façade of painted canvas to mask the reconstruction of the side of the Carignano Palace facing the Piazza Carlo Alberto, a job that took from 1864 until 1871. A second time he was consulted was over the restoration of the Bargello, the Palace of the Podestà in Florence, that was carried on between 1857 and 1865. It had been argued that the restoration had been too drastic, if restoration was a justifiable term for what had been done. In particular it was alleged that the mural decorations of the interior were much too florid. Azeglio's opinion was given in support of the painter responsible, who, he believed, had restored the rooms to what they had probably been like in their original state. His other public works commission was to sit on the jury to approve the designs submitted

---

[1] Carcano, op. cit., p. 510.   [2] Ibid., p. 512.   [3] *Confidenze*, p. 283.

for the west front of the Duomo in Florence. This was at last to be completed, and, it was hoped, in a style that would harmonize with the rest of the cathedral, and in particular with the campanile. The design accepted was by de Fabris and the front was completed in 1887. Azeglio, like the other commissioners, received a fee of a thousand francs, which he quietly gave to the Florentine orphanage.[1]

He was still painting during these years and in February 1862 he completed one of his finest paintings, if not his very finest, 'Ulysses meeting Nausicaa'. This was intended not only to be his masterpiece, but also to be his 'souvenir d'amitié' for the city of Turin in whose gallery it hangs with others of his works. After this he made no significant mention of paintings in progress until 1865 when it appears that one of his pictures was being sought on behalf of the King of Portugal, who had just married into the House of Savoy. Azeglio's friends, not named, were acting as intermediaries. Azeglio was most anxious that there should be no haggling. An Englishman had apparently been willing to pay 4,000 francs for this picture, but the King was not to be asked so much. It was true that another painter had asked him 30,000 for a picture, but Azeglio would rather give him a painting as a wedding present than overcharge him. At the same time Prince Oddone, Victor Emmanuel's third son, had asked Azeglio for something. Azeglio did not know what kind of subject the Prince would prefer. He would like to do him one of trees, the thing 'I do least badly—the sea worst of all'. And for this he would ask no more than 1,000 francs.

For a later age his writings of this period are more interesting than his paintings. Besides his political pamphlets he now wrote his memoirs. It was in February 1863 that he first began to speak of them—a work of 'longue haleine'—a 'frame in which all can be contained, that will permit me to empty my sack'. 'I shall try to be just, which means sincere, as though I were writing from the next world.'[2] He toyed for a while with the idea of writing them in French in order to reach a wide circle of readers outside Italy, but 'as my intention is to write a book that will be useful to our new generation I have to say things that would be platitudes in French, for the ideas, degree of civilization, and public opinion of the French are not the same as ours'.[3] 'Italy's first need is reform of the Italians . . . the great and mighty Italian of today is but

[1] *Confidenze*, p. 314.   [2] Rendu, op. cit., p. 265.   [3] Ibid., p. 271.

rusty iron: the humble—who knows? Perhaps something may be made of them.'[1]

The work went ahead steadily: he planned three volumes of 400 pages each, but in July he had written 350 pages and had only reached his twenty-second year. He was following his system of 'writing whatever comes into my mind'.[2] He believed it would please people and an old friend had told him it would be more successful than *Fieramosca*. By the autumn of 1865 he had made enough progress to hope that two volumes would be out in the spring of 1866, and these would take him to 1849. He could now see that the memoirs had taken a definite shape—'not to tell the public all the idiocies I have done in my life. My own affairs are just a pretext to talk a bit about everything and everyone, as, if one were to write a new *De Officiis*, no one would read it, so this new species (and I will take out a patent for it) of making a catechism in the form of so many anecdotes will be readable if nothing else.'[3]

The *Ricordi* does not take Azeglio's story beyond 1845 and even so the last eleven years were botched together by his friend Torelli under the supervision of Rina and her husband. Azeglio's original version had broken off about the time of the publication of *Ettore Fieramosca*, though the final section of the memoirs dealing with his political mission to the Papal States, his interview with Charles Albert, and the writing of *Casi di Romagna*, is authoritatively his. The intervening part was made up by Torelli from fugitive writings by Azeglio, not very convincingly either, since internal evidence shows that passages were written at different dates. Some of Torelli's patchwork is misleading: his account of the circumstances of Azeglio's journey to Rome in 1845 written into the *Ricordi* is controverted by the evidence of Azeglio's own letters.[4]

When he began his memoirs the very last thing Azeglio intended was to write an account, and still less a justification, of his political career. The accident that they came to be broken off well before 1848 was reached ensured this: but even had Azeglio written more, he would not have been likely to have written the traditional statesman's autobiography, all too often an anthology of past speeches and an *ex post facto* defence of past actions. He was anxious to put the whole of himself, not the politician, on to paper, and he was not in any case really a political animal. He wished, he

---

[1] *Confidenze*, p. 268.   [2] Ibid., p. 280.   [3] Bianchi, *Lettere*, p. 378.
[4] On the origins of the *Ricordi* see Ghisalberti, op. cit., pp. 11–68.

said, to avoid not merely self-justification, but narrative also: to pause late in life, to judge the acts of his youth and early manhood, to judge and not just to retail. This was to be a work of self-analysis and as such he hoped that it would make a contribution to the moral education of Italians. In order to add to its value as a series of moral judgements he would pay tribute (as indeed he did) to men whom he had found cause to admire, no matter what might have been their social status, or however humble their careers.

Such were his aims. But as ever his pen ran away with him. Narrative and the description of the Italian social scene give his memoirs interest to a reader a century later. He does not lose sight of his plan to reveal moral excellence and to praise it: his parents, brothers, and friends receive due credit for their intellectual and moral integrity and for their philanthropy. He gives an impressive and moving account of his father's batman, who shared his master's miseries as a prisoner of war with the unswerving devotion of the traditional faithful feudal retainer, begging bread for both and, like the Marchese, risking his life by attendance at clandestine Masses, during the Terror. 'My father brought him back and presented him to my mother as a friend, and I still have the satisfaction of paying his pension to his heirs, whom may God preserve, multiply, and bless.' He could see the good also in the peasants of the Campagna, despite the violence of their lives and the instability of their tempers, and never doubted that these faults were the result of centuries of misgovernment corrupting natural goodness.

High-minded as Azeglio might have been in his intentions and in much of his achievement, frivolity kept breaking in. There were many aspects of his private life that he would not reveal: he was one of those who kiss but do not tell: yet he left his reader in no doubt that he had not lived in a cloister before his marriage. In youth, he said, he had had a nature so impressionable, so passionate that he could not fully describe the violence of the emotional storms he had lived through. 'But now, *Dieu merci, c'est fini*, as Richelieu said.'[1] The least forgivable sin was to recount one's conquests, for 'the most stupid of all vanities is that of passing for a Don Juan Tenorio'.[2]

---

[1] But for Azeglio it was not finished: according to Vaccaluzzo, there was still Laura Zanucchi, sister of Byron's Guiccioli.

[2] *Ricordi*, pp. 218, 219.

An entire chapter,[1] the fifteenth, was devoted to 'Love', and it was as shocking to those who had to prepare his memoirs posthumously for publication as Gibbon's famous fifteenth chapter had been to many of his readers. Between them Rina, her husband, Torelli, Tabarrini, and the publisher Barbèra cut out substantial parts of this chapter, and only in the edition prepared by Professor A. M. Ghisalberti can it be read as Azeglio wrote it. Let it be said quickly that the deleted pages were not scandalous or pornographic: their fault was flippancy and cynicism. Nor were they very original. Azeglio was by no means the first writer, for instance, to suggest that romantic love is a literary creation and that those who experience it may do so because they have read about it and having read believe that they too must undergo it. 'Let us forget the eclogues and the idylls. Have you ever seen a peasant forget to go out to his daily labour, or another forget to make his polenta because he was in love? . . . This blessed "love" that turns, or has turned, so many heads in Europe—what does it become in the Orient with its illiteracy, its polygamy, and its harem slaves? Do you think that from Constantinople to the north-west coast of America there are many who for years have sighed for a fair cruel one? They have more likely sighed for the money to buy one.' This may not strike one as very dazzling wit: but it is ironical if not funny that it should have been written by the author of two best-sellers about precisely this type of love. And he ends his chapter flippantly. 'So I close my section on love, and I have said too much: for I have no illusions about the number of conversions to be expected as a result of my reflections. In effect, in this question of love, who does not wish to find out for himself? Try it, try it, my lads. And in fifty years' time you will preach to those coming after you as I am doing to you, and perhaps with as much effect. God forgive me.'

This is the *Ricordi* at far below its best. Yet though Azeglio intended to subordinate narrative to reflection, self-analysis, and self-criticism, the narrative parts are far more valuable than the reflections, even if few of these are as frivolous or as jejune as most of the chapter on love. His description of his father's educational methods, of his early years in Florence, of the Countess of Albany, Alfieri, and Fabre are vivid: but whilst the childhood recollections of many autobiographers have a clarity of vision and depth of feeling that tends to diminish as the writer passes to consideration

[1] *Ricordi*, pp. 211–24.

of adolescence and maturity, Azeglio's memoirs gain in attractiveness. Most amusing and most valuable as an evocation of a past way of life is his account of his years spent in Rome and the Castelli, where until the 1840s the nineteenth century seemed not yet to have begun. Apart from the account of his initiation into politics, the later part of his memoirs is somewhat disappointing, even allowing for its composite origin: but even so it does convey something of the feeling of living in Milan under the Austrians, when the man at the next table in the coffee-house might be a police spy, the waiter probably was, and one's concierge certainly would be one: where there might be laxity for years and brutality for months: but where there was the Brera, the Scala, and the literary circle centred on Manzoni.

And the *Ricordi* strikes one as a happy book. It suggests not only that life had been enjoyable but that the re-telling of it had been fun too. This happiness is in curious contrast with the bitterness, the disillusionment of the letters he was writing at that same time. Honey and gall flowed from the same pen, the one in the account of his early years, the other as he surveyed the world as he saw it in old age.

During these closing years Cannero was his home for most of each year, though he would usually go to the western coast for the worst part of the winter. His new villa was not large and sometimes guests had to sleep out at the near-by inn. His garden ran down to the lake and its development was a newly-found hobby. 'For me, our old flowers, roses, carnations, jasmines, are always the favourites and those flowers without scent and the foliage plants that seem to have been varnished I leave to others.' By 1864 he had planted some 500 roses and the garden was mature enough to be really pleasing. Life followed a gentle routine.

In the morning I get up rather early, and whilst my room is being tidied I go down into the garden to see the gardeners, for there is always something being muddled: then I go up again and work till ten; lunch, then garden again till half-past three: a walk, and at half-past four a meal: then another walk. From half-past eight to ten, reading, and at ten, to bed. . . . The Ferris are near at hand, and each evening—billiards. The familiar priest of Oggebbio is here—the heresiarch—and so time goes by and death comes nearer.[1]

From time to time he went to Turin, it might be for political motives, or to see to the Gallery. In winter, in December or

[1] Paoli, op. cit., p. 176.

January, he would leave Cannero for a milder climate. The winter of 1861–2 he spent in Turin on gallery business, but the cold made him miserable: then he went back to Cannero. The following winter he divided between Genoa, Spezia, and Florence. In June he was in Milan for a few days and saw Manzoni, now aged eighty-five but 'rejuvenated': they were only to meet once again. Then in August he went to Evian to take a cure. He stayed at a boarding house mainly frequented by French guests and was bored to death, and at times infuriated by the lack of privacy. But this holiday gave him the chance to see Rendu, to whom so many of his letters, especially on political matters, had been addressed. Back in Cannero he received a visit from Emanuele, who brought the Shaftesburys with him, causing alarm to the household at the presence of a Lord and Lady. At the end of the year (1863) he went by way of Genoa to Pisa, where the weather was so pleasant that he decided to winter there regularly in future. From Pisa eventually to Florence, to stay with the brother of Bettino Ricasoli: for though he had written critically of the 'Iron Baron', and radically as they differed in temperament, they were fond of each other. He seemed to have stayed regularly in Casa Ricasoli when in Florence, whilst Ricasoli used Azeglio's apartment when he in turn was in Turin. In December 1864 Azeglio went to Turin to speak on the transfer of the capital to Florence, and thence to Pisa again: but this time the weather there was appalling. In due course he went home to Cannero, again via Turin in order that he might vote in the general election, 'lest I imitate the church bells, which do not go to Mass but call others'. Once back in Cannero he stayed until the end of 1865, when he went back once more to Turin, but with unhappy presentiments. He was not feeling well and the previous winter he and his manservant had taken turns in being out of sorts, Massimo with colds and the man with gout. But looking across the square at the opposite building 'and realizing that in its attics there are men with no servants, no fuel for fires or soup for nourishment or wool in the mattresses, I see that I am not in the last stages of desperation. As Louis XIV's courtier said . . ., "Sire, nous mourons tous . . . ou presque tous".' This winter of 1865–6 he therefore resigned himself to staying in an hotel, though the life of hotels and restaurants was becoming unbearable to him. 'Curious, after being married twice, to be doomed to live as a lodger, all that is left of my marriages being the necessity of paying 6,000 francs to keep Sora Luisa . . . And yet they say I am a man of talent.'[1]

Amongst the visitors who had stayed with him at Cannero during these years had been members of his family: Rina and her husband with their daughter: Emanuele: his natural daughter Bice, still a widow, a fact that worried him: old political friends and correspondents—Rendu and his wife, Minghetti, Ricasoli, and Minghetti's friend Pasolini. The eminent painter Gonin had been there: best known now for his portraits, he was also responsible for covering what seems like acres of wall-space in public buildings with representations of battles and state functions. And finally there had been one Signor Romano,[2] who came in August 1864 and started Azeglio on a craze for table-turning, automatic writing, and séances that obsessed him for the rest of his life.

This was a period when all over Europe spiritualism was the rage—in London as well as Paris and in Italy, where Elizabeth Barrett Browning was interested. Automatic or 'medianic' writing was a common phenomenon. People of all kinds and classes were writing in strange tongues. In Turin an illiterate girl was reported to be writing in Arabic. There were rapping and dancing tables and chairs; mediums were in trances, transmitting messages from the eminent or the anonymous dead all over the continent; and those who had always been the most sceptical or the most materialist seemed often to be the most anxious to be convinced— or deluded. Of all Azeglio's friends it was Persano, the least imaginative, who was the first to be told of the new interest. A letter from Cannero on 14 August 1864 made the first announcement.

These last few days there has happened to me a curious experience that still continues. There came here a friend and, as we were speaking of various matters, the talk fell on spiritualist experiences. I laughed at the idea, but as he is a person incapable of deceit curiosity was aroused in me. We made experiments and I assure you I have seen things I would not have believed possible. By what causes they are produced I do not know, but I can tell you that what we have seen is inexplicable by the natural laws applicable to matter.[3]

To Teresa Targioni Tozzetti in the same month,

[1] Bianchi, *Lettere*, p. 382, and O.P.T.

[2] He is so spelt with a capital in manuscript in O.P.T., making Romano a proper name: in print he has appeared as a 'Signore romano'.

[3] Persano, op. cit., p. 195.

There came here a little while ago a Signor Romano, who spoke of strange experiments made by him in spiritual matters. I laughed at them but he offered to make me both see and touch. In short the end was that Bice saw apparitions, that I have had oracles, and for a time we spent the entire day asking questions and getting answers from —— and from ——. In truth I do not know where the devil these effects I have seen come from. . . . I could speak of a hundred things, to write of them is impossible, so, the next time that I am in Florence. . . .[1]

Persano was puzzled by this outbreak of mysticism. So a second letter of scientific argument was sent to him.

Scholastics argue, 'I do not believe such a thing therefore it is not so.' But Bacon, Galileo, and others say, 'Such a thing is evidently so, and therefore I believe it.' It only remains to find if in fact a thing is so or not. The conclusion of all this is that saying 'I believe' or 'I do not believe' is meaningless. What does have meaning is to say 'Is it, or is it not so?' To verify—there is no other way than to forget preconceived ideas, to examine the facts and deduce the logical conclusions. This I am now doing, as ever. I am studying. So far I have understood and profited little.[2]

At the end of the year came his last meeting, already mentioned, with Manzoni, when Azeglio 'talked for nearly an hour of nothing but tables that turn and dance, of spirits and suchlike things with which he believes himself to be in communication'. But on this occasion Azeglio was perhaps as anxious to keep the talk off politics as on spiritualism. Manzoni's daughter, Vittoria Giorgini-Manzoni, visited Cannero and became not merely interested but apparently a shade frightened. 'In his last years he [Azeglio] led a strange life, almost shut away at Cannero and entirely absorbed in his spiritualist affairs. I myself have seen and heard things truly amazing and inexplicable at Cannero. But my spiritual director advised me never to speak or even think of them.' She was wrong, nevertheless, on two points. Massimo was not shut away in Cannero nor entirely absorbed in these spiritualist affairs, for this was the time he was writing his memoirs in addition to entertaining and travelling around a good deal.

News of his eccentric activity reached Panizzi in the British Museum and he wrote to ask Azeglio about his discoveries. Clearly somewhat on the defensive, as he had been with Persano, Azeglio explained once more that his interest was purely scientific: that he had had experiences that no materialistic explanation

[1] *Confidenze*, p. 292.   [2] Persano, op. cit., p. 193.

could account for, but that he had been 'put into communication with an intelligence whose personality and credibility are impossible to verify. Hence the final result is of little importance for anyone who is not purely materialistic. I have never been such a one and so have no gain from my experiments beyond having taken part in phenomena that earlier I would have believed impossible.' He recommended Panizzi to read *La Doctrine spirite*, which, he believed, gave the best account of the origin of evil. One may doubt whether Panizzi ever took the trouble.

The Ferris have been mentioned as among the guests at Cannero. After Azeglio's death Gaetano Ferri published a tract on spiritualism[1] in which he told how Azeglio had introduced him to spiritualism. 'For two months at Massimo's villa, helped by a succession of friends, we obtained phenomena and intelligible communications which convinced us, Massimo earlier than me, that a new horizon was being unveiled to humanity and that spiritualistic science was not for girls or swindlers but a means of passing beyond the limits of unhappy earthly experience.' He described table-turning, 'intelligible sounds with no possible earthly cause', piano keys struck by spirits, 'medianic and direct writing', 'tangibility', moving lights . . . everything that the neophyte could hope for.

Yet all this activity by supernatural agencies was in vain. Never did they do the one thing Azeglio desired, and at times when most urgently wooed they might do nothing at all. His sceptical man-of-the-world nephew wished to see or hear some of these abundant miraculous phenomena: but all to no avail. Not a whisper of sound nor the merest glimmer of supernatural light could be evoked. But Massimo still assured his nephew that had they had the services of one of his most agreeable guests of the previous year, a most lovely woman with great gifts as a pianist and as a medium, Emanuele might well have seen or heard something to convince him.

The other disappointment lay—as so often happened—in the messages themselves and in their spiritual authors. The two whom he was most anxious to hear from were Cavour and Cesare Balbo. Who knows what arcane wisdom they might have possessed, what solutions to the Roman question they might have propounded, what advice to the Italian electors? But nothing intelligible came through from the other side. 'Cavour, if it really was Cavour, says

[1] *Angelino suicida* (1868).

I must be patient and I will succeed. I try similar exercises in writing with Cesare Balbo: but I cannot yet succeed in writing any ideas.' It is sad that the coolness that had existed between them at times during Cavour's lifetime should have been carried beyond the grave, that so great a mind should have so little to impart. But would it not have been sadder if Azeglio had been led to believe that he had had some message from his great contemporary and had published it to an astonished, offended, or hilarious world?

Another worry was that he had been made something of a laughing-stock in England in 1864 on account of Luisa. Though he had not seen her for years he was incensed to have her and her infidelity brought into the open in a book that Emanuele sent him from London. It was by a Miss Susanna Horner, on the life of Giusti.[1] Some of Miss Horner's errors amused him—as her making Luisa the daughter of Manzoni. But she sent him into paroxysms of rage by antedating the liaison between Luisa and Giusti. Azeglio begged Emanuele to correct Miss Horner on this point should he ever meet her. By the time she became Giusti's mistress, 'I had definitely renounced her company' (though, as we know, he was making her an allowance and writing frequently to her especially on politics). He would hate it to be thought that, if 'cocu', he was complacent. This letter is quite unprintable in its references to Luisa and her lover, showing how deeply he felt himself insulted.[2] A second and calmer letter to his nephew says that after he had left Luisa it was up to her to arrange her own life: his interest in it had ended. Clearly it was not her relationship with Giusti that enraged him: he was at heart mortified by his failure to make a success of married life. His half-mocking comments on his homelessness confirm this. But he bore no enduring resentment against Luisa and when she came to visit him as he was dying it was not he who made recriminations.

In his growing loneliness Rina could be of little comfort to him. She and Matteo visited him from time to time but they were living their own lives. Matteo had taken charge himself of the management of the Ricci estates, wisely, thought Azeglio, who said: 'We of the study are usually comestible material for stewards and secretaries. I have known this from my own experience, and, thank God, learnt it in time.' In 1863 they were at Cannero,

[1] Giuseppe Giusti, 1809–50, a Tuscan best known as a satirical poet.
[2] These unpublished letters are in O.P.T.

when 'My memoirs, like Rina and her child, are gaining weight. I begin to hope that the sad fate that oppressed all on the female side of the Manzoni family may spare her.' She and Matteo were going to set up a permanent residence in Turin at this time and not live, as Massimo put it, 'with that swine of a father-in-law at Macerata'.[1] Rina was back at Cannero in the October of that year, and though she may not have known it her father had been debating whether to leave the villa to her or to his nephew, on condition that he should pay Rina some compensation for it. For 'my kind son-in-law Matteo is an angel, but any single idea of taste, tact, or suchlike would never enter his mind. I for my part am fond of Cannero and would not like it to go to Philistines who would spoil it.'[2] Yet this idea was not satisfactory: after all, as Emanuele had no direct heir and did not seem likely to have any, the villa must eventually go to Rina in any case: so by the end of the year it was his decision that it should be hers.

Worries over Rina, Luisa, or Cannero were trivial compared to those over Bice. She was thirty-three in 1860 and a widow. Her husband, Ronco, had invested their money badly and after his death she had only her dowry and an investment that had a capital value of 20,000 francs at best, perhaps less. Her husband's lawyers were giving her an annuity for a limited term of years until things became clearer. In all her income was about 5,000 francs, so she had to accept help from her father, who gave her an allowance and a home for six months of the year at Cannero. Clearly the only satisfactory and permanent solution for her was to marry again.

Somehow, sometime, and somewhere she had met an Englishman, Henry Grant, whose father had had a business in Leghorn and was now living in retirement in Palermo. The father seemed to be comfortably off, if not actually 'living like a lord', as Azeglio believed. But the son seemed to have no prospects at all and, since he was eight years younger than Bice, delay was dangerous. As he had no observable qualifications for any workaday profession, he tended to assume that it was up to the British Government to provide for him: a consulate seemed to be the ideal solution. Bice was of the same opinion and her father was prevailed upon to use his influence. A whole series of letters between Massimo and Emanuele was devoted to the furtherance of Grant's career. Massimo had to go to work on Emanuele, who in turn had to

[1] Unpublished letters in O.P.T.   [2] Ibid.

convince the British Foreign Office that it was somehow the duty of the Government to provide a snug little sinecure, preferably in Italy, for this young man for Massimo d'Azeglio's sake. Massimo was not at all happy about asking such favours, and, as he knew, there were plenty of candidates for consulates, whilst few could have as limited qualifications as young Grant. He had no degrees: the passing of some kind of examination seems to have been a condition of appointment, but he showed no sign of applying himself to any study. And Barings, whom he had quoted as a reference, disclaimed all knowledge of either him or his father. Even the depth of his attachment to Bice was not convincing to Azeglio. Was he really so keen to marry her? Or was it rather Bice who was keen to marry him? Her father thought it was the latter and he was annoyed at her lack of practical common sense. 'I had found for her a man of mature years, a gentleman, with sixty to eighty thousand *lire* a year of income, willing to set up an elegant house in Nice . . . etc. etc., . . . whom I believed willing to take her without dowry. . . . But . . . *chansons, chansons*—I was not able even to discuss the matter.'[1] Elsewhere Massimo described him as 'a polished little man, a darling'. But she was, as ever, carried away by romance.

After Azeglio's death the seemingly reluctant bridegroom came up to scratch and he even received his consulate. But not in the Palermo he had longed for, nor even in Italy. They sent him— and Bice went with him—to Warsaw. Though eight years his senior, Bice outlived him and his death left her once more ill-provided. Luckily for her Emanuele had left her a modest income by his will, to supplement the little that she had from her father. She lived to a ripe old age to be a serene, grandmotherly-looking person.

Early in December 1865 Massimo left Cannero to go to Pisa, planning to stay for a little while in Turin on the way. He set out despondently, for he was certain that in Turin he would catch a cold, as always happened, and despite the powders for inhaling that Emanuele had sent him from London it would hang depressingly on. Pisa, when he reached it, would be warmer: but life there was a life of hotels and restaurants, a wearisomeness to him. But he never arrived there. He took his expected cold in Turin: it turned more serious and soon it was clear that he was approaching a crisis. Stefano Stampa, a stepson of Manzoni, was with him

---

[1] All quotations from letters in O.P.T.

W

and Emanuele was sent for. Luisa arrived from Milan and was greeted by Massimo wittily, touchingly, yet mockingly. 'Alas, Luisa, it was always like this—you arrive just as I am leaving.' It is sad to have to say that she left before he did. She professed high moral indignation at finding him in the care of an illegitimate daughter and made this a justification of her departure. She may have taken equal objection to the presence of Laura Zanucchi, but we cannot tell.

Emanuele, warned by telegraph, arrived in time to see his uncle still living, 'serene, full of resignation, the least grieved of all in his bedroom', according to Stefano Stampa's account to Manzoni. But Emanuele was almost too late. The end came very suddenly when Azeglio had been feeling somewhat better. His family had left him for a little while, for all were tired and Emanuele, after his journey from London, was worn out. Only a friend, Stefanoni, was with him, and Azeglio died in Stefanoni's arms as he was raising him on his pillow.

XVIII

CONCLUSION

A CONTRIBUTOR to the July 1852 number of the *Edinburgh Review* added to his review of three books on Piedmontese history (only one of which received even a passing mention in his very Macaulayan essay) a comment on recent events in Turin, the Connubio and the exclusion of Cavour from the new Azeglio ministry.[1] Though puzzled by Cavour's motives in coming to 'an unnatural understanding with the so-called "liberal" party', the writer clearly considered Cavour to be the man of the future. 'The state of Piedmont, from centuries of abuse, is a downright Augean stable and the late Minister of Finance was the very Hercules for its purification. . . . The army, court, and diplomacy were matters of strict monopoly. It was this evil that Cavour sought to remedy by the adoption of the revolutionary principle—to new measures, new men.' Whilst he believed that 'the country can well dispense with neither d'Azeglio nor Cavour', the reviewer's opinion of Azeglio was cool, if carefully balanced, and neither the events of the rest of Azeglio's career nor the scrutiny of a subsequent century invalidate it to any serious extent.

Massimo d'Azeglio is a poet, an artist, a man of taste and pleasure: he is, further, disabled by wounds and infirmities. Great exertions, with the exceptions of occasional fits and starts, cannot be expected nor justly demanded of him, but he is nevertheless indispensable as *magni nominis umbra*. Without him, so long as he lives, no government in Piedment can inspire either respect or confidence. . . . D'Azeglio has been and is a contemner of all save personal distinction, proud to have earned his bread by his pen and easel: but he has not strength of mind enough to tear himself loose from all connexions of family and caste: he exaggerates the danger to be apprehended by too open a war with that old noblesse which in my opinion is as impotent for evil as for good. D'Azeglio therefore talks of reform, of promotion of true merit, but has in reality ventured to do little in his own department, and not allowed much to be done in those of his colleagues.

There is justice in the charge that 'great exertions, with the exceptions of occasional fits and starts' were not to be expected of

---

[1] This article is referred to in Chapter XII above, p. 227, note 1.

Azeglio. His whole career as Prime Minister revealed an inability to undertake sustained hard work, but to ascribe this to his wounds and infirmities was too charitable. As one could see from his own records he wrote his novels in the same fitful way as he conducted public affairs, long spells of inactivity being punctuated by bouts of activity. Only his *Ricordi* seems to have been written at a steady rate.

The reviewer could not have known all the instances of Azeglio's contempt for all save personal distinction, and his refusal of the Collar of the Annunziata and of a pension were still to come. Azeglio talked much, perhaps too much, of honour but he could act decisively when he believed his country's or his own to be endangered, as when he resigned his Milan appointment over the 'rifles for Garibaldi' affair.[1] Yet there had been occasions when he fell short of his own standards, in Rome in 1847 in his association with men like Ciceruacchio, in his Orders of the Day of 1848, and in some of his dealings with the Papacy during the struggles over the Siccardi Laws.

There is justice in the charge that he had not followed the policy ascribed by the reviewer to Cavour of finding new men for new measures. He was implacably hostile to men of the left like Guerrazzi and Rattazzi, and to the whole class of professional politicians entering public life usually by way of the legal profession. His hatred of Mazzini and of Garibaldi became almost pathological. Yet on the other hand he would not give office to extremists on the right like della Margarita and Revel, though he accepted their support in the Chamber: and he chased obscurantist clerics like Fransoni and Marongiu-Nurra into exile. Inevitably he fell back upon members of the Piedmontese aristocracy, though not always of the highest rank, in forming his cabinets: men like Provana di Collegno, Pes di Villamarina, and his own nephew went to represent their country abroad. Like the English Whigs of the 1830s, according to Melbourne, they were all cousins, but Azeglio was convinced that his caste and theirs, by virtue of long traditions of service to Piedmont's army and monarchy, were the true guardians of their country's honour. Disinterested himself, he believed that they too were more likely to be so than the new men, and on this ground would have defended himself against the charge of lacking the will to 'tear himself loose from all connexions of family and caste'.

[1] See p. 278.

To describe him as *magni nominis umbra* in 1852 seems unflattering, but it was not wholly unjust. Even with three years of office behind him he was still to many outside Italy the author of patriotic historical novels and of electrifying pamphlets like the *Ultimi casi di Romagna* or the *Lutti di Lombardia*, and as such he was seen as 'poet and artist' rather than as Prime Minister and man of action. The suggestion that Piedmont needed both Azeglio and Cavour was more flattering and more just. It is true that Azeglio was soon to go out of ministerial office and Cavour to return to it, and that they would never again be colleagues in a cabinet: but Cavour again and again in time of crisis would appeal to Azeglio—to write a memorandum, to go to a congress or on a mission to Paris, London, Milan, or Bologna. On each occasion, putting aside his pique at the way in which Cavour had treated him at the time of the Connubio, overcoming his opposition to the ends Cavour had in view and to the means he was using to attain them, Azeglio accepted the call to duty.

Looking back, as one has been doing, on a judgement passed on Azeglio over a hundred years ago, one realizes that though it was in many ways percipient it still missed the real importance of his work for Piedmont, for though Azeglio's greatest services to his country had already been performed, a writer in 1852 was too near his subject to see it in perspective. Azeglio's first major achievement as a responsible politician was certainly his success in securing such favourable terms of peace from Austria after the débâcle of 1849, not merely in the reduction of Austria's claims for financial compensation but in gaining indemnity for so many against whom the Imperial Government might well have taken retaliatory proceedings. He had maintained the constitution despite pressure from outside Piedmont, and attacks on it from both right and left wings of the Chamber and from the corridors of the Palace. As Prime Minister he had accepted responsibility for the invidious task of re-ordering the relations between Church and State, without which the modernization of Piedmont would have been superficial or tardy. To have seen as much as this accomplished within three years was not a bad record for one who was as inexperienced in practical affairs and as unexcited by them as Azeglio was. These things should go to his credit, to offset his frequent wrong-headednesses, such as his vendetta against Garibaldi, his scorn for so many other politicians, his dread of the acquisition of Rome as capital, and his regrets that southern Italy had ever been brought into unity with the north.

The politician, however, was only one Azeglio. There was also the writer. His two finished novels might have their melodramatic absurdities of plot, their over-simplification and exaggeration of characterization, but they had zest and speed of action, the qualities that his unfinished *Lega lombarda* lacked. The posthumous publication of his *Ricordi* and then of collections of his letters showed him writing with ease, spontaneously and informally, often angrily, sometimes savagely or scandalously vituperative in parts of his letters, sometimes wise and judicious. Over and over again in the *Ricordi* and the letters comes the entertaining anecdote, the bright incisive epigram or apt quotation to make one realize how excellent a writer he was when writing at his ease.

But even writing was to him, after all, a sideline. It was by painting, if not for it, that he lived for most of his life. After his death his reputation declined: nor can one claim that he was of the first rank. One writer, perhaps not too well remembered himself, Fournier-Sarlovèze, published in 1902 an essay on Azeglio as one of a series of 'Artistes Oubliès'. Less unkindly, Gozzano visualized his pictures as they might have been seen in a drawing-room of the eighteen-fifties, with:

> Venezia ritratta a musaici, gli acquarelli un po' scialbi,
> le stampe, i cofani, gli albi dipinti d'anemoni arcaici,
> le tele di Massimo d'Azeglio, le miniature
> i dagherrotipi. . . .[1]

Forgotten or remembered, overpraised or undervalued, paintings of his in Italian galleries still have their attractiveness and still testify to his genuine and hard-earned craftsmanship.

And when all attempts to estimate his significance as political writer, as practising politician, as novelist, and as painter are completed, one returns to think of that evanescent phenomenon, the total charm of the man, of his gift of being at home with peasants in the Castelli, aristocrats in Rome or Florence, writers and painters in Milan: of the Minister-President singing to the young people to his own accompaniment after an official recep-

---

[1] Venice depicted in mosaic, watercolours somewhat faded, prints, trinket-boxes, albums painted with anemones of long ago, canvases by Massimo d'Azeglio, miniatures and daguerrotypes. . . .

tion, or of the ageing man amongst his roses at Cannero. One has read somewhere that when Bingham, at one time Chargé d'Affaires in Turin, was once asked the offensive question, had he ever known a pleasant Piedmontese, he at once answered: 'Yes— Massimo d'Azeglio.'

BIBLIOGRAPHY

I. ORIGINAL SOURCES CONSULTED

(*a*) Archives of the Opera Pia Taparelli, Saluzzo (O.P.T.):
   Letters to Emanuele d'Azeglio from Massimo, Roberto, Costanza d'Azeglio, and from Prospero Taparelli d'Azeglio to Roberto and his family.
(*b*) Papers of Admiral Count Persano in the possession of Doctor Rodolfo Pellion di Persano, Turin:
   Letters of Massimo d'Azeglio to Count Persano and Massimo d'Azeglio's unfinished story in English written for Countess Persano.
(*c*) The Biblioteca Reale and the Archivio di Stato, Turin:
   Various letters to and from Massimo d'Azeglio, Provana di Collegno, Archbishop Gaisruck, Grossi, Gino Capponi.
(*d*) The Public Record Office, London:
   Reports of Her Majesty's Ministers in Turin. Papers F.O. 67, Vols. 163 to 195 for the period of Massimo d'Azeglio's premiership.

II. LITERARY WORKS OF MASSIMO D'AZEGLIO

La Sacra di San Michele. Turin, 1829.
Ettore Fieramosca. Various editions. Translated as *The Challenge of Barletta* by Lady Louisa Magenis. W. H. Allen, 1880.
Niccolò de' Lapi. Various editions. Translated as *The Maid of Florence* by W. Felgate. Bentley, 1853.
Bozzetti di vita italiana. Barbèra, Florence, 1910.
I miei ricordi (ed. A. M. Ghisalberti). Einaudi, Turin, 1949. First translated as *Recollections* by Count Maffei. Chapman and Hall, 1868. Translated as *Things I Remember* by E. R. Vincent, Oxford, 1966.
Scritti postumi (ed. M. Ricci). Florence, 1871.
An unfinished story in English, in *Italian Studies*, Vol. XII, 1957.

III. POLITICAL WRITINGS OF MASSIMO D'AZEGLIO

Bianchi, N. (ed.), *La politica di M. d'A.* Roux e Favale, Turin, 1883.
Rubris, Marcus de (ed.), *Scritti e discorsi politici di M. d'A.*, 3 vols. La Nuova Italia, Florence, 1931 (*S.D.P.*).

IV. COLLECTED LETTERS OF MASSIMO D'AZEGLIO

Bianchi, N. (ed.), *Lettere inedite di M. d'A. al Marchese Emanuele d'Azeglio*. Roux e Favale, Turin, 1883.

Briano, G. (ed.), *Lettere di M. d'A. al fratello Roberto*. Carrara, Milan, 1872.

Carcano, G. (ed.), *Lettere di M. d'A. a sua moglie Luisa Blondel*. Milan, 1870.

Paoli, C. (ed.), *Lettere a Giuseppe Torelli e frammenti in continuazione dei 'Miei ricordi'*. Carrara, Milan, 1870.

Persano, Carlo di (ed.), *Lettere di M. d'A. a Carlo di Persano*. Turin, 1878.

Rendu, E. (ed.), *L'Italie de 1847 à 1865: Correspondance politique de M. d'A.*, accompagnée d'une introduction et de notes par E. Rendu. Didier, Paris, 1867.

Rubris, M. de (ed.), *Carteggio politico di M. d'A. e L. Galeotti*. Sten, Turin, 1928 (Galeotti).

Rubris, M. de (ed.), *Confidenze di M. d'A. dal carteggio con Teresa Targioni Tozzetti*. Mondadori, Milan, 1930 (*Confidenze*).

Sforza, G. (ed.), *M. d'A. alla guerra dell'independenza nel '48. Documenti inediti*. Ferraguti, Modena, 1911.

Tommasi, C. (ed.), *Lettere inedite di M. d'A. a suo genero, Matteo Ricci*. Milan, 1878.

Tommasoni, T. (ed.), *Lettere inedite di M. d'A. e F. Gualterio a Tommaso Tommasoni*. Rome, 1885.

V. LETTERS OF MASSIMO D'AZEGLIO IN OTHER COLLECTIONS

Fagan, L. A. (ed.), *Lettere ad Antonio Panizzi*. Barbèra, Florence, 1880.

Pantaleoni, D., *D. Pantaleoni e M. d'Azeglio, Carteggio inedito*. Turin, 1888.

Minghetti, M., *I miei ricordi* (3 vols.). Roux, Turin, 1888.

VI. BIOGRAPHICAL WORKS

Cantù, C., 'Massimo d'Azeglio', in *Collana di storie e memorie contemporanee*, Vols. 36, 37. Corona e Caimi, Milan, 1868.

Ferri, G., *Angelino suicida* (for M. d'A. and spiritualism). Bocca, Turin, 1868.

Ghisalberti, A. M., *Massimo d'Azeglio, un moderato realizzatore*. Edizioni dell'Ateneo, Rome, 1930.

Rubris, M. de, *Il cavaliere della prima passione nazionale*. Cappelli, Bologna, 1930.

Rubris, M. de, *L'araldo della vigilia*. Sten, Turin, 1929.

Santangelo, P. E., *Massimo d'Azeglio, politico e moralista*. Einaudi, Turin, 1937.

Vaccaluzzo, N., *Massimo d'Azeglio*. Anonima Editoriale Romana, 1930.

VII. OTHER BIOGRAPHICAL SOURCES

ROBERTO AND COSTANZA D'AZEGLIO

D'Azeglio, Roberto (ed.), *Souvenirs historiques de la Marquise Constance d'Azeglio*. Bocca, Turin, 1884 (*Souv. hist.*).

Colombo A., (ed.), *Carteggi e documenti diplomatici inediti di Emanuele d'Azeglio* (2 vols.). Società per la storia del Risorgimento Italiano (Comitato Piemontese), 1920. (The second volume was set up in type but not published. Proofs are available in the O.P.T. Archive.)

Schettini, M. (ed.), *Giornale degli anni memorabili di Costanza d'Azeglio*. Cino del Duca, Milan, 1960.

PROSPERO (PADRE LUIGI) TAPARELLI D'AZEGLIO

Carlo, Eugenio di (ed.), *Un carteggio del R. P. Luigi Taparelli coi fratelli Massimo e Roberto*. Anonima Editoriale Romana, Rome, 1926.

Pirri, Padre Pietro, *Carteggi del R. P. Luigi Taparelli d'Azeglio*. Biblioteca di Storia Italiana Recente, Turin, 1932.

CAVOUR, CAMILLO BENSO DI

Chiala, Luigi (ed.), *Lettere di Camillo Benso di Cavour*, 6 Vols. Roux e Favale, Turin, 1883.

Commissione editrice dei carteggi di Camillo Cavour (ed.), *Cavour e l'Inghilterra, Carteggio con V. E. d'Azeglio* (2 vols in 3 books). Zanichelli, Bologna, 1961.

Ruffini, Francesco, *La giovinezza del Conte di Cavour*. Bocca, Milan, 1912.

Thayer, W. R., *The Life and Times of Cavour* (2 vols.), Houghton Miflin, Boston, 1911.

Whyte, A. J., *The Early Life and Letters of Cavour*. Oxford, 1935.

Whyte, A. J., *The Political Life and Letters of Cavour, 1848–1861*. Oxford, 1930.

CLARENDON

Maxwell, Sir H., *The Life and Letters of Lord Clarendon*. Edwin Arnold, 1913.

MALMESBURY

The Earl of Malmesbury, *Memoirs of an Ex-Minister*. Longmans, Green. 1884.

MANZONI

Colquhoun, A., *Manzoni and his Times*. Dent, 1954.

Rosa, G. Titta, *Aria di casa Manzoni*. Ceschina, Milan, 1955.

METTERNICH

The Memoirs of Prince Metternich. Bentley, 1880.

PALMERSTON
Ashley, E., *The Life of Lord Palmerston*. Bentley, 1876.

PIUS IX
Pirri, Padre P., *Pio IX e Vittorio Emanuele II dal loro carteggio privato. La Laicizzazione dello stato sardo 1848–56* (*Miscellanea Historiae Pontificiae*, Vol. VIII, Book I). Pontificia Università Gregoriana. Rome, 1944. (*Cart. priv.*).

Hales, E. E. Y., *Pio Nono*. Eyre and Spottiswoode, 1954.

PRINCE CONSORT, THE
Martin, Sir T., *The Life of the Prince Consort*. Smith, Elder, 1875.

PROVANA DI COLLEGNO, MARGHERITA
Diario politico. Ed. A. Malvezzi, Hoepli, Milan, 1926.

RICASOLI, BETTINO
Hancock, W. K., *Ricasoli and the Risorgimento in Tuscany*. Faber and Gwyer, 1926.

RUSSELL, LORD JOHN
Spencer Walpole, *The Life of Lord John Russell*. Longmans, Green, 1889.

VIII. POLITICAL THOUGHT OF THE RISORGIMENTO PERIOD
Gioberti, Vincenzo, *Del primato morale e civile degli Italiani*. Utet edition, Turin, 1946.

Balbo, Cesare, *Le speranze d'Italia*. Utet edition, Turin, 1944.

Brunello, B., *Il pensiero politico italiano dal Romagnosi al Croce*. Zuffi, Bologna, 1949.

Salvatorelli, L., *Il pensiero politico italiano dal 1700 al 1870*. Einaudi, Turin, 1949.

Salvatorelli, L., *Pensiero e azione del risorgimento*. Einaudi, Turin, 1963.

IX. HISTORIES OF THE RISORGIMENTO PERIOD
Berkeley, G. F.-H., *Italy in the Making, 1815–1846*. Cambridge, 1932.

Berkeley, G. F.-H. and J., *Italy in the Making, June 1846–1 January 1848*. Cambridge, 1936.

Berkeley, G. F.-H. and J., *Italy in the Making, 1 January 1848–16 November 1848*. Cambridge, 1940.

Cambridge Modern History, original version, Vol. X, Chapter IV (Carlo Segre), Vol. XI, Chapters IV, XIV, and XIX (E. Masi).

Jemolo, Arturo, *Chiesa e stato in Italia negli ultimi cento anni*. Einaudi, Turin, 1948.

King, Bolton, *A History of Italian Unity*, 2 vols. Nisbet, 1934.

Pieri, Piero, *Le società segrete ed i moti del 1820–1821 e 1831.* Vallardi, Milan, 1948.

Smith, D. Mack, *Cavour and Garibaldi, 1860.* Cambridge, 1954.

Solmi, Arrigo, *The Making of Modern Italy,* Benn, 1925.

Trevelyan, G. M., *Garibaldi's Defence of the Roman Republic.* Longmans, 1907.

Trevelyan, G. M., *Garibaldi and the Thousand.* Longmans, 1910.

Trevelyan, G. M., *Garibaldi and the Making of Italy.* Longmans, 1911.

Trevelyan, G. M., *Manin and the Venetian Republic.* Longmans, 1923.

INDEX